HIGHWAYS AND BUYWAYS:

NATURALISTIC RESEARCH FROM THE CONSUMER BEHAVIOR ODYSSEY

Russell W. Belk
Editor

International Standard Book Number: 0-915552-27-2

International Standard Serial Number: 0098-9258

Russell W. Belk, Editor

Highways and Buyways: Naturalistic Research from the Consumer Behavior Odyssey

(Provo, UT: Association for Consumer Research, 1991)

PREFACE
William D. Wells

By the middle of the 1980's, the consumer had all but disappeared from "scientific" consumer research. In the most prestigious journals, the method of choice was the controlled experiment: college student subjects made artificial responses to artificial stimuli in situations which had none of the annoying details of real life. Most of these experiments were about Theory, which in turn was about other theories, none of which had much to do with how mom buys bread.

The method of second choice was the mathematical model. Numbers replaced feelings, thoughts and actions, with no regard to whether the real life analogies ever followed the rules the numbers did. Again, the models were not about how real consumers buy gasoline, or how real audiences use television to enrich their days. The models portrayed pathetic never-never lands without emotion, character or plot.

As a result, consumers--the original and only proper focus of consumer research--had all but vanished. Worship of logical posivitism had turned the discipline into a self-contained, self-reinforcing, depopulated world.

One consequence of all this was that "scientific" consumer research became less and less interesting to audiences outside of academe. For anyone interested in the real behavior of real consumers, the most prestigious journals offered fewer and fewer insights, less and less help.

A second consequence was that discovery also disappeared. Too many journal articles had an all too obvious "grind it out so that I can get promoted" quality about them, as distinguished from "I can't wait to tell you about some tremendously exciting work."

Thirdly, and most ominously, very few of the authors in the most prestigious journals took their research seriously. Despite occasional--and clearly secondary--references " to managerial implications," the focus was almost invariably inward, on other articles, rather than outward on how real consumers actually behave from day to day. It was as though the fictional world of Theory had become reality, and the real world with real people in it had simply disappeared.

Given this downward spiral, Russell Belk's Odyssey proposal came as a most welcome ray of hope. An established scholar, with a team of well-known, respected colleagues, proposed to restore consumers to consumer research--not as epiphenomena, but live and in color, as the central figures in the work!

The product of that proposal--this volume--provides at least three rewards. First, despite disavowal of any attempt to help sell services or products, the Odyssey turned out to be useful in the very best sense. One cannot read this volume without learning something about how real consumers make decisions about what to buy.

Second, the Odyssey put the joy of discovery back into its proper place. These chapters burst with enthusiasm. Judging from this volume, discovery is fascinating for its own sake.

Finally, and possibly most important, this book conveys a seriousness of purpose which many other academic research efforts lack. Instead of looking inward at the literature, the Odyssey participants looked outward at consumers. Instead of following the most expedient route to yet another publication, the Odyssey participants invented strategies to bring their powers of observation into first-hand contact with the true subject matter of the field.

At one point in its development, the Odyssey was called "weird science." Not weird at all. True science. Careful observation and insightful description of what makes real people tick.

HIGHWAYS AND BUYWAYS:
NATURALISTIC RESEARCH FROM THE CONSUMER BEHAVIOR ODYSSEY

TABLE OF CONTENTS

IV. Evaluation

The History and Development of The Consumer Behavior Odyssey[1]
Russell W. Belk

In the summer of 1986, approximately two dozen academic consumer researchers worked for varying periods of time from a 27 foot recreation vehicle conducting qualitative research as we traveled from Los Angeles to Boston. We employed a variety of naturalistic methods to explore American consumption. This project has come to be known as the Consumer Behavior Odyssey. While we faced somewhat fewer obstacles than Odysseus, our own epic journey opposed traditions in the field and sought a fresh way of acquiring knowledge about consumers and fresh perspectives about the domain and nature of consumer behavior. Later chapters will present the major findings and themes that the Odyssey and follow-up data collection have developed. This chapter first provides some historical perspective on the project. How did the Consumer Behavior Odyssey project come about? What was the intellectual climate that motivated a large group of people to participate in such a project? What was it like to work on the Odyssey?

BEGINNINGS

Perhaps it is best to begin this history with a glimpse at the document that first gave it a social reality: a letter I sent to nine people in January of 1985. The letter read as follows.

January 9, 1985

Dear_____ :

May I bounce an off-the-wall idea off you? This letter is going to a small group of friends (Hirschman, Holbrook, Kassarjian, Levy, Olson, Rook, Sherry, Wallendorf, and Wells) who are weird enough to entertain this proposal, but honest enough to throw cold water on it if that's what it deserves. So please give me reactions, suggestions, and expressions of interest, disinterest, or desire to disassociate yourself from the following long term joint research proposal.

A Consumer Behavior Odyssey

In a nutshell, the idea is for a small group of us to travel from coast to coast one summer in order to qualitatively document various buyer and consumer behaviors via videotaped in-situ consumer interviews, largely unobtrusive still photos, and impressionistic journals. The goal would be to approach people shopping, buying, and consuming products and services, in a largely unstructured way without a priori hypotheses or quantitative/structured measures, and obtain an archive of records for whatever teaching/research/learning purposes we or others could (a posteriori) devise. For instance, edited experiential journals might be published along with or separately from a book of edited photos. Edited videotapes could be put together in documentary format with or without commentary. In distributed versions as well as the archives, it is my initial thought to let the records speak for themselves as data and to avoid theorizing and elaborate interpretation, at least within the scope of the group research commitment. Anyone would then be free to analyze and make of these data what they will.

While presumably not all observers/recorders/researchers would be interested in participating in all phases of the project, it is my thought that the total project embrace a wide variety of buying and consuming situations that could ultimately be juxtaposed and compared across geographic regions (including urban versus rural), ages, races, sexes, social classes, and products and services. For instance, data collection sites and occasions might include high-end department stores, low-end discount stores, new and used auto dealerships, garage sales, flea markets, auctions, Salvation Army stores, tourist attractions, real estate inspections, supermarkets, motels, fast food and 4-star restaurants, backyard barbecues, picnics, weddings, brothels, country clubs, bars, dance halls, pet stores, pet shows, the Metropolitan Opera, rock concerts, etc., etc..

I suppose the closest precedents for something like this are things as diverse as the buyer scenarios collected by Tucker in *Foundations for a Theory of Consumer Behavior*, Bill Owen's photo essay *Suburbia*, the photo and essay study *Learning from Las Vegas* by architects Robert Venturi, et al., the recent best-seller (that I have not read), *Blue Highways*, the allegorical *Journal of Albion Moonlight* by Kenneth Patchen, and the gonzo journalism of Hunter S. Thompson. The general project reflects McGuire's ("Seven Koan") recommendation to observe people, not data, and the rare opportunity we have in the field to observe consumer and buyer behaviors. There is an instructive literature, largely in anthropology, sociology, and American studies on how to do research of this sort, but nothing of quite this magnitude seems to have been done in any field. A more

[1] I would like to thank Jeff Durgee, Morris Holbrook, Debbie MacInnis and Melanie Wallendorf for their helpful comments on an earlier draft of this chapter.

multidisciplinary project would certainly be feasible, but that's more ambitious than I think we need to be.

In terms of costs and funding, the nicest scenario would be to get grants to cover food, lodging, travel, and perhaps some good compact 3/4" videotape equipment for a rental van full of researchers (who might join and depart at various points) for one to two months. Post-editing, writing, developing of still photos, and archival cataloging, storage, and assembly would be other details to work out.

But before thinking in this much detail, let me solicit your comments, criticisms, statements of (dis)interest, and suggestions. Suggestions for other potential participants, research angles, and funding possibilities are especially welcome. I suspect that summer '85 would be too soon to get such an odyssey organized, so summer '86 sounds like a reasonable target date.

Thanks for listening. I look forward to your reactions.

Sincerely,

Russell W. Belk
Professor of Marketing

I was inspired to write this letter by one of the revelatory feelings I tend to get when I know at a profound intuitive level that something is right. It was written at a time when I had spent the past couple of years arguing that the field of consumer behavior had been construed too narrowly (e.g., Belk 1982, 1983, 1984a, 1984b). I had also given several presentations involving such non-traditional sources of consumer behavior insight as literature, poetry, comic books, painting, photography, music, rock videos, film, and grave goods. I felt a need to break out of the narrow straitjacket of the managerial orientation that others in the field had called for. There had to be more to consumer behavior than laboratory research on cognitive processes had been able to reveal. Consuming is a natural and inevitable part of daily life and research that attempts to also be a part of daily life seemed a logical way to study it. Accordingly, I sent the letter to the most innovative and open-minded people I knew in the discipline. I didn't really think about whether I might be jeopardizing my career potential with such a move. I just knew it felt necessary and right.

The State of the Field at the Time

At the time of this letter, the philosophy of science most typically employed in academic consumer behavior research was logical empiricism. There was also ferment at the time; there had been discussions -- both private and public -- at national conferences and smaller workshops, and in the journals, about alternatives to logical empiricism. But, for the most part, this was the philosophic tradition guiding consumer research. The philosophic approach of logical empiricism (a.k.a. logical positivism, falsificationism) rests on a set of epistemological assumptions which lead researchers to search for *the* truth about a presumably singular and knowable reality, often in the artificial environment of a laboratory setting in which everything else is presumed to be held constant. To a small number of us this received wisdom seemed increasingly unsatisfactory and untenable. It seemed to provide, at best, only a partial perspective on consumption. Something important was missing.

The field of consumer research was dominated substantively at that time by a view of consumers as information processors. The primary conceptual focus was brand choice decisions made by individuals. If information processing takes place, it seemed reasonable that it would occur as consumers chose brands in the marketplace. As such, consumer research was for the most part focused on buyer behavior, and not on consumption behavior at all. It was focused on contemporary times, with little historical perspective. And it was ethnocentrically based on U.S. patterns of buying behavior.

Structurally, there was also some controversy emerging, but for the most part, consumer research was housed in business schools and was conducted from the perspective of a business trying to sell more of its products in order to make more profit. People outside marketing departments were not seen as consumer researchers, although their work might be regarded as interesting by those who were considered consumer researchers. At this time, people within the field often talked about consumer research as being interdisciplinary. But what was typically meant by this was that people within business school marketing department PhD programs might take a few courses in psychology and subsequently "borrow" (though not often pay back) psychological concepts and apply them to the dominant perspective of consumer behavior research. Because cognitive psychology was dominant within psychology, information processing became the dominant conceptual approach employed in studying consumer behavior. Since there were profits to be made in understanding contemporary U.S. buying patterns for branded products, and since most consumer behavior researchers had business school academic appointments, the dominant perspective was widely embraced.

Methodologically the field looked to experimental design as its ideal, sometimes supplemented by survey data. The prescribed procedure was to develop a hypothesis (most often based on a psychological theory), run an experiment, and employ analysis of variance and other multivariate procedures for testing the hypothesis statistically. The introduction of experimental research and multivariate methods had helped to largely quash the more qualitative motivation research movement of the 1950s.

Dissent Becomes Action

Thus philosophically, conceptually, methodologically, and structurally, there was, and had been, dissent. There had been a few courageous dissidents who had questioned the dominant approaches, especially in the first half of the 1980's. Interestingly, although they were paradigmatically on the fringe, these dissidents were sociometrically at the core. The positivist philosophy was being questioned and debunked by Paul Anderson (1983, 1986), and through his organization of the AMA Workshop on Marketing Theory held in Blacksburg, Virginia in May 1985. This dominant philosophy was also being questioned through the circulation to an invisible college of interested consumer researchers, reading lists which Jerry Olson constructed while on sabbatical.

The limited conceptual focus on buyers rather than consumers had been questioned much earlier by William T. (Tom) Tucker (1967) in a book that presented a series of ethnographic descriptions of consumer behaviors. But his message for the most part fell on deaf ears. He was ahead of his time in his thinking and the message was delivered just at the time that the field was striving for "scientific" legitimacy via the "multivariate revolution" and its potential for computer manipulation of large amounts of quantitative data.

The focus on buying rather than consuming had been criticized by Elizabeth Hirschman and Morris Holbrook (Hirschman and Holbrook 1982; Holbrook and Hirschman 1982). That a focus on the meanings of consumption rather than purchase might lead to the use of methods other than experimentation had been amply demonstrated by Sidney Levy over a substantial period of time, including one publication that appeared at roughly the same time as these others (Levy 1981). Contrary to a frequently expressed hesitation concerning the individual hazards that might accrue to newcomers trying approaches that differ from those of the mainstream, it was demonstrated that such a branching out was possible when Dennis Rook, whose dissertation Sid Levy chaired, received an honorable mention in the

1985 Robert Ferber Award for Consumer Research competition for the best *Journal of Consumer Research* article based on a recent doctoral dissertation (Rook 1985). New methods for understanding consumption were being unveiled including the use of photography as a research method (Wallendorf 1984), the use of personal introspection guided by psychoanalytic interpretation (Holbrook 1986), and the use of materials from the humanities to investigate consumer behavior (Belk 1986). It was also becoming clear that social scientists from other fields could make a significant contribution to consumer research without adopting a managerial perspective. John Sherry, an anthropologist by training, published an article based on anthropological theory in the *Journal of Consumer Research* (Sherry 1983), and scholars from a number of disciplines were beginning to recognize consumer research as a legitimate area of study (e.g., Lears 1983, McCracken 1985, Horowitz 1985).

At the same time, there was a growing debate about whether consumer research was well-served by being oriented toward the interests of managers and businesses. A double session was held at the 1984 Association for Consumer Research meetings in Washington, D.C. entitled 'The 'Vices' and 'Virtues' of Being Relevant: Perspectives on Consulting." The session included personal position papers by Jack Jacoby, Jagdish Sheth, and Jerry Wind speaking on the virtues of consulting activity, versus others by James Bettman, Russell Belk, and Morris Holbrook on the vices of consulting activity for consumer researchers. A large audience listened to the somewhat heated discussion, even though the presentations were less volatile than the exchange of materials by Holbrook and Jacoby in the months preceding the conference and the somewhat subdued versions published in the proceedings of the conference. Paul Peter, who had previously circulated a cleverly written paper entitled "On the Role of the Neppian Pheebs" to a number of colleagues, pointed out in the discussion following the presentations that it appeared to him that for an academic consumer behavior researcher to do consulting work for business was a bit like doing consulting work for Goliath to help him defeat David. Paul was not alone in taking this position. The critical self-examination of the structural position of the field continued at another double session the following year entitled "Whither ACR?" The session included presentations by Paul Anderson, Russell Belk, Alden Clayton and Diane Schmalensee, Geraldine Fennell, Elizabeth Hirschman, Morris Holbrook, Melanie Wallendorf, William Wells, and Richard Lutz (whose call for conference papers that returned to consumer behavior's "roots in marketing" had precipitated the reactions that led to this session).

The point of this extended list of names, dates, and places is that by 1985 the field remained dominated by one position, but was increasingly raising questions concerning the appropriateness of this position. A substantial and sociometrically-central minority of opposition was growing in size, strength, and support. It was within this context that my letter was formulated and received. What this January 1985 letter did was to provide a forum for attempts to coalesce the questioning into a collectivity. It seemed to offer the opposition group a demonstration project around which we could organize and mobilize.

Having said this, I must reveal that my entire graduate training focused on experimental social psychology and multivariate quantitative methods. However my Minnesota dissertation chairman, Ivan Ross, is both a psychologist and a broad and interesting human being who inspired me with a healthy skepticism toward the taken-for-granted. Although I have never had a course in anthropology or sociology (except for one course in social psychology taught by a sociologist), I had done a little reading in these areas. Still, I was obviously a babe in the woods. Fortunately, the idea for the Consumer Behavior Odyssey fell on fertile ground and the Odyssey was able to attract others (Durgee, Heisley, Sherry, Wallendorf) who had actually had some training in qualitative methods through courses in sociology or anthropology.

Response to the Letter

The first two responses to the letter, which I subsequently distributed to other potential participants, were from Hal Kassarjian and Bill Wells. Hal Kassarjian wrote, in part:

January 18, 1985

Dear Russ,

I received your letter of January 9 and read it with a great deal of interest. To be perfectly honest, I felt in me an excitement and almost a thrill. Its a feeling I hadn't had in this field in many years. When ACR first started, when early ACR conferences were being organized, when JCR was being planned I had felt that same thrill. A feeling that we were embarking on something important or at least fun.

Consumer research has been dull for the last half a decade. Perhaps it is because the technocrats have overpowered the field and squeezed it dry of fun. There are a few people left in this field who can enjoy it and I think

you have written to them about this idea. Levy, Hirschman, Wells, and the others. Much of what there is in the field today is simply not fun or even very interesting. I think that is the reason why the Holbrook-Jacoby (not to mention Belk, Wind, Bettman, etc) session on consulting was so popular at the last ACR meetings. Finally something interesting to listen to rather than a paper on scripts or short-term memory.

If this project could be pulled off, I think it would be the major contribution of the 1980's. First of all, it would be fun and people will be anxious to see what was done. Secondly, it should, as you suggest, produce a plethora of raw data that others may or may not use. But much more important than that, it may accomplish what Tucker was trying to do in his *Foundations for a Theory of Consumer Behavior*. He failed.

In my opinion, what Tucker was trying to say is, "explain these vignettes." [Marketers]... and psychologists and anthropologists, explain Juan Navarro's purchase of a shirt, the Rigby family purchase of maple furniture (or whatever it was), explain the purchase of the Volkswagen or Peach Faced Parrot. He failed to get his message across. It was too early; we didn't exist as a field as yet. There were too many exciting concepts yet to be borrowed, to worry about explaining the purchase of a shirt.

With a project like this and the masses of data it can produce, we can go back to what Tucker was saying. Take your attribution theory and your information processing and your schemas and explain the purchase of an orange peeler at the county fair, a tee shirt at a Texas rodeo, a Rolex watch in Beverly Hills, a Coca-Cola tray at a flea market, or even a ugly bottle blond at a brothel.

The only problem I see is that it really should be atheoretic. No prior hypotheses and no elaborate interpretations or expectations (as you suggest). I am not sure we can handle a free floating opportunity; I am not sure we are good enough. For example we have invented formula writing for our articles (e.g. JPSP, JEP and even JCR) because we are not good enough to write real prose.

Here, we would have to learn the skills of a journalist. This is a research method we are not all that good at. We would need to film with the eye of a director and a film editor. To be useful, it would have to look like a segment of "20/20" or a documentary. It will have to be skillful; with the eye of a story teller or a journalist or a TV cameraman to be successful. I think Levy has that skill as does Wells and some of the others. I think it can be done.

I think the rented van is the only way to go. I think people will have to stay with the project for say 3-4 weeks minimum or they would not get the hang of it. I think we will all need to become familiar with filming and a touch of acting so that it is not the technology that drives us but the gathering of data. And I think we may need to weave in some theories from the field once in a while - on tape - even if it is only to say - go ahead ... - deal with this situation. But these are all details to be worked out. The fact that I get excited even about details reflects my excitement about the project.

Yes, its a big job and it will require a lot of money. But it can be done. If a few people sitting around a table can launch a new Journal (JCR) that was to "lose" 50,000 1970 dollars before it even appeared, a van can be rented. If someone like Cohen was willing to risk more than half a year's salary to guarantee hotel charges to get ACR started, it seems to me that this project can be pulled off.

I think it needs careful planning and some expert help. I would sure like to see a journalism type involved in it. Maybe at some conference you can have people come a day early or stay a day late to work on it. Perhaps at the AMA meetings in Arizona, next month, a planning meeting can be arranged to prepare for a full meeting of participants at the August AMA meetings. Final planning can be at the ACR meetings in Nevada.

Russ, I want in on it. I'm not sure why? Maybe because it will be fun to spend a month with colleagues really studying the consumer rather than reading manuscripts and crunching numbers. Maybe it will just be fun to go to a Texas Rodeo, a wedding, a garage sale, or a dance hall with someone to discuss what it is we are seeing. Maybe something important will come of it, but even if it turns out to be a amateurish flop and disaster, it will be fun. Even the sloppiest of data will make one helluva story. I think it has the potential to be the most exciting thing that has happened in this field in a decade or longer.

If nothing else, it will be great fun to talk about it and plan it. Count me in! And thank you for putting my name on your distinguished list. I consider it an honor. And, by the way, I think others will also consider it an honor to have been part of the project, and the real problem will be to keep out the technocrats and the rigid researchers and keep in the weird ones and outcasts from the main stream.

Keep me in touch and perhaps you might want to pass around the letters that you do get.

Sincerely,

Hal Kassarjian

Hal's letter sparkled with excitement and Hal's delightful humor. The letter from Bill Wells (then Senior Vice President and Director of Marketing Services at the advertising agency of Needham Harper Worldwide) was equally encouraging and made funding seem a real possibility:

January 16, 1985

Dear Russ,

Thanks for including me in the group considered weird enough to comment on your Odyssey idea. A high honor!

As you know, I've been distressed by academic researchers' tendency to migrate from real consumers to theoretical never-never land. Your Odyssey idea, appropriately executed and publicized, should go a long way toward pulling at least some of them back.

I'll help in any way I can. MSI seems like a good place to centralize funding efforts. I will be glad to support your plan with them, and to lobby with people I know on the MSI board. You will also need help getting permission to do on-site observations, interviews, and tape recordings. We have some influence with Honda, HFC, McDonald's and Sears.

If you plan to move ahead, you might want to discuss your plans at the MSI-Division 23 conference on advertising and consumer behavior. That meeting is scheduled for July 11-12. It's being held at Needham. Let me know if you'd like to do that.

Good Luck!

Cordially,

Bill

PLANNING THE ODYSSEY

Initial Plans: 1985 Winter American Marketing Association Educators' Conference

Clearly, there was support for the idea, even though it was still relatively amorphous. The next step was to get together and talk. A group meeting was arranged for the following month at the February American Marketing Association Winter Educator's Conference in Phoenix. Present at this meeting/dinner in Phoenix were Russ Belk, Valerie Folkes, Beth Hirschman, Hal and Traute Kassarjian, Jerry Olson, John Sherry, and Melanie Wallendorf. It was clear that there was a unique group spirit here when someone decided we should order the entire dessert tray. A ritual quickly developed in which each person would take a bite of each treat and pass it on to the next person until all desserts had been consumed; we called it the venereal dessert.

At the dinner we discussed the Odyssey and agreed that the coming summer was probably too early to be ready for such a venture, and that the summer of 1986 was indeed more feasible. We concurred that the travel format, while not essential for such research, would allow as many researchers to participate as possible, with some potentially acting as a scouting party that would travel ahead of the larger group. We quickly became aware of the equipment needed to carry off this project. We also became aware of the additional training and preparation many of us felt we needed. It was decided that we would begin circulating reading lists among ourselves.

Follow-up Activity

Soon after the conference in early March 1985, I circulated another memo to the expanding group of interested people. This memo suggested that we all begin acquiring necessary methodological skills (e.g., photography, videotaping, interviewing, writing, participant observation, and oral history taking), as well as looking for others who might have needed skills (especially in documentary production). This memo also raised the possibility, suggested by Bill Wells, of obtaining funding through the Marketing Science Institute. I volunteered to serve as a clearinghouse for information. The next due date was April 15, 1985 for people to respond with an indication of interest. The next planning meeting was scheduled for the October 1985 meetings of the Association for Consumer Research in Las Vegas.

In June of 1985, I circulated a summer reading list to a still growing group of interested people. The two page list of methods readings contained only two entries from the field of marketing along with three papers from a phenomenology session at the previous ACR conference. All other suggested readings were from outside the field. John Sherry subsequently helped expand this reading list with additional anthropological treatments of methods. This was a learning endeavor which we hoped would extend the range of methodological understanding of not only the participants, but of the field in general.

In July of 1985, John Sherry made a "pitch" at the Needham Harper conference that Bill Wells had mentioned in his letter. Among those in attendance was John Farley who was ultimately instrumental in granting funding from the Marketing Science Institute. In September, just before the 1985 ACR conference, I sent out another memo to an ever-growing set of potential participants. An evening meeting was scheduled for the ACR conference in Las Vegas in mid-October 1985. This memo announced that Tom O'Guinn

would join the project, adding someone with substantial background in photography and film production. Up to this point, no others with such skills had been identified. The memo also announced that John Sherry had pitched the project to MSI people at the Needham Harper conference, and that I had made a preliminary inquiry about funding possibilities.

Although I may have made some enemies in doing so, at several universities where I gave talks in the year preceding the Odyssey I included (in addition to an explanation of the proposed Odyssey project) a takeoff on Jonathan Swift's "Modest Proposal". These comments parodied the consumer information processing perspective by proposing that since consumers don't really behave in the manner by CIP models, we should make them do so by implanting computer chips in their heads, along with transceivers and antennae for receiving advertising information and transmitting processed reactions. With the incorporation of attitude model attribute weights, variation in consumer choice was eliminated in this proposal and a marriage of the economic and cognitive models of human behavior was thereby achieved. All of this was meant as a light-hearted poke at the dominant approach and a further justification for the need to shake free of our traditional assumptions and to seek the consumer *in situ* in order to develop a more grounded understanding of what consumption means to people. I now think this approach may have succeeded philosophically in establishing the intent of the Odyssey, but may also have somewhat narrowed the constituency that might have otherwise taken the chance of becoming involved with the Odyssey.

The 1985 Association for Consumer Research Meeting

It was clear that there was momentum to the project by this time. This was most evident when a group of about 40 people showed up for the Las Vegas dinner. No one believed that everyone who came to dinner would actually participate in the research, but it was an indication of the level of curiosity and interest of the field. If Hal Kassarjian was worried that the technocrats might invade the project, Melanie Wallendorf was worried that untrained or unskilled people would weaken the project. But I wanted it to be open to anyone who was interested. The project was to be a learning experience and I think we all had much to learn, in part from each other.

Since this first meeting of the group over dinner was cumbersome, we adjourned to a hotel meeting room afterward. Because there were many in attendance who had not been on previous mailing lists, the meeting was primarily informational, with expressions of interest, and suggestions -- sort of a huge focus group. Another meeting was set for a second night and was attended by about 18 more hard-core participants. At this meeting we began to assess skills and agree to take on specific roles for the project. For instance, Rick Pollay was to be our archivist, Melanie Wallendorf was to compile people's expressions of interests for the summer, and I was to concentrate on funding.

During the ACR meetings, we learned that the Marketing Science Institute and its then executive director John Farley had agreed to give us a $1000 seed grant for a demonstration project to show that we could do such research and that it could be fruitful. If the pilot project was successful, there was an unstated promise that MSI would consider additional funding for the main project. Bill Wells also invited us to prepare a wish list of things we would like funded for the project.

Given the size of the seed grant and the necessity for completing the demonstration project quickly, we decided to go with an intensive week of research involving a small group consisting of Hal Kassarjian, John Sherry, Melanie Wallendorf, and me. Since John and I had previously done work with gift-giving, this was one focus considered. But Melanie knew of a swap meet in the Southwest that offered a convenient location for three of us and the promise of good weather. It was decided that this swap meet would be the focus for our demonstration project and that we would carry out the data collection in November. Melanie would visit the site once first on a scouting mission.

I sent out another memo after the ACR conference to summarize what had been decided there. With optimism, the memo concluded that "the force is with us." The pilot was to be conducted November 21-24, 1985 at what we have subsequently called the Red Mesa Swap Meet in Pueblo, New Mexico (a disguised location). The Odyssey project would begin in Los Angeles on June 14, 1986 and would be in the Chicago area by July 10, 1986. The travel itinerary would finish in the New York City area in August 1986. At that time it was our plan to stay in houses and backyards while en route, with each participant seeking his/her own funding for any food and lodging expenses. An austere budget planned around this self-subsidy of personal expenses still totaled $50,000. Just prior to the pilot project, I heard from Bill Wells that Needham Harper would pick up the $4700 it would cost to rent a van for the summer project. This had been the largest single item on the wish list, so we were elated. All we needed to do now was an impressive job on the pilot project. We were excited!

The Pilot: Red Mesa Swap Meet

The pilot was a wonderful experience. The substantive findings are summarized in Belk, Sherry, and Wallendorf (1988). But this report does not adequately reveal our feelings in conducting the project or how this project shaped the eventual conduct of the larger Odyssey project. These aspects deserve more attention here.

Because of an illness in his family, Hal was not able to come to the swap meet for data collection, but rather participated by serving as one of the three auditors (the others were Robert Prus and Dennis Rook) on the report we wrote. During the pilot project John, Melanie, and I encountered many of the types of problems the Odyssey would face daily ("where is the cord?" "I think we are low on battery power," "the van won't start," "I am dead; I don't know how I can do this again tomorrow," and "I don't know how I am going to get caught up on my field notes."). These problems centered on the depletion of energy in ourselves and our equipment as well as questions about how to continue. But we also encountered the joys of intensively working together, the thrill of an interview that "got good stuff," and the solidification of a working style that grew into a daily Odyssey pattern. We learned that such research is exhausting, exhilarating, and demanding. We decided that on the full Odyssey we would need to be adaptive, confer regularly, and learn to rely upon the unique skills of each participant.

I doubt that MSI ever got more effort, energy, or material out of $1000 than they did out of the seed grant that got us started. It was partly a labor of love, partly that this effort promised larger rewards in potential funding for the summer project, and partly that it was now time to "put up or shut up" about the project. I had conducted focus groups before and had just completed a video class, but doing depth interviews in the field was *terra incognita.* I was simultaneously excited and frightened. We ate, slept, and breathed the swap meet and each successive interview became a little less terrifying as I learned that people are basically friendly, helpful, and rewarded by someone who takes a sincere interest in what they have to say. I think it took until sometime during the summer to fully convince Melanie that we were giving something to our informants by listening (rather than just taking). Still, John and Melanie were much better at this than I was.

When we got out of the field from the pilot (and I had our fieldnotes, photos, artifacts, audiotapes, and videotapes before me and a convincing report to draft for our sponsor), the real fun began. I always liked the challenge of making sense out of quantitative data, and teasing themes out of qualitative data is more exciting by far. I knew these themes would have to be scrutinized by Melanie, John, our auditors, and several informants, so they had to be clear from the data. At the same time, they had to be interesting and unique enough to show the promise of these methods. This was before we got laptop computers, shared software, and search routines, so I made multiple copies of our notes, scribbled marginal comments about potential themes, and piled them up before me to see what we had. Sometimes our on-site discussions and Daily Odyssey Audits (John's phrase with intentional double entendre in the acronym) held each evening had begun to flesh out these themes; in other cases they "jumped out" of the data; and in still other cases they might occur to me days later as I was out on a morning run. Gradually it all took shape and I thought it was a good document, although still a preliminary report that the others had yet to see, with member checks and external audits to follow. Nevertheless, as I sent this preliminary report to the Marketing Science Institute, I had a very good feeling about the chances of further funding. I was now a firm believer in what I had previously taken as an act of intuitive faith: qualitative research has enormous potential for consumer research.

Final Planning

By mid-December of 1985 (less than a year since the original letter, and less than a month out of the field from the pilot project), after the preliminary report on the pilot project had been filed with MSI, an update memo was sent to the list of people interested in the Odyssey. With this memo, I sent all who had expressed interest a questionnaire form designed by John Sherry on which they were to indicate their plans regarding participation in the project. It was time to begin to make more definite plans for the summer of travel and data collection.

At the end of February of 1986, I sent a copy of the final report to MSI on the pilot project to all potential participants and updated everyone on the emerging specific plans for the summer. At this point, the list of people who definitely planned to participate was becoming more finalized into a core group of active participants--more or less the two dozen who would participate in the full Odyssey. Others offered to help in various ways. Dennis Rook would be spending the summer in Bali, but volunteered his apartment as a launching pad for the project in Los Angeles. Alan Andreasen also agreed to do some preliminary site work in that area for us, as did Vic Johar. Keith Hunt would be teaching over the summer and couldn't travel with us, but was willing to help with arrangements prior to launching the project and offered lodging at his house if we would be

in the area. Keith has so many children that an extra 5 or 6 people at his house wouldn't make a big difference, he assured us. An advance party of John Sherry, Sid Levy, Deb Heisley, and Mary Ann McGrath were set up to do scouting work in the Chicago area. In addition, Foote, Cone and Belding Advertising pledged sufficient money to cover our second largest expense category, namely film and audio tapes. Less than a month before we entered the field, John Farley informed me that MSI would indeed supply additional funding for the project. We would still need to contribute individually (many of our universities also helped), but the project was viable.

Trying to coordinate who would be with the Odyssey at what times was becoming complex. Melanie created a sheet showing people and sites and distributed it to everyone in May of 1986. By this time, Melanie and I had each ordered laptop computers to be delivered in Los Angeles. Tom O'Guinn had arranged the use of University of Illinois video equipment and had purchased 200 blank 3/4-inch videotapes and literally a refrigerator-full of 35mm film. Joe Cote had arranged free lodging in a Hilton Hotel on a space available basis for a week. Kay Belk, who contributed the title "Highways and Buyways," silkscreened Odyssey t-shirts for all participants. Scott Roberts, John Schouten, and Rich Semenik were doing some scouting work in the West and awaiting our arrival at a point where they would join us. Valerie Folkes, Vic Johar, and Hal Kassarjian were awaiting our arrival in California, where they would work with us. Morris Holbrook was doing preliminary site work in an Eastern resort area where he and Jeff Durgee would join us. Elsewhere, Bernie Jaworski and Debbie MacInnis were scouting an Eastern urban location where they would join the Odyssey. Beth Hirschman invited us to stay at her house in Connecticut when we were in the East. While I was at a European conference, Hal Kassarjian, after conferring with Keith Hunt and Melanie Wallendorf, located a van we could rent.

CONDUCTING THE ODYSSEY

In mid-June 1986, Tom, John, Melanie, and I arrived in Los Angeles and started the project which at times looked like a new series entitled "The Four Stooges" and at times looked like good social science. For better or worse, we were now a team. The particular people along for the journey changed over time as we traveled across country, except that I was there for the duration and Melanie made it coast-to-coast. The Consumer Behavior Odyssey went to swap meets, antique sales, art shows, fast food outlets, into people's homes, to souvenir shops, hotels, grocery stores, parades, riverboat cruises, hospitals, county fairs, shelters for the homeless, and to nursing homes. We interviewed people as diverse as foreign and domestic tourists, entrants in a custom car show, owners of goats in a goat show, the Amish, nuns, a family traveling across the country by covered wagon, artists, suburban housewives, circus performers, street people, collectors, and an old man with three garages full of a lifetime's possessions.

The interviews were largely unstructured, although they became more focused as our understanding developed over the course of the summer. Such is the emergent nature of the method. We employed a research methodology that has best been explicated by Lincoln and Guba (1985). The approach is characterized by the emergence of themes in a constant comparative method, employing member checks, auditing, and memoing. The sample is purposive and selected to constantly challenge and assess emergent ideas. These procedures were developed and adapted in the pilot project at Red Mesa Swap Meet and are described in Belk, Sherry, and Wallendorf (1988) and Wallendorf and Belk (1989).

Although this project was unusual within consumer research, it is similar to traditional anthropological and sociological field studies and psychological depth interviews. Yet it was unusual by not remaining within one context. Instead, we defined our context very broadly as American consumption as seen through the eyes of the consumer, but with the insight and technology that our interdisciplinary team of scholars could add. We employed what Whyte (1984) calls "hunt and peck ethnography." A guiding assumption of this approach is that the deeper themes or issues exist across locales, across sites, across people.

Nothing can fully convey the rich memories I have of the trials, rewards, and experiences of the Odyssey summer. Three incidents that occurred near the beginning, middle, and end of the project may allow some glimpses into this sea of memories however. The first occurred in Los Angeles one morning/evening (we worked until 1:00 or 2:00 AM, as was typical despite getting up at 6:00 AM). We decided that we would practice our interviewing skills by conducting video interviews of each other in which the assignment was to find out what possessions each of us had brought for the trip and what meaning these things had. I believe this had initially been Rick Pollay's idea. The interview of Tom O'Guinn was most revealing. We had learned something of Tom's lifestyle in the day or two preceding the interview, mostly by tripping over the array of his equipment and clothing that occupied an ever-expanding portion of the apartment. During the interview we were shown a single tennis shoe (Tom was

sure he had the other somewhere), three different kinds of dental floss, a battery charger that Tom was sure worked with something he must have along, and a large pharmacy of emergency medical supplies-- just in case. Tom did not travel lightly in any sense of the word. His wit and humor during the interview added to the hilarity, helped break the ice, and allowed the sort of release that proved essential to keep up our pace and keep our group intact. A second incident occurred in the desserts of the West. I was driving the RV while Melanie and Hal worked on fieldnotes (a never-ending task on which we could at best approach occasionally catching up) and Tom bulk-loaded film from large rolls into camera-sized rolls. I spied a covered wagon and campsite near the side of the road and slammed on the brakes. There was a little grumbling, but when everyone recovered I pointed out the wagons and we were off on one of those fortuitous interviews that were the source of some of our best data. A third incident happened at an outdoor antique show one day on the East Coast when the crew was down to Melanie and me. Things started when after a particularly rich on-camera interview, I started talking to our male informant in greater depth while Melanie started interviewing his female partner. She decided to videotape the interview and learned what a logistical challenge this can be without a separate camera person. Lest I be deprived of learning of this challenge she left the camera to do another interview just as I was starting another on-camera interview. As I rewatch this tape, the audio is quite clear thanks to the hand-held mike, but the video includes mostly some nice foot shots.

What I remember more than anything, however, is the people who made the Odyssey possible. This includes our informants, supporters such as Bill Wells and John Farley, our families, and most of all, the Odyssites who devoted their skills, knowledge, time, efforts, and money to the project. Without them (and Melanie Wallendorf, Tom O'Guinn, and John Sherry contributed the most dearly), this project would not have been. Everyone who participated made the Odyssey a better project and there were even some casualties. Alladi Venkatesh (Venky) showed up in Chicago with his forearm in a cast, and Tom O'Guinn broke his finger "in action."

OUT OF THE FIELD: THE ODYSSEY CONTINUES

Once we had finished the field work, the Odyssey was far from over. When I returned the van to the rental company just outside of Boston in late August, some 25 boxes of research materials were shipped back to Utah. Once they arrived, the task of sorting, labeling, and indexing began. In addition, incredibly, there was just over a month to prepare a promised session on the Odyssey for the Association for Consumer Research Meeting. Melanie was co-chair for the conference and had the attendant details to handle. As ACR President that year, I also had to prepare a Presidential Address (readers may remember it as "the dog food level of things" speech). While some credible papers and a slide show were presented at that year's ACR Odyssey session, entitled "How We Spent Our Summer Vacation," we all felt it was far too early to be able to confidently say anything substantive. It wasn't really until the 1987 conference that we were ready to discuss analyses and findings.

In the intervening year, participants disguised fieldnotes, made duplicates of all videotapes, slides, and print photographs, and indexed all of these materials so they could be installed in an archive at MSI following the conference. We tried to accomplish some of the necessary joint work at conferences, and at one point, Tom and I joined Melanie in Tucson for a mini-marathon long weekend of photo and slide coding. In addition, the pilot study report to MSI was expanded into a paper for journal submission (Belk, Sherry, and Wallendorf 1988), and several presentations of the Odyssey material were made at universities and other professional organizations.

As our final report, John Farley of MSI suggested that we prepare a visual report rather than a paper, in order to capitalize on the visual nature of the videotaped interviews and photographs. In response to this suggestion, Melanie and I produced a 40-minute video on the Odyssey entitled "Deep Meaning in Possessions: Qualitative Research from the Consumer Behavior Odyssey" (Wallendorf and Belk 1987). As had been the case with most of the project, producing the video was another task for which we were ill-prepared. We had no training or experience in video production, but nonetheless set out to do this confident that having learned to run a video camera, shoot still photographs, use our laptop computers, use computer software for managing and searching qualitative data, drive and operate a recreation vehicle, and conduct fieldwork, we would learn how to produce a video simply by doing it. I had excerpted some video and slide material for an interim report/presentation to MSI in November of 1986. This material formed the rough core of the subsequent video. Learning that we could use editing equipment that Tom had secured at the University of Illinois and at a local television studio, I joined Deborah Heisley, Melanie, and Tom there in February, 1987. Tom had some previous experience with editing equipment, but we were faced with an array of unfamiliar equipment and very little in

the way of instructions. Nevertheless, with two nearly sleepless nights and days, and one totally sleepless day and night, we came close to completing what we thought was our finished product. By that time Melanie was doing a sabbatical at Utah, so we returned to Salt Lake City with our prized video to make some finishing touches at the University of Utah. When the media people there saw the technical flaws in what we had done, they suggested that we start over. We sadly accepted their advice and began several months of trying to schedule time to work on the video. During this time we were assisted by Scott Roberts, who was then a doctoral student at Utah. Thanks to a professional production crew and several months of work, we finished a video of which we are proud, even though it was not perfect and took much longer than we had initially planned. The video is distributed by the Marketing Science Institute for a nominal price and is currently used in a number of classes in marketing departments and related fields. Watching the video should provide a more complete perspective on the Odyssey and its methods and findings.

The data collected by the Consumer Behavior Odyssey are housed in an archive at the Marketing Science Institute in Cambridge, Massachusetts. This archive consists of approximately 1000 single spaced pages of field notes and journals (in hard copy and in word processing files), roughly 4000 still photos, about 40 hours of videotaped interviews, and hard copy and computerized versions of indices to these materials. This archive is available for use by other researchers. While this archive houses materials from the summer-long Odyssey, data collection did not stop there for us. The basic procedures used during the Odyssey have been employed in dozens of projects since. Subsets of the Odyssey team (involving Belk, Durgee, Heisley, Holbrook, McGrath, O'Guinn, Roberts, Schouten, Sherry, and Wallendorf) have been involved on these projects and have acquired additional audio, video, photography, and computing equipment and expertise to facilitate this research.

THE PAYOFF

By moving not only across the country, but also by moving away from the concepts, methods, and philosophy of science that have previously characterized academic consumer research, what have we learned? The remainder of this book demonstrates the substantive and methodological findings of the project. Immediately following this chapter is a poem by John Schouten that distills multiple images and aspects of fieldwork on the Odyssey. It is followed by three views of the methods employed.

Excerpts from Morris Holbrook's log presents a narrative describing field experiences in a way similar to, if more poetic than, others' fieldnotes and journals. Bernie Jaworski and Debbie MacInnis describe their experience in serving as informants before joining us as researchers. And Dennis Rook reflects on the experience of having his apartment occupied and (to his surprise) studied by the Odyssey crew while he was gone. He also reflects on the subsequent experience of being autodriven by John Sherry using photos of his "stuff" (some of which are included here) as stimuli.

The next section of the book presents an array of substantive findings from the Odyssey, sometimes supplemented by follow-up work. The sacred and profane paper is one of two contributions in the book that has been published previously, and is included because these themes emerged as the *leitmotif* of the Odyssey. Tom O'Guinn's touching greatness paper is a photo-based analysis of the fascination of many Americans with celebrities. John Schouten's poem "Sorting" is included next as it evocatively and succinctly describes some of the same phenomena that I need many more pages to attempt to present in my paper on possessions and the sense of past. That paper is followed by Jeff Durgee, Morris Holbrook, and John Sherry's analysis of the drama of performances through five very different entertainments encountered on the Odyssey. In a final photo essay in the book (reprinted with the permission of the *Journal of Popular Culture*), Deb Heisley, Mary Ann McGrath, and John Sherry show the cycles of an urban farmers' market and describe the corresponding development of their research project at this market. Jeff Durgee, Morris Holbrook, and Melanie Wallendorf then present a thick description of the lives of upper middle class women as they are played out in and through their homes. The substantive papers conclude with an analysis of collecting by Morris Holbrook, John Sherry, Melanie Wallendorf, and me.

The concluding section of the book contains two evaluations of the Odyssey. Annamma Joy, with the advantage of the greater distance of someone who was not along on the Odyssey, presents an evaluation of the project from the self-reflexive perspective now current in anthropology. She helps to further contextualize the present research vis-a-vis other qualitative research that has recently been published on consumers. I conclude with some observations on some small and large lessons learned from the Odyssey.

But in another sense, what we learned is not the same as what we found. As John Sherry noted in a memo circulated after we completed the field work, "what we learned from each other and through each other may ultimately eclipse whatever substantive findings we eventually publish." What we learned has much more to do with the basic human passions that led each of us to participate in the project. What we learned is that those passions constitute the essential strength of the kind of social science we do as well as the essential nature of the world we study. We learned that the fears that held us back previously, and still continue to hold others back, aren't worth listening to. We have made a brave leap when we didn't know how to jump, and found that it brought us joy. Through this research and through each other we have encountered something of the fullness of life.

REFERENCES

Anderson, Paul (1983), "Marketing, Scientific Progress, and Scientific Method," *Journal of Marketing*, 47 (Fall), 18-31.

Anderson, Paul (1986) "On Method in Consumer Research: A Critical Relativist Perspective," *Journal of Consumer Research*, 13 (September), 155-173.

Belk, Russell W. (1982), "Acquiring, Possessing, and Collecting: Fundamental Processes in Consumer Behavior," *Marketing Theory: Philosophy of Science Perspectives*, Ronald F. Bush and Shelby D. Hunt, eds., Chicago: American Marketing Association, 185-190.

Belk, Russell W. (1983), "Worldly Possessions: Issues and Criticisms," *Advances in Consumer Research*, Vol. 10, Richard P. Bagozzi and Alice M. Tybout, eds., Ann Arbor: Association for Consumer Research, 514-519.

Belk, Russell W. (1984a), "Against Thinking," *Scientific Method in Marketing*, Paul F. Anderson and Michael J. Ryan, eds., Chicago: American Marketing Association, 57-59.

Belk, Russell W. (1984b), "Cultural and Historical Differences in Concepts of Self and Their Effects on Attitudes Toward Having and Giving," *Advances in Consumer Research*, Vol. 11, Thomas Kinnear, ed., Provo, UT: Association for Consumer Research, 753-760.

Belk, Russell W. (1984c), "Manifesto for a Consumer Behavior of Consumer Behavior," *Scientific Method in Marketing*, Paul F. Anderson and Michael J. Ryan, eds., Chicago: American Marketing Association, 163-167.

Belk, Russell W. (1986), "Art Versus Science as Ways of Generating Knowledge About Materialism," *Methodological Perspectives in Consumer Research*, Richard Lutz and David Brinberg, eds., New York: Springer Verlag, 1986.

Belk, Russell W., John F. Sherry, Jr., and Melanie Wallendorf (1988), "A Naturalistic Inquiry in Buyer and Seller Behavior at a

Swap Meet," *Journal of Consumer Research,* 14 (March), 449-470.

Hirschman, Elizabeth C. and Morris B. Holbrook (1982), "Hedonic Consumption: Emerging Concepts, Methods, and Propositions," *Journal of Marketing,* 46, (Summer), 92-101.

Holbrook, Morris B. (1986), "I'm Hip: An Autobiographical Account of Some Musical Consumption Experiences," *Advances in Consumer Research,* 13, 614-618.

Holbrook, Morris B. and Hirschman, Elizabeth C. (1982), "The Experiential Aspects of Consumption: Consumer Fantasies, Feelings, and Fun," *Journal of Consumer Research,* 9 (September), 132-140.

Horowitz, Daniel (1985), *The Morality of Spending: Attitudes Toward the Consumer in America: 1875-1940,* Baltimore: Johns Hopkins University Press.

Lears, T. Jackson (1983), "From Salvation to Self Realization: Advertising and the Therapeutic Roots of the Consumer Culture, 1880-1930," *The Culture of Consumption: Critical Essays in American History 1880-1980,* Richard W. Fox and T. J. Lears, eds., New York: Pantheon, 1983, 1-38.

Levy, Sidney J. (1981), "Interpreting Consumer Mythology: A Structural Approach to Consumer Behavior," *Journal of Marketing,* 45 (Summer), 49-61.

Lincoln, Yvonna S. and Egon Guba (1985), *Naturalistic Inquiry,* Beverly Hills, CA: Sage.

McCracken, Grant (1985), "Clio in the Marketplace: Methodological and Theoretical Issues in the History of Consumption," *Historical Perspective in Consumer Research: National and International Perspectives,* Chin Tiong Tan and Jagdish N. Sheth, eds., Singapore: Association for Consumer Research, 151-153.

Rook, Dennis (1985), "The Ritual Dimension of Consumer Behavior," *Journal of Consumer Research,* 12 (December), 251-264.

Sherry, John F., Jr. (1983), "Gift Giving in Anthropological Perspective," *Journal of Consumer Research,* 10 (September), 157-168.

Tucker, William T. (1967), *Foundations for a Theory of Consumer Behavior,* New York: Holt, Rinehart and Winston.

Wallendorf, Melanie (1984), "Social Stratification, Object Attachment, and Consumer Life Patterns," paper presented at the 1984 meeting of the Association for Consumer Research, Washington, D.C..

Wallendorf, Melanie and Russell W. Belk (1987), "Deep Meaning in Possessions: Qualitative Research From the Consumer Behavior Odyssey," (videotape), Cambridge, MA: Marketing Science Institute.

Wallendorf, Melanie and Russell W. Belk (1989), "Assessing Trustworthiness in Naturalistic Consumer Research," *Interpretive Consumer Research,* Elizabeth C. Hirschman, ed., Provo, UT: Association for Consumer Research, 69-84.

Whyte, William F. (1984), *Learning From the Field: A Guide from Experience,* Beverly Hills, CA: Sage.

Life among the Winnebago
John Schouten

Wooden Indians,
mechanical miners,
barkers with beards and bad teeth
bid us enter and buy;
women with legs like bread dough
and men with John Deere
caps or Epcot Center belt buckles
amble through curio shop doors
with passionless faces:
we have taken up life with the Winnebago.

Those of us who eschew the city bus
for the daily tournament of freeways
put a home inside a bus
and tie ourselves with black umbilici
to oases like Rec Vee Park
or Chief Hosa Campground,
everchanging landscapes
of aluminum in the pines.

We eat the native foods
(Coca-Cola, yuppie cheese, light beer, Twix bars)
and perform the necessary rituals
of acculturation (the symbolic bath,
a facsimile of suburban food preparation);

we seek artifacts by which to explain,
to understand
the structure of life in this elusive tribe,
following their movements with tangles
of microphones and videotape and Kodak
in all its forms,
tip-tapping field notes
WordPerfectly for the annals
of science that lie
in file drawers
and shoe boxes and floppy disks
and photo albums and coat pockets throughout
the land of the Winnebago.

From the Log of a Consumer Researcher: Reflections on the Odyssey[1]
Morris B. Holbrook

In Memory of
Arthur Tenney Holbrook, 1870-1968

PREFACE

When I was a boy, I used to travel every summer with my family to stay at our place on the Brule River in Northern Wisconsin. The stream was spring-fed, ice-cold, and brim-full of small brook, brown, and rainbow trout. We spent our days fishing with fly rods, poling canoes upstream, floating back down, and (on occasions of extreme bravery) swimming in the crystal-clear, frigid water. In the evenings, we read old books from the musty shelves, sang campfire songs, and played cribbage.

Everything in this tranquil place had its own special name. To the constant consternation of novitiate guests, a boat was a "canoe"; its front, back, and sides were its "bow," "stern," and "gunwale"; its oar was a "paddle." I dutifully mastered these terminological refinements. More difficult for a small boy to remember, our house was "the lodge"; and its central living space was "the council room."

Tucked into the top drawer of a large desk near the window of this council room, my family kept a book called "The Log." Every day or so, my dad or grandfather would take pen in hand and, in a meticulous version of his best physician's scrawl, would enter a record in this logbook. Such entries contained the names of all guests and visitors, the number and sizes of trout caught on the river that day, the magnitudes and durations of significant storms, the dates and times of canoe-poling feats or sports-related accomplishments, and any other informational tidbits that he chose to immortalize in this fashion. Sometimes, lists of numbers would appear in the log; sometimes, passages of well-crafted prose.

---

[1] This chapter presents excerpts from the log kept by the author during the period of his participation in the Consumer Behavior Odyssey. It is intended to provide a narrative unfolding of the research experience encountered on the Odyssey. Different excerpts, pertinent to more specific themes, appear in other chapters of the present volume and in three previously published papers [two in *Advances in Consumer Research*, Vol. 14-15 (1987-1988) and one in *Research in Consumer Behavior* (1988).] Copies of the full document, without deletions, may be obtained by writing to the author at 504 Uris Hall, Graduate School of Business, Columbia University, New York, NY 10027.

One year, when I was about ten, something extraordinary appeared under our Christmas tree. It was a book written by my grandfather, based on the accounts he had entered into the log over a lifetime of trips to the Brule River and published at his own expense, complete with photographs. Everyone who has ever read this book has loved it. It contains wonderful evocations of life on the river. It beautifully conveys my grandfather's sense of humor and magically captures his spirit of playfulness. It plumbs the depths of his soul by recreating his most cherished moments. It is called *From the Log of a Trout Fisherman*.

I suppose that, ever since I initially encountered my grandfather's marvelous accounts of his experiences on the Brule, I have secretly wanted to write my own log. His introspective, deeply personal narrative provided the first quasi-phenomenological portrayal of a lived world that I had ever read. Given that it came from a man who had studied under William James at Harvard, I ought not to have been surprised by its eloquence. But, in those days, I did not know such things. I only knew that it felt good to read and that, someday, I would like to try something similar.

But I lacked a suitable subject. For many years, my life's most dramatic moments consisted of studying for school (which largely involved reading other people's books), playing the piano (which only David Sudnow has managed to make experientially interesting), and football practice (which I would rather forget). Probably with justification, I found it hard to imagine these as topics in which others would find any interest. Only recently did I discover "consumption" as a heading under which I could meaningfully collect some of my more self-reflective thoughts. I have put together such musings in short pieces entitled "I Awake," "I'm Hip," "The 25-Cent Tour of a Jazz Collector's Home," "I Am an Animal," and "The Turtle." But these amount to little more than tiny vignettes, brief stories that some would charitably call introspective or interpretive in the humanistic tradition but others would harshly characterize as egocentric or narcissistic in self-indulgent excess. Having grown up reading people like Samuel Johnson, not to mention my grandfather, I do not shrink from such accusations. Yet, until now, I have lacked a subject broad enough to command my sustained attention. Finally, in the Summer of 1986, I got my chance.

During the Summer of 1986, several consumer researchers banded together on an excursion that they called "The Consumer

Behavior Odyssey." They rode in a van -- a 27-foot recreational vehicle -- from California to Massachusetts, observing different aspects of consumer behavior in a wide range of settings along the way. During a two-week period in July and August, they and their RV stayed with me at our house in the Pocono Mountains of Pennsylvania. This house is a modest weekend retreat in a developed area called Hemlock Farms. Hemlock is not exactly the Brule River, but at least it is in the woods.

This log represents my experiences -- just before, during, and after that visit by the members of the Consumer Behavior Odyssey. I intend it as a companion piece to the field notes and journals written by my friends and colleagues who participated in the Odyssey by riding on, sleeping in, and often nearly clinging to the van. Like good naturalistic inquirers, they followed accepted anthropological practice by endeavoring to split their observations between the more objective and interpersonally verifiable (as contained in their field notes) and the more subjective and personally introspective (as contained in their journals). But, from the start, I questioned the tenability of this distinction and opted instead for a medium that combined both in what I called a "log," partly to distinguish it from the documents created by my traveling companions and partly to remind myself that I followed in a tradition started by my grandfather.

My log reports reactions to what I observed around me on the Odyssey. It stems from the data collected in my travels, but it reflects the filtering of those data through my own sensibilities. In other words, it tries to capture the research experience as I lived it in the Summer of 1986. Thus, in a sense, one might say that my colleagues have written about the Odyssey *across* (across the country, across consumption situations, across informants) whereas, by contrast, I have written about the Odyssey *within.* I have peered, as far as I can, into the depths of my own responses to our observations of consumption phenomena. And here is what I have found.

JULY 29: *LEAVING*

Yesterday, in getting ready to leave town, I experienced a really bad scene -- weighed down by tremendous pressure...to cram sixteen hours of last-minute work into a ten-hour day.... All this meant that I did not start my packing for the trip until about midnight when I turned the dregs of my dwindling attention to the issue of what I would need for two weeks on the Odyssey.

I had been buying film, notebooks, and pens; so these went into one pile. I sorted through my tapes and filled a little carrier with interesting jazz cassettes. Along with these, I

would need my ancient Walkman and various extension cords. I added this stuff to the pile.

The question of what to bring for reading -- and whether it was worth the bother -- preoccupied me for some time. First, I sorted through my various stacks of papers and pulled out everything I thought was a near-emergency. Then I gathered together some working papers, Xeroxes, and reprints that I'd been wanting to read. Then I snatched up about eight or nine of the books that I ordered several weeks ago while working on a semiotics paper...and threw all this into my shoulder satchel and a bag from J&R Records.

By this time, it was 2:00 a.m.... I was very keyed up and, despite being so tired, had a lot of trouble drifting off to sleep. This was really the first time that I've become viscerally excited about the Odyssey and all its promising uncertainties....

Today, Tuesday, I awake with the radio alarm at 6:50 a.m. I enjoy some tender moments with Sally and then arise with difficulty, very sleepily beginning to throw any clean clothes I can find into a gigantic shopping bag. This includes mostly socks, underpants, t-shirts, polo shirts, khakis, jeans, and a few odds and ends (belts, suntan lotion, Kleenex). After orange juice and a financial consultation with Sally, it is past time to leave.

This will be our longest separation (by far) since we were married 21 years ago, and I'm not looking forward to it. Originally, I think I took it for granted that Sally would spend at least part of the time with the research group in the field. But, with her psychotherapy practice, this begins to look less and less likely (except, maybe, on the weekend).

I barely reach the car by the 8:00 a.m. deadline when they start to give parking tickets and then find that I literally *cannot* make it move forward. Total panic! Ultimately, I pinpoint the problem in the parking brake, which is not releasing properly. After fiddling with this recalcitrant device for some time, I finally persuade it to snap loose so that I can get the car going. Maybe I should suspend use of the parking brake for a while....

On the way up the Hudson, I stop at school to drop off some emergency mail.... After buying two large black carry-out coffees at Chock Full o' Nuts, I finally take off from Columbia at 8:45 and head for the West Side Highway.

The Hudson River Drive is free of traffic going north, but the southbound lanes feature one of the worst traffic jams I've ever seen. All vehicles are literally stopped dead in their tracks from 125th Street to the George Washington Bridge. In the midst of all this, as a symbol of inefficiency, a police car sits with its siren blaring and its lights blinking, but with absolutely no hope of moving as much as an inch in any direction.

After passing through what seems like even more than the usual number of near-accidents involved in escaping from Manhattan, I cross the bridge, successfully breaking out of the right-hand lane to avoid being swept helplessly up the Palisades Parkway, and head west on Route 80. I open my first cup of coffee and rejoice that WBGO is playing an Art Pepper record as I leave town. This piece is a fiery blues from the late lamented Artist's House label (former home for one of my rare consulting projects)....

Once free of the City traffic, I decide to see if I can successfully write and drive at the same time. I find that I can -- up to a point -- but only if I don't look at the paper. Conceivably, I muse, what I have written thus far will be totally illegible. Also, the practice is doubtless rather dangerous. But, at least it keeps me involved....

I make such good time to the Delaware River Bridge that I decide to stay on Route 80 to East Stroudsburg where I can pick up a couple of needed items (peanuts, paper towels, and toilet paper) at the Weiss supermarket.... On entry, I feel overwhelmed by this store. It is about four times the size of even the largest NYC grocery and fills me with a sense of containing countless products that I desperately need to buy and will be instantly sorry I haven't the moment my friends arrive and start asking for them: "Do you have any parsley, Morris? Where do you keep the celery? Excuse me, but is there any cayenne pepper in the house?"

To cope with the bountiful variety of the offerings at Weiss, I adopt the simple heuristic of walking around the store and picking up everything that looks important until I can't carry any more in my arms. During this voyage through the aisles, two people ask me if they can get me a shopping cart. I must look very strange, if not pathetic, but I assure them that I am shopping in this unprecedented manner on purpose as a self-limitation to my purchasing activity. Finally, I know I must stop when I need to ask a lady to put a can of peanuts on top of the growing pile in my arms. After this last desperate gesture, I can barely stagger to the checkout counter.

It turns out that what my arms can carry is: two rolls of Scott paper towels, four rolls of Scott toilet paper, one bag of instant-lighting Kingsford charcoal, two pounds of ground round, two half-gallon bottles of Diet Pepsi, two half-gallons of Diet 7-Up, and one big can of Planter's peanuts. While picking up these items, I overhear an elderly couple who (as if out of a marketing textbook) are literally agonizing over which toilet paper is the best buy for the money. I picture them on social security, barely able to scrape together enough cash to afford to wipe their behinds, but together and therefore happy nonetheless.

Meanwhile, I am confident that my own toilet paper selection (Scott) was probably the *worst* buy for the money. I have compensated for this by grabbing the Diet Pepsi -- on sale at 99 cents, about 70 cents cheaper than at the Red Apple down the block from us on 87th Street, where the prices preserve direct proportionality to the general scuzziness of the atmosphere and decor.

I leave the supermarket at 10:30 and stop at the Burger King -- site of the only known public bathroom in East Stroudsburg -- to pick up a Whopper for what will undoubtedly prove to be a rather cold and soggy lunch in a couple of hours. My order prompts the comment that they have just started serving hamburgers so that I shall have the official honor of being their first lunch customer of the day. I quip that I hope the burger isn't left over from last night and am assured, with horror, that serving day-old burgers would violate company rules....

I climb back into the Olds and drive up Route 209, stopping at the beer depot to pick up a case of Budweiser in cans before hitting Route 402 North. My second fantasy about the Odyssey people is that they will guzzle vast quantities of beer and wine -- I know I will -- and so I have laid in a fairly generous supply of both these commodities. I hope that I can be a good host, but I have little experience with this sort of thing. How does one take care of people who live in a van with their own supply of electricity and water? Besides lending them a hose and an extension cord, I am not sure *what* one does.

As I pass the Pickerel Inn, heading toward the Hemlock Farms entrance, I notice that it is already 11:07. Writing notes in the car turns out to be a completely absorbing experience, and the time has flown. I entertain the sudden fantasy that I might find the van waiting for me at Horseshoe Lane, with several angry friends pissed off that I wasn't there to meet them. But I calm myself with the thought that it is much more likely they will arrive in the late afternoon, in the evening, or even in the middle of the night. I expect Jeff Durgee at 4:00; so we'll see what happens.

At the Hemlock Farms gate, I tell the unbelievably officious guard that I expect some visitors at Horseshoe Lane. This uniformed employee makes me spell my name three times, inquires solicitously about the names of all my visiting friends, and wants to know their exact times of arrival. I hope and pray that the van will pass his scrutiny without incident.

When I first heard that the Odyssey would be coming cross-country in a van, I pictured one of those cute little Dodge wagons with the pointed noses. In Chicago, the sight of the actual behemoth that my friends had rented in California filled me with something between astonishment and dread. I am sure that it will be the largest privately owned vehicle ever to seek access to Hemlock Farms. While I know of no specific rule against inviting your friends to visit you in something larger than a hairy mammoth, I still cannot picture this gigantic RV breezing past our gestapo-like sentry without some sort of incredible hassle....

On arriving at the house, I unpack the car, put away the groceries, stash my clothes, and open all the windows. I get WBGO going on the FM, retrieve the rest of my lukewarm coffee from the Olds, and settle into the Sears gazebo. Here, surrounded by our slim white chairs and the rusty hibachi, I experience a moment of utter tranquility. A grasshopper, probably injured, lurches across the terrace. The sun comes and goes from behind its cloud cover. Distant rolls of thunder seem to underline the heaviness of the humid air. From the house, I can here a Latin-tinged jazz band performing Chick Corea's "Spain" with some heavy bongo drums and screaming trumpets. The announcer says that it was Tito Puente. Meanwhile, I wait.

I wait for the arrival of my friends and who-knows-what kind of activities to come. I do not even know in advance which friends and colleagues will remain on the van by the time it reaches me. I'm more or less counting on Russ and Melanie, probably Rick, maybe Tom, probably not John, and almost certainly not Hal (who said that he would again join the van at Beth's house). Jeff will arrive separately. John Pfeiffer might join us, as might Wendy Bryce, T. J. Olney, or Grant McCracken. It should prove quite interesting to see who actually shows up. During the delay, I've got the doubtless soggy Whopper, the need for exercise, and plenty of paper work to keep me busy....

The van, with Joe Cote at the wheel, arrives at about 2:00 p.m., edging down the driveway and barely missing trees on both sides. On board are Russ Belk, Rick Pollay, and Melanie Wallendorf. After general greetings and welcomes, they show me the RV, I show them the house, and we settle down to a general discussion of possible venues for the next few days. I have collected piles of promotional literature from the surrounding area; so we go through these with everyone calling out various points of special interest.... To my relief, it seems that people do show some curiosity about several possibilities in the vicinity.... Later, over dinner at Verano's Italian Restaurant, the group considers a list of possibilities that Rick Pollay has compiled and votes on the first three choices of each member. This democratic approach clearly demonstrates a general interest in the Green County Fair, but that is about all it demonstrates. Other options receive more

mixed support -- for example, Buckhill Falls, bed-and-breakfast inns, weight-reduction centers, candle shops, and white-water rafting. In a triumph of democracy, we leave all such decisions for the future and decide to spend tomorrow practicing on each other to introduce new members to the necessary interviewing skills and equipment-handling procedures....

Joe, Jeff, and I share a few thoughts on our feelings about the direction of the research. I express my own reaction to the field notes and journal entries completed up to the arrival of the van in Chicago. These hinge on what I sense is a gap between the relatively matter-of-fact field notes and the more interpretive journal entries. According to the perspective of Naturalistic Inquiry, accuracy, completeness, and consensus regarding the field notes are the touchstones of rigor and truthfulness. This emphasis extends to a preoccupation with research audits and member checks. I acknowledge the potential value of such procedures but fear that an over-emphasis on the mechanics of collecting and recording field notes might lead to a "new orthodoxy" in which we just latch onto a surrogate for the old positivism. For me, increasingly, the emphasis on data collection needs to be tempered by an openness to interpretation -- including interpretation that is subjective, personal, and introspective. The clearest opportunity for such an interpretive thrust lies in the journals; so I favor a greater value placed upon the diary-like journal entries and their potential contribution to developing interpretations of what is happening in the research process....

Melanie, Rick, and Russ retire to the van. Apparently, they prefer its womblike coziness to the relatively spacious but unfamiliar house. Also, as the ingroup who have been together for several weeks, they are protected by the van's privacy from the outgroup of relative newcomers. Meanwhile, Jeff takes Christopher's bed, Joe chooses the "library," and I keep my usual spot in the bedroom upstairs....

JULY 30: *INTERVIEWING EACH OTHER*
When I awake at 8:00 a.m., Melanie has already left to take Russ to the Newark Airport (en route to the AMA Doctoral Consortium at Notre Dame). I offer Jeff and Joe their share of the remaining juice (about three ounces each). Jeff accepts; Joe declines.... A curious phenomenon, thus far, has been that those who arrived on the van continue to live "off the van," returning to their cocoon for food, beverages, and other sustenance.... In this, the van stands as an emblematic womb -- linked to the house by its umbilical hose and extension cord, linked to its inhabitants by a kind of invisible chain that keeps pulling them

back inside to perform all necessary functions of the body and spirit....

After a while, Rick appears. We discuss our plans for the day's activities, which include a projected round robin of interviewing each other on camera. Soon, we realize that, in discussing what we plan to do, we have slipped into actually doing it. Rick has begun to hold forth on his collection of advertisements. We therefore decide to stop the breakfast table chatter and to get the cameras rolling in earnest. At 9:45, we turn our efforts in this direction....

Joe, Jeff, Rick, and I take turns interviewing each other and practicing the art of operating the video camera and audio tape machine. My turn on the camera comes first and coincides with Jeff's interviewing Rick on the subject of his advertising-related artifacts. They have prepared the round table with a display of these "advertiques" and now dive into the topic of how, why, and where one would amass such a collection. The conversation is clearly fascinating. However, I find myself completely absorbed by the visual aspects of the task. The simple act of panning, zooming, and focusing offers a myriad of possibilities for framing the picture and moving from one shot to another. These are visually intriguing, and I can practically feel the right side of my brain rev up while the left side clicks off. I find myself immersed in what is happening spatially and how I can use the camera to try to capture it. About an hour goes by before I realize that standing in one place and struggling to steady this heavy camera has made me tired.

Next, it is my turn to interview Joe on the subject of pet consumption. Around a general discussion of Joe's Rhodesian Ridgeback, Terra, I try to elicit some material on the status of pets as family members. We explore the subject of whether a dog might serve as a surrogate baby and related topics....

After a quick break for lunch, it is my turn to be interviewed -- in this case, by Rick on the subject of jazz collecting. Rick leads me through what I think is a well-conducted interview on my jazz fanaticism. Much of the material repeats stuff I've discussed in the "Bird," "I'm Hip," and "25-Cent Tour" papers. However, I do have one minor flash of self-insight when Rick asks me what I find so compelling about musicians like Chet Baker and Art Pepper, who have expressed so much pain in their playing. I suddenly realize that what moves me so deeply is *not* the pain that they convey per se, but rather the extraordinary power of their *ability to express it*. The clear analogy is my reaction to great acting in the theater or movies, where I am so often moved less by the emotions at stake than by the expressiveness of the acting. The ability to express those feelings is the crux of

the matter -- whether the emotion happens to be love, joy, sadness, anger, or fear.

The taping concludes with an interview of Jeff by Joe on the subject of Jeff's rowing activities. I play the role of audio engineer and thus have plenty of opportunity to attend to the interview. It provides a wonderful example of fanatic consumption....

We finish the taping at about 4:00. Desperately in need of exercise, I discretely excuse myself and retire to the balcony upstairs to do my huffing and puffing. This location requires me to use the bare wood floor and to listen to my music through headphones, but those compromises seem worth it for the sake of a little physical exertion.

After exercises, I write for about an hour in the log and then join the others for some chat before beginning to watch the day's tapes.... The tape of my interview with Joe brings back all sorts of feelings as I relive the experience of what I was trying to accomplish with my questions. I am again aware of how hard I must resist my temptation to interrupt and how difficult it is to steer the conversation back on itself in a way that does not seem totally arbitrary but that still returns Joe to issues that I want to pursue. For example, I really have to work to try to establish a link between pets as children and Joe's family relations. I find myself once again tensing as I try to struggle for unobtrusive ways to bring out these tenuous connections.

After the Morris-Joe interview, we break for dinner, which turns out to be hamburgers cooked by me and three previously opened bottles of red wine with some rolls that Melanie brought back from Dover on her return trip from the Newark airport.... When we have finished eating, Rick and Joe plan potential sites for tomorrow while Jeff and I clean up the kitchen. I identify some key locations on the map. Rick proposes taking the van with a view toward spending the night. I object that the van might be a little crowded for five people, two of whom might rather not sleep in a van, but am gently informed that this viewpoint is absurd.... Everyone agrees to depart at 8:00 a.m., and we all retire at about midnight....

JULY 31: *CHUCK OLDBOY'S CIMMARON AND BEYOND*

We arrive at Chuck Oldboy's Cimmaron at 9:00 a.m. and slip past the guard at the gate with the excuse that we have come to eat breakfast (ergo to spend money).... We cannot find the restaurant; so Melanie asks at the desk, and it turns out that we need to take a shuttle bus to the place where we can eat. This dining room is the size and color of three barns placed end-to-end and, like everything else at Cimmaron today, has an empty feeling.

Roughly five percent of the tables are occupied. The maitre d'hotel guides us to a table next to a group of eight who are talking about Leavittown.

The most exotic things on the menu are French toast, English muffins, and Danish pastries. The main fare consists of things like omelets, pancakes, and hash browns. Just beneath the hot chocolate for 85 cents, the menu proudly announces (without apparent intended irony) that "the Chef and the Staff at Cimmaron wish you a happy joyful day."

After a long (not so happy joyful) delay, the waiter finally comes to take our order. Melanie, Rick, and I request bagels and cream cheese with tea or coffee. The waiter asks if everyone is on a diet. Apparently, most customers go for the more substantial meals, as we might also infer by watching the heaping mounds of edibles that soon begin to arrive at the table next to us.

The cavernous dining room is filled with white table cloths, crimson napkins, matching chairs, and huge portraits of four stars who look like rejects from Woody Allen's "Broadway Danny Rose." Rick and I muse on why the place seems so dead and decide that this effect results from the large spaces with few people to fill them, the lamentable Muzak, the lack of living plants, the listless air of the staff, and the low energy level of the guests (who seem to wander around aimlessly with absolutely nothing to do).

I take Melanie and Jeff to see the pool, which contains numerous bulbous bodies bobbing up and down. According to Melanie, the five women whom we see in the pool, bouncing like boisterous beachballs, are performing some sort of ritual aerobic dance. Presumably, this explains why they revolve in a big circle like slightly demented show ponies....

The glass in the pool area has grown opaque from condensation between its double panes. This prompts the comment from a young bearded lifeguard that Cimmaron will soon close the pool area for renovations.... According to this lifeguard, the "old" management let things run down. This "old" management turns out to be none other than Chuck Oldboy himself. He used to come here in a helicopter to sing. But he did not put money into the place. It deteriorated and got poor word of mouth. Our lifeguard speculates that Chuck bought the place because he thought that gambling might be legalized in the Poconos. However, the locals fought this innovation, tooth and nail. When the potential legalization fell through, Chuck lost interest and let the place decline. This led to the bad word of mouth, which the new management must now overcome.

Still according to this lifeguard, the new management is a group of bankers from Oregon. They are trying to fix the place up and hope for better word of mouth and more traffic. The lifeguard thinks that the best hope for success lies is sales conferences, business meetings, and trade conventions. Recently, they have had several group gatherings here. This has been good for business, but he does not know much about how the conference attendees behave because he is not supposed to get friendly with them. Unlike a boat, Cimmaron discourages the staff from fraternizing (or sororitizing) with the clientele. It occurs to me that this might be a *wonderful* place for next year's ACR conference. Just before it goes bankrupt, Cimmaron might offer some truly economical rates. Besides, how else could you top Las Vegas?...

On the stroll back to the lobby, we stop at the bulletin board that lists coming entertainment attractions: Maureen McGovern (July 26), Greg Bonham (August 1), Rhonda Hansome (August 1), Sal Richards (August 9), Corbett Monica (August 15), Julius LaRosa (August 16), Scott Record (August 27), and Lionel Hampton (August 31).

Nearby, in the bar area, people are playing a question-answering trivia game. About 30 vacationers are seated with pads of paper, answering questions like "What Aesop animal assumed that the grapes were sour anyway?" "What did Moses do for a living before he was called by God?" or "What island is the boot of Italy kicking?"... The lady standing next to me says that they do "something like this" in the bar area every morning. I find it interesting to speculate about what else could possibly be like this.

I take a cup of coffee from the pot near the registration desk. Jeff and I wander into the night club. The curtain is down, and some gentle piano chords drift from behind it. Soon, a muffled vocalist sings along. The night club is enormous. It probably seats a couple of thousand customers and must feel devastatingly empty with so few people around.

Next to the nightclub area, we find color photos of (among others) Frankie Vali, Norm Crosby, Alan King, Lola Falana, Donny and Marie Osmond, Robert Goulet, and Ben Vereen -- an almost perfect compilation of my eight least favorite performers. Apparently, this place caters to the same crowd that constitutes the major target audience for the "Tonight Show."...

Melanie and I join the group that Jeff made friends with at breakfast, allegedly to play some poker. I give them all my pennies (which more or less disqualifies me from further participation in the game) and then concentrate on talking with a trim, nicely dressed lady who tells me all about her discontent with Cimmaron as a vacation site.

It has been raining hard all day and much of yesterday. She feels that, under these conditions, there is nothing to do here. It is OK for younger people. But she and her husband do not play tennis and pingpong or swim much, and there is little else to do indoors. Accordingly, this group of about six friends have organized their own poker game with pennies for chips. But she does not play poker; so she seems willing to talk with me.

She first came to Cimmaron about five years ago when it was much nicer and they gave you free pizza by the swimming pool and had a cocktail hour with free drinks at the bar. She feels that Cimmaron was nice then. They gave you more for your money and much more food, which was also better prepared.

The last time they came here was after Chuck Oldboy had bought the place, and things had really deteriorated -- no more free food, worse service, renovations closing various areas, and intense overcrowding due to the presence of a national convention of tap dancers.

That time, their vacation was especially unpleasant. This hurts because her husband can get away for only a few days each year. He works as an electrician for "Circle Time," which operates a chain of stores in the boroughs and on Long Island. They live on the Island with their 23-year-old son who attends a local community college part time and wants to be an electrical engineer -- or just an electrician like his dad if the more ambitious plan does not work out. They do not charge their son rent, but she sometimes wishes that he would contribute more to the household expenses.

Because of his responsibilities with Circle Time, her husband can only take a few days off (Monday-Thursday) and must leave immediately after breakfast tomorrow. For this reason, she feels especially upset about all the rain in the past 24 hours, feels bored, but feels especially frustrated right now because she has *just* heard that there is a problem with her husband's blood medicine. She just returned from shagging pennies in her room, where she happened to get a call from her son saying that there was an error in her husband's prescription so that he has been taking the wrong dosage.

She feels: (1) *worried* about her husband (who was recuperating from pneumonia when she first met him, who got the same thing on their vacation last year, and who has been suffering from blood problems ever since, such that if he takes too much medicine, he bleeds and, if he takes too little, it clots); (2) *angry* that she got no phone message from the hotel but just happened to be in the room when her desperate son called on one of his repeatedly unsuccessful attempts to reach her; (3) *frustrated* that the medical clinic gave him the wrong dosage (which puts her in mind of a

malpractice suit); and (4) *disappointed* that, once again, her tiny annual vacation has been ruined....

I ask my informant why they returned to this place after their bad experience with the crowds of tap dancers. She says that *last* year they had an even worse time visiting Villa Florence in the Catskills, which they had trouble finding down in some valley and where her husband got walking pneumonia. She did not enjoy Villa Florence, even though she is Italian and they served Italian food for breakfast, lunch, and dinner. According to her, the place was "too food orientated" and there was nothing to do but eat and sleep. This bad experience apparently persuaded them to return to Cimmaron, partly as the lesser of two evils and partly in hopes that it might have improved. Also, she feels the entertainment is better at Cimmaron -- particularly a multi-talented singer-magician-comic named Marty.

For her, this year, Cimmaron has improved somewhat but still lacks good food and service. The first night, their chicken and veal (not to mention their steaks) were not fully cooked so that her table complained. After that (by inference, because of the complaining), the cooking improved. (This lady feels that, if things are unsatisfactory, you *have* to complain or they won't know. The last time she was here, she complained so much that they did not charge her for her room. I am surprised that they let her come back.) But, in spite of her remedial actions, the restaurant is still empty ("you could count the people"), the service is still slow ("today it took two hours for breakfast"), and they still do not give you enough to eat ("except at breakfast")....

All things considered, my informant strikes me as heroically thin in spite of the general obesity of the people around her. She also shows a kind of tough stoicism in coping with her emotions on what *has* to be a very disappointing occasion. Here she is -- in this God-forsaken tacky place, beset by rainstorms and bored out of her mind on her one four-day vacation of the year -- with poor food to eat, lousy service, and nothing to do except watch her seven friends play poker and worry about her husband who might bleed to death or get a blood clot at any moment thanks to the incompetence of her son (who just panicked instead of calling information to get the Cimmaron phone number), the hotel staff (who only slipped a note under her door to tell them about the medical emergency), and her doctor (who is himself away on vacation, probably a lot more pleasantly than she, one surmises). In that light, this lady seems rather noble, managing to keep her cool and to remain amazingly cheerful in the face of having her already short vacation ruined by the weather, illness, and culinary vagaries. I enjoy a moment of admiration for her remarkable self-control before responding to Jeff's announcement that it is time to head for the van to push off for Buckhill Falls....

We arrive at Buckhill Falls, which I have said is about ten miles from Cimmaron but which turns out to be about fifty feet away (thereby helping to establish my current reputation as the group's most incompetent navigator), at about 1:00 p.m. I spend the first few minutes finishing some notes in the van and then head up the hill in search of answers to the question of what on earth people find so fascinating about this place....

I take two photos of the main falls framed through the trees. It seems incredible to me that anyone would pay $3.50 to come and see this dinky little trickle of water....

At the top of the hill, I find a mediocre view of a valley and a couple of small mountains that I photograph only for the sake of documentation. A family of three has preceded us there.... They come from just south of Allentown and happened to be passing by on their way up north of Hawley to visit some family or friends. This was their first tourist-type stop of the one-day trip, and they feel it is something they should see since they live nearby and have never seen it. In general, they seem satisfied that they have come and think they might return after they are old enough to buy a ticket at the reduced price for senior citizens. They say they think it must be *really* pretty in the autumn with all the fall colors....

I talk to a couple who have driven here from the western part of Pennsylvania. They definitely think the view is worth it in terms of the climbing and the ticket prices. They have arrived rather out of breath, with him worrying that his camera is not working properly. To be safe, he takes two pictures of the valley. He thinks maybe he needs a new camera. I, too, take some shots of the valley to document my impression that this is really a most ordinary view, comparable to what one sees all along Routes 80 and 84.

My informants are on their annual vacation. They have driven here in their camper, have spent the night in a camper park south of Stroudsburg, and will pass a few days wandering around the area, looking at scenery, and shooting pictures. They have just come from New Jersey, near Hackettstown. They had gone there because they have never seen New Jersey before and thought they should look at it while they were here. They have grown children who are not with them and feel that their 21-foot camper is quite comfortable for two people because, if it rains, you can stay inside and do something. Somehow, they make the RV sound like Cimmaron-on-wheels.

There is something rather engaging about interviewing people *while* they are actually engaged in consumption. I am

amazed that *everybody* seems to think that this experience is worth it. Here they are, often obese, lugging themselves up this big hill to look at something that is *less* spectacular than what they can see for free all up and down the sides of the road. And yet -- while huffing and puffing and reeling financially from the blow of the outrageous ticket prices -- they *still* feel glad they came and think it was worth it. Cognitive dissonance run rampant? A flow experience? Who knows? I don't. Either do they....

We leave Buckhill Falls at about 3:00, headed for the candle shop, massage parlor, factory outlets, and other points West. The candle shop is one place where the tactile and olfactory matter enormously. People touch and smell almost everything. Numerous families with multiple children crowd and scrape through this tacky little two-story store -- sniffing the colored candles and fondling the little wax statuettes. Some carry plastic baskets full of prospective purchases. Others stare vacantly at the paltry merchandise. One bedraggled woman clutches a tiny baby that has the good sense to look completely miserable. I secretly gloat with self-satisfaction over having passed this wretched shop literally countless times without ever having felt the slightest temptation to enter.

In the parking lot, several men stand near their cars, apparently having sent their womenfolk into the store without them. In this, their good judgment appears thoroughly vindicated, the only danger being that their girlfriends or wives might appear at any moment with armloads of bought wax. One couple in a white Pontiac pauses before leaving to take a photo of the red-and-white striped building. Perhaps, someday, this snapshot will evoke happy memories of their fun-packed visit to this Pocono paraffin paradise....

On the way back up Route 402, we pass the Greenfield Manor weight-loss center. Melanie, Jeff, and I agree that this would be a fabulous venue for some depth interviews on body image, transformation of self, complementary changes in grooming rituals, anticipated effects on social relations, etc. We vow to approach the fat farm people for permission to observe....

We arrive back at Hemlock by about 7:30, early enough for me to squeeze in some exercise. This seems especially important right now in light of my day of sitting in the van, my aching back, and my late lunch on Route 209 at "Burgers 'R Us," whose "Big Dude with Cheese" has sunk to the bottom of my stomach like sludge, whence it sends out evil and bitter sensations of indigestion. I therefore throw myself into the calisthenics with gusto and manage to fight off the dyspepsia long enough to stage a full workout....

Meanwhile, Rick's job is to prepare the sauce for a pasta dish that Melanie has planned to prepare. Because I cooked hamburgers last night and because I am still undressed, I decide to let the others get started on the cooking. But, after about 15 minutes, I go down in search of their company...and beer.... Joe, Rick, and Jeff put together a tasty sauce for Melanie's pasta along with a nice salad and a pleasant wine. I busy myself with trying to create a friendly ambience in the living room, with subdued lighting and the free candle from the candle shop. I persuade the others to forsake the kitchen and eat at the round table atop the platform. I feel that this setting provides a sort of cozy atmosphere for what turns out to be some good conversation centered around the events of the last couple of days and plans for tomorrow. We seem to converge on the fat farm as our next target site.

AUGUST 1: *GREENFIELD MANOR*

I awake at 7:59, about a minute before the alarm is scheduled to ring, to the sounds of soft rapping and thumping from below. Because I live in dread of malfunctioning alarm clocks and this seems like a good test case, I force myself to wait for the clock to erupt into its buzzing tumult. It turns out that this particular chronometer delivers a sort of symphonic crescendo that starts with a soft click changes into a quiet murmur and then quickly swells into a violently grating wail. Apparently, I have always been so dead asleep when it has sounded in the past that I have never before heard anything except its obstreperous squeal. This supplies one more piece of evidence for my theory that some of my soundest sleeping gets accomplished just before, during, and after the alarm clock goes off....

We leave the house at about 9:30 and drive down Route 402 to the Greenfield Manor weight-loss center. With some trepidation, on my part at least, Jeff, Melanie, and I walk to the front office and introduce ourselves to the proprietress -- a stocky, pleasant looking, well-dressed lady of about 60 years in age, named Francine. We explain ourselves to Francine. To my relieved surprise, she welcomes us warmly, encouraging us to come right in and ask our questions. She says she'll join us shortly but, meanwhile, suggests that a couple of her guests show us into the dining room.

I half expect to see feed troughs lined up in rows along one wall but instead encounter a very tidy, fresh-smelling, pine-paneled area with about ten tables, all neatly set in preparation for lunch. The manor sleeps 33 people; so I infer that there must be about that many place settings in view. My tour guide -- one of the guests at the hotel (a slightly heavy, dark haired lady of about 50 from Central Park West) -- tells me that she has found the place a wonderful retreat for purposes of dieting and exercise. CPW has come for ten days to relax, have fun, lose weight, and learn how to do aerobics properly. In particular, she wants to learn how to monitor herself so that she can feel when her pulse reaches the desired rate of 130-140 beats per minute. CPW says that she participates actively in the manor's exercise programs, which begin right after breakfast at 9:00 and run until lunch at 12:30. She does the walking and aerobics classes; she also swims, but has not yet worked up to jogging. CPW's husband is a real runner and does the bridal path in Central Park, which is a little longer than around the reservoir, once a day at lunchtime instead of eating. She cannot exercise with her husband, but she does hope to keep up an active regimen when she gets back home. CPW has an exercise bike, which she finds boring, though people have told her that she should try listening to music or watching television while pedaling. TV does not help because there is nothing worth watching except on Channel 13, she says, in what strikes me as a typical New York elitism. She might try music because her son has a portable tape player. CPW says that she will try to maintain her better eating habits when she leaves this place, though she knows that this will be hard to accomplish. She knows that you can't lose very much weight in just a few days, but has come for both the good eating habits and the exercise training, with hopes of continuing the latter when she returns home. Since she works, CPW will have to cut back on her exercise, but intends to do something in the evenings when she gets home from the office. She does not worry that she will feel too tired to exercise after a full day of work because, at the manor, she has discovered that exercise picks you up. For her first couple of days here, CPW had a headache and felt sluggish, but then someone told her to go for a walk. She did and, by the time she returned, felt refreshed and wonderful. She thinks that exercise makes you feel good and wants to continue.

During my conversation with CPW, an older lady of about 70 pushes past us several times, walking with some difficulty and nearly spilling her (forbidden) cup of coffee (which she has smuggled downstairs from her room). (Cigarettes are also prohibited in the manor and must, if at all, be smoked outside.) She is heavy set, but not enormously fat, with medium-length white hair, piercing blue-grey eyes, and an extremely animated countenance. She lives in Wilmington, is an old friend of the proprietress (Francine), and has come here many times. She already knew about the place from knowing Francine, whereas CPW had read the manor's tiny (holding up thumb and forefinger) advertisement in the *New York Times*. Wilmington does not come here for the exercise. Rather, she cannot get around easily, but does enjoy the routine, the people, and the atmosphere.

We are immediately joined by a fairly rotund 65-year-old with grey-red hair who, like Wilmington, has been visiting Greenfield Manor for many years. She lives in Paterson and also heard about the place from the tiny ad in the *Times*. However, after coming here repeatedly, she has established friendships with innumerable fellow patrons. There is a lot of repeat business here, and she already knows many of the people who return frequently. This gives the place a feeling of "home" to her. That homelike feeling is further enhanced for her by the fact that her regular room, which she reserves year after year, is the nicest room in the manor. Francine promised this to her the first time she called and, to her husband's initial surprise, kept her word. Her husband stays home while Paterson comes up here to eat moderately and shed a few pounds. She always takes off some weight, but it creeps back during the winter months, especially whenever she visits her family in Berlin. Because of encroaching arthritis, Paterson can no longer join the exercise program (which she once frequented with abandon). Sometimes, she and Wilmington limp part-way around the walking course with the others, but they quickly run out of steam and don't exercise much at all. Rather than engaging in aerobics or calisthenics, Paterson finds this a wonderful place to relax, to chat with friends, to read, to think, and (one surmises) to escape from her husband (a fitness freak) for a few days of tranquility. Again, she emphasizes the homelike atmosphere and demonstrates this point by leading me upstairs to her room, commenting on the way that the one flight of steps is good for her and thereby recalling an earlier comment that she gets enough exercise by just doing the housework. Her room, indeed, *is* quite nice with a large double bed, a dresser, a card table covered by a pink table cloth (which Francine places there so that she can read or write), a little black-and-white TV (which she brings from home and plugs into the antenna hookup on the wall), and a private bathroom (which looks capacious but which I do not presume to enter). The room looks out over an expansive lawn onto Route 402, whence emanate the whooshes of some passing cars. These do not bother her during the day and subside at night. The room also has an air-conditioner, which she needed last week but not now.

We return to the living room and rejoin Wilmington. I ask about the typical guests at the manor and learn that there is really no

such thing. Almost all the visitors are women, with only one or two men staying here at any one time. They range in age from teens to near-octogenarians. Both Paterson and Wilmington can recall many pairs of teenage girls who have checked in for a visit. The oldest guest whom either can recall was 76 years old. Most are between 40 and 60 years in age. Further, not all of the women who come here are fat. Many are thin and simply want to get in better shape. Also, many are former fatties who want to avoid sliding back into their previous ways. One fabled woman, currently staying at the manor, took off 160 pounds over a period of time and has checked in for a tuneup. I do not meet this heroic lady, but I do encounter a chirpy little 45-year-old blonde who prances through the living room several times -- wearing a stretch swimming suit under a t-shirt, wagging her slim fanny, and claiming facetiously that she has lost 150 pounds in only two days. She has a lively spirit, appears to enjoy joking about the fact that she is not exactly skinny, and clearly relishes the opportunity to show off her best asset (namely, her derriere). Apparently, she likes to flaunt the fact that, though hardly svelte, she is thinner than everybody else in the place.

I ask Paterson and Wilmington about the greatest weight losses they have witnessed and the farthest distances people have come to stay here. Both these achievements appear to have coincided in the accomplishment of one chubby 25-year-old who journeyed all the way from Hawaii, stayed three months, and lost 40 pounds. I ask Paterson about the effect of this remarkable transformation. Unfortunately, she was not there at the end to compare the before-versus-after difference. At any rate, her own "transformations" come from feeling *cleansed*. She has tried fasting -- nine days at another weight-loss place with medical supervision. She felt wonderful and totally cleaned out as a result of this experience. However, fasting for several days is too dangerous to do without full medical supervision and, consequently, Francine (who has no doctor on her staff) will not permit it.

These ladies and, in fact, everyone at the place (including or even especially Francine) seem to have a clear sense that any weight loss will be temporary at best. However, in Paterson's phrase, they feel *cleansed*. This theme is picked up by a man named Jack, here with his wife, Betty.

Jack, who now joins our group, is almost alone among one or two other males staying here. Earlier, to Wilmington and Paterson, I had suggested that, with about 30 unaccompanied females running around, many men might find this an attractive place to visit. They replied, rather wistfully, that most guys would not want to meet a bunch of women like them (meaning overweight). I commented that men who tended to be heavy themselves might want to meet ladies with the same proclivities. They agreed that sometimes "common interests" do attract.

This attraction theory seems born out, in part, by Jack. As he sits down, I realize that Jack is, if anything, more obese than any of the ladies I have interviewed. Yet, he has come largely at the insistence of his wife Betty. Jack and Betty have been here three times together. Jack, too, feels *cleansed* by the experience of being here for a few days. He comes mostly to rest and to relax, avoids participating in the exercises, and most of all does *not* take photographs. At home, he works as a professional photographer who used to do weddings (at $1500 per day on the current market) but who now focuses mostly on commercial photography, by which I infer he means products (such as Pabst Beer, whose logo adorns his t-shirt and for whom he says he has done some work) and people in the entertainment industry (such as a "famous actor" whom he discreetly refrains from mentioning by name). However, he *never* takes pictures on his holidays, which would be too much like work. If he visited a wonderful scenic area, he *might* use an Instamatic, but would probably just buy post cards. So much for being intrinsically interested or involved in the art of photography. And so much, as well, for the possibility of raiding his collection of before/after fat photos.

For Jack and Betty, there is no "after," only a "before." Betty arrives and turns out to be painfully obese. After what was presumably a rather mild workout of some sort, she is so out of breath that she can hardly regain her composure. Now, she joins the group and at first sits panting on a piano bench nearby -- inviting a visual comparison between herself and the piano, which (it being only a spinet) she easily dwarfs. She is the only person I have encountered here so far who has what I would call a *profound* weight problem.

Betty has come here ten or twelve times (a good trick in the five years the place has been open for business). She once lost a lot of weight, but quickly gained it all back. Some of this weight first appeared when she gave up smoking. Betty says that, when she quit tobacco, she lost her creativity as an amateur writer of short stories or poems (it's not clear which). I ask her if the tradeoff was worth it (referring to the linkage between tobacco and creativity); but she misses my point, assumes that I mean the smoking/eating connection, and declares that being heavy is healthier than smoking. According to Betty, medical studies have shown that, in your middle years, you are better off if you are a little hefty. By this logic, she would be *very* well off indeed.

But, of course, she understands that she has a drastic problem in this regard. Indeed, Betty seems quite intelligent. However, she seems to comfort herself a bit unrealistically with the thought that you can be *too* thin. On this score, she is definitely out of danger.

Earlier, to establish rapport, I have confided my own weight problems (former heaviness and continuing tendencies toward succumbing to temptation). Meanwhile, Joe Cote (who has joined the discussion) commiserates with Wilmington and Betty about their most disastrous temptations -- such as ice cream, candy, and bread. Wilmington replies with her characteristic wit that, for her, candy is no particular problem. She just *loves to eat*.... Virtually anything that is available will do, though she and Paterson agree that an especially problematic recurring temptation is a "glass of wine."

Wilmington also appears to aim, indirectly, at consoling Betty by expounding her theory that obesity is genetic and by announcing that, if she had it all to do over again, she would take up the study of genetics and discover a cure. Wilmington illustrates this nature-versus-nurture hypothesis with a rather touching story about her own daughter who, in every way, resembles her late husband's family -- with dark hair and a dark complexion but, most of all, with no tendency to get fat. As a little girl, this daughter would buy a candy bar, eat a little piece, put the rest in the fridge, and keep it for a few days. (Jack agrees that such restraint is a physical impossibility for a heavy person.) Wilmington's daughter has grown up to be a (distinguished sounding) psychoanalyst. One of her kids, at ten, has a tendency toward pudginess. Another remains skinny as a rail no matter how much she eats. Wilmington attributes this to differences in metabolism and remarks sardonically that she herself has *no* metabolism and, as a result, *no* energy. Her witty insights and animated conversation belie this claim: she is loaded with intellectual if not physical energy. But I get the point that Wilmington wants to make. She wants to relieve some (though not all) guilt by establishing factors beyond her control. Soon, she comments that one of her granddaughters looks just like her late husband's family. I ask mischievously if that is the skinny granddaughter. She knows damned well that I am tweaking her genetic theory but admits anyway that, no, it's the pudgy granddaughter. I would not have raised such a potential discrepancy with anyone who did not have such a nice light touch. Wilmington excels in this respect. She is anything but fat and jolly. She is heavy with a marvelously elfin sense of humor.

Wilmington's light touch also characterizes her tongue-in-cheek theory of the fashion industry, oriented both toward injecting humor into her weight problem and toward protecting her own self-image. She feels that the world of fashion is dominated by homosexuals who have no fondness for the female form and who therefore design their clothes to fit inhumanly skinny models with figures so emaciated as to appear unhealthy. Also, to her distress (shared by the other ladies in the group), the clothing stores carry sizes only up to about 12 or 14 so that there is nothing in the typical retail outlet that she can wear. Occasionally, she and Paterson buy men's items, such as jogging suits or shirts, but this purchasing strategy does not work very well for party dresses. In general, Wilmington feels that people are pressured by commercial interests to "be thin" -- in defiance of their genetically determined "set points," which just happen to lie at "be fat." Indeed, the "megabuck" weight-loss industry would crumble if word got out that you *can't* defeat your biologically predetermined weight level. So, in her worldview, nature dictates what you will weigh while designers establish what is fashionable. A century ago, it was stylish to be a real woman with a little plumpness on you. Today, the pendulum has swung to favor extreme skinniness (as in the Twiggy look a few years ago, with miniskirts that did not flatter most people). I resist the temptation to suggest that, logically, textile manufacturers should rejoice at the thought of a demand for larger dress sizes and instead try to console her with the thought that maybe soon her "pendulum" will swing back in the other direction. But Wilmington outfoxes me once again, replying with her usual animation and bright grey eyes, "Not in *my* lifetime."

At this point, we are joined by Francine, the proprietress, who graciously asks if we have any questions. I immediately reinforce her by telling her that everyone has been *raving* about her place -- how well it is run, how nicely it is kept, how clean it is, and how friendly it feels. This feedback is completely truthful, and she responds appreciatively.

Francine began this business about five or six years ago. She was a school teacher in Queens. At 38, she had gone back to school for her MA in English and had then taught English and film appreciation in high school for 10 years. (This makes her about 55-60, I would guess.) She had always had a weight problem - - plump as a little girl and more ponderous with each successive child. She and a friend visited a weight-loss center and decided that they could do better themselves. They searched for a suitable place and finally found this spot -- a former inn with a restaurant and, what clinched it, a private bath in every room. Starting in 1981, she has built up the place by investing heavily in renovations, redecoration, a new pool, an exercise room, and an annex

with additional sleeping quarters. The friend dropped out in 1982 because the facilities needed an additional $40,000 and the friend was afraid of the risk. Francine willingly assumed the necessary debt with some encouragement from her CPA husband (who passed away about three years ago).

Rather than offering a fancy beauty parlor or a luxurious spa with lots of expensive services, Francine's philosophy is to provide a streamlined, inexpensive place that people can afford. A few celebrities have come here (names withheld for obvious reasons), but she prefers plainer folks (many of whom, judging from the parking lot, do happen to drive Mercedes).

Francine is obviously quite proud of what she has accomplished. She broke even the first year, made money the second, and did well by the third (much to the amazement of her husband, the accountant). She keeps the place open from May through October (seven months) and spends the rest of her time in Queens (with hopes of eventually moving to Manhattan), with an annual trip to visit London and a British health spa. During the winter months, Francine closes down the manor and lets her son use it for ski trips. By living in this way, she earns enough to be comfortable. She does not need much. She has enough. She does not have eyes to make more money by expanding or by opening up another establishment (which "they" invited her to come down to Wilmington to do). In fact, she prides herself on offering a fair price -- one that is less expensive than anyone can believe and that keeps her friends coming back. Last year, the manor got a write-up in *Shape* magazine. They quoted the wrong price ($240 per day instead of per week). (Jokingly, she says that, at those rates, she expected Elizabeth Taylor to come running.) This incorrect price information scared away business. But, to atone in part, she later got listed by the same magazine as one of the ten best new weight-loss establishments.

Earlier, we had spoken briefly with Heidi, a portly lady in a jogging suit with heavy peroxide and makeup so thick that it seemed to give her face a permanently puckered expression. Heidi lives in Bergen and raves about last night's production of "Barefoot in the Park" at one of the local theaters (better even than Fonda and Redford, she says). She eagerly recommends the same theater's up-coming production of "Funny Girl." But, in spite of this surface cultural patina, Heidi strikes me as somewhat less refined than her compeers. She has a bit of a Bronx-style accent, rather flashy taste in clothes, and little apparent involvement in the weight- or health-orientation of the manor. She does not do the exercises and knows she'll gain back any weight she happens to shed (so does not try very hard to lose any). When somebody mentions the existence of bears in the woods, Heidi jokingly vows never to go into the woods again. On rainy days, Heidi goes shopping in Stroudsburg (where she probably finds some of her flashy wardrobe). She has visited the Stroud Mall but not the candle store (at least, not *yet*). However, for all her torpor, Heidi does show interest in a nature trail where she wants to take Paterson. Later, after lunch, they depart on this expedition into the nearby forest. Heidi drives her Mercedes....

AUGUST 2: *THE GREEN COUNTY FAIR*

I first stir at 7:20 with Sally (up for the weekend) crumpling paper nearby, but drift off to sleep again only to be jarred into full consciousness by the importunate Sunbeam at 7:55.... We depart in a cheerful frame of mind at about 8:50, heading out the north exit from Hemlock to Route 84 on our way to Centertown. As we learn on our arrival at 10:00 a.m., the Green County Fair opens at noon; so we shall have about two hours to kill.

Toward that end, I embark in the general direction of the goat show, which seems to be the only action in the vicinity. My first sight is a row of about six female goats indifferently displaying their rear ends to a judge who thoughtfully strokes his chin as he ponders the derrieres of these four-legged charmers. I shoot several photos of the goats, their masters and mistresses, and the judge. The goats seem very calm. Finally, the judge picks up a microphone and rattles off a bewilderingly complicated explanation of why goat 1 dominates goat 2 dominates goat 3 and so on. The complexity of his explanation evinces an intricate multiattribute scoring system that, I later learn, classifies criteria into categories such as general appearance, straightness of the back, slope of the rump, and size of the udder. Clearly, the procedure resembles the Miss America pageant -- except that, here, talent is even more irrelevant and the criterion of breast size is made somewhat more explicit.

After waiting until he has a free moment, I approach the winner and ask him how it feels to take first prize. He is pretty blase about the whole thing because, for him, this is a fairly frequent event. He has a family of about five animals that take turns winning these contests. He and his own family spend every weekend traveling all over the area entering and winning competitions. He rattles off a long list of places they have recently visited. I ask him if he does it for fun or business, and he says it's mostly business. Prizes help to sell his goats for breeding purposes, apparently the name of this particular game. I ask how far people travel for these competitions. From all over the country, he says. This year's national event is in Texas, but he does not think he'll go

because it is too far to drive. One lady he knows did take three goats to California last year on an airplane and won something. I inquire if she bought them seats on the plane. He says they rode in the baggage compartment. We both agree that the animals were probably quite frightened.

I wander over to another area where several people have set up folding chairs and are watching the show with great interest. After the next round of judging with its bewildering explanation over the public address system, I approach a distinguished looking grey-haired man wearing top-siders, jeans, and a Gant-type short-sleeved shirt. I ask him what "all that" meant, and he very patiently explains the scoring system. According to my informant, everything centers on the characteristics likely to promote the longevity, reproductive capacity, and milk-giving performance of the goat. These functional characteristics include a flat back (to avoid spine problems), a sloping behind (to promote entry for mating purposes), and a large udder (for milk) that is tightly hung (to avoid dragging on the ground). He says that, though he has no entry in today's contest, he watches it with great interest to get a feel for this particular judge's key criteria. Strategically, he figures out what each local judge looks for and then makes selections from his stock of 50 animals to determine which eight or so to bring to a given show. Silently admiring his marketing savvy, I ask if today's judge favors his herd. "About in the middle," he says. There are two big-winning competitors here today, and he's anxious to compete against them. I ask if he and his wife (pretty and dressed entirely in white, which seems especially incongruous amidst the filth that surrounds us) are excited. "More tired," he replies. I inquire whether they do this for fun or business. "*Not* fun," she emphasizes. He explains that the shows are motivated mostly by the desire to win ribbons for purposes of increasing the value of their animals for breeding. He and his wife do this as a hobby that "got sort of out of hand." She runs the goat farm and almost breaks even. He helps her on weekends. During the week, as his full-time job, he runs his own advertising agency....

After taking some notes, we leave the van at 11:30 with the camera, the tape machine, and several miscellaneous packs of gear, all headed for the fairground.... We walk through one undercover area of displays (mostly because it is misty if not actually raining), and I pause to watch a salesman of electronic keyboards at the booth of Keys and Pipes, Inc. from Birmingham, NY. A couple with two young boys and one older teenage son show some interest in a particularly unmusical-looking piano-like object. The salesman begins his pitch by explaining to the man that he will get a free rubber boat complete with oars and an outboard motor if he buys a keyboard (priced at $700 and up). While the two men enthusiastically examine this nautical vessel, I corner the wife and ask her if she would buy such an instrument. She says that it might be good for the kids to learn music. They are in second and third grade, 11 months apart in age. They will learn to play the recorder at school, but she wants them to have the opportunity to study music because there are teachers in the area, though she does not want to push it because they already play baseball. She herself does not play but might want to try a keyboard like this one (a Viscount that bears a disconcerting resemblance to my own Casio 701). However, she thinks it might be better for the kids to learn on a real piano. I ask her which she thinks would be easier to play, and she says an electronic instrument.

In spectacular verification of this prophesy, her husband returns from looking at the rubber boat and gets the real sales demonstration. Just prior to this, her 9-year-olds have themselves demonstrated what *they* would do with the electric piano by fighting bitterly over who got to push the buttons while their mother screamed at them. She says that she would need to buy two to keep peace in the family. Now the salesman starts an obviously canned spiel. He "positions" the keyboard as like a player piano with a box that plugs in and contains the equivalent of twelve of the old piano rolls. As he speaks, he inserts a little cartridge and pushes some buttons until the electric piano begins to emit a truly contemptible version of "Stardust." The man, amazingly, seems to enjoy this rendition. So the salesman switches to the next mode of man-machine interaction by explaining to the man and his sons that they can control the volume by using the pedal for "expression." This "expression" pedal will allow them to vent their emotions by varying the loudness and swelling to a crescendo at just the right moment to convey a peak of excitement.

However, just in case the expression pedal does not offer enough room for artistic outlet, one can move to an even higher level of man-machine interfacing at the flick of another switch. Now, this switch allows one to perform the tune for oneself by following the red lights that flash when each successive note needs to be played. Unfortunately, this manner of performing does not permit any rhythmic continuity, but it does generate a sort of faltering melody with snatches of harmonic accompaniment. The man pushes keys fitfully with predictably embarrassing results. Then his 16-year-old son takes over and, by alertly following the flashing lights in the proper order, punches out a melody that *almost* sounds like "Stardust." After this

display of adolescent virtuosity (no doubt honed on extensive experience with video games), this family wanders away -- never, I suspect, to buy a Viscount.

I share a few thoughts with the salesman, who promptly tries to sell me a keyboard. I tell him that I play the piano and already own two electronic instruments, one almost identical to what he has been trying unsuccessfully to sell, plus a real Steinway baby grand (which I mostly play). He then establishes that I live in New York City and have a summer house nearby. With this as a lead, he pounces and tries to sell me a reconditioned piano for our summer home.

Actually, the Viscount salesman is a nice man, and he *knows* I'm not going to buy a piano -- partly because I've told him that I'm just waiting for my friends, carrying this enormous camera, and partly because I've already insisted that I don't want another piano, especially not one that would just sit around in the damp woods at Hemlock Farms and inexorably go out of tune. But his inveterate selling instincts just won't quit. He *can't* turn it off. As we move on, I wish him good luck, hoping for his sake that there are many people in the region who need or want a rubber boat....

We wander further and move into another area where we...tape an interview with a young blonde-haired girl of about 23 years who sells ferrets. She sees these pets as her children -- especially Elvin, whom she removes from the cage and fondles and kisses. She "falls in love" with some of her ferrets and hates to sell them. Her business is called "Superior Ferrets," and her name is Stacey.

Stacey takes great pains in the quality of her breeding and refuses to sell animals to anyone who wants them for the wrong reasons. She will not send her ferrets home with just anyone. Her animals are her babies; she is mommy; her boyfriend Brent (who does not wear a shirt or speak) is daddy. Indeed, these ferrets serve for Stacey as child substitutes.... She was hurt in a car accident and cannot have kids. These are her babies, she says; these are her life....

Stacey's $70 ferrets have extensive pedigrees with complete bloodlines because, according to her, people want to know this information, just as she wants to know her own bloodline. She thinks that people choose ferrets in a way that matches their own personalities. How do they know which ferret is right for them? They just know.

Stacey wears a "Superior Ferret" t-shirt. She says she could see a million ferrets and still love them. I believe her but wonder, secretly, if she has ever considered *in vitro* fertilization, surrogate motherhood, or adoption....

I next interview a man named Bruce who raises and sells parrots. He breeds twelve species, most of which reproduce fairly readily. Bruce spoon feeds his birds with tender loving care. He has parrots living and breeding in every room of his house except his bathroom. In all, he has about sixty birds around the house and plans to move to larger quarters. He wants the birds to have more space; but clipping their wings is essential for their own welfare.

Bruce's daughter, Hope, is there with him and tells us that she joyfully plays with the parrots, particularly a yellow bird named Tequila, which is her favorite. She has had Tequila for a few years. A parrot usually lives from 70 to 100 years. That's one of the great things about these birds; you don't have to worry about grieving over their death. She would rather have a parrot than a dog or cat because she does not want to feel sorrow over the loss of her pet.

I ask Bruce how he got into raising parrots. He traces it back to when his wife was very ill and her parrot guarded her until she recovered. He, too, has a personal favorite -- a Macaw named Blue -- that would protect him with its life. Blue is exactly like a human friend. Bruce has a *bond* with this bird. Yet he does want Blue to be able to mate so as to fulfill her (sexual) needs. Blue shows signs of wanting a mate by turning her back and rubbing up against him.

Parrots can cost as much as a Cadillac. His domestic babies cost about $250. But, like Stacey (the ferret lady), he won't sell them to just anyone. Rather, a potential customer must prove worthiness. You don't just sell a parrot to anyone because the bird is intended to be a sweet lovable friend. A friend for life. So he screens people very carefully. It's important when you're dealing with something alive to make sure that people know there's a *responsibility* attached to owning it. So he has a buyback policy and will take the bird back at any moment (with a full refund). (In this, his birds resemble the mogwai in "Gremlins.") The only such return happened because, one night at a dinner party, Tequila imitated the sound of the owner's wife making love. Apparently, this woman's sense of humor fell short of the parrot's.

Bruce believes that his parrots understand the language they use. Some have vocabularies of up to 500 words. He believes that they communicate intentionally, that he can carry on a conversation with them, and that the birds understand him. He feels very good when one of the birds tells him it loves him.

Bruce thinks that parrots have emotions and feelings. If you leave a bird for a week, it gets angry. In partial disconfirmation of his communication theory, they don't actually *say*

they're angry; but you can tell because of the way they *act*. Last year, when he returned home from a week at the hospital, his favorite bird bit him on the cheek. Parrots also feel grief. He recently lost a bird; its mate is now grieving and may never mate again. Parrots feel joy, too, as when the two birds were mating; they would kiss and display great affection. But parrots show *no fear*. They fear nothing in defending what they love.

When pressed, Bruce concedes that some people fear parrots because they bite. Imported birds often do bite. His birds, by contrast, are raised with tender loving care and won't bite. The ones that have bit him have acted because of a past history of abuse. Bruce can make friends with a bird, even one that hasn't been properly handled and can handle it safely. Thus, he won't admit that people have any reason to fear these birds. Here, Bruce seems to be practicing some denial. He acknowledges that his own birds (albeit imported) have almost torn his eye out and have dislocated his fingers, that his most cherished friend bit him because he went to the hospital for a week, and that -- by handling birds incorrectly -- many people get bit by them. But he *still* won't admit that people have *any* reason to be afraid of parrots.

Bruce sells only the young birds. If a parrot stays around long enough to have a name, then he keeps it. Once it has a name, you can't let it go. He doesn't mind selling the birds for money because it's a business. But he does accept the *responsibility* to sell to the right customer. He is not an unscrupulous salesman who will do anything to make a buck.

Bruce believes that people buy a parrot to have a friend, one that will be with them for the rest of their lives. It's a companion for the duration. This status of the bird as a consumer durable is a major selling point. So he doesn't sell birds; he sells friends. He agrees that they are like children because they will live longer than you do....

Though Bruce disavows any intention of salesmanship, I feel overwhelmed by the sudden urge to buy a parrot. Perhaps fortunately (in view of our avocation as cat fanciers), I did not bring my checkbook to the Green County Fair. If I had the funds handy, I might find myself returning to New York with a feathered friend sitting on my shoulder, nibbling at my ear, and perhaps saying that it loves me....

Earlier, when I first saw the statue of Big Chief, we were walking into the fairground in the rain with me carrying the video camera and lacking my Mamiya. I asked Russ to take photos, but I want some for myself too. Now, I venture into the night to capture some time-lapse shots of the Chief in all his glory. Bright lights illuminate the big statue from all angles.

I am almost speechless with admiration for the sense of humor displayed by the otherwise unsung artist who created this monument to mischievousness. First, I photograph the Chief from the front. He raises his right hand in the Indian "how" gesture; his left arm stretches stiffly downward at the other side. The positions of this arm, his hand, and especially his left thumb appear unusually awkward, even for the work of a primitive artist. What can account for this sculptural anomaly? The answer lies in the side view of Big Chief -- the view that greets all visitors to the fair almost as soon as they walk through the gate. This commanding perspective on the Chief from his right side transforms his otherwise awkwardly held thumb into a perfectly proportioned and accurately placed phallus, hanging out for all to plainly see. Now, we leave the fairground, as I silently bid farewell to this noble savage.

AUGUST 3: *THE RENAISSANCE FESTIVAL*

After sleeping late, we kill about an hour and a half debating on where to go today and packing the van. At about noon, we pull out of the drive (itself a 15-minute adventure), bound for the Renaissance Festival in Sherwood Forest Park, down near Buffern, New York.

On arriving, we head for the Mud Show (which...features four young buffoons in a sort of slapstick romp through a filthy pit filled with deep slime). We shoot quite a bit of footage of these clowns building audience excitement and hustling for coins. The spectators respond enthusiastically and are especially receptive to the aspects of the performance that include wallowing in the mud and putting it into the mouth. In one superb piece of terpsichorean mastery, the ruffian actors place large quantities of dirt into their mouths and spit (most of) it out. The crowd goes wild.

After the show, one of the actors (a tall thin young man of about 22 or 23) comes over, takes an interest in the camera, and begins talking with Jeff. I get the tape rolling, reposition the tripod, and begin filming the interview.

This fellow intends to pursue a career in comedy. He graduated last year from Columbia University, where he majored in Urban Sociology and worked with a comedy-improvisation group. He has been driving a cab, but got this opportunity for a comedic gig and grabbed it. (I think about my ambitions for Chris to go to a good school like Columbia and wonder how I would react if he did all that and then ended up in a pit eating mud.)

Jeff asks our informant how it feels to commune so intimately with Mother Earth. In response, the buffoon minimizes the importance of his culinary actions. Before

long, he begins clowning for the camera and occasionally lapses into what sound like canned routines. He does have a serious side, however, and makes some earnest statements about his career plans. He first realized he had a flair for comedy when he gave the valedictorian speech in high school (as first in his class, an achievement that he mentions several times). Everybody laughed in the right places (thereby providing positive reinforcement). Now, he works on improvised comedy -- something he illustrates at the end of the interview when he indicates his phone number by raising the corresponding number of fingers to represent each digit. The last digit in his phone number is "1." So he concludes the conversation by giving us the finger....

AUGUST 4: *HONEYMOON HEAVEN*

The alarm wakes me at 8:00. I shave, brush, and work out to the sound of Hampton Hawes and Oscar Peterson.... I shower, put the kettle on the stove to boil, and begin rapping at Melanie's PC.... We dilly and we dally for a while and then decide to venture to East Stroudsburg for laundry, chores, and anything else of interest that we can find along the way.

On the trip down Route 402, I begin typing some more of my handwritten log entries. This endeavor proceeds fitfully due to the bumps and bounces, every one of which flings my fingers off the keys and causes typos that I have to keep backtracking to fix. For the rest of the morning and most of the afternoon, I persevere in the typing, while the others fiddle with laundry, bicycle repairs, bulk film loading, groceries, and beer.

When we have completed these chores, we decide to drive to Mt. Adams and to check out the honeymoon resorts. First, however, we stop at Nostalgiaville, where...I wander around taking photos of firearms, deer heads, musical instruments, woodworking tools, beer signs, and other atmospheric props.

From here, we travel to the Breezy Peaks Lodge for a look around. This place is indescribably awful. I thought that Cimmaron scraped the bottom of the hostelry barrel, but Breezy Peaks sinks leagues below anything that Chuck Oldboy could imagine in his wildest wetdream.

Breezy Peaks' main building boasts ugly furniture, dirty carpets, hideous pictures on the walls, and crowds of guests that look deprived, depraved, depressed, demented, degenerate, debased, or various combinations thereof. We shoot some photos of the activity board, some especially tacky furnishings, and tasteless formal portraits of a couple in their heart-shaped bath tub. But I cannot bring myself to turn the camera on what honestly does look like a group of people suffering from severe mental disorders. This sight makes me sad, uncomfortable, and filled with the desire to leave Breezy Peaks Lodge *now*. After a brief tour of the squalid dining facilities (jacket and tie required, apparently *any* jacket and tie) and the cheapshot gift shop (with tennis balls at $4.95 per can, *twice* the going rate), we flee.

Settling into a pleasant, cozy restaurant for sandwiches and beer, we enjoy some good conversation about evangelism and other phenomena encountered in previous phases of the Odyssey. During this chat, I am somewhat distracted by the presence of a huge projector-TV screen showing Roger Clemens pitching a Red Sox game against Chicago. I wonder how my Yankees are doing. I fear that they are not doing well. I think about Chris at summer camp on Cape Cod and wish I had time to write him....

We drive the one-hour trip back to Hemlock Farms and arrive at about 12:45. I feel very tired, rather humiliated by the tawdry side of the Poconos that we have seen today, and glad to be home where the deer if not the antelope play.

AUGUST 5: *THE WOMEN OF WOODVILLE*

When the van has been packed and loaded with water and wine, we depart in the general direction of Woodville, PA, where we plan to spend some time visiting Martha Park Keeler -- an old school chum of Melanie's and now a decorator (who has offered to let us interview some of her clients, friends, and family)....

Our first interview in Woodville is with Nan Schlinger (a.k.a. "Bunny" by virtue of a nickname with which she seems to identify, as indicated by her large collection of rabbit-oriented statues, sculptures, and figurines).... Bunny welcomes us warmly and settles us onto the terrace where I begin by shooting some stills during the initial stages of the interview in progress. Soon, I enter the house and take snapshots of everything in sight -- thinking little, shooting reflexly....

Everything in this house has the feeling of being *new*. Everything *smells* new, clean, and freshly painted. Doors stick because of the new paint whose odor permeates the premises. This new smell contrasts vividly with the visual impact made by the traditional decor. The older objects -- photos of family, weddings, graduations; books; rabbit artifacts -- seem lost in this pervasive aura of *newness*.

To document this impression, I try to capture two particularly salient manifestations of the prevailing *decor nouveau*. First, I photograph...a comfortable pair of chairs near a window that looks out on a very similar new brick split-level house directly across the yard. Presumably, this is where Bunny sits -- darning socks or stitching flags -- while she waits for her husband to return from work on cold dark winter evenings.

The second emblematic shot shows the hearth scene -- surrounded by a picture on the wall, various small statues on the mantel itself, two tables on either side with lamps and innumerable family photographs crowding their surfaces, a beautiful brass fireplace set -- and, last but not least, the fireplace itself: absolutely empty with its brand new white bricks gleaming brightly....

We next arrive at the house of Martha's parents, Mr. and Mrs. Rick Park.... Valerie Park greets us at the door, wearing a white dress and full of warm welcomes. She steers us toward the patio in search of enough light for the video camera....

After snapping Valerie and Russ in conversation, I slip back inside and start photographing the garden room. Immediately, I begin to observe profound symmetry everywhere I look.... Soon, upstairs, I encounter a magnificent bedroom with everything put neatly away and hardly any signs of habitation except a stack of magazines topped by *Architectural Digest* and a copy of William F. Buckley's latest spy novel..... The bed is flanked by two identical lamps and by two wallpaper-disguised doors on each side, with a double curve of small pictures hung carefully above it and a flowery bedspread that exactly matches the wallpaper....

I notice that my batteries in the flash are beginning to wear down. By the time I finish the upstairs shooting, the flash will barely recharge, and I still have most of the downstairs to do. Panicked, I run to the van to see if there are any batteries in my shoulder satchel. None. I see two boys with a bicycle in the yard next door. So I wander over with my best "hi, I want to be your friend" smile and offer them five dollars if they'll bike to the nearest store and get me two double A's. One of the lads disappears briefly and returns with two batteries. Overcome with gratitude, I give him the five dollar bill....

With my engines thus revitalized, I return to the house and begin canvasing the first floor. Again, more symmetry greets me at every turn. I capture the symmetrical displays on the dining room wall, including the spoon collection and the other wall decorations.... I move through the dining room and begin on the rubber plants, which were the first things that Valerie showed us when we entered.

Valerie obviously loves her rubber plants and takes great pride in how she can cut them back and root them. Earlier, she showed me how to drip paraffin on the exposed stumps to stop their milk-like bleeding. I started to comment on how they resemble wounded people, but the group moved on without me. Now, I am just snapping the five or six sprouting rubber trees when the others return and commandeer my attention to shoot some (additional) photos of the spoons and the bedroom. Not wanting to brag about the extent to which I have already penetrated the inner sanctum, I comply.

After this exercise in redundancy, I launch into some photographs of center stage, the living room.... I shoot the central seating area with some red roses positioned effectively against a white armchair. The house is full of plants and fresh flowers. Though incredibly neat and tidy, it exudes a warm lived-in feeling. I photograph some objects that remind me of my own parents -- some eagle bookends, some flowers, the dining room table and Chippendale chairs. In many ways, this house is decorated in a style my mom might like. It reminds me of home....

On the way back to the van, I pause to take some photos of the tree-lined street on which the Parks live. Maples and oaks line both sides of the road and arch together over the top to form a wonderful cathedral-like ceiling of green leaves. This recalls my childhood neighborhood with its marvelous tall trees before the Dutch elm disease wasted them all. I feel a moment of intense nostalgia as I see some yardworkers in a pickup truck take out their lawnmowers and start to work the way I used to do when I spent long summers cutting the grass in my parents' yard. I think about the old house that has now been sold and the old street that has lost its trees; and, for a moment, I feel sad....

After our day of interviewing, we drive the short distance to Martha and Mark Keeler's house. They cordially greet us as we lumber into their driveway and hook up to their electrical outlets, promptly blowing the circuit breaker a few times with our air conditioner, setting off their burglar alarm, and thereby causing the police to call.... Mark seems nice and very anxious to please a bunch of total strangers who have moved into his space with a major piece of vehicular equipment that has converted his driveway into a campground and made his own respectable Cadillac look somewhat out of place....

My worst fears about sleeping in the van are more than confirmed. While the mattress is pretty comfortable, the air conditioner blows frozen blasts of icy wind directly at my face and neck. I realize that I'll need to spend the night with my head under the covers, something that I have not attempted since I was a small child and thought that a wolf came into my room every night. I wonder why these great van-haunting outdoorspeople cannot survive in this cool climate without their gigantic fuse-blowing artificial air machine. Predictably, I toss and turn all night.

AUGUST 6: *NEW AND OLD, ARTIFICIAL AND REAL*

I drag myself out of bed at about 8:00 and decline Melanie's persistent offers of a warm shower (though, Heaven knows, I need one). Instead of bathing, I ponder questions concerning how I might go about turning some of that hot water toward the purpose of making coffee....

Martha arrives, and we start our interview. During this exchange, I try hard to keep her own thread going while still sticking to some of our main themes. We touch on entrepreneurship and how her decorating business emerged from an unhappy marriage in which she wanted kids and a career as an independent business woman while her husband wanted childlessness and a desk job for her (9-to-9 in New York City). Ultimately, Martha also wanted out of that particular marriage. So she took the plunge, attended the Parsons School of Design, moved back to Woodville, and began her own decorating business....

Unlike her first husband, Mark has supported her venture, while her dad has also encouraged her entrepreneurial flair. Indeed, Martha believes that she has learned her business skills from her father, who owns and manages a successful company that manufactures hollow candies (such as the chocolate Easter rabbits that roam the stores every March and April). Further, Martha's mother has served as a role model for many of her decorating activities....

In general, Martha feels that her own house shows a kind of "schizophrenia." The front part (living room, dining room) is decorated in a traditional style intended for guests and formal meetings. The back part (kitchen, family room, deck) is more contemporary for family and intimate gatherings. This distinction thereby sets up a contrast between the old and the new. I inquire which part reflects the "real" Martha. She appears unable to answer and pauses a long time.

My own hunch is that the traditional furnishings in the front part of the house represent what Martha feels she *is* -- as defined by old school ties, social status, Junior League membership, and parents who worry that her actions reflect back on their own reputations. This "front" embodies that from which she would like to assert her independence. Implicitly, such independence would involve a break from tradition in everything, including furniture. Thus, part of her likes the contemporary. For her office, she designed hi-tech furniture (which clashes violently with that area's wood-paneled walls). She also has modern things in her back rooms (surrounded by the clutter of children's toys).

In other words, the modern side of Martha's house has not fully coalesced, and this disarray parallels some tensions in her personal life. She cannot quite make a break from the old ways or completely assert her independence. She feels that, with a new baby on the way, she might have to cut back on some of her commitments. I ask her, if she had to choose one, would she keep the Junior League or her decorating business? After a *long* pause, she says, "the business." But the length of the delay seems to indicate her degree of conflict.... In the living room, I find an emblem of this conflict -- a large abstract oil painting hung next to a set of built-in shelves housing a collection of quaint figurines.

Our interview also touches briefly on the contrast between the artificial and the real. In her work, Martha uses fake flowers and cloth or plastic plants -- both because they are easier to care for and because some places do not have enough light for live foliage. Indeed, her garage contains several imitation ficus benjaminas waiting to be used in various decorating jobs. Martha's own master bedroom features both a vase of phony flowers and an artificial ficus, which resides in a brightly lit spot between two windows bathed in sunshine. Martha also feels that sometimes one cannot arrange to own real animals, no matter how much one loves them. For example, she adores horses and dogs (*not* cats) but cannot keep such livestock because Mark has "allergies to everything that walks or crawls." Hence, they own no live pets. Later -- when photographing the family's hearth -- I notice that, unlike some of the others I've seen in Woodville, it serves to burn real logs. Given our earlier conversation, I am quite surprised to see a large dog asleep directly in front of the fireplace. However, upon closer inspection, Martha's dog turns out to be stuffed. Empty. As hollow as the centers of her father's chocolate Easter bunnies....

AUGUST 7: *TYPING*

After our exertions on the excursion to Woodville, I crash. I realize increasingly that I have only the slimmest chance of finishing the typing of my log entries before leaving tomorrow for my holiday with Sally and Chris. I therefore coax Russ and Melanie into spending the day on such bookkeeping activities....

Consequently, after rising, exercising, and showering, I sit at the round table and start typing to the sounds of Andre Previn and Russ Freeman. Six hours later, I am still at it. By this time, from sitting tensely in the slant-backed chair, my lower back is aflame with agonizing pain. I desperately want to reach closure on this task; so I persevere. But afterwards, I feel physically and mentally drained and in no mood to visit the Clyde

Beatty Circus (an option that Russ and Melanie have cheerfully proposed as a possible way to spend our evening).

It makes only moderate demands on my rhetoric to persuade the others to designate this as an evening of reflection, conversation, and catching up on the video tapes I haven't seen yet. In fact, they graciously offer to take me to dinner, and I jump at the chance, making a reservation at the Settler's Inn for 8:30....

We take the van to Settler's so that I can watch videotapes on the way. I screen the footage on Nan Schlinger and Valerie Park, using this opportunity to verify the overall impressions that are already in my log. I would backtrack and make changes only if I found something factually incorrect. I don't.

Dinner is most pleasant. We talk about issues like "What does it all mean?" "Where do we go from here?" and "How should we present this stuff at ACR?" We find no answers to any of these questions, of course, but we have a nice chat.

During the drive back to Hemlock, I watch more tapes. On our return, I retreat into the house with a PC, the diskettes, and some hard copies of the notes written by Melanie, Russ, and Rick. I sit up until about 2:00, reading the printouts and scrolling through the discs....

AUGUST 8: *GOING HOME*

I arise again at 8:00, push myself through the familiar grooming and exercise rituals, exchange some tender thankyous and farewells with Russ and Melanie, and leave for home and Sally at about 11:00 a.m....

On the trip back to New York, I ponder my experiences during the past ten days. When I drove out to Hemlock Farms on July 29, I had a deep sense of uncertainty over what to expect. I was right. The ensuing events have differed considerably from anything that I might have anticipated.

First, the monster RV hardly raised an eyebrow at our security gate. Apparently, the guard really is intended for security and not to hassle the residents of the "Property," as the real estate agents like to call it. Presumably, thieves do not usually arrive in mammoth six-wheeled recreational vehicles that stick out like sore thumbs; so vans are OK.

Second, I devoted much less time to being a host in our house than I had originally expected. For the first couple of days, I tried to play this role. But, especially after Joe and Rick left, I began to understand that the others really did prefer being in the van; so I spent as much time as I could on wheels.

Third, I learned that the boundaries of my eagerness to live on a van extend from about 9:00 a.m. to about 10:00 p.m. I vastly prefer sleeping in my own bed and also feel much more comfortable trying to exercise, shower, and change in a house....

Fourth, I do not think that this particular Odyssey could have functioned without the van. The RV provided a good place for a group of people to work for about eighteen hours a day. For everyone but the driver(s), a long trip meant a chance to type field notes, journal entries, or log material; to watch videotapes; to compare thoughts; to eat; to sleep. Thus, the van introduced very real efficiencies in terms of time.

Fifth, I'm not so sure that efficiency is everything. As elsewhere, there may be an efficiency/effectiveness trade-off. In this case, some effectiveness may have been lost to the driven quality that characterized the feverish collection of data, writing of notes, entering them into the PC, and other compulsive research activities (my own included). As I have discovered, it is easy to get sucked into the need for a sense of completeness. I still wonder, however, if it might not be better either to proceed more slowly and reflectively or to collect the materials now and write them up for Christmas. After all, that is what my grandfather did when he wrote *his* log.

Sixth, I wonder if the emphasis that some of us place on the distinction between field notes and journal entries might not be misdirected. True, it adheres to the traditional practice in naturalistic inquiry. Yet, often, the field notes amount to little more than a partial transcript of what is already on tape, whereas the journals sound like "Dear Diary" material that has no real support in concrete events. Hence, the all-important interaction between objective reality (if there is such a thing) and the researcher's subjective impressions (or personal introspections) may tend to slip through the cracks. I am aware that, by tradition, anthropologists and ethnographers prefer to do it this way. But that does not necessarily make it right for purposes of projects related to this particular Odyssey.

Seventh, as an alternative, I have tried to focus on writing a "log" that combines aspects of field notes and journals by describing my own experience of our sites and interviews. These experiences involve an interaction between the objective reality of the data and the researcher's own subjective interpretive responses. A positivist wants to eliminate the latter. But, increasingly, postpositivists have recognized the impossibility of such a reduction. The log format may help us put the researcher back into the research. I hope so.

Eighth, such a device will help us only to the extent that we really do care about our experience of the research process. When I began the Odyssey, I thought that the main point was to study other people (as consumers). Increasingly, however, I have realized that, for me, the main point has been

to study *myself* -- myself studying *other* people as consumers and myself *as* a consumer. The Odyssey experience seems well-suited to providing the latter kinds of insights. Most of what I have learned on the Odyssey and tried to convey in my log concerns the nature of that research experience.

Ninth, I remain aware that any conclusions coming out of my log should be viewed as preliminary and tentative. The log provides an interpretive, personal account of what one researcher experienced during a ten-day portion of a summer-long journey that involved many people. Their reports will doubtless differ from mine and should be studied and compared accordingly.

Tenth and last, I am more grateful than I could have anticipated for being allowed to participate in this research experience. The Consumer Behavior Odyssey was, for me, a great adventure in which several colleagues permitted me to share their most private and profound thoughts and feelings. Where else could I have found such friends and fellow travelers? Where else, indeed, could I have pursued a project so vast, so heroic, and so inspiring as to raise Ulysses -- that archetypal traveler -- from the dead?

On Being an Informant on the Consumer Behavior Odyssey

Bernard J. Jaworski
Deborah J. MacInnis

The paper represents a retrospective analysis and interpretation of our experiences as informants on the Consumer Behavior Odyssey Project. The data for this analysis consists of four forms: our field notes, the videotape of our interview, recollections of the experience beyond the field notes, and emotion/cognition triggered by an analysis of the experience. Various topics are discussed including (1) the mechanics of the interview, (2) reactions to the interview, and (3) reflections on the experience one-and-a-half years later.

INTRODUCTION

Approximately a year and a half has passed since we were interviewed by the Consumer Behavior Odyssey researchers. At the time our field notes revealed that the interview was an enjoyable "consumption" experience, the topics covered were diverse, and the emotions that surfaced during the interview were considerable. We still share these views today. The purpose of this chapter is to document the types of thoughts/emotions that surfaced during the interview, provide a retrospective commentary/interpretation of the interview, and raise a few issues concerning the conduct of future naturalistic investigations. While the context of the chapter is novel, both Loud (1974) and Mullen (1935) have reported their reactions to documentaries concerning their lives and/or social environments. Hence our reactions to the process are not novel.

Prior to a discussion of these issues it is worthwhile to consider the motivation for this chapter. First and foremost the intent of this article is to provide a glimpse of Consumer Behavior Odyssey data collection from the perspective of the informant. We consider the type of questions asked, the style of interviewing, the structural arrangements of the group, the interaction of Odyssey members and other issues. Second, we hope that novel issues concerning the process of naturalistic data collection surface.

One additional issue is worth raising before we turn to substantive concerns. During the week that the Consumer Behavior Odyssey was in our home area, we assumed multiple roles on the project. Initially, we served as "site coordinators". Basically, this involved identifying research sites that best matched the interests of the group. For example, we identified ethnic neighborhoods, areas that were recently flooded, and outdoor markets. The researchers then selected a subset of sites to target. A few days later we

were interviewed by Russ Belk and, to a lesser extent, other Odyssey members. The day following the interview we traveled with the Odyssey to a nearby Polish festival. Since we had limited field experience, we felt most comfortable assuming secondary roles. That evening, in an trailer park, we were "autodriven" by Russ Belk and Melanie Wallendorf (i.e., we saw the tape recording of the interview at our home). We believe our reactions to the autodrive process were recorded at the time.

In order to adequately address our roles as informants, we divide the paper into three basic sections. In the first section, we consider structural issues related to the interview, such as the types of questions asked, the nature of the interview, and the roles of Odyssey members. The second section focuses on our reactions during and immediately following the interview. Here we discuss our feelings about the topics covered and the range of questioning. The third section considers our reflections on the experience after reviewing the videotape of the interview one-and-a-half years later. This section represents our responses to the videotape.

THE INTERVIEW

The Odyssey is coming, the Odyssey is coming! Bernie vividly remembers this long, bulky recreation vehicle pulling up to the curb in our tree-lined, lower-middle class neighborhood. While the sight of this RV was quite unusual, parking the vehicle proved to be quite a challenge. After squeezing into a spot, out jumped Russ Belk, Joe Cote, Rick Pollay and Melanie Wallendorf. The first thing Bernie noticed was the energy and enthusiasm of the group. He remembers commenting on how much energy, drive and enthusiasm they had - especially after several weeks on the road. Privately, he also recalls mentioning to Debbie that he was surprised by their collective demeanor noting that he was not sure he could have maintained their level of intensity and goal-directedness after living and maintaining such an active, unusual lifestyle.

Relatively early in the process, we reached the conclusion that Melanie and Russ played a dominant role in site and topic selection. Several reasons may have accounted for this role. First, they were the driving force behind the Odyssey and were the only researchers to have traveled with the Odyssey from its beginning in Los Angeles. Relatedly, we quickly gained the impression that their research agenda was developing and focusing as the Odyssey moved East. Hence, their notions of appropriate research sites, participants and topics were perhaps more developed than Joe's or Rick's.

Before describing the actual interview, we should put the interview in its appropriate context. The interview was held on Thursday, July 24, one day following Bernie's dissertation defense and two days following Debbie's dissertation defense. We were both working on the final revisions of our dissertations. Our apartment was in the process of being dismantled for the move to Arizona. Many pieces of furniture were being, or had been sold to other graduate students in the business school. We were planning to have a tag sale to sell of the remaining possessions on Sunday, July 27th. On Monday July 28th, a fellow graduate student was going to move in with us. She was scheduled to take over our apartment after we moved to Arizona. Because her lease had expired she either had to stay with us or sleep on the streets. Since the latter alternative was clearly unacceptable, we had an unexpected house-guest during this very hectic time. It was strange though, because her presence made us feel like we were being rushed out of the apartment. Graduation was the following Saturday (August 2nd) and both sets of parents were coming to visit for several days. We were planning to fly to Arizona on August 8th along with our dog and two cats. The movers who were taking the stuff we had planned to keep were coming between graduation day and August 7th. Needless to say, it was a rather hectic time.

The Set-Up

The process of setting up all the audio-visual equipment took Russ and Joe several minutes. First, the video camera needed to be set-up with a tripod. Next the tape needed to be positioned and the microphone attached. Joe assumed the role of cameraperson, Russ was to lead the interview, Melanie was floating throughout the apartment, and Rick arrived a few minutes into the interview. We sat on the floor near Russ while Keisha (our dog or "baby substitute") stayed near us for most of the interview.

The Interview

The interview covered a number of diverse topics. While Russ seemed to have a set of research questions in mind, they were not "visibly" apparent to us. That is, he did not have a note pad with questions nor did he seem to "force" the discussion to make sure certain topics were discussed. However, he did probe for more details when certain issues were raised. The general pattern appeared to be to touch upon a given topic (i.e., planned acquisitions after assuming roles as faculty

members), discuss some details related to the role transition, and move onto a new topic. The new topic typically was related in some way to the old topic. For example, after discussing planned purchases in Arizona, we discussed joint decision making and then joint research. Bernie's field notes reflected both the process and the number of topics. He noted:

> The interview was semi-directed. Although Russ clearly had an agenda, it was also clear that he was willing to diverge from it should some interesting comment or side issues arise. In general, I had no problem with the content of the interview or with the style of questioning....

Concerning the topics covered, he noted:

> A number of diverse topics were covered including our role transition, planned purchases, possessions we were planning to sell, images about [our] new role as faculty members, [and] the purchase of our new automobile....

In addition to the questions asked by Russ, Joe and Rick also asked a few questions. These questions were always framed in the context of Russ's questioning. Often they required us to elaborate or provide more detailed information. To provide some perspective on the types of questions asked, the direction of questioning and the flow of the interview, we have provided a rough sketch of the interview schedule in the Appendix.

Russ assumed a very casual interviewing approach. His approach seemed to be more of a friendly, "I'd like to get to know you" style as compared to a confrontation or mechanized form of interviewing. To get a feel for the process, we thought it appropriate to report a verbatim excerpt from the interview. Given space limitations and the difficulty in transcribing interviews (e.g. this excerpt took 3 hours to transcribe), we have selected a three to four minute discussion of "selling our Chevette".

> Debbie: ..you know, the same thing happened with the car... We have a 1979 Chevy Chevette that has 150,000 miles on it, ..so it's not exactly..the..it's not
>
> Russ: Now is that going too? to Arizona?
>
> Debbie: That's being sold..
>
> Bernie: No.
>
> Russ: O.K. But you just bought a new Camry?

Bernie: Yes.

Debbie: Right. But that's in Arizona.

Russ: Oh. O.K. .. You got it there..

Bernie: We bought it there.

Debbie: We bought it in Arizona.

Russ: Have you seen it yet? The actual car?

Bernie: No.

Debbie: No. Not the actual car.

Bernie: Yes. But we sort of knew what we were getting..We got out there, we got to the dealership we argued ..finagled..and everything else and we ordered it..The only thing is that we were not sure what the color it would be..because they gave us some choices..

Russ: O.K. so if you do not get the new car until you get there and you sold ...you're selling the old one here.. How do you get there and how does your furniture get there?

Bernie: O.K. we're leaving here on the 8th of August..We're flying out.. I'm giving my car to the person we sold it to on or about the 6th or 7th.. When we arrive on the 8th, the person... the bank where I got the loan.. I got to know the guy on the phone, .. he is going to pick me up at the airport.

Russ: O.K. that is good.

Bernie: ..and drive me over,.. and we will have the car that day...So it is only a one or two day period where we won't have a car.. and I'll just borrow..down below there are some graduate students... and I'll just use their car..for that day or two.

Russ: Oh O.K.

Bernie: But to finish Debbie's thought there..is that we were selling this car..even though it has 150,000 miles on it.. I have done alot of work on it..The body is in very good condition, .. so I mean its not..its something where if you spent let's say six or seven hundred dollars I know it would last for several at least for a few years...enough for a sort of a graduate student hack car.

Debbie: [says something we can't make out]

Russ: uh huh.

Bernie: It turns out that our neighbor next door here...was working..and he came over and said I have someone who I work with who would be interested in your car...So I went to see this guy and it turns out he is a fellow who has a family with I think he has about six kids..He looks to be about thirty..

Debbie: He's a security guard...[stops as Bernie interrupts.]

Bernie: He's a security guard...He's ah..black...I 'm not sure what education he has but my feeling is that he doesn't have alot so I sold it to him for 450 dollars and I felt pretty good about it because I feel like, you know the car,..... let's say I could have gotten 700...I'm not sure but let's throw that number out... I felt good about giving it to this guy for 450... and I didn't feel like I was ripping him off at all...I mean I felt like you know 450..[we miss some of the verbatim because Joe has to change to new tape] and all of a sudden he buys it...I didn't misrepresent anything... exactly what had been done what worked ..what he was getting into...The nice thing about it is that he really loved the car...he took it around...went to get his wife and loaded three of the kids in the car and went driving around for about an hour and a half...and he loved it...I felt so good about it...You know I wish I, I wish I had a little bit...even if we had a couple thousand in the bank, I would have said listen, just keep the car...it would have made me feel really good.

Debbie: In fact we were thinking that if we didn't sell the car there's a couple of people we have met around here just through walking our dog that are not real well off.

Bernie: For example, we walk through this cemetery each day and take our dog for a walk.. And there is this guy over there his name is Bud and I don't know what he earns for an income, but I'd say maybe 5 or 6 dollars and hour plus he has a house on the grounds. But he simply doesn't [have much. He had to] take a part-time job..He is a very bright guy, .. no formal education... I was saying to Debbie it would be nice if we had a few thousand in the bank and simply bring the car over and say here, take it.

While this excerpt of the interview lends itself to various interpretations, our primary concern is to illustrate the types of questions and responses. The only other significant structure-oriented dimension of the interview concerned Keisha's constant demands for affection. Frequently this interrupted the flow of conversion.

After the interview itself, we were asked to walk around the apartment and talk about our "stuff". We talked about what had been in the room (some of it had been sold to other grad students), what was left, and whether we were taking it or selling it. The entire interview lasted approximately 2 hours. After the interview we all went to a Vietnamese restaurant, in part, to celebrate the defense of our dissertations.

IMMEDIATE REACTIONS TO THE INTERVIEW

Early Friday morning we began a trek to the nearby Polish festival after a few hours of data collection in the city. At some point during the next two days we had the opportunity to record our reactions to the interview using the PC's in the recreation vehicle. Below we report verbatim our field notes concerning our reactions to the interview.

Bernie's Reactions to the Interview:

...The interview was fun. It was an enjoyable 'consumption' experience.... I would be willing to bet that many of the interviewees would consider the interview [to be enjoyable].

I really didn't like to talk about the car purchase. I thought we were ripped-off and it was not easy to share the experience. It brought back the same feelings all over again.... I would guess that the interviews bring out strong affect. Many of the topics discussed are not "light"; rather they are very personal... A lot of emotion is expended in the course of the interview..

...at a few points I thought that Russ might be trying to get "more data" or "read more into situations" than the situation allowed. I couldn't help but think I don't process certain things deeply. For example, the two bureaus we were giving to our landlord/neighbor/friends did not have a tremendous amount of meaning...even though they were my grandmother's. When Russ began to question us, only then did I begin to consider their sentimental value. Up to that point I never really thought about it. That is, on a day-to-day basis I don't even think about them. It is only in situations where you are given a choice of saying "keep" or "sell" that you consider their value...

I couldn't help but notice that Melanie was not in the room. At one point I thought she might be scouting our possessions....In situations where the individual is being interviewed, but some of the group 'interviewers' leave or do not pay attention, I wonder what the interviewee thinks..

Debbie's Immediate Reactions to the Interview.

I really enjoyed being interviewed. It was fun talking to Russ about our experiences. I noticed, however, that he had a tendency to say "Oh Okay" in response to our comments. I wondered several times during the interview what he meant by that. Did it mean Oh, OK, I know what you mean. Or was it, OK, I have to acknowledge what they said, even though I'm not getting any real meat here. Or, was it OK, I have no idea what you guys are talking about, let me try to direct it somehow.

I felt the interview made me learn a lot of things about myself. For example, I never really realized how much I do treasure my office space, and how I really do feel that Bernie violates it when he comes in there. In fact, now that I think about it, whenever he comes into my office I always ask, "What do you want"; as if to say, why are you here? The thing is that I realize I'm selfish with my office space, but I have no motivation to change it.

I also realized how much of our stuff is related to special occasions, friends, places, etc. Pictures, decorative items are all tied to those we have known. We have always had some close friends wherever we have been. Having things they have given us around is as much a confirmation of our friendship with them as it is a recognition of where we have been... Of our roots. When we remember them, we remember ourselves.

I am really puzzled by the fact that we have a lot of stuff that I really dislike and think is ugly, but that I still hate to sell. For example, why will I feel upset if we only get $100 for our upholstered living room furniture when I really hate the stuff? We talked about the sacred-profane notion. Added to that is an equity notion, I think. It's like saying,"Look, I paid $1200 for this stuff. It's still in reasonable condition.It's worth at least $200!" The feeling involved in the whole selling of personal possessions issue is very complex. I'm having a very difficult time articulating it. Some might be: (1) the actual value of the stuff itself in some sort of objective sense (2) the feeling of personal identification (I really like this thing; it's me) (3) The feeling of instrumental identification (I had a lot of experiences in which this thing was involved, (even though I don't like it), but you look at it as just an object). In other words, you don't know the history of this thing in terms of its relevance to my life.

The fact that the interview was a learning experience to me was interesting and somewhat positive. But I'm worried whether other people find out negative things about themselves through the interview. What are the ethical implications of this?

Our only regret in writing this section is that we wish we had more detail in our field notes. Bernie recalls typing his field notes on the way back home from the Polish festival. In addition to trying to figure out Word Perfect, he recalls being under time pressure to get the thoughts on paper before arriving back in the city. Debbie remembers being carsick from writing and reading her notes while in the moving RV. As a result, she couldn't write as much as she would have liked. Immediately after we returned home was had to begin the process of getting ready for our tag sale.

REFLECTIONS ONE AND A HALF YEARS LATER

Debbie's Reactions to the Interview

a. Reactions to Watching Myself.
    One of the first things that struck me was how different I looked. I seem to have aged considerably in a short year and a half. I was amazed at how I talk and what my laugh sounds like. I was also acutely aware of my nonverbal responses during the interview; the fact that I often sat with my arms folded or hugging my knees (perhaps indicating some trepidation and self-consciousness about the process of being interviewed and/or filmed), the fact that I talk with my hands, that when I'm thinking about something I don't maintain eye-contact with the individual, and the fact that I play with my hair a lot (another nervous gesture?). None of these things were very pleasant. The process of watching the tape was somewhat painful.

b. Reactions to the Interview Process.
    I became acutely aware of the fact that despite my nonverbal defenses against being interviewed, the process was quite conversational and relaxed. Bernie was just about lying down on the floor and was his usual animated self. We were clearly not

hesitant about talking, and our answers to Russ' questions were quite frank. I wondered whether this was a factor attributable to Russ' interviewing savvy, or whether we simply felt comfortable with him due to our similar status as academics, our understanding of the kinds of things the Odyssey was studying, and/or the fact that we were so burnt out from finishing our dissertations and would have talked to anybody about anything.

    Despite the fact that Bernie and I spent most of the two hours doing the talking (we hardly let Russ get a word in edge-wise), I remember feeling frustrated over the fact that we brushed over many topics that we would have liked to talk about in greater depth. We could have gone on and on about any one of the major areas we talked about: transition imagery, product dispositions, the car buying process. And we wanted to do so. More in-depth discussions would have left me more satisfied. I just didn't get the feeling that I had "told all" and really given them an idea about various aspects of our lives. As an interviewee there was a real desire on my part to make sure the response was fully explicated.

c. Reactions to the Interview Content.
    Emotions. Watching the tape brought back a lot of memories, most of which produced considerable anxiety: the stress of finishing our dissertations, the fact that our house was being torn up and our possessions given away, the potential problem of two sets of parents visiting for several days for our graduation, worry over teaching once we got to Tucson, distress over the fact that we felt we had gotten ripped-off in our car purchase, wonder over how we were going to make ends meet financially until we got our first paycheck, fear that Keisha (our "baby substitute" dog), and Humphrey and Boo Boo (our cats) wouldn't make it to Tucson alive after traveling in the baggage compartment of the plane for seven hours, and distress over leaving some very good friends. It was a tense time, and there it was, relived on film! It was awful! The autodriving technique is a very powerful one for reliving experiences. I started to wonder what the autodrive technique might be like to those people interviewed by the Odyssey members who had *really* been through some traumatic experiences; such as the flood victims. Perhaps the re-creation of the emotion would cause them a tremendous amount of negative emotion, and bring back memories they would have wanted to put behind them.

    Aside from the emotional re-experiencing of the time in which the interview was conducted, I also learned a lot about my consumption behavior by watching the tape. Interestingly, some of these things were *not* apparent to me while we were interviewing.

This point also raises the important issue of field note recording. Several of the issues raised in my field notes I had completely forgotten.

The Meaning of Possessions. The meaning of possessions was a dominant theme in our conversation, which was natural since were in the process of either packing up or selling our stuff. Several interesting things about our possessions became apparent as I watched the interview. I realized that I tend to personify some of my things. For example, I talked in the interview about "rescuing" a table of my grandfather's (that later became my desk in college) from an old garage. When talking about fixing up some of our old pieces of furniture, I talked about "revitalizing" them.

The dispositions of our possessions were also symbolic of our transition. I remember that while we were not planning to take most of our furniture with us, because it was too expensive to move, it was not very good (graduate student furniture), and because I *hated* some of it, I felt like I was giving away kittens when we sold it. You know you can't keep them, but it's still sad to give them away. Here had been a family or collection of pieces that had represented the center of our existence for at least four years, and we were breaking it up. It was the most concrete signal of the transition. It represented the break up of a stage of my life. Not that I didn't want to move on and stop being a graduate student! But I had bittersweet feelings about the transition. We were leaving some good times behind and moving to an unknown situation.

Related to the above is the notion that selling our possessions at the tag sale was difficult because people just picked over them and treated them as things, just somebody else's junk. It was junk, but it was *my* junk, and I resented the fact that people couldn't see it in its context of my life. Some possessions have real meaning in terms of self-history or self-identity, regardless of their aesthetic or functional value. I hated haggling over the price. It was making something that had a role in my personal history a simple exchange good that was going to a stranger. I would rather have just given it to somebody than to haggle over the price.

Catharsis. At the same time there was almost a thrill of getting rid of some things. It represented change and an acknowledgement that we *were* making a transition; that things *were* going to be different. It was exciting! It was also great to get rid of things I had hated for so long; Things that were ugly (I hated our living room furniture), things that didn't work right, or were so pathetically out of style. I remember being embarrassed about having such awful clothes in grad school and saying that I couldn't wait to put them in a pile and light a match to them.

Poor as we were, we had accumulated quite a bit of things since we were married, and it was exciting to pare down to only the essentials. I stated in the interview that I was worried that once we started working we would buy too much stuff simple because we had the "means" (i.e., the money). I was worried because I didn't want to become overloaded. I didn't want to drown in the things I had purchased. Luckily, I had overestimated the "means" we would actually have left over for discretionary purchases. Although in this year and a half we have acquired a house, furnishings, and new clothes, we haven't yet had to deal with the problem of becoming overloaded.

Giving. We felt like we were incredibly fortunate to be moving on to a better, more lucrative lifestyle, and because we had that opportunity, we wanted to give our stuff to people who were not as fortunate as us (i.e., people in our neighborhood who didn't have much, other grad students). It made us feel really good. First, we were sure that the stuff went to a place where it would be welcomed, appreciated and needed. Second, we wanted to feel like we were helping out people who had and still have tough times; something for people who deserve a break in life.

Gifts as Symbols of People. I realized that many of the things we were taking were gifts (artwork, wedding gifts) given by friends or very close relatives. While not all of these things represented my most favorite possessions, it was unthinkable to get rid of them. It would be like throwing your friendship away. For example, we moved a painting by my grandmother of a bunch of flowers in a vase. It's not very good by artistic standards, and neither Bernie nor I like it very much as a piece of art. But it was a part of her. She died this past year. I'm glad I have it.

Imagery. I suppose it should come as no surprise to hear this from me, of all people, but our future plans were so obviously filled with imagery. Anticipatory imagery makes up such a huge part of our consumption experiences. Ours were so rich and developed. And we built upon each other's imagery every time we talked about some aspect of our transition. Some of our images were so incredibly unrealistic, and we looked back and laughed at them when we watched the tape. For example, we felt that in the evenings after teaching and research we would have time to prepare gourmet meals, drink fine wine, and listen to music. I think we have done this once or twice in the past year and a half. However, the images were necessary and they were a definite part of the planning process, realized or not.

Complex Decision Making- Although I had not realized it at the time, watching the tape made me realize the very complex nature of the car purchase decision making process. In part, the process was one we savored, since it represented the realization of a fantasy for us (a new car--after driving the old Chevette), and because it represented a break from working on our dissertations. So maybe we made it more complex that it needed to have been. In part, it was a complex process because we bought the car in Arizona rather than where we were living. Word of mouth influence from friends was perhaps the dominant information source, followed up by information from nonpersonal, non-marketer dominated sources (e.g., *Consumer Reports*) and then literature provided by the dealership. We did everything we could to avoid talking to the salespeople. It's as though we felt they had absolutely no credibility because they had such a great incentive to try to sell us a car. Their hard sell tactics are just too much! We wanted to run everytime we walked into a dealership (we had the same feeling everytime we talked to a realtor when we were searching for a house after we moved to Tucson). We enjoyed the search aspects of the process and certainly did not view them as burdensome or costly in any way. It was the actual buying (negotiating) and financing (payment) process that engendered all the bad feelings.

Space as a Consumption Good. Bernie mentioned on tape that my office at home was regarded as a "sacred" place that he wasn't allowed to enter unless he had some work related activities to talk about. Things really haven't changed. I now have a home office in our new house and I still hate to be bothered when I'm in there. The violation of a "possession" known as space was also apparent in our reactions to the new tenant moving into our apartment. We had gotten to know her through graduate school, and while she was a wonderful, pleasant person, we both felt her presence and her stuff in what was "our" apartment was a true violation of our space. I would imagine that needs for space rank quite high in the needs hierarchy for some consumers. It is an interesting consumption domain, but to my knowledge, underresearched. It is also interesting to note that our perspectives on space have changed. It is interesting to note that during the interview process we noted that the sabbatical house were renting was large (1600 sq. feet). That amount of living space seems small to us now.

Bernie's Reaction to the Interview

a. *Reactions to Watching Myself.*

I agree with Debbie, watching oneself interact with others or discuss life experiences is an interesting experience. Actually, I didn't dwell on my physical features when I watched the tape for the first time. However, several other things shocked me. First, I couldn't believe how much I interrupt Debbie. She barely had a chance to talk when were discussing certain topics. In the course of everyday conversation I don't think I do this as frequently. However, when I get excited about a topic, then I seem to bulldoze through the issues. The second thing I noticed was how much I use my hands to discuss or illustrate points. While this might be somewhat interesting in its own right, the thing that struck me is how much my mannerisms, movements and hand gestures resemble my father's. The last point that I found surprising was the speed at which I talk. My students sometimes complain about how fast I talk. I now know exactly what they are talking about - particularly since I attempted to transcribe a few minutes of the conversation.

b. *Reactions to the Interview Process.*

I had the same reactions to the interview as Debbie. Namely, I *wanted* to hear us talk more about different aspects of our life at that time. In retrospect, it was a very stressful time. However, a number of interesting things were happening - I now wish we had the time to say more (or perhaps were given the time to go into more detail). Actually, I would be willing to bet this feeling would be representative of those informants who discussed their collections. I'm sure that when they are autodriven that they feel they did not provide enough detail for a listener to pick up the subleties of the collection. More importantly, I would think that the collector would want to hear himself/herself talk about things that are *very* important to him/her.

c. *Reactions to the Interview Content.*

Emotion. Similarly to Debbie, I also thought a great deal of emotion was expended in the course of the interview. It vividly brought back some terrible experiences (the course loads, buying a car, having no money) and some great experiences (defending the dissertation, selling/"giving" the Chevette away, reflecting on friendships). Perhaps the most vivid emotion concerns the purchasing of the new car. To this day I can still recall the negotiation process and the feeling that we were ripped-off during the financing. It pains me to write about it. On the other hand, the interview brought back some very pleasant memories. For example, it was great to relive the old apartment. We worked exclusively at home during graduate school and it was nice to tour the apartment by watching the film.

One other point is worth mentioning. In the course of watching the video, I had the opportunity to observe Debbie. It was obvious that the tape brought back a great deal of emotion for her - it was etched on her face.

Everytime that Keisha appeared on the TV screen, Debbie smiled.

Financial Theme. One overarching theme covered virtually every topic discussed: money. I simply could not believe how much money- or lack thereof- influenced the way we saw the world at that time. For example, in selling the Chevette, I remember being disappointed that I could not give the car to the security guard. He and his wife loved the car - as did his kids. But we needed the 450 dollars at that time. The sad epilogue to the story is that he could not come up with the money to pay for the car. As a result I sold it to another security guard working at the same church. As it turned out the person I sold it to would also be classified as part of the lower or under class. I feel great that I could sell it to him. I often wonder if the car is still running. I hope so.

The financial theme found its way into a number of other topics. For example, we talked about joining a health club in Tucson, purchasing new clothes, being about to go out to dinner, shopping for groceries, imagery related to purchase and buying an airline seat for the dog. Obviously, when one discusses consumer behavior, financial concerns are frequently at the forefront. However, in our case, it seemed to dominate many of the topics. I suppose it makes some sense since graduate school provides a weird mix - a great deal of intellectual stimulation on the one hand and material poverty on the other.

I forgot. There were several topics that were discussed that I completely forgot. Even with some "cued recall," I still would not have remembered them if I did not see the tape. For example, at the start of the interview, I was discussing my ideas for a "auction of belongings" by invitation only to the graduate students at the business school. I thought it would be a good way to sell the furniture and at the same time give these students/friends a good deal. We were not out to make a great deal of money. I'm not sure why we chose not to follow through on it. This is but one example of things we discussed that I would not have recalled. Obviously, this simple example illustrates the importance of recording field notes immediately after returning from data collection activities.

Friends. It was very sad to talk about some of the people who we knew then. The cemetery caretaker - Bud - is one person who comes to mind. For the three years we lived in that apartment, we took Keisha for a walk 4 times a day - every day of the year. Ninety-five percent of the walks were through the cemetery so that Keisha would not have to be on a leash. As one might expect, we struck up a casual friendship with Bud while were on our walks through the cemetery. More often than not the conversation was about the weather,

cutting the grass, or cemetery politics. Nothing very heavy. Yet, we saw him almost everyday. I really wanted to give him a present for allowing us to so freely walk undisturbed on his turf (there were leash laws/signs all around). I regret to this day that we forgot to say goodbye and did not leave him some small token of our appreciation. Unfortunately, it is sad to think that he is probably still plodding away with very few financial rewards and appreciation - even though he takes his job very seriously.

The interview also triggered memories about graduate students who were in our cohort or are still in school. Fortunately, we have kept in touch with a number of these friends. There is no question that graduate school builds some type of bond between peers. I kiddingly tell Debbie it must be like being combat buddies. There is no way to communicate the experience that was shared. Only by passing through the experience at the same time -sharing the highs and lows- could one truly appreciate the effort.

The Car. I hate to talk about the car purchase. Interestingly, each month as we pay the bill, we are reminded of the experience. We are also reminded as we (1) bring the car in for routine service (thank God it hasn't required any repairs), (2) drive by the dealership, (3) talk with friends about their new car purchase and (4) budget for each month's expenses. Melanie and Russ - please do not follow up on this purchase!

CONCLUSION

The good news is that we have settled into our new home in Arizona and currently we enjoy a very comfortable life. Interestingly our normal routine is not much different from graduate school- except that we now have to teach.

The dog and cats survived the plane trip to Arizona. We tried to buy Keisha a seat on the plane but the airlines wouldn't let us. Fortunately it was a one-way, direct flight so the probability of losing them was slim. They seemed to have settled into the warm Arizona climate quite nicely. Our only concern is that coyotes live in our rather untamed neighborhood so we need to make sure everyone is inside the house after dark. Given the importance of our animals in our lives, it should come as no surprise to learn that one of our first purchases in the new house was the construction of a five foot tall wall that enclosed the back yard so that our "babies" could be protected from coyotes, tarantulas, rattlesnakes and other creatures of the desert.

On the consumption front we have begun to lessen the burdens of graduate school poverty. Much to Debbie's delight, we have managed not to overconsume, although this is probably because the domains in which we want to consume are so broad. Although the first few months were spent shopping for reasonable clothes (i.e., beyond T-shirts and scruffy jeans), we now have a wardrobe that is not comprised entirely of pregraduate school attire.

We have also furnished our bedroom, kitchen, family room and two home offices. As one might expect, Debbie's office was fully furnished about 3 or 4 months before Bernie's. We still have a way to go, however, we are making progress. Interestingly, the "financial theme" still tends to worm its way into our lives. With a new house that needs a lot of work we somehow never seem to have enough money. We also seem to be extremely goal directed in our consumption habits. The house has become an area of achievement of sorts. We are always planning to get this or that "done", as if the completion of the project marks some sort of achievement. Interestingly too, our home, reflects more of us personally than any other house in which we have lived. Our financial means have allowed us this pleasure. We think we are all set for Melanie or Russ to begin to follow-up on purchases related to role transitions!

REFERENCES

Loud, Pat (1974), *Pat Loud: A Woman's Story*, New York: Coward, McCann and Georghegan.

Mullen, Pat (1935), *Man of Aran*, New York: E. P. Dutton Co.

APPENDIX
Overview of the Interview: Questions and Answers

Questions by Russ	Answers
	We are in the middle of talking about a grad student auction we would liked to have had
What happens Sunday? (re: tag sale)	Motivated by move to AZ; Talked about amount of stuff we have accumulated since we got married
You got married how long ago?	Bernie gives our life history
And you were slowly accumulating stuff over this period?	Debbie talks about a table that she got from her grandfather.
Is your grandfather still alive? Is that when you acquired it?	No. Debbie explains the acquisition process.
What does this furniture mean to you?	Debbie explains that it has been her desk in college and has been through a lot of her personal history
So it means more of you than it means your grandfather?	Yes
	Bernie talks about some bureaus we got from his side of the family; his grandmother. Discusses how he restored them.
You're getting rid of your (Bernie's) grandmother's furniture?	Yes
How did you decide to keep Debbie's grandfather's stuff and get rid of your grandmother's stuff?	We explain that we are giving them to some special friends who are going to have a baby.
Another little aside...Do you know what sort of furniture you want once you move to AZ?	
	We talk about how our oak coffee tables were custom made by an Ithaca crafts-person. Talk about how we hate our upholstered living room furniture. Hated it from the start. It was a different color than we thought when we bought it.
Even if you had $15,000 you wouldn't take this furniture?	The stuff would stay.
[Rick Pollay:] How are you disposing of these tables?	Discuss selling most of the stuff to other grad students
Is there any sense that they'll remember you because they have it?	Not really. Just want to help them out.
Let's go onto the topic of your new car. OK, So you are selling your car and you have a car in Arizona. How do you get there and how does your furniture get there?	Talk about present car. Chevette with lots of miles on it. Flying to AZ. Giving car to person who is buying it a few days

APPENDIX (CONTINUED)
Overview of the Interview: Questions and Answers

Questions by Russ	Answers
	before we leave. Person buying it is a custodian with 2 kids. Not much money. We sold him the car for a song. Felt good to help him out. Discuss how we were thinking about giving car away to guy in our neighborhood who is the groundsperson of a small cemetery. He makes very little money. Doesn't have a car.
Tell me what you think of this. You're living in a lower-middle class neighborhood. They're in your current status. You're leaving this status but you're not. Is there any sense of paying them back?	Not really paying them back. Just want to help them out. We know what its like to have no money.
Let's go back to the car purchase. One of the first things that you're going to buy is a car. Tell me about this. Bernie and Debbie buy a car.	Discuss how we got a guide from *Consumer Reports* on how to negotiate for a car. Discuss how it bore no correspondence to what actually happened.
Do you both drive about equally? Is this a joint purchase?	Bernie drives most of the time. Debbie hates to drive. But it is a joint purchase. Bernie wanted an automatic hoping that it will increase the likelihood of Debbie driving. Bernie discusses images of buying a sports car (MR-2) but decided it was impractical. Narrowed choice down to Honda Accord and Toyota Camry. Discuss likes/ dislikes, options and value of both. Lot of friends bought Camrys. Read a lot about them in *Consumer Reports*.
You said a bunch of people on the faculty had already purchased a Camry. Another informant said this was a minus for him. Did that enter into your decision making?	It probably made us more comfortable.
OK. So you got a Camry. How did you go about purchasing it and where did you purchase it?	Discuss the bargaining process. (too painful to go over in depth)
Is this your first new car?	
How did the actual bargaining process go? Did you say take it or leave it? Did you say yes immediately?	Went to his office. Discussed process in detail.
You said he was a typical salesman. Was he experienced?	

APPENDIX (CONTINUED)
Overview of the Interview: Questions and Answers

<u>Questions by Russ</u>

<u>Answers</u>

You are both marketing PhD's. You know about the marketing concept. Did he typify the marketing concept?

Yes. Playing the concept. Talked about his tactics.

So to sum up, you're happy with your new car even though you haven't seen it?

We mention that what we are *really* upset about is the whole financing deal. We felt like we got ripped off because the dealer told us we didn't have any credit established and would have to pay high interest rates. Bernie relates the story about the financing we got through an AZ bank. We discuss the process as a "nightmare" .

Lets get you away from your nightmare and move onto a more pleasant topic. What is your order of priority for acquisition when you get to Tucson. Wait a minute, let me set this up...Are you moving to a bigger place?

We talk about our plans to rent a faculty sabbatical home for a year so we can save up money to buy a house and still avoid buying furniture. Discuss the size, interior and exterior of the sabbatical house we rented. We say it is pretty large (1600 square feet).

What's the image of what you'll wear?

We will dress rather formally (tie and jacket, dress, suits) We have to assume the role as faculty and clothes will help us do it.

Have you ever taught before?

Never. Which is why we need to rely on the clothes to assume the role.

What else besides clothes?

Discuss joining a health club. We really enjoy exercising.

Discuss eating out.

Taking bikes?

Yes. Definitely.

What else is on your wish list?

Major purchases are delayed until we can afford the house.

So all these expenses will go up?

Yes. Discuss fear of going out of control. Have delayed gratification for so long, are afraid we'll just buy something because we have the money, not because we need it. Don't want to become overloaded.

What about travel. Is that in your plans?

Yes. Haven't done much since have been in grad school. Mostly to conferences. Discuss trips we've gone on in the past.

You say "we" a lot. Are most of your purchases joint? For clothes for example?

Discuss process of clothes buying.

Do you get groceries together?

Yes.

APPENDIX (CONTINUED)
Overview of the Interview: Questions and Answers

Questions by Russ	Answers
And professionally you're going to do research together?	Discuss how we enjoy working together even though our interests differ. Working together also makes us feel less competitive with one another.
[Joe Cote;] We heard you were going to take your pets along. Was there any question about this?	Pets are kids. Really nervous about taking them on plane. Afraid they'll die in the baggage compartment or get lost somewhere. Tried to buy a seat for the dog. Wanted to keep her right beside us in the plane but airline wouldn't let us.
You don't have to answer this but... some people see kids as the next thing up from pets. Do you see kids in your future?	Not immediately. We want to enjoy ourselves for awhile. Discuss images of what we want life to be like once we move to AZ.
[Rick Pollay:] If you're so talented in imagery, don't you set yourself up for a lot of disappointment?	Not really. There is some initial disappointment, but it's never been so strong that it actually ruined things for us.
Would it be any different if you weren't able to achieve [your imagery]?	Discuss when it might be frustrating if imagery cannot be attained.
Do you ever buy a lottery ticket?	All the time.
[Rick Pollay:] You have a lot of imagery about the future. Any imagery about the past?	Yes, recently. Due to move. Interesting psychological aspects of making the transition. Think of all of the bad things about present place and how new place will be so much better on those dimensions. Way of creating psychological distance from old place. But as actual moving date gets closer, remember all the good things. Become sentimental. Lots of fond memories. Want to see places "for the last time" as if saying goodbye to them.
Russ gives us some post cards of the city he picked up. Run through these and pick out those that have special meaning; those that are this city to you.	Discuss photos. Memories of various places.
[Rick Pollay:] Any exchange of gifts among people so you have a memento of them?	Show gift of stained glass window done by our landlord and his wife (special friends). Discuss how we are not exchanging gifts with other people. People are very generous with their hospitality, but rarely are gifts exchanged. Discuss how we used to get together with friends more before we went to grad school. Have lots of

APPENDIX (CONTINUED)
Overview of the Interview: Questions and Answers

Questions by Russ

Answers

pictures of social gatherings. Haven't done much picture taking in this city.

So you've taken a lot of pictures in other places you've lived, but you haven't taken many here?

Harder to get together. Discuss fact that almost all of the art work that we are taking with us is art that people have given us or places we have lived. Provides memories of those people/places.

I Was Observed (*In Absentia*) and Autodriven by the Consumer Behavior Odyssey
Dennis W. Rook

ABSTRACT

Four Consumer Behavior Odyssey principals (Russ Belk, Tom O'Guinn, John Sherry, and Melanie Wallendorf), were house guests in my Santa Monica, California, apartment when they launched their summer fieldwork in June, 1986. I was far-out-of-town in Southeast Asia during their stay, and this discussion begins with my thoughts and feelings about being "observed" *in absentia.* In addition to residing in my apartment, the Odyssey team conducted an extensive photographic inventory of its contents. In July, 1986, John Sherry conducted an autodriving interview with me, using the photographic slides as stimuli for eliciting information about the origins and meanings of my possessions. The bulk of this paper discusses my reactions to the autodriving interview as a methodological tool for consumer researchers, and also, as a meaningful experience for "researched consumers."

June 26, 1986

"Oh Dennis, they stayed for such a *long* time. I think two weeks! The wife she was very nice. I think she is married to the one who looks like a hippie. And another man was very nice; he has a family, and we talked a lot. And there were others -- men -- who I don't know about. They just came and went. They all laughed a lot, and were very nice."

Elsa Joseph (wf-82)
Santa Monica, California

This conversation began just as I arrived on my doorstep after travelling continuously for 26 hours from Bali to Jakarta to Singapore to Hong Kong (I think!), and finally back home to LA. I was balancing four pieces of luggage, including an embarrassingly maxed-out "expanda-bag" overstuffed with tourist haul. I was exhausted but grateful to be home. It was about 9:00 AM, and Elsa pounced as soon as she heard me fumbling with my apartment keys. She was ready to talk. In my muddled, jet-lagged brain I somehow deduced that Elsa was talking about, respectively, Melanie Wallendorf, Russ Belk (the "hippie"), John Sherry. Tom O'Guinn and Hal Kassarjian fell into the "other men" category, but I wondered with some concern, how many "others" were there? Despite my fatigue, I was amused at Elsa's attempts to interpret this group's social relationships, not to mention her lifestyle assessments.

Elsa Joseph was my next door neighbor and friend; she was then 82 years young, and a bundle of energy who drove a big 1975 Buick Wildcat, and who immediately "adopted" me upon my arrival in Santa Monica four years earlier. Elsa force-fed me frequently; I think she would have catered my dinner parties if I had been more opportunistic. We looked after each others' mail, plants, etc., when one of us was out of town. Before I left for a one-month visit to Southeast Asia, I told Elsa that a "few" colleagues would be staying in my apartment for a "few" days while they were conducting some "important consumer research" in the Los Angeles area. Elsa was both security conscious and territorial, and I reassured her that my guests were prominent professionals and lovely people with whom she would feel comfortable.

"Two weeks?", I pondered. Three thoughts occurred almost simultaneously. First, I wondered if Elsa was trying to make me feel guilty. Did my Odyssey house guests terrorize her with all-night "member check" parties? Did they invite their "informants" to the apartment for validity procedures? At this point, I think I whimpered something along the lines of: "They said they were *only* going to stay a couple of days." But I rebounded quickly, considering my jetlag, with: "Well, their research here must have been *very successful*!" Touche, Elsa; let me unpack first, and then we'll dish it.

This merged into my second thought: Hey, they must have really enjoyed LA. I was a Los Angeles booster then, and viewed this much maligned megalopolis as a relative paradise niche with an urban beat, and I felt gratified that my friends had discovered its summertime pleasures, in addition to realizing their research objectives. As my key opened the door, it hit me that all these people had *LIVED HERE FOR TWO WEEKS(!)*, and a third thought occured to me: "Boy, I'm glad I lent out the porno." Just kidding, I didn't even have a VCR then. This mini-confrontation with Elsa had alerted me to the Odyssey team's extended presence in my nest, but my thoughts were still focused mostly on hauling the "expanda-bag" over my threshhold. Once I opened the curtains to examine my apartment, I looked for visible signs of their stay.

The filth was unbelievable; evidence of decadent living pervaded my apartment, and common decency precludes any mention of the condition of the bathrooms. Sorry, just

Highways and Buyways © *1991*
Association for Consumer Research

kidding again. I cannot help but imagine that more than a few consumer researchers in the summer of '86 harbored prurient fantasies about the Odyssey's leaders who *LIVED TOGETHER!* for an entire summer, travelling from coast to coast pursuing what some colleagues then considered a "weird" research agenda. But surprise, the apartment was meticulous. This group was clearly operating under the Boy Scout principle of leaving a camp site just as you found it. In fact, I was actually frustrated that there was almost no physical evidence of the Odyssey's presence in my home. Charming "thank you" notes had been left; a request to pick up some developed film that Tom O'Guinn had shot; and a note regretting a coffee pot accident that was accompanied by a perfect replacement.

I began to feel that I had missed out on something special and significant. This feeling was solidified as I began to receive copies of the detailed field notes that the Odyssey team began to disseminate to Odyssey participants and supporters. I read these with avid curiosity. They reported the team's arrival in Los Angeles, discouraging lost baggage incidents, and a variety of logistical and technical difficulties in getting started: the RV, the sound and film equipment, etc. They also chronicled the involvement and support of local consumer researchers whose academic bases ranged from Irvine to San Bernadino to Westwood to University Park -- a geographic area roughly the size of Rhode Island. Nothing about any parties, though. Finally, the field notes resonated with the excitement that the Odyssey project aroused among its participants, and they described the evolution of personal relationships and roles within the research team.

At this point, my personal enthusiasm for the project was accompanied by considerable envy and regret that I had not been more intimately involved. I also began to reflect on how different this team approach to learning is from the more prophylactic empiricism of surveys and lab experiments. It is somewhat paradoxical that the conventional sociological and anthropological approach that the Odyssey pursued would eventually stir up so much methodological controversy.

Not only did the Odyssey's research conform to conventional social science field work, its approach -- as I discovered later in my work at DDB Needham in Chicago -- is similar to prototypic commercial uses of qualitative research, where both field teams and emergent design are commonly employed. I quickly became accustomed to the routine of flying off to some research site to conduct focus groups from 6:00-10:00 PM. Here emergent design was *pro forma*; if a topic was exhausted, or a creative concept bombed in

the first group, the second group was not wasted on pursuing a dead issue. Following the group interviews, agency and client personnel conducted debriefings (member checks), sometimes until midnight. Findings were negotiated over Bud Lights.

In addition to these more global thoughts, my concerns in July, 1986, were more personal and immediate. The Odyssey was committed to probing and interpreting the meanings of people's possessions, and I couldn't avoid wondering what they thought of *MY STUFF*. The field notes they disseminated made it clear that they were really, in the vernacular, "getting into people's shit." And they had begun in Los Angeles; interpretive energies were pent up and ready to be unleashed; and they were staying in my apartment, surrounded by some admittedly idiosyncratic material artifacts I had collected over the years.

THE NEXT FEW WEEKS

My curiosity was mixed with some anxiety; what did my stuff tell my Odyssey colleagues about Dennis? At this point in my life, I was a voracious reader of psychodynamic literature, particularly Freud and Erikson. Intellectually, I knew the symbolic nature of one's possessions, but at this point in my life, I had not yet immersed myself in the adventure (and expense!) of psychoanalytic dialogue. So I was uneasy, a feeling that was heightened by subsequent conversations with my Odyssey house guests. Russ, Melanie and John all expressed some degree of discomfort in having lived amidst my possessions without the benefit of my presence to explain their origins and meanings. As Bernie Jaworski noted in reviewing this manuscript, this situation was analogous to archeological expeditions, crime scenes, and murder mysteries. My absence allowed interpretations (crime scenes?!) to arise without any grounding in my own perspectives. "Now I'm really exposed," I thought.

Specific comments also added to my concern. At various times mentions, sometimes jibes I thought, were made of (1) my cast iron parrot ashtray, (2) my really big bed with "tight" red sheets, and (3) my bedroom's collection of mounted animal horns (a "horny" bedroom?!). I was subsequently informed that the Odyssey had gathered an extensive photographic inventory of my entire apartment. The Odysseyans expressed considerable concern that this had been conducted without my permission, but by now I could only think "what the heck," and summoned a useful phrase I had learned in Southeast Asia earlier that summer: "No problem." I too couldn't help but be curious about the meanings of my stuff.

FIGURE A
Toy Grocery Store (c. 1940)

JULY 26, 1986: AUTODRIVING WITH JOHN SHERRY

A few weeks later, I flew to Evanston, Illinois, to attend the First International Conference on Marketing and Semiotics, at Northwestern University. At some point during the Conference, John Sherry proposed that he conduct an autodriving interview with me about my home and the possessions in it, using the photographic slides the Odyssey team had collected as stimuli for our discussion. This certainly seemed in the "semiotic" spirit of the week, and I was now more than ready to talk. Autodriving's history and method are summarized in a recent article by Heisley and Levy (1990), so I will only highlight the summary details of this interview.

The session took place in John's office on July 16. It lasted slightly over 90 minutes, and it was conducted, more or less, in a classical in-depth style. I was asked to view the slides that were organized thematically around each room in my apartment. Beyond this basic structure, the interview was essentially non-directive, and I did the bulk of the talking. John encouraged me to talk about whatever struck my fancy in each slide, and he left it open for me to talk about the origins, acquisition, organization and meanings of

many different objects. John asked if I had a favorite room, and since I said "no," he suggested we start in *his* favorite room: the kitchen.

The Kitchen

Most of the discussion about the kitchen centered about items that have no culinary function. In retrospect, my kitchen had gradually evolved into more of an art gallery and shrine than a food preparation center. We talked about my miniature "antique" toy grocery store (see Figure A), and about the considerable amount of framed "art" on the walls: food ads from a 1918 *Ladies Home Journal*, a menu from Rook's Restaurant (no relation) in Zion, Illinois, a colorful 1940s fruit crate label. I also had almost-a-collection of postcards on the refrigerator door: a Ken Brown "Tournament of the Twinkies," a "numbered duck" postcard from a lunch at Paris' Tour d'Argent, and a picture of the Santa Monica mountains in flames in 1980. I suggested to John that these represented my sense of humor and belief that the kitchen should be a "fun place." The one object that evoked the most feeling was a framed picture of my German Shepherd "son" Neil, who had died in my last year of graduate school. I told John I put his picture by the kitchen window

FIGURE B
Cast Iron Parrot Ashtray (c. 1950)

because he always liked to sit in the window in my Evanston home, presumably watching out for "Dad's" return. There was little discussion of the kitchen as a food preparation center. I was single and ate out often. I was even vying with my colleague Mike Kamins for USC's "most-recruiting-dinners" award. The prize seemed to be about a ten-pound weight gain!

The Living Room

Next we began to look at slides from the living room. John mentioned that one focal point here for the Odyssey team was my 32-inch tall, floor-standing cast iron parrot ashtray (see Figure B). This strong visual "statement", John explained, recalled the chapter in William Tucker's (1967) classic book about "The Peach-Faced Parrot." John further explained that Melanie has a friend who refers to the state of alcoholic inebriation as getting "shit-faced." Late at night the Odysseans would sit around my living room

and, stimulated by the parrot and exhaustion-induced silliness, joke about being "peach-faced" and "shit-faced." I think you had to be there. I mentioned that I had acquired the ashtray (cheaply) at an auction, and had owned it for about 15 years. I described it as "wild and crazy," and suggested that it reflects my appreciation of "cheap potpourri and kitsch." I didn't know at this time that my parrot would debut in both the opening and closing shots of the Odyssey's premier film as a semi-secret symbol of those late nights in Santa Monica.

Another high visibility item in the living room was a large (55" by 70") velvet painting of -- not Elvis -- but a classic California-style Spanish bungalow located alongside a babbling brook in a rustic canyon (Figure C). The painting is titled "Hollywood," and dated 1927, which occasionally causes me to speculate that this may be one of the very first contemporary velvet paintings! John asked

FIGURE C
"Hollywood" Velvet Painting (c. 1927)

what this means to me and my answer was simple: the ultimate dream home. I explained that such homes were now on the market in Los Angeles' nicer canyons with prices *beginning* at $1,000,000. With some resignation I told John, "Well, if I can't have the house, at least I have the velvet painting."

By far the most dominating object in my living room was a 1946 Wurlitzer Model 750 Jukebox. It was the first model made after World War II, and the first to have "bubble lights." It was also only semi-functional; the bubbles no longer worked, the automatic record selector was jammed, and even the needle had been lost in my move to Los Angeles. I described this to John as my "most frustrating" possession. On the one hand, it was the most attention-getting, and attracted many "wows" and "cools" from first time viewers. On the other hand, it didn't work like it should; I described it to John as a giant, colorful "lava lamp." I had discovered that it

would cost a small fortune to rehabilitate, and there always were more pressing needs.

Nonetheless, I clung to it. The jukebox had lived in three separate residences in Evanston, and I moved it with me to Los Angeles in 1982. It made another transcontinental trip back to the Chicago area in 1987 (still unrehabilitated). I finally "gave up" and sold it in 1989, rather than move it again to Evanston from Downtown. In looking back, it is remarkable how long the process of object de-cathexis can take!

We talked about other objects in the living room, mostly more framed "art." As the discussion progressed I came to realize a need for more and better organization of my "stuff" into "collections." My thoughts then reflected ideas I have just recently encountered in the Belk, Wallendorf, Sherry and Holbrrok (1990) piece, "Collecting in a Consumer Culture," in this volume. I was beginning to focus more explicitly on "maintaining my space", as they

FIGURE D
Assorted Black Memorabilia (c. 1930s-present)

describe this process. I couldn't wait to get back to Santa Monica and put things in proper order. I had quite a bit of "show business" memorabilia: posters, autographed glossies -- all of which had some personal connection with friends of mine who occupied various roles in "the business." Even my mother made it into this collection with color-retouched photos taken during her childhood dancing career. Intermingled among them were more tranquil graphics: a Billy Jackson landscape of the Champaign/Urbana countryside, several still lifes painted by my grandmother and great grandmother, Hawaiian nature photographs taken by my sister. I began to redecorate in my mind even as I talked with John. It was a productive interview, killing two birds with one stone!

Probably the most controversial objects in the living room belong to my "Black Memorabilia" collection (see Figures D and E). I actually can't remember how this one got started, maybe with an innocent Aunt Jemima salt & pepper shaker. Today the collection includes about three dozen objects, among them a large minstrel show poster, many salt & pepper shakers now, a "mammy" broom and notepad, "Dixie" postcards and sheet music, a "Coon Chicken Inn" souvenir plate, "Darkie" toothpaste packages, a lawn watering "boy", hair gloss preparations, and other unusual

objects, a few of which I am reluctant to display. The curious thing is: of the 30-plus pieces in the collection, I have purchased no more than 10. The rest have been gifts. I speculate that my collection not only helps focus my friends' and family's gift-giving impulses, but it provides them with an opportunity to engage in innocuous wickedness by buying something that seems relatively "taboo" for Dennis.

The Bedroom

I had been somewhat primed for this part of the interview by earlier casual comments made by my Odyssey house guests, so I jumped right in, asking John: "So what's the big deal about my 'tight red sheets'?" In listening to the taped interview later, I realize that I hardly let John get a word in edgewise. With more than a little defensiveness, I lectured John that if you didn't tuck the sheets in tightly, they would "just flap." I explained that this would be "wrong," and added that it was hard even to talk about it, or to imagine an alternative. I can only speculate now that my childhood toilet training must have been quite rigorous. On the other hand, without a little compulsiveness, America's beds never get made!

Moving into the closets, John said he was impressed with how organized they were.

FIGURE E
Lawn Watering "Boy" (c. 1940)

I countered that I wasn't very satisfied with them at all, and wished there were more shelves so I could "organize things better." By this point in the interview, but only in retrospective listening to the tape, it is clear that in 1986 I was at least moderately obsessed with "organization." Also, after almost an hour of interviewing, I was becoming more relaxed, reflective and anlytical.

I had some prior, conscious awareness of the phallic imagery that pervaded my bedroom. Friends made jokes about the tall vertical shafts of my four-poster bed, and about the large, prickly cactus plants that lined the wall by the window. My collection of large animal horns was displayed on the interior walls. John picked up on the phallic imagery, too, and I joked with him about compensatory behavior, and free-associated about handcuffs, etc. (see Figure F).

The Bathrooms

John observed that there was "not too much messy anywhere" in the apartment. I explained that "you could comfortably eat an omelet off my mother's bathroom floors," and that I had tried imperfectly to uphold this family tradition. I also confessed that when I was an undergraduate, I was a "complete slob" who regressed with little resistence to the hygienic lowest common denominator that is often associated with student group living.

After skirting the issue for a few minutes, John admitted that because my doctoral dissertation studied consumers' grooming rituals, he was surprised that I had not appointed my own bathrooms more extensively. He implied that the Odyssey team had expected more of me, and were disappointed in the mere functional status of my *salles de bains*. I explained that it wasn't because I wouldn't *like* to have a more luxurious bathing and grooming environment,

FIGURE F
Longhorn Hat Rack (c. 1945)

but my bathrooms were "small and nasty." The "master" bath off my bedroom couldn't have been more than 40 square feet, and such a cubicle discouraged development. Also, I was a renter and unsure how long I would keep the apartment. I invested more in grooming products than fixtures, but readily acknowledged that someday I would enjoy spending big bucks on a bathroom spa.

The Office

I used my second bedroom as an office. In it I had the usual appointments: bookshelves, a desk, computer and printer, a sofa-bed for guests, and more "art" works on the walls. At one point I blurted out: "I love my computer." John noted that this was the first item toward which I had expressed "love." I then joked that perhaps I should be rushed to a psychiatric emergency room. I further explained that when I was a graduate student, I had "hated" the computer; back then it seemed to be an unfriendly object used for statistical torture. Now I valued the PC for "communicating and being organized." I also explained how it had become an object in my everyday morning ritual: go to the bathroom, start the coffee, boot the computer. I mentioned how I looked forward to its morning greeting, with the friendly and familiar beeps and whirr sounds that invited me to get down

to work. Living alone allows for certain lifestyle eccentricities to emerge.

John also inquired about a framed picture I had on the wall of a group shot of the 1908 Board of Directors of the Milwaukee Railroad, assembled in the ballroom of the Pfister Hotel. I explained that these somber-faced, tuxedo-clad "business men" represented my personal transition from my previous career in government social service to the world of "marketing." Many individuals of my generation harbored, as adolescents, vaguely anti-business attitudes, and I was now attempting to work beyond this. I figured that if I could face these dour, intimidating figures everyday, the more yuppified brand managers of the contemporary marketplace would be "no problem." This visual therapy appears to have worked; the picture is now in storage on my back porch.

1990: REFLECTIONS ON THE MEANINGS OF MY "STUFF"

It was almost exactly four years ago that I participated in this autodriving interview. To prepare myself for writing this chapter, I sat down on several separate occasions to listen to the audio tape John Sherry made of our 1986 interview. In listening to the taped interview with John, it now seems clear that the themes and motivations underlying the acquisition, usage and display of my possessions are complex and reflect my movements and transitions along various, basic personal continuua. This general approach to interpretation was introduced to modern marketing audiences by Levy (1981) and applied more recently by Hirschman (1988), and by Belk, Wallendorf and Sherry (1989). The following discussion relies on a structural approach to examine the personal learning I gained from the autodriving interview. It also uses a "casual" psychoanalytic perspective to consumer behavior, as exemplified in early work by Levy (1968), and more recent work by Holbrook (1988), and myself (1985, 1987).

Conscious/Unconscious

One of the acknowledged benefits of in-depth interviewing is that it reveals unconscious material. Evidence of these dynamics abounds in John's interview with me. While some aspects of my collecting were quite conscious, others were not. Also, some aspects of my conscious collecting were motivated by unconscious elements. For example, although I was aware that I had gradually gathered a collection of "show business" memorabilia, I was only dimly in touch with how this material reflects my own artisitic yearnings. I have many friends in the performing and plastic arts; I, however, have few artistic skills, certainly none that would economically support a "life in the theatre." So this ever-growing collection not only represents meaningful personal connections to various art worlds, it allows expression of my own artistic impulses. This explains why I have stuffed such unlikely areas as my kitchen and office with "art" objects, as well as more conventional, functional ones. My in-depth interview with John helped bring this persistent but unconscious pattern into my conscious awareness.

Sacred/Profane

The interview also helped me realize my attraction to both sacred and profane possession domains. Lurid movie posters competed on my walls with more serene landscapes. Today an eclectic religious "shrine" (prayer candles, Madonna icons) stands next to a collection of Mexican Day-of-the-Dead ceramics. At some level, I believe this represents an attempt to integrate my (sacred) rural origins with my (profane) urban lifestyle, as well as some ambivalence about making choices between the two. Although my family moved from rural southern Illinois when I was only four, memories of the quiet, slow-pace, physical beauty, and "simple" people persist and still appeal. Psychoanalytically, this also suggests my use of collections to sublimate aggressive or anti-

social impulses in appropriate, "artistic" ways. I think this also explains part of my recent attraction to Southeast Asian artifacts which often combine sacred religious themes with more profane, temporal motifs.

Maturity/Immaturity

Many of my collectibles might fall into the category of "toys for boys." From my earliest collecting days, I began to acquire objects that seemed "fun" to me. The parrot ashtray, the toy grocery store, and objects long traded away or sold attracted me because of their fun, amusing features. I spent most of my childhood in Protestant suburbia, surrounded by clones of June and Ward Cleaver, eating Betty Crocker recipes and living in "colonial" decors where "neutral" color schemes were equated with mature virtues, propriety, and good taste. As a teenager I began to reject this version of modern living: give me some color and spices, please! And enough with the "colonial" look. Everything seemed too dull and serious. My collecting life began -- in part out of an identity crisis that expressed itself in "artistic" acquisitions, some intentionally purchased to stir up Mom and Dad.

As I talked with John, I found myself occasionally referring to "adult" purchases I had recently made. For example, I described my newly purchased set of bedroom furniture as "adult furniture." Even something as seemingly trivial as framing pictures now, in retrospect, seems to represent taking a more mature (and less hostile) orientation toward my possessions. As I student, I was content to stick a poster on a wall with a staple gun or thumbtacks; my more "adult" self required framing, which signifies a more abundant and even nurturing attitude. While the "fun" and "kooky" themes are still prominent in my collecting behavior, they have been infused with more expansive themes, not just a rebel yell.

Comedy/Tragedy

In addition to the whimsical and fun aspects of my acquiring and collecting, there is a "serious" side, too. This was one of the central learnings I achieved in the autodriving interview with John. In explaining the origins and meanings of various objects, I found myself making frequent reference to the role of my ex-wife, Marcella. One of our common joys was "junking" through thrift and antique shops, and taking our chances at auctions. It was easy to forget -- until the interview -- how many of "my" acquisitions represented joint consumption. It also reminded my how much fun this had been. When our marriage began to dissolve, our consumption patterns took an unusual course. Unlike the situation in the 1989 movie, "The War of the Roses," we began to buy even more lavish gifts for each other, unconsciously hoping that the widening crack might close through escalation of behaviors that had brought us together and been so mutually gratifying. It didn't. So, beneath the enjoyment I find in living with some of my treasured possessions is an occasional sense of tragedy that they were acquired in a relative paradise now lost.

Chaos/Structure

As I mentioned earlier, the theme of "organization" popped up on several occasions during the interview. Looking back, I see that I had too much "stuff" that was too little organized. I had too many burgeoning collections (not all of which have even been mentioned so far): ceramics, prints, animal horns, hats, Black memorabilia, toys. I also had singular but dominant items that didn't seem to fit into any particular collection category: my juke box, the velvet painting. A brooding sense of personal chaos was emerging at this time. As described in the Belk, Wallendorf, Sherry and Holbrook (1990) article on "collections" in this volume, I see that I was entering the refinement and organization phase. Some of my collections were in a terminal phase -- my animal horns and wooden toys, for example. I was de-cathecting these and would acquire no more. I was also trying better to organize others that were growing -- ceramics, prints, and Black memorabilia. During my interview with John, this vague sense of disorder grew more acute, and I became aware of my need for more coherent organization and display of these collections.

Aspiration/Frustration

My possessions not only symbolize who I am and what I value, they represent both vague and specific acquisition goals, and more general lifestyle aspirations. My velvet painting illustrates the core of this idea. As the Rolling Stones informed a generation not particularly eager to receive the message: "You can't always get what you want." This certainly applied to Southern California real estate in 1986. Modest homes in Santa Monica that sold in the mid-1970s for $35,000 were now on the market as $300,000-plus "tear downs." And my canyon dream home was a million dollar proposition. A condo compromise or a fixer-upper in a marginal neighborhood at this point had little appeal or excitement value. So I settled for the velvet painting; maybe I could spend part of next summer writing that screenplay that would generate a bidding war between studios. You can always dream, and everybody in LA has a hyphenated profession.

REFLECTIONS ON THE AUTODRIVING EXPERIENCE

One of the great research myths today centers around the notion that people are too busy to be interviewed, and that they will only agree to an interview if they are offered increasingly (and distressingly) large financial incentives. I think this is largely an artifact of the way we conduct research, and how we treat respondents. I have worked with more than 1000 focus group respondents; many *do* seem to want only to provide "quickie" like/dislike responses, collect their cash, and be on their way. In many cases I don't blame them; the research is boring, often merely a survey-in-disguise that is uninvolving, technical and demanding. On the other hand, I have encountered very different responses from research that is conducted in-depth and on a one-to-one basis. On more than a few occasions, respondents in these conversational situations have actually expressed their thanks for the opportunity to think deeply about something, and to share their thoughts, speculations, and uncertainties. This is the kind of research that the Consumer Behavior Odyssey sought to develop and encourage.

This is the kind of research that John Sherry conducted with me. I found it -- despite my initial trepidation -- extremely gratifying. We talked for ninety minutes, and could have gone on longer if John had not had a luncheon obligation. My sentiments echo those of Jaworski and MacInnis (1990) in this volume; the autodriving interview was both fun, meaningful and revealing. As market and consumer researchers, we are presumably motivated by the principle of "knowing the consumer." From my personal experience, autodriving is a research tool whose recent rediscovery promises to help achieve this end in ways that are gratifying and meaningful to both the researcher and to the research participant.

REFERENCES

Belk, Russell W., Melanie Wallendorf and John F. Sherry (1989), "The Sacred and the Profane in Consumer Behavior: Theodicy on the Odyssey," *Journal of Consumer Research*, vol. 16, no.1 (June), pp.1-38.

_____ , Mealnie Wallendorf, John Sherry and Morris Holbrook (1990), "Collecting in a Consumer Culture," in *Highways and Buyways: Naturalistic Research from the Consumer Behavior Odyssey*, ed. Russell W. Belk, Association for Consumer Research, forthcoming.

Heisley, Deborah and Sidney J. Levy (1990), "Autodriving: A Photoelicitation Technique," manuscript in review.

Holbrook, Morris B. (1988), "The Psychoanaltic Interpretation of Consumer Behavior: I Am an Animal," in *Research in Consumer Behavior*, eds. Elizabeth C. Hirschman and Jagdish N. Sheth, Greenwich, CT: JAI Press Inc., pp. 149-178.

Hirschman, Elizabeth C. (1988), "The Ideology of Consumption: A Structural-Syntactical Analysis of `Dallas' and `Dynasty'", *Journal of Consumer Research*, vol. 15, no. 3 (December), pp. 344-359.

Jaworski, Bernard J. and Deborah J. MacInnis (1990), "On Being an Informant on the Consumer Behavior Odyssey," in *Highways and Buyways: Naturalistic Research from the Consumer Behavior Odyssey*, ed. Russell W. Belk, Association for Consumer Research, forthcoming.

Levy, Sidney J. (1968), "Mammon and Psyche," in *Explorations in Consumer Behavior*, eds. Montrose S. Summers and Jerome B. Kernan, Austin Texas: University of Texas Press, 119-133.

_____ (1981), "Interpreting Consumer Mythology: A Structural Approach to Consumer Behavior," *Journal of Marketing*, vol. 45 (Summer), pp. 49-62.

Rook, Dennis W. (1985), "The Ritual Dimension of Consumer Behavior," *Journal of Consumer Research*, vol. 12, no.3 (December), 251-264.

_____ (1987), "The Buying Impulse," *Journal of Consumer Research*, vol. 14, no. 2 (September), 189-199.

Tucker, William T. (1967), "The Peach-Faced Parrot," in *Foundations for a Theory of Consumer Behavior*, ed. William T. Tucker, New York: Holt, Rinehart and Winston, pp. 105-115.

The Sacred and the Profane in Consumer Behavior: Theodicy on the Odyssey[1]

Russell W. Belk
Melanie Wallendorf
John F. Sherry, Jr.

ABSTRACT

Two processes at work in contemporary society are the secularization of the sacred and the sacralization of the secular. Consumer behavior shapes and reflects these processes. For many people, consumption has become a vehicle for achieving transcendent experience. In this chapter, this ritual substratum of consumption is explored. Properties and manifestations of the sacred inherent in consumer behavior are detailed. Similarly, the processes by which consumers sacralize and desacralized imensions of their experience are described. The naturalistic inquiry approach driving the insights in this chapter is advanced as a corrective to a premature narrowing of focus in consumer research.

It has been argued that revelatory incidents are the primary source of insight in ethnographic fieldwork (Fernandez 1986; Sherry 1988). These are highly charged encounters suffused with meaning. Because these incidents are directly experienced by the researcher, the significance of the phenomenon under study is more fully appreciated than might otherwise be possible. A number of such revelatory incidents have caused us to reevaluate some of the field's fundamental constructs for understanding marketplace and consumer behavior. Consider the following abbreviated examples:

---

[1] Reprinted with permission of the *Journal of Consumer Research*. Financial support and intellectual encouragement from John Farley and Marketing Science Institute, Bill Wells and DDB Needham, David Berger and Foote, Cone, and Belding enabled the data collection on which this chapter is based. The authors also thank Howie Becker, Mihaly Csikszentmihalyi, Andrew Greeley, and Deborah Heisley for insightful comments on an earlier draft. Professor Wallendorf appreciates the hospitality of the Departments of Marketing at the University of Utah and Northwestern University, where uninterrupted time and other support was provided to complete this manuscript during a sabbatical. All three authors acknowledge the support of their respective institutions and the other members of the Odyssey research team during the data collection phase of the Consumer Behavior Odyssey.

Among the wares for sale at the edge of the midway of a bustling Southwestern swap meet are decorative brooms and handcrafted dolls which closely resemble Cabbage Patch Kids. The vendor, a vibrant middle-aged woman named Sarah, fashions the dolls with loving detail born of remarkable social circumstance. After the birth of her first child--a son now embarking upon a trying preadolescence--an automobile accident prevented Sarah from conceiving other children, most notably the daughter she always wanted. During her recovery, Sarah began "making the babies." In joining the dolls' fabric bodies and faces, Sarah sees the babies "come to life." She views her skill as a special gift, just as babies are a gift from God. As she talks about her dolls, she adopts a different linguistic register, shifting into baby-talk, and caresses their foreheads as she speaks. Prior to closing the sale of each doll, Sarah performs a deliberate transaction. She kisses the doll before releasing it to a customer, wishing it well and knowing all the while how happy the doll will make other children.

Describing his arrangement of sculpted ceramic figures alternately as a "surrealistic fantasy" and a "dream" Garth Warren watches viewers strolling past his exhibit at the open air art festival. The young Southern Californian artist has created a series of figures ("Eygot," "Wewants," "Sleep Drive," "Swollen Pride") complete with framed misspelled proem cautionary tales, which represent aspects of his own personality (notably "consumerism") which he purports to dislike greatly. He is building a portfolio suitable to entering galleries, and is using this show to gain some exposure. Significantly, he is little concerned with business matters, and finds pricing his artwork troublesome. He gives many of his pieces away for nothing, and is as content with a talkative looker as a paying customer. His younger sister, however, is sales-oriented, and has undertaken to protect Garth from his own philanthropy. Using a pricing policy that is at turns intuitive and strategic, she is not above reviling critical lookers or altering her brother's work to suit a prospective buyer. Garth's philosophy of "If people smile, it's enough; they don't have to buy" contrasts strikingly with the sister's philosophy of "I make sure he gets what's coming to him." Theirs is a symbiotic relationship in which commerce assumes a custodial role with respect to art.

The middle-aged proprietor of Mr. Ed's Elephant Museum and Gift Shop speaks with considerable pride of opening his present business. Operating on intuition he likens to predestination, Mr. Ed risked starting a venture sustained through the display and sale of elephant replicas and peanuts. His museum houses a collection of hundreds of elephant replicas he has amassed for the enjoyment of others and for posterity. His gift shop is similarly laden with elephantiana. Despite the apparent similarity of contents, Mr. Ed regards the two areas as sublimely distinct. The museum items will never be offered for sale at any price, regardless of their similarity (or even apparent inferiority) to items in the gift shop. Mr. Ed can conceive of no compelling argument (including his own hypothetically imminent destitution) for moving a piece from the museum to the gift shop. Mr. Ed maintains with axiomatic, heartfelt certainty that to attempt such a move would be "wrong."

Each of these vignettes reflects a dimension of buyer and seller world views previously undescribed in consumer research. Each is an example of the ritual substratum of consumer behavior. These observations make it apparent that consumption involves more than the means by which people meet their everyday needs. Consumption can become a vehicle of transcendent experience; that is, consumer behavior exhibits certain aspects of the sacred. It is the premise of this chapter that this sacred dimension can be clinically described and interpreted, thereby enhancing our understanding of consumer behavior. In the following pages, we explore the qualities of sacredness and the underlying processes of transformation manifest in consumer behavior.

Theory and research in the sociology of religion suggest that a fundamental distinction structuring social life is between what is set apart and regarded as sacred and what is regarded as profane or ordinary. In some societies, the sacred involves magic, shamanism, animism, and totemism. Such societies often accord sacred status to components of the natural environment that are revered, feared, worshiped, and treated with the utmost respect. In contemporary Western religion, the sacred/profane distinction is also important, although the elements of experience considered sacred differ. Contemporary Western religions define as sacred certain gods, shrines, clothing, days, relics, and songs. While less a part of nature, these objects are regarded by the faithful of contemporary Western religions as sacred, and there are parallels with the regard for certain natural objects by participants in non-Western religions. Both sets of objects fulfill a need to believe in something significantly more powerful and extraordinary than the self--a need to transcend existence as a mere biological being coping with the everyday world.

For many contemporary consumers, there are also elements of life with no connection to formal religion that are nonetheless revered, feared, and treated with the utmost respect. Examples include flags, sports stars, national parks, art, automobiles, museums, and collections. Whether we call the reverence for these things religious, contemporary consumers treat them as set apart, extraordinary, or sacred, just as elements of nature are sacred in naturistic religions and certain icons are sacred to followers of contemporary, organized religions. Although the specific focal objects differ, the same deeply moving, self-transcending feelings may attend each, and the same revulsion may occur when these objects are not treated with respect. Religion is one, but not the only, context in which the concept of the sacred is operant.

Explicit recognition of the sacred status accorded to many consumption objects illuminates aspects of contemporary North American consumer behavior that, while basic and pervasive, have not been explained by prior theory and research. The substantial body of social science theory on the role of the sacred in religion is used here in developing an understanding of sacred aspects of consumption. This body of related theory is used in analyzing and interpreting the Consumer Behavior Odyssey data (Belk 1987c; Wallendorf and Belk 1987; Holbrook 1987; Kassarjian 1987; Sherry 1987a; Wallendorf 1987b) and in building a theory of the sacred aspects of consumption.

The conditions and characteristics of consumption interpretable through the constructs of sacred and profane are detectable through introspection and a close reading of a diverse literature set. However, the processes of meaning investment and divestment--the sacralization rituals we treat at length in this chapter--are resistant to such distanced exposition. To reflect the insights immanent in armchair and field, we employ a compromise strategy of presentation. That is, *conditions* for and *foci* of sacredness are explored principally through literature evaluation tempered by fieldwork. *Processes* are examined principally through analysis for field data tempered by literature. This work is intended as a conceptual contribution to parallel disciplines and as an empirical contribution to consumer research.

After explaining the naturalistic methodology through which the insights in this chapter were derived, we review the sacred and profane in scholarly theories of religion. To understand what these theories can contribute to our understanding of consumer behavior, we next explore shifts in contemporary boundaries between the sacred and the profane. In so doing, we illuminate what is considered sacred in the secular world of consumption. Going beyond merely categorizing objects or experiences as either sacred or profane, we then develop a theory of the central processes by which transcendence is achieved through consumption, using data from participant-observation and depth interviews from the Consumer Behavior Odyssey. Finally, we outline areas of consumer research that can benefit most from this theoretical perspective.

METHOD

The importance of the distinction between sacred and profane aspects of consumption emerged in interpreting our data from a pilot project (Belk, Sherry, and Wallendorf 1988). Subsequently, the Consumer Behavior Odyssey collected data primarily through naturalistic, qualitative fieldwork as detailed by Lincoln and Guba (1985). Data analysis and interpretation with corroboration from the religious and social science literatures were guided by the constant comparative method of Glaser and Strauss (1967) and techniques specified by Miles and Huberman (1984) and Becker (1986). We used natural settings, emergent design, multiple sites, purposive sampling, cross-context testing for transferability, depth and intimacy in interviewing, triangulation of data across researchers and data collection media, and triangulation of interpretation across researchers. Despite a long history of usage in anthropology and sociology, these approaches have been employed less commonly in the study of consumer behavior and, thus, are explained briefly here.

Before and during fieldwork, and throughout postfield coding and further analysis, we immersed ourselves in the literatures that address the sacred/profane distinction. Our reading of these literatures was both close and emergent, and has shaped and reflected the interpretation presented here. Unlike positivistic research, which supposedly evaluates extant literature to discover gaps to address through additional research, the Odyssey did not begin with a literature-based problematique. Rather, fieldwork prompted library research, which in turn led to additional fieldwork. What was at one moment a need to interpret consumer behavior in context, became at the next moment a desire to deconstruct and reconstruct scholarly theories. We employ a presentation style that reflects this balance between library and field.

Emergent Design

Data collection and analysis were guided by emergent design. This approach differs from surveys or experiments, which assume that the researcher understands the phenomenon prior to doing the research, so that hypotheses and fully specified data collection and analysis plans are possible.

In naturalistic inquiry, no such assumption is made. Instead, researchers build an understanding of the phenomenon as it occurs *in situ*, later testing the veracity of that understanding, also *in situ*. The first step is to observe and record the phenomenon in detail. Researchers then specify their understanding and construct guidelines for further data collection to test the emerging understanding. This iterative process continues in what Glaser and Strauss (1967) call the constant comparative method. Rather than data collection followed by analysis, data collected previously form the basis for an interpretation, which then defines what data still are required to test the interpretation. The process continues until conceptual categories are saturated and reach a point of redundancy, making further data collection unnecessary. For example, by the time we interviewed the collector of elephant replicas mentioned earlier, we had explicit hypotheses concerning the separation of sacred possessions from profane, usable commodities available for sale. This collector echoed the views of prior informants that collections are sacred and thereby differentiated from salable commodities.

Neither the number nor type of interviews needed to reach this point of saturation can be specified a priori. This results in a substantial amount of time spent by the researchers themselves gathering data and developing "thick description" (Geertz 1973). Initial interviews are largely nondirective (Briggs 1986), but later blend into more directed, semistructured ones.

Sites and Purposive Sampling

This article is based on data from a pilot study conducted in the fall of 1985, as well as data collected by the Consumer Behavior Odyssey in the summer of 1986 (see Kassarjian 1987 for the project's history). The Odyssey's goal was to develop a deep understanding of consumption, broadly defined. To accomplish this goal, a rotating team of academics employed naturalistic methods while traveling across the United States. Themes from the pilot study were pursued, but other themes and concepts also emerged as the project advanced.

Data for the pilot project were collected at a swap meet (Belk, Sherry, and Wallendorf 1988). A major theme detected was that consumers made sacred and profane distinctions in their behaviors and uses of space, time, and objects. At the completion of the pilot study, this theme was not fully developed into theoretical propositions and was understood only with regard to the phenomena present at this site, but it appeared to be powerful enough to warrant broader investigation.

During the Odyssey, we first checked whether the sacred/profane distinction noted in the pilot study was apparent at other swap meets. This approach differs from that of single-site ethnographies and was stimulated by our sense that these were broadly applicable theoretical concepts. Finding that the concept generalized well to four other swap meets, other outdoor periodic sales events were sampled, including two antique flea markets, a farmers' market, and a yard sale. Other outdoor events that combined the sales interactions already observed with entertainment or celebrations were added, including a Fourth of July festival, three county fairs, two community festivals, three art festivals, one historical festival, and two ethnic festivals. To generalize beyond outdoor events, we included fieldwork at two indoor antique fairs or auctions. We also did fieldwork at indoor sites housing more permanent sellers, including three museums, a gas station, a bookstore, an ethnic grocery store, several restaurants, and a fast food restaurant. To generalize to sites that are more permanent to consumers, we also went to informants' homes.

Homes were sampled purposively to represent sacred space, in contrast with commercial sites, which are generally more profane. In sampling for sacredness, we spoke with people about their collections and other objects given special status, such as cars in a car show. These data were contrasted with data gathered at temporary homes such as recreational vehicle parks, a summer trailer park, six resorts and hotels, a national park campground, a weight loss resort, a nursing

home, and two homeless shelters. People in the midst of a long-distance move were interviewed, as were people encountered on the street or highway rest stops. Other sacred sites purposively sampled included a temple, a chapel, and two evangelical services. No interviews were conducted utilizing CB radios, although this approach was tried. Although differences in the specific focus of the sacred varied, we saw no indication that the sacred and profane processes discussed here applied only to certain sites or geographic areas in the United States.

Depth Interviewing

Data were collected through depth interviews and observations requiring unstructured responsiveness to consumers (Briggs 1986) as well as the development of intimacy between researcher and informant (Wallendorf 1987a). Informants were told that the interaction was part of a project attempting to understand American consumers. Possibly the field of consumer research has not explored sacred aspects of consumption previously because the sacred aspects of consumption are less likely to emerge in experimental and survey research interactions.

Data Record

Although fieldnotes were written for all interactions with informants, many interactions were also recorded on videotape. Although not problem-free, our experience with videorecordings leads us to challenge the speculative claim of Hirschman (1986) that videorecording should be avoided due to its intrusiveness. Videotaping captures the rich detail of an interview, while simultaneously leading researchers to examine their membership roles in the field (Adler and Adler 1987). Video and still photography are data collection techniques finding increasing support among experienced ethnographers in sociology and anthropology (Briggs 1986; Collier and Collier 1986; Ives 1974; Werner and Schoepfle 1987).

Since informed consent necessitates some level of intrusiveness (Punch 1986), video photography is not the problem it would be if covert participant-observation were being attempted. The extensive literatures on deviance indicate the wide range of behaviors accessible to research using undisguised, naturalistic methods and speak to the possibility and importance of acknowledging informants' rights to informed consent. Video captures informants' explanations constructed in response to researchers' inquiries, called "perspectives of action," as well as informants' actions in their social setting, called 'perspectives in action" (Snow and Anderson 1987, after Gould et al. 1974). It provides rich temporal and nonverbal detail reminiscent of Bateson and Mead's (1942) early work with film and still photos and Leahy's photo ethnographies in the 1930s (Connolly and Anderson 1987).

Still photography was used to document sites and participants. These visual records were combined with written researcher records in the form of fieldnotes, journals, and photo and video logs. Fieldnotes consist of detailed notes about each interaction written on a daily basis by each researcher. Fieldnotes are the primary data record and the only material in those cases when video or still photo records were not made. Supplementing the fieldnotes are the more introspective journals of each researcher, which contain reflections, emerging interpretations, and memos to other researchers.

The pilot study data consist of 121 single-spaced pages of fieldnotes and journals, 130 still photographs and slides, two hours of videotaped interviews, and an artifact file. The Odyssey data include approximately 800 pages of fieldnotes and journals, 4,000 still photographs and slides, 137 videotapes lasting 15-18 minutes each, about a dozen audio tapes, and the artifact file. Odyssey data are archived at the Marketing Science Institute in Cambridge, Massachusetts. Pilot project data materials were audited by three scholars, whose reports on the trustworthiness of interpretations are available. The point of listing the quantity of data is not to imply that it is related to the quality of data, but rather to indicate the extensiveness of the documentation from which this work draws. As is typical in ethnographic research, the depth and richness of the data is indicated by including verbatim excerpts from fieldnotes within the chapter.

Triangulation

Two forms of triangulation employed enhanced the thickness of description and sharpened the accuracy of researchers' observations. These two forms are triangulation across researchers and across media. Since Odyssey data collection was conducted by a team, several researchers often wrote fieldnotes on the same interview. These were written separately and without discussion prior to writing, permitting the assessment of completeness and convergence. Differences in emotions experienced may be expected to occur in journals, given the subjective nature of human interaction. However, triangulation across researchers minimizes discrepancies in the recording of factual information and improves the recall of the research team. As the team gained experience as a research instrument, the observational skills and perceptual biases of

individual members allowed a division of labor to emerge that reduced redundancy in description and increased effectiveness and comprehensiveness in recording interactions; for example, we divided the labor required to simultaneously interview an informant, attend to the video camera, and shoot photographs. Triangulation across media involved examination and comparison of video interviews, photographs, and fieldnotes.

Triangulation is also useful in assessing the mutuality or uniqueness of the interpretation. We blended the perspectives of a bi-gender team (as recommended by Levinson 1987) of three consumer behavior researchers with theoretical and methodological training in psychology, sociology, and anthropology. These differences led to few disagreements regarding the appropriateness of the sacred/profane interpretation, although there were minor differences in the highlights given to this theme. For example, a psychological orientation leads the interpretation toward a definition of sacred experience as individually motivated, while the sociological focus is on consequences for societal integration and cohesion. Generally, we found our differing theoretical perspectives mutually compatible rather than mutually exclusive. Where such differences exist, they are noted in the text.

Interpretive Contexts

In building the interpretation, the data were obtained and structured by context. We use the term *site* for a particular type of physical location where data were collected (e.g., a swap meet), and the term *context* for categories of consumption phenomena, a distinction comparable to the "focal settings" and "cultural domains" identified by Snow and Anderson (1987). Contexts that emerged were gifts, collections, heirlooms, pets, time, souvenirs, art, mentions of "special" items, photographs, physical space, holidays, and pilgrimages. In building and testing interpretations, contexts were examined sequentially, with each succeeding context acting as a check on the interpretations supported by preceding ones (as in Lincoln and Guba's suggestion that researchers use referential adequacy materials to check the credibility and confirmability of an interpretation). Just as saturation was used to guide the emergent sampling design, redundant support over different contexts was used to assess generalizability of findings. We do not present propositions that were disconfirmed as we moved across contexts.

Analysis

During fieldwork, we circulated memos on our emerging understandings. As data collection progressed, these memos specified propositions to be challenged through purposive sampling. Contrary to the conception of interpretive methods described by Calder and Tybout (1987), naturalistic inquiry uses purposive sampling and constant comparative method to test by developing, challenging, and reformulating the emergent conceptualization.

Fieldnotes, journals, and photo and video indices were computerized for use in systematic data analysis. This data analysis was completed using ZyIndex, a computerized program for qualitative data management and analysis (see Belk 1988a). Analysis of each context also included examination of photographs and videotapes. Triangulation between researchers occurred with separate examinations of computer analyses and visual records.

Based on understandings developed in the pilot project and memos concerning emerging interpretations, two focal processes were identified: the transformation of profane commodities into sacred objects, and the maintenance and loss of sacredness (desacralization). Data for each context were coded using margin notations concerning each process. The transferability of these propositions was tested by sequentially analyzing contexts. Consistent with the constant comparative method (Glaser and Strauss 1967), propositions were revised in successive comparisons with new data until saturation and redundancy were achieved. What we refer to here as testing is in fact a large series of tests continued until the theory fully captured the phenomenon. Limitations and modifications are noted as the results are presented. The discussion is organized by process and draws from each context.

THE SACRED AND THE PROFANE IN RELIGION

What is Religion?

William James's (1961, pp. 42, 45/orig. 1902) behavioral definition of religion still serves well:

> (Religion) shall mean for us the feelings, acts, and experiences of individual men in their solitude, so far as they apprehend themselves to stand in relation to whatever they may consider the divine. . . . We must interpret the term "divine" very broadly, as denoting any object that is godlike, whether it be a concrete deity or not.

In its avoidance of a particular theological perspective, this definition is hardly singular among social scientists. For example Roberts (1984, p. 90) states:

> Religion has to do with a unique and extra-ordinary experience--an experience that has a sacred dimension and is unlike everyday life . . . the experience of the holy. Such an experience is often called nonrational, for it is neither rational nor irrational.

Such definitions stress the special quality of sacredness that makes something religious. Marcel Mauss (quoted in Ferrarotti 1979, p. 674) contrasted this observation with the more common assumption that religion involves particular deities:

> It is not the idea of god, the idea of a sacred person, that one finds over again in any religion, it is the idea of the sacred in general.

To understand how this perspective on religious experience applies to contemporary consumer behavior, we must specify the properties of sacredness.

Properties of Sacredness

The sacred can best be understood by contrasting it with the profane, as in the extensive theoretical treatments by Emile Durkheim and Mircea Eliade. Their perspectives are similar, although Durkheim's notion of religion is more sociological, focusing on societal consequences, while Eliade's is more psychological (Stirrat 1984). We present 12 properties of sacredness synthesized from the writings of Durkheim, Eliade, and subsequent theorists. Of these, hierophany, kratophany, opposition to the profane, contamination, sacrifice, commitment, objectification, ritual, and mystery all apply in both individual and social treatments of the sacred. Communitas and myth are primarily social concepts, and ecstasy and flow are primarily psychological.

Hierophany. Hierophany is "the *act of manifestation* of the sacred . . . i.e., that *something sacred shows itself to us*" (Eliade 1958, p. 7), conveying the idea that, phenomenologically, people do not create sacred things. Instead, sacredness manifests itself experientially as "something of a wholly different order, a reality that does not belong to our world" (Beane and Doty 1975, p. 141). In Eliade's psychological view, hierophany involves the notion that the sacred does not manifest itself to everyone. A sacred stone continues to appear like other stones except to those who believe it has revealed itself to them as unique, supernatural, or *ganz andere* (totally other).

Durkheim (1915) also sees the sacred as being beyond individual creation; however, in his sociological view, the sacred emerges collectively when society removes certain things from ordinary human use. Something is defined as being sacred through a social process that brings a system of meaning to individuals (hierophany), resulting in societal cohesion.

Kratophany. The sacred elicits both strong approach and strong avoidance tendencies (Durkheim 1975/orig. 1896). This ambivalence creates an overwhelming power, the manifestation of which is called kratophany (Eliade 1958). Although the vernacular usage of the term sacred implies only that which is good and desirable, Durkheim distinguishes between beneficent sacred powers, such as those associated with gods, protectors, and holy places, and evil sacred powers, such as those associated with corpses, sickness, and impure objects (Pickering 1984). Both are imbued with sacred power through strong ambivalent reactions (kratophany) that combine fascination and devotion with repulsion and fear. Because people simultaneously seek the beneficence of the sacred and fear the evil it can unleash, they approach it with a care appropriate to its kratophanous power.

Opposition to the Profane. The extraordinary sacred is defined partly by its opposition to the ordinary profane. Profane refers to that which is ordinary and part of everyday life, not to that which is vulgar or offensive, as in vernacular usage. Although Durkheim recognized various degrees of sacredness, the extremely sacred was held to be inviolably distinct from the profane. "The sacred . . . cannot, without losing its nature, be mixed with the profane. Any mixture or even contact, *profanes* it, . . . destroys its essential attributes" (Durkheim 1953, p. 70). Such sacrilege includes trespass on the sacred by profane persons; only a priest or shaman can cross from the profane to the sacred realm, and only after appropriate purification. A primary societal function is the exercise of social control to maintain the separateness of the two spheres, protecting the inviolate status of the sacred and maintaining its position as set apart.

Contamination. Both beneficent and evil sacred things have the power to contaminate through contact. However, in contradistinction to medical usage of the term, contamination in this context generally indicates the spread of positive sacredness rather than evil (negative sacredness). Objects blessed through sacred ritual are thus said to be contaminated with sacredness. A religious example of contamination is the Christian ritual sacrament of communion, in which a congregation eats symbols of the body and blood of Christ (in some traditions, transubstantiation is said to occur). Similarly, possessions of sacred persons become venerated icons because they are contaminated with sacredness; places where sacred activities occurred are contaminated with sacredness that the faithful seek to attain through pilgrimages (O'Guinn 1987; O'Guinn and Belk 1989; Turner and Turner 1978).

Sacrifice. As an act of abnegation and submission, sacrifice establishes communication with the sacred by purifying and preparing the sacrificer (Hubert and Mauss 1964). Sacrifice usually involves a "gift to the gods" of otherwise profane material goods, such as domestic animals in pastoral societies (James 1962). But sacrifice can also involve asceticism, fasting, sexual abstinence, self-mutilation, and martyrdom (Mol 1976). Sacrifices prepare one to commune with the sacred, bring about a strong degree of commitment to sacred experience, and indicate appropriate deference to reinforce the extraordinary character of the sacred.

Commitment. Individuals feel a "focused emotion or emotional attachment" to that which is considered sacred (Mol 1976, p. 216) Psychologically, such commitment directs attention to the sacred, which becomes a strong part of one's identity. This aspect of sacredness shares some features with what has been called involvement in the consumer research literature. However, sacredness goes beyond the concept of involvement, as will be explained more fully later.

Sociologically, collective formation of shared commitment to a definition of the sacred is the integrative basis for society (Durkheim 1915, 1960/orig. 1902; Weber 1962/orig. 1920). Regardless of what is chosen to signify the sacred in society, shared commitment results in what Durkheim terms mechanical solidarity, in which religious participants replicate the social order by maintaining commitment to the collective definitions of sacred and profane. Individual commitment to the sacred is so strong that initial experience with the sacred may result in conversion--an identity change resulting in an unshakable conviction.

Objectification. Objectification is "the tendency to sum up the variegated elements of mundane existence in a transcendental frame of reference where they can appear in a more orderly, more consistent, and more timeless way" (Mol 1976, p. 206). Through representation in an object, the sacred is concretized. This allows things of this world to take on greater meaning than is evident in their everyday appearance and function. A stone may continue to appear as a stone, but it is a sacred object when its origin is understood through a creation myth to be the tear of an animal. We find this aspect of the sacred to be particularly important in understanding the sacredness of some contemporary consumption.

Ritual. Rituals are "rules of conduct which prescribe how a man should comport himself in the presence of . . . sacred objects" (Durkheim 1915, p. 56). Rituals are often performed without deliberate thought to the rationale that guides them. They are functional through their performance, apart from their content (Bossard and Boll 1950). Like sacrifice, ritual prepares one to approach the sacred and may be enacted as an individual or, more commonly, as a group. Ritual surrounds the contact of profane persons with the sacred to ensure that the evil powers feared in kratophany will not be unleashed. Ritual also protects the sacred from contact with mere mortals and alleviates human anxiety about this contact (Malinowski 1954).

Myth. Myths often surround the sacred and are used historically to document its status through narratives, iterative tales, or speculations about existence (Kirk 1970). Such accounts define our place within the world and maintain sacred status through repetition (Eliade 1964; Mol 1976). They socialize participants' understandings of the collective definitions of the sacred and instruct new participants such as children and recent converts.

Mystery. The sacred "has conferred upon it a dignity that raises it above the ordinary or 'empirical'" (Pickering 1984, p. 159). It cannot be understood cognitively, for the sacred commands love, devotion, fear, and related spiritual or emotional responses rather than rational thought. This mystery is characteristic of phenomena that do not fit human behavior models based on presumptions of self-interest or competition, but rather derive from a desire for more profound experiences and meanings (Nisbet 1966). When something loses this mystery, it loses its sacredness and becomes ordinary and profane.

Communitas. Communitas is a social antistructure that frees participants from their normal social roles and statuses and instead engages them in a transcending camaraderie of status equality (Turner 1969). It is most likely to occur when the individual is in a "liminal" or threshold state betwixt and between two statuses, such as may occur on religious pilgrimages (Turner and Turner 1978) and in initiation ceremonies, fraternal

organizations, countercultural groups, and occasionally among research teams (Sherry 1987a). This spirit of communitas emerges from shared ritual experiences "which transcend those of status-striving, money-grubbing, and self-serving" and act as "proofs that man does not live by bread alone" (Turner 1972, pp. 391-392).

Ecstasy and Flow. The sacred is capable of producing ecstatic experience, in which one stands outside one's self (Colpe 1987). Durkheim (see Pickering 1984) describes a joy that arises from the transcendent reality of sacred things. According to James (1961, p. 55/orig. 1902),

> Like love, like wrath, like hope, ambition, jealousy . . . it (religion) adds to life an enchantment which is not rationally or logically deducible from anything else.

The sacred can take a person outside of self, matter, and mortality, but such ecstatic experiences are momentary rather than constant (Greeley 1985). Ecstasy marks the extraordinary character of sacred experience and distinguishes it from the common pleasures of everyday life.

A psychological interpretation refers to the effect of participation in the sacred as flow (Csikszentmihalyi 1975) or peak experience (Maslow 1964). Flow experiences include a centering of attention, a loss of self, a feeling of being in control of self and environment, and an autotelic aspect such that the activity is its own reward (Csikszentmihalyi 1975).

Victor Turner (1977) has subsequently distinguished communitas as involving a "shared flow." Like the differences between Durkheim and Eliade regarding sacred experiences, the differences between flow or peak experience and communitas are not so much in the nature of the experience as in whether it is a group or an individual phenomenon. Although group ritual does not appear necessary for ecstatic experiences (Hardy 1979; Laski 1962), such rituals can and do bring about sacred experiences. To begin to explore the applicability of the concept of the sacred to contemporary consumption, we must consider the contemporary boundaries between the sacred and the profane.

SHIFTING BOUNDARIES BETWEEN THE SACRED AND THE PROFANE

The sociology of religion has noted changes in contemporary society that make interpretations of the sacred and the profane somewhat different than Durkheim's--in which the sacred resided in the sphere of religion and the profane resided in the secular world. Changes in contemporary life indicate that the sacred/profane distinction is no longer isomorphic with the religious/secular distinction (Becker 1957). Two trends work together to support the applicability of the concept of the sacred to the secular context of consumption. The first trend involves the gradual secularization of contemporary institutional religion, while the second involves the gradual sacralization of the secular. Both processes reflect shifting boundaries between the sacred and profane.

Secularization of Religion

The secularization of religion is a widely noted pattern. For example, Ducey (1977) found growth in nontraditional church services and decline in traditional services in the United States during the 1979s. Nontraditional services substituted the profane for the sacred, such as lay for clerical dress, contemporary guitar for classical organ music, and oral participation by parishioners in addition to sermons by the pastor. These changes reflect culture's dynamic definitions of the sacred and the profane.

Others have found a gradually more secular celebration of traditional religious events, such as Christmas (Belk 1987a; Bock 1972; Luschen et al. 1972), and a marked decline in family religious rituals, such as prayers at meals and bedtime, and collective readings from sacred literature (Bossard and Boll 1950). The discontinuance of Latin in the Catholic Mass exemplifies a secularization of religion involving demystification, lesser separation of sacred and profane times, and lesser preservation of ritual and myth.

The use by contemporary religions of radio and television media also demonstrates secularization through the broadcast of sacred rituals into what may be profane spaces of times (O'Guinn and Belk 1989). "Televangelism: secularizes religion also by its association with the secular medium of television" (Frankl 1987). By becoming more linked to the secular, religion may have undermined its own sacredness, opening the way for other foci of sacredness. That is, as religion provides less of an extraordinary experience, people look elsewhere for experiences that transcend everyday life.

Sacralization of the Secular

The emergence of the sacred in secular contexts has coincided with the secularization of institutional religion. As the Catholic church lost control of politics, knowledge, art, and music, each of these spheres developed sacred status of its own. To characterize this trend, Rousseau formulated the term "civil religion," which refers to finding the essence of religion in what is traditionally regarded as secular. The notion has been treated in greatest depth by Bellah (1967, 1985), whose theory of civil religion attempts to resolve the ambiguous role of religious symbols in secular society (Fenn 1986). Contemporary sacralization of the secular is seen as occurring in the cultural arenas of politics, science, art, and consumption. Evidences from each of these areas will be briefly reviewed.

Nationalistic celebrations reflect the sacralization of the secular within politics (Demerath 1974; Shiner 1972). National holidays are celebrated more widely than many religious holy days; national anthems are sung with all the reverence of hymns; national flags are icons; and contemporary national heroes and monuments have supplanted the widespread worship of religious saints and shrines (Beist 1978; Roberts 1984; Rook 1984; Warner 1959). Market forces accelerate and focus this sacralization of nationalism, creating invented traditions, such as Scottish clan tartans (Hobsbawm and Ranger 1983), and replacements for evil eye and hex symbols in official-looking commercial security system and security patrol signs on the doors and windows of many American homes (Rook 1987). Europeans venerate royalty (e.g., Williamson 1986) with a mystique imparted by long-standing rituals and symbols (Hayden 1987; Shils and Young 1953). The crown jewels are regarded as icons that are as unthinkable to sell as it would be to turn the Statue of Liberty into condominiums.

A second area where the secular is sacralized is science. Rather than religion, science is considered the ultimate arbiter of truth in societies that venerate rational thought and causal explanations (Capra 1975), much to the dismay of fundamentalists. Weber called the substitution of scientific for religious belief "the disenchantment of the world," while Schiller called it "the disgodding of nature" (quoted in Berman 1984, p. 57). The miracles of god and nature have gradually been replaced by scientific explanations (Inkeles 1983). Now it is science rather than religion that is viewed as imparting knowledge, although a number of authors see this as an unfortunate divorce of eros from logos (Bateson and Bateson 1987; Berman 1984; Highwater 1981; Hyde 1983; Keller 1985; Pirsig 1974; Plato 1955/orig. 400 B.C.) that leaves us with an incomplete understanding of the world.

A third arena that provides evidence of the sacralization of the secular is art and music. Since the Reformation, religious content in music and art has declined and secular themes have increased (Berger 1967). Yet, both are sacred to many consumer. Art, like science, is not only sacred, it sacralizes. Placement in a gallery, museum, university, or other scientific or artistic institution can sacralize objects (Clifford 1985). Museum curators are among the priests of the art world. Prominent collectors are also accorded expert status to authenticate artwork and act as "missionaries' in promoting art to the uninitiated (Lynes 1980).

In a definition reminiscent of the sacred/profane distinction, Becker (1978) differentiates between art and craft, noting that both may be aesthetically appealing, but a craft object has a use. This accords with the idea that the sacred is set apart and beyond mundane utility and also accords with the noble portrait of the starving artist, which Becker (1982) finds accurate given the difficulty of having one's work defined as art.

The presence of the sacred is as evident in popular music as it is in the so-called "High arts," but there are clearer deities-- charismatic rock stars. The sacralization of rock music is accomplished by each generation of youth, which draws its collective identity from the songs of these rock stars (Martin 1979) via a process that Goodman (1960) calls "the sacramental use of noise." The ecstasy here derives from the liminal experiences of sex, violence, and mysticism (e.g., drugs) associated with this music (Martin 1979), as well as deriving from the music experience itself (Holbrook and Hirschman 1982).

This leads us to consider evidence of the sacralization of the secular from the realm of consumption. Although consumption historically has often been opposed by institutional religious teachings (Belk 1983), it has gained sacred status in our consumption-oriented and hedonistic society (Campbell 1987; Mol 1983). Mol illustrates the "cosmic straddling, deep commitment, solemn rites, and expressive symbolism" that may attach to art, sports, music, and even secular objects such as some clothing and automobiles. That consumption has become a secular ritual through which transcendent experience is sought has been noted, but not empirically explored, in the consumer behavior literature (Hirschman and Holbrook 1982; Holbrook and Hirschman 1982; Leiss, Kline, and Jhally 1986; Rook 1985; Sherry 1987b, 1987c; Wallendorf and Arnould 1988; Williamson 1986). Just as Protestantism helped secularize religion in Weber's (1958/orig. 1904) view, the rise of individualism has made it possible to define the sacred as that which brings secular ecstacy to the individual. According to Campbell (1983, p. 293):

> Although nominally "secular" in character (this principle) . . . derived from the idea of a "covenant" or compact between each individual and his own "self," in which in return for acknowledging one's duty to serve the spirit of self, that spirit would in turn

bring happiness to the individual. Heaven in such a doctrine is the fulfillment of self."

It is the sacralizing of certain aspects of consumption that will serve as the focus for the remainder of this article.

What is Sacred?--The Domains of Sacred Consumption

As a result of the secularization of religion and the sacralization of the secular, the sacred/profane distinction has become applicable to the secular context of consumption. While anything can potentially become sacred (Acquaviva 1979), sacred status is not distributed randomly across the elements of a culture. Instead, consumers enact the sacred/profane distinction within common domains of experience. Potentially sacred consumer domains, like potentially sacred religious domains, fall into six major categories: places, times, tangible things, intangibles, persons, and experiences. We will discuss the meaning of the sacred/profane distinction for contemporary consumer in each of these as a means of building a definition of sacredness.

Places. In agricultural societies, one's homeland is the sacred center of the world. Even contemporary displaced cultural groups such as the Navajos experience a fractured social fabric as a result of losing their land (Scudder 1982). Some sacred places, especially those in nature, have the beauty, majesty, and power to evoke ecstasy and flow without help from myth, ritual, or contamination (Brereton 1987; Lipsey 1984). In other cases, these means may be needed to sacralize a place.

Places may reveal their sacredness through hierophanous signs, as with the Aztec city of Tenochtitlan, founded where an eagle landed on a blooming cactus (Brereton 1987). A place may also become sacred through contamination through events that occurred there (e.g., Jerusalem). Places where sacred persons were born, performed miracles, received mystic revelations, and are buried become sacred through contamination. Rituals may also sacralize a place as with groundbreaking ceremonies, burials, and house-warming parties.

Once a place is regarded as sacred, it may command reverential behaviors such as pilgrimages, removal or wiping of shoes, silence, purification prior to entry, or sacrificial offerings. If they do not already exists, boundaries may be marked and shrines erected. The sacredness of some spaces is defined by the activities that occur there. In religion, churches, temples, and shrines are viewed as sacred. But distinctions are also made between sacred and profane areas in the secular world. A secular place commonly designated as sacred is the geographic area of a person's childhood. Pilgrimages are often made to these areas on vacations, especially when accompanied by other family members. Going back can be either a positive or negative sacred experience, depending upon how much the place has been changed and how much of one's former identity, familiarity, and mastery is retained (Belk 1988b).

The primary locus of the sacred in the secular world of consumption is the dwelling (Eliade 1959; Jackson 1953; Tuan 1978). It is sacred because it houses the family, because it is a home (Kron 1983). The most sacred and secret family activities occur there, including eating, sleeping, cooking, having sex, caring for children and the sick, and dressing (Saegert 1985). It is separated from the profane world "outside" (Altman and Chemers 1984; Rapoport 1982) through the careful attention given to entry thresholds (Deffontaines 1953; Rapoport 1981). In societies organized around nuclear families rather than collective groups, the dwelling imposes order by centering the world for its inhabitants (Duncan 1985). Within the home, private spaces serve as inner sanctums in a society favoring individualism (Tuan 1978). The hearth is often a communal family altar where family photos are enshrined and greeting cards connecting the family to others are displayed (Collier and Collier 1986; Jackson 1953; Levi-Strauss 1965).

Consumption also has its public cathedrals that enhance the mystery and sense of otherworldliness of the sacred. Such places have been instrumental in the development of consumer culture. Perhaps the most influential of these has been the department store. Rather than following the wheel of retailing pattern of entering the market as low-price institutions, turn-of-the-century department stores entered the market as extravagant show places where functional and financial considerations paled in the magnificence of their grandiose architecture, theatrical lighting, and sumptuous display (Bowlby 1985; Williams 1981). Today, the simple department store is eclipsed in grandeur by the shopping mall (Kowinski 1985; Mann 1980; Zepp 1986), where shopping has become a ritual in a consumption-oriented society.

Other cathedrals of consumption in the past two centuries have included the grand opera house (Naylor 1981), the theatre (May 1980; Sharp 1969), the museum (Rochberg-Halton 1986), world's fairs (Benedict 1983; Rydell 1984), and the grand hotel (d'Ormesson 1984). Such places gave consumers a taste of opulent luxury, often even being named "palaces" in the early 1900s. Although

consumers could not aspire to live in such grand places, attending events there enlarged desires and created a sense of reverent awe for luxury and consumption.

Times. Just as sacred and profane places are separated, time is separated into sacred and profane periods. Sacred time is not merely an interval that is otherwise profane. Once sacred time begins, it seems infinite and without meaning. For example, creation myths form a history within a different time plane than that of the profane world. The sacred past is recoverable through rituals such as New Year celebrations that reenact a creation myth (Eliade 1958, 1959) or festivals such as Christian Easter, which reenacts the resurrection of Christ and renewal of nature. During initiations, graduations, weddings, funerals, and birthdays, we participate in the sacred.

Sacred times occur cyclically during the day (e.g., Islamic prayers, the morning coffee break), week (e.g., the sabbath, a leisurely reading of the Sunday newspaper), month (e.g., new moon ceremonies), and year (e.g., the harvest feast, birthday celebrations). As with entry into sacred places, purification rituals may accompany entry into sacred time to separate it from profane time. Special clothing, fragrances, prayers, utensils, and foods may accompany sacred time (Farb and Armelagos 1980; Leach 1961; Wolowelsky 1977). Sacred time may even serve in lieu of sacred places, as with the Jewish calendar, which has been suggested to be replete with sacred times due to the long exile of the Jews from their sacred homeland (Zerubavel 1981).

Sacred time also occurs episodically in secular consumption contexts; e.g., for the fan attending a sporting event or concert or for a gourmet sitting down to a fine meal. Irreverent behaviors, such as interruptions, inappropriate noise, or too casual an attitude toward the focus of attention at these times, are considered not only rude but sacrilegious. Such actions profane events that devotees think should be regarded with awe and appreciation. Ritual garb, behaviors, foods, and vocabularies or silence may also be expected during these sacred intervals. As Rheims (1961, p. 29) notes:

> Museums are the churches of collectors. Speaking in whispers, groups of visitors wander as an act of faith from one museum gallery to another. Until the end of the nineteenth century it was customary to visit the Hermitage Museum at Leningrad in a white tie. The almost ritual habits practiced in the sales-rooms in London and Paris have been the same for two hundred years. The Hotel Dourot (an art auction site) is

a sort of temple. It has fixed ceremonies, and its daily hour from ten to eleven has a completely religious atmosphere.

During a rock concert the behaviors considered appropriately reverential differ, but are still defined as sacred to participants. These behaviors include use of marijuana, lighting matches to indicate reverence at the end of a concert, ecstatic dance, and purchase of tour t-shirt relics. Here it is the quiet, seemingly uninvolved concert-goer who is considered inappropriate.

Tangible Things. Sacred tangible things include icons, clothing, furnishings, artifacts, and possessions that are symbolically linked with and objectify the sacred. Shrines honor sacred relics and separate them from the profane world (Geary 1986). In naturistic religions, animals may be totemic and sacred (Houghton 1955; Levi-Strauss 1962), whereas in vegetation cults, trees and plants are regarded as sacred symbols of life, creation, renewal, youth, and immortality (Eliade 1959). Sacred religious objects are sometimes fine pieces of art, but are sometimes quite simple things like the bone, top, ball, tambourine, apples, mirror, fan and fleece shown to novices in the Lesser Eleusinian Mysteries of Athens (Turner 1972). Ordinary as these things may appear to be, they are made sacred by myths, rituals, and signs. They are the media by which a society's "deep knowledge" is passed on to succeeding generations. Objects may also be defined as sacred because of their rarity and beauty, marking them as inherently non-ordinary (Clark 1986), as with precious metals and gems (Eliade 1958).

Sacred objects are not treated as ordinary objects, but rather seem to require special handling. They are revered with a "Bow, a prostration, a pious touch of the hand" (Eliade 1959, p. 25). They are consecrated, used in prayer, sung about, and used to trigger inspiration and ecstasy. Further, they may be believed to have magical powers, both beneficent and evil. As Eliade (1958) notes, rare stones and metals are often believed to have aphrodisiac, fertilizing, and talismanic qualities. They may be considered poisonous, able cure diseases, preserve dead bodies, protect from harm, or bring prosperity.

Sacred objects are imbued with kratophanous power. Some possessions within the home are also sacred, even though they may be as humble-appearing as odds and ends on a bureau, a pincushion lid, a cigar box, faded American Legion poppies, and assorted pills and patent medicines (Morris 1948). Particularly favored possessions represent aspects of the person's life that are regarded as sacred (Wallendorf and Arnould 1988).

A sacred possession for many in the United States is the automobile (Levy 1978; Marsh and Collett 1986; Neal 1985; Sherry 1986a). As satirized by Mol (1976, p. 152):

Once upon a time there was a country that was ruled by a god named Car. In the beginning it did not amount to much. Then it came to pass that out of Dearborn, Michigan, there came a man who took Car and said "Let there be mass production," and slowly Car took over the country. Car temples were built, car stables were put up and special stores sprang up where people could go and buy gifts for Car. Weekends became ritualistic: On Saturday the people would wash Car gently with soap and on Sunday they would pet it with a soft rag to remove any stray dust and ride around the countryside. Car ruled the country for many years, demanding annual sacrifices of several thousand people and keeping most of the people in a downtrodden state as the people tried to meet financial pledges they had made to Car.

Thus, ordinary consumption items can serve as sacred icons.

Intangible Things. Immaterial things considered sacred include magic formulae, dances, crests, names, and songs (Beaglehole 1932). More contemporary examples include fraternity and sorority rituals, secrets between friends or lovers, and family recipes for stuffing the Thanksgiving turkey. Like tangible sacred things, intangibles exhibit kratophany and are approached with both attraction and fear (Clodd 1920).

Persons and Other Beings. While Durkheim held that individuals in general are sacred in modern Western society (Pickering 1984) due to values of possessive individualism, what is meant here is that certain persons are sacred and set apart from others. Gods, prophets, and saints are religious examples. The lives of saints take on a sacred character through good deeds, self-abnegation, sacrifice, martyrdom, and piety. At a slightly less sacred level are the leaders and officials of the church. They are not thought of as choosing their positions, but rather are "chosen" or "called," most often by a non-rational, hierophanous vision. In many religions, they too live a life of sacrifice, self-abnegation, poverty, chastity, and good deeds.

Some sacred persons have prophetic charisma that gives them magical power over followers (Weber 1968/orig. early 1900s). This power can be greater than that residing in impersonal things, so that the charismatic leader can redefine ideas of what is sacred. Over time, the power of the charismatic leader is routinized in a bureaucracy, which then confers sacred status on particular positions, and subsequently to those who occupy these positions. The sacredness of a charismatic leader, then, shifts over time from the person to a structure, to positions, and then to role occupants.

As an immediate manifestation of the self, the body may be regarded as sacred. It is ritually bathed, anointed with oils, groomed, arrayed in sacred clothing, and decorated, as with tattoos (Hope 1980; Rook 1984, 1985; Sanders 1985; T. Turner 1977; Wallendorf and Nelson 1986). Clothing adorns the body to symbolize group membership, as in the clothing signs that devotees of long distance running use to distinguish themselves from joggers (Nash 1977). Miner (1956) has deftly pointed out that contemporary body care rituals regard the bathroom as a shrine, the medicine cabinet as a treasure chest of magical potions and charms, and doctors and pharmacists as priests.

Pets are a type of sacralized animal (Sussman 1985; Tuan 1984). Apart from the way pets structure family interactions, their sacralization shapes human food preferences. Just as cannibalism is taboo, eating a pet or any animal considered suitable as pet is unthinkable (Harris 1985). In ancient Polynesia, pigs were family pets (Titcomb 1969), but in modern agribusiness, the pig "has been reduced to the status of a strictly utilitarian object, a thing for producing meat and bacon" (Serpell 1986, p. 6).

Experiences. The experiences of prepared individuals at sacred times and places are themselves sacred, as with the travels of pilgrims. The distinction between sacred and profane travel can be made according to purpose and destination; travel to a shrine is sacred, while a journey away from home for business is profane (Fabien 1983). While the religious pilgrimage is a traditional form of sacred travel (Turner and Turner 1978), a part of any touring involves a seeking of the sacred. Worship of the pure, uncrowded natural site recalls naturistic religion. There are also new sacred sites, including such playful centers as Disneyland and Walt Disney World. The nostalgic motifs of these centers are designed to convey the visitor into a sacred time (Moore 1980) by evoking what Durkheim calls a nostalgia for paradise (Cohen 1979; Culler 1981; Giesz 1969; Tuan 1978). Sightseeing has become a modern ritual (MacCannell 1976) within the sacred, non-ordinary time of a vacation (Graburn 1977). It is a festive, liminal time when behavior is different from ordinary work time. An important part of the tourist's quest is to bring

back a part of the sacred experience, place, and time. The objectified result is frequently a photograph or souvenir (Gordon 1986; Stewart 1984). An outsider may regard these as kitsch, but they are sacred for the pilgrim (Giesz 1969; Whetmore and Hibbard 1978).

Eating is a sacred experience in many contexts (Farb and Armelagos 1980), primarily when food has meaning beyond mere physical energy replenishment. Meals are eaten ritually at certain times, in certain places, with certain implements and procedures (Jones 1982). Eating is a ritual connecting the nuclear family, and there are a number of holiday occasions in which extended family and friends are bonded by sharing food that symbolizes life. For North Americans, these include Thanksgiving, Easter, Passover, Christmas, and birthdays (Wolwelsky 1977). Contamination through food is a strong symbolic perception, as evidenced by the rumors embodied in consumer oral tradition that deal with profanation and taboo (Koenig 1985; Sherry 1984). Certain foods, such as Big Macs and Kentucky Fried Chicken, can become sacred icons that nostalgically represent culture (Curry and Jiobu 1980; Kottak 1975).

Additional sacralization of experiences and of persons, places, and times attend the ritual consumption of spectator sports. Guttman (1978) reviews the original religious basis of spectator sports and argues that, while no longer religious, sports are still sacred. In spectator sports, the fan participates in an experience in which teams and heroes are revered, stadiums are temples that may be the site of pilgrimages, and artifacts may serve as sacred relics. Fans participate in various pre-, post-, and during-game rituals (Birrell 1981; MacAloon 1984; Stein 1977; Voigt 1980), and sports seasons are sacred times for them. Myths involving players, teams, and the principles they are thought to exemplify help sacralize sports, with the Super Bowl being the largest mythic spectacle in the United States (Birrell 1981; Cummings 1972; Real 1975).

Although not comprehensive in listing everything that is regarded as sacred, this discussion points out areas of secular consumption in which the sacred is experienced. This discussion highlights parallels between religious experience and the broad range of places, times, tangible things, intangibles, persons, and experiences that contemporary consumers may regard as sacred. What is of interest is not a mere listing of what is regarded as sacred, since almost anything can become such a focus, but rather the processes supporting individual and collective definitions of sacred consumption and the distinctions separating sacred from profane consumption. Rather than listing everything that may be labeled sacred consumption, we will outline the processes by which consumers understand and preserve particular aspects of consumption as set apart, extraordinary, and sacred.

Interpretive Summary of What Is Sacred

We have detailed a number of properties of the sacred, and have shown how conventional scholarly interpretations of religion enhance our understanding of consumer behavior. Our discussion of shifts in the boundary between the sacred and the profane demonstrates the selectively permeable nature of these domains of experience. Religion has become secularized, and the secular sacralized in contemporary Western society. In this context, consumption may become a primary means of transcendent experience. Rather than experiencing the kind of extraordinary meaning previously attained primarily through religion, contemporary consumers define certain objects or consumption experiences as representing something more than the ordinary objects they appear to be. In this, they participate in what the sociology of religion calls the sacred. The focal interest here is not on *what* is regarded as sacred, as almost anything can be imbued with this meaning. Rather, our primary interest is in the *processes* by which particular consumption becomes and remains sacralized.

Before examining the processes by which consumption is sacralized and preserved as sacred, it may be helpful to recapitulate our understanding of the sacred. We take the sacred in the realm of consumption to refer to that which is regarded as more significant, powerful, and extraordinary than the self. Sacred occurrences may be ecstatic; they are self-transcending. Such self-transcending experiences may, but need not, be aided by a social context involving fellow believers who also revere the object or experience. The profane, by contrast, is ordinary and lacks the ability to induce ecstatic, self-transcending, extraordinary experiences. Profane objects are treated casually rather than reverently and are not a focus of devotion.

Perhaps the closest existing analog in consumer research to our concept of the sacred is the involvement construct. Conceptually, high enduring product involvement (Houston and Rothschild 1978) is related to, but is not the same as, sacred consumption. It is likely that many of the high enduring involvement automobile owners identified by (Bloch 1981) and Richins and Bloch (1986) regard their automobiles as sacred. However, high enduring product involvement and sacred consumption are distinctly separate concepts. The notion of

sacredness in consumption is not restricted to products: it may also attach to people, places, times, and experiences. More importantly, high enduring product involvement is not a sufficient indicant of sacredness. A consumer who watches television frequently and who regards it as an important source of life satisfaction need not regard television or television programming as sacred. For television to be sacred to a consumer, it would also need reliably to provide self-transcending, extraordinary experiences, and be capable of being profaned. High enduring product involvement is often characteristic of those for whom a particular type of consumption is sacred, but not all who exhibit high enduring product involvement will regard the consumption as sacred. Involvement is a component of sacred experience, but is insufficient to fully capture the experience of sacred consumption. The involvement construct does not explain the processes of movement between sacred and profane that are explained in the theory of sacred consumption explicated in the remainder of this chapter.

Nor is recent work on self-concept and fluid body boundaries sufficient to encompass the sacred in consumer behavior. Whether objects are viewed in Western, masculine perspective as extensions of self (Belk 1988b) or in more feminine, Eastern terms as incorporated into self, no sacralization need occur in either event. Ultimately, the meaning of the sacred may lie in the discovery or creation of connectedness, but without a confluence of the properties we have described, sacredness will go undetected.

We know of no extant quantitative measures of consumption sacredness, which is why we have described the properties of the sacred in such detail, emphasizing the variety of the experience rather than relative degrees of intensity. We have not called for the development of quantitative measures because the nature and experience of the sacred may be antithetical to such measurement. The ontological and epistemological assumptions of positivist methods are not sympathetic to the mystical and experiential nature of sacredness, but instead are oriented to a different universe of discourse. Qualitative assessment becomes important in developing an understanding of sacred consumption processes and in discovering the dimensions along which their properties might be measured eventually. We will now examine the processes characteristic of sacred consumption.

RESULTS: PROCESSES OF SACRED CONSUMPTION

Anything may become sacred. Sacredness is in large part an investment process. Consumers construe meaning in various fashions and in different degrees of ontological intensity. Objects (broadly construed) potentiate and catalyze experience of the sacred. This experience may be ritualized at the level of ceremony or even of habit; it may be subject to much exegesis, or so deeply subconscious as to resist everyday inspection. The sacred adheres in that which is designed or discovered to be supremely significant; in this regard, industrialized society is no different from any other society, hegemonic and ethnocentric Western values notwithstanding. However, groups and individuals satisfy the universal need to experience the sacred quite differently. A comprehensive analysis must describe not just what is considered sacred, but also the *ways* objects and people move between the sacred and profane realms. Our analysis will focus on two processes that occur regarding sacred and profane aspects of consumption; sacralization processes and maintenance processes that perpetuate sacredness.

Sacralization Processes

How do certain possessions attain sacred status? Is sacredness something that is acquired with the object, as power steering is acquired with an automobile, or is it something that happens after the object is acquired? Our data indicate that there are at least seven ways through which an object can become sacralized in contemporary consumer culture: ritual, pilgrimage, quintessence, gift-giving, collecting, inheritance, and external sanction.

Sacralization Through Ritual. An ordinary commodity may become sacred by rituals designed to transform the object symbolically. Much ritual behavior in contemporary consumer culture has been secularized--in effect reduced to ceremony or habit--but some ritual may be reclaimed, or singularized, and consciously returned to the realm of the sacred. These rituals may be public or private, collective or individual.

Sacralization through ritual is evident in informants' descriptions of the process of moving into a new house and turning it into a home. (For additional material on the architectural dimensions of sacralization, see Oliver 1987 and Slesin, Cliff, and Rozensztroch 1987). A man in a homeless shelter who was moving into his own room in a boarding house estimated that turning this space into a home would happen quickly; he expected that his new room would feel like home the first night that he slept there. For him, merely sleeping in a the room for one night, combined with the knowledge that it was his, was sufficient ritual for transforming it into a home.

However, for lower middle-class people spending the summer in a trailer campground, making the place feel like home involved extensive work to the exterior of the trailer and the rented space, as indicated by the following excerpt from field notes:

> There is an amazing amount of work which has gone into outdoor settling and decorating. The sites have wood piles, awnings, colored gravel to be raked around the yard, white painted rocks to line the driveway, American flags, lawn statuary of all types including animals which are in fact native here such as squirrels, hanging lantern lights in abundant variety, and plastic chain strung around the space like a fence. There are lawn chairs of heavy metal, twirling daisies and other whirligigs, woodburned signs with the residents' names on them, planters with flowers, and even some annual flowers planted in the ground.

Kopytoff's (1986) call for a "cultural biography of things" provides the concept of singularization for interpreting this behavior. Singularization is the process by which a commodity becomes decommoditized (see also Appadurai 1986). A relatively undifferentiated object is individuated by the consumer through this process, which is paramorphic to management's intent in the practice of branding (Gardner and Levy 1955). Singularization can be tracked in the successive investments and divestitures of meaning associated with a consumer's relationship with an object. Since excessive commoditization homogenizes value, and in this sense is "anticultural," decommoditizing rituals ensure that some things remain unambiguously singular (Kopytoff 1986). Thus, in a Durkheimian sense, culture (through its bearers, i.e., consumers) sacralizes portions of itself; consumers transform a house into a home. Sacralized objects embody the power inherent in cultural integration. Although singularization does not guarantee sacralization at the level of culture, it does allow consumers to bring order to their own world of goods and make sacralization a possibility.

In the trailer campground, artificial nature was brought in to singularize the home. This was not unique to camper parks where people spent the entire summer; similar rituals for settling and designating as sacred were observed at a recreational vehicle park where most people spent only one or two days.

> Some campers have a great many plants about their sites, as if trying to cultivate the illusion of being at home in their

yard, or of somehow having tamed nature while living in its midst.

Rather than finding this a waste of time, the owner of the first camper park mentioned was proud of the work many of the residents had done to decorate their sites. They were proudly demonstrating the lower middle class orientation toward home ownership and care of possessions (Coleman 1983; Levy 1966) by working diligently on their space--even while on vacation. One woman who lived in this park was getting a new trailer. She said that it would take a while before the new place would seem like home, and outlined the ritual transformations she and her husband would use to make it a home. They planned to build a deck around the new trailer, and she was making craft objects to decorate the interior. In addition to the desire to make the trailer more aesthetically pleasing, these rituals serve to singularize and transmute the trailer into a home.

Sacralization may be accomplished in part by imposing one's own identity on possessions through transformations. The urge to change, customize, or just symbolically approrpriate, as with photographs (e.g., Sontag 1973), appears to be strong, as illustrated in this comment by a woman who was renovating the house she shares with her husband and children:

"The first day that we were able to be here, which was two minutes after settlement I guess, we ran in. My husband's stepfather came and photographed inside and outside; and (then we also took pictures of) stages of change as we redid last summer. It's just fun to get those out and remember how, oh, it was awful." (wf, 35)[2]

The photographs are a reminder of the time when this was a profane house. The celebration of such sacralizing transformations is common. A teen-aged male described his months-long work altering his first automobile to make it just the way he wanted it. He ritually cares for the finished car with twice-a-week baptismal washings and a once-a-week anointing with wax.

An elderly informant explained that she and her husband had spent much of their adult lifetimes fixing their home just the way they wanted it. They then purchased a second farm home that they renovated extensively, including putting in a lake. Furniture pieces made from walnut trees removed from the lake site were given to each of three children as

symbols of the transformation of the farm into a singularized home.

"It was such fun to do. Even though you didn't make them yourself, you felt like you were responsible for them." (wf, 65)

Her description unconsciously echoes a mythic theme in *The Odyssey* (Homer, Book 23: 190-204) in which the bed of Odysseus and Penelope is hewn from Zeus's sacred olive tree. Although this informant hired a cabinetmaker, she feels responsible for the pieces because the ideas carried out were hers, as was the case in the restoration of the farm house. The transformation of the trees into furniture provides a tangible object to represent self and family heritage. This was supported by her 35-year-old daughter who observed in a separate interview:

"It's very lovely furniture. But it makes it more than personal; it's like a piece of me." (wf, 35)

The furniture is a ritual symbol of the daughter's connection to her family.

Sacralization Through Pilgrimage. A second means by which an aspect of consumption may be sacralized is through a secular pilgrimage. By secular pilgrimage, we refer to a journey away from home to a consumption site where an experience of intense sacredness occurs. The most extraordinary pilgrimage we encountered among informants was being made by a middle-aged couple and their son traveling by horse-drawn, covered wagons. They had sold their house, truck, and possessions, and had given up jobs and school-based education to roam freely through the American and Canadian West. What was being sacralized through this pilgrimage was the self via self-sufficiency wrung from hardship, and through contamination by the natural sites they visited.

Other secular pilgrimages encountered were being undertaken by people in motor vehicles or on bicycles and were to last either months or weeks. These often involved historic destinations such as Gettysburg, Washington, D.C., and the mansions of Newport, RI. Whereas the first two destinations celebrate nation, the third celebrates the American ethos of wealth and worldly success. Through such pilgrimages, the sacredness of the site is maintained.

Such places are seen as shrines and are often visited on mass pilgrimages by tourists to attain a sacred state of being through contamination. This includes shrines with positive power, such as the Statue of Liberty, as well as those exhibiting kratophanous

---

[2]Parenthetical notations with fieldnote material indicate race, gender, and age.

power, such as the Vietnam Memorial (Lopes 1987; Spencer and Wolf 1986). Secular pilgrimages typically occur during the liminal time of vacation when one is temporally away from the everyday, ordinary world.

In some cases, we encountered groups of pilgrims who had banded together much as the religious pilgrims chronicled by Chaucer (1948/orig. circa 1400). Three males and one female in their early twenties were camping near each other in a national park, although they had only encountered each other that evening. Two were doing long tours by bicycle and the other two had done so previously. A shared sense of values as well as a shared liminal state (Turner and Turner 1978) prompted their camaraderie, as was also true of those participating in the Consumer Behavior Odyssey (Belk 1987c; Sherry 1987a).

Not all persons we encountered traveling were involved in secular pilgrimages. Those moving to a new home were invariably rushing to their next destination, and the interim travel was an annoyance rather than an experience to be enjoyed as a favored state of grace. They were anxious to get to what was sacred to them: a place they could call home.

Sacralization Through Quintessence. Not all sacralized objects are as unique as handcrafted walnut furniture or a cross-country bicycle trip. Some sacred objects seem ordinary, yet are regarded and treated as extraordinary. Initially this puzzled us, particularly for objects that are sacralized and cherished precisely for their similarity to other objects. We observed the sale of jewelry "As seen on Dynasty and Dallas," complete with photographic murals of Linda Evans. We observed the use of Don Johnson cardboard mannequins to sell jackets similar in appearance to those worn on his television show "Miami Vice." While the concept of contamination is at work there, there appears to be something more operating to sacralize commodity objects. It was even more apparent in one automobile enthusiast's explanation that he was a believer in Chevrolets and came from a family of "Chevy people," while another was a "Ford man." Simply put, how can mass-produced, anonymous, commodity-like objects acquire sacred status?

One enlightening concept is quintessence. Quintessential objects possess a "rare and mysterious capacity to be just exactly what they ought to be . . . unequivocally right," according to Cornfeld and Edwards (1983). Objects cited by both Cornfeld and Edwards and Sudjic (1985) as quintessential include the Mont Blanc Diplomat pen, the Swiss Army knife, the Cartier Santos watch, Dom Perignon champagne, the Polaroid SX-70 land camera, Levi's 501 jeans (see also

Solomon 1986), the Zippo lighter, the American Express card, the Wham-O frisbee, the Volkswagen Beetle, Coca-Cola, and Ray Ban sunglasses. What do these products have in common? According to Cornfeld and Edwards (1983, n.p.):

> The pleasure such things offer us is wonderful and illogical; it is very like the pure joy a child feels when he unexpectedly comes into possession of something magically desirable . . . . For while we may use quintessential things for commonplace purposes, they serve as talismans and guideposts, touching our souls with souls of their own.

Sudjic (1985, p. 18) echoes this mystical totemic language.

> Caring about green wellies, or about customized Cortinas are both examples of the practice of using cult objects in a tribal way, for members to identify each other, and to exclude outsiders.

Armstrong (1971, pp. 26, 29) designates an object exhibiting such quintessential qualities as an "affecting presence."

> The . . . affecting presence (is) . . . a self-contained, perpetuating actor on the one hand and a human-perceptor related affectant on the other . . . . Ontologically, the affecting presence is a perpetuating affecting act--a near-being with its unique "personality" continuously exerting its own existence, though it is known only in transaction. It is independent of any source of "meaning" or energy external to itself; being a self-sufficient entity, it is it own "meaning" and provides its own energy.

The metaphors employed in these descriptions indicate that these are sacred objects. They are branded commodities, but give the impression that they are beyond mere commerce. This suggests that sacred objects need not be one of a kind. As with the "Chevy man," for some consumers it is the brand and model that is sacred rather than a specific, personally owned object. Sacred objects are not always singularized (Kopytoff 1986), particularistic, or unique objects. Instead, the item may be seen as unique from other brands, as with the smell of Lysol to some Irish Catholics or the flavor of Oreo cookies to their devotees. Uniqueness theory (Snyder and Fromkin 1980) recognizes a range of such individuation strategies. An example of the mysticism that may attach to such quintessential brands is the furor caused by Coca-Cola's 1985 decision to abandon its age-old formula in favor of a tastier one. Despite positive indications from taste tests, for consumers the magic and mystique were gone. As the quintessential products listed previously suggest, quintessence generally is achieved over a long period of time and is not a process that emanates exclusively from efforts by the producer.

This temporal dimension of the sacred is bound up with authenticity. While museums of art reproductions were once common, our society is currently unwilling to accept such displays as sacred. In our interviews with collectors, authenticity--discerned in various ways, including signatures, numbered prints, first editions, and items produced during a certain period of time--was commonly cited criterion in selecting items for a collection. The quest for quintessence is a quest for authenticity--"The Real Thing" in Coca-Cola's well-chosen vocabulary. However, quintessence is seldom as universal as Coca-Cola's. It may be supported by a cult of "true believers," as with the "Chevy man" mentioned earlier. Alternatively, it may be supported by the celebration of newness in an object, as newness renders the object quintessentially perfect.

Some places were rendered quintessentially sacred by consumers' desire for authenticity. For some informants, the more commercial a place was seen as being, the more it was disparaged. The more natural, real, or authentic it was perceived as being, the more it was treated as a sacred place. Perceiving a place as real is more a matter of having it fit one's prior images or imaginative reconstructions than it is a matter of being factually, historically, or locally accurate, as noted in this field note excerpt concerning a Japanese tourist in his early twenties.

> He exhibited typical Japanese unwillingness to offend by claiming to have difficulty picking a favorite place he's been in America, but he liked the West due to the cowboy flavor of Arizona and New Mexico, and he wants to move to a smaller area of America. He doesn't like the crowded areas and said that the West is like the real America for him.

Disneyland was described by tourists as a marvelous place to bring the family. Still, a tourist at a Midwestern historical museum stressed:

> "It is important to get away from such commercial places and learn about real history." (wm, 50s)

The type of place viewed as quintessentially sacred varies with the informant, but the function of sacred places in vacation pilgrimages remains constant. These places potentiate experience of the sacred by embodying hierophany and kratophany, by enabling communitas, and by being limned with myth by their promoters, as with Disney World (Kottak 1982).

Tourists also regarded as quintessentially sacred those places that they have visited that are exceptionally natural, uncrowded, and unspoiled by other tourists. One woman made such a discovery on her vacation with her husband, as described in this field note excerpt:

> They had not planned to go to Prince Edward Island but heard so many people in Nova Scotia say good things about it that they decided to go. In fact, it was one of their favorite parts of the trip. One 12-mile stretch of the beach was the most beautiful place she had ever been. She said it looked like "God had reached down his hand and touched it." (wf, 60s)

Such places are sacred not only because they are perceived as authentic and unspoiled; there is also some naturism or reverence for nature reflected. An emically driven interpretation is that visiting this place showed the family's resourcefulness in discovering its quintessential beauty and made the family members special and unique for having been there, further singularizing their own sacredness.

Although the intuitive feel for the condition of quintessence may be right, additional work is needed to explore fully the range of such human-object relations (e.g., Csikszentmihalyi and Rochberg-Halton 1981; van Imwagen forthcoming; Wallendorf and Arnould 1988). In this regard, Scarry (1985) notes that apart from attachments to objects that come to represent connections to particular people (a singularized, sacred object), we also are comforted by anonymous and mass-produced objects. They are regarded in many ways as alive, as the bearers of the message, "Whoever you are, and whether or not I personally like or even know you, in at least this small way, be well" (Scarry 1985, p. 292). Quintessential objects bind us culturally, societally, and even globally to a sense of sacred uniformity, which coexists with our desires for individuation (Boorstin 1973; Breen 1988).

Sacralization Through Gift-Giving. Informants identified a fourth means for sacralizing an object, namely through gift-giving. Gifts often have special meaning, and selection of gifts to give to others is clearly different from a commodity purchase. The sacred/profane distinction is evident in

Malinowski's (1922) continuum with pure gifts at one end (no thought of return is involved) and pure trade at the other, and in Mauss's (1925) distinction between pure gifts and pure commodities. When informants purchased objects as gifts, they engaged in one phase of a sacralizing process. Consumers take gift objects from the profane world where they are purchased, systematically remove price markers, and decoratively wrap them (Waits 1978). They ritually exchange these gifts in a ceremony that may involve the mandatory presence of others, decorations, and special clothing (Belk 1979; Caplow 1984; Sherry 1983). These actions separate items from the profane world of commerce, singularize them (Kopytoff 1986), and turn them into gifts.

Since a gift is usually an expression of connection between people, it may take on sacred status. However, some gifts, such as the "free gifts" received in return for purchases or charge account applications, remain profane commodities. Not all gifts are sacred, and not all gifts are equally sacred.

Gifts are hallowed by connection to other sacred elements of life. Tourist sites provide consumers an opportunity to capture the sacredness of the site by buying a gift for those at home, or a souvenir for oneself. In the range of sites we sampled, gift shops were abundantly present: at cheese factories, restaurants, battlefields, castles, theatres, truck stops, recreation vehicle parks, and almost all other tourist sites encountered. Pre- or pseudo-singularized objects (i.e., mass produced artifacts ennobled by the label "gift") available at these shops were purchased and resacralized by consumers; the objects were transformed into gifts or souvenirs. To indicate where the object was obtained and to sacralize it further, the name of the site was often inscribed on it (Gordon 1986; Stewart 1984), as with t-shirts imprinted with images of the Statue of Liberty bought by two elderly informants for their grandchildren. Alternatively, metonyms--objects so closely linked with an experience that they literally embody it (Lakoff and Johnson 1980)--were selected for souvenirs, as with the inexpensive Indian jewelry bought for friends at home by a Japanese college student touring the American Southwest. This contamination by a sacred site visited on a pilgrimage enhances the sacredness of the transformed object (Kelley 1987).

Another type of gift that is often sacralized is one imbued with handwork and labor. Shortly before she died, one informant's grandmother sewed her a sampler; it is a gift that the grandaughter deeply cherishes. It is not the literal content of the poem on the sampler, which the informant could not recall from memory, but rather its symbolic content that makes it sacred for her. Because the

sampler was given to her as a surprise, it is more sacred than the crafts she asks her mother to make. These latter items are closer to commodities, and she refers to these requests as "placing an order." Because she asks for them, they are not as cherished as the gift of the sampler.

In this pattern of meanings, the value-expressive, self-symbolizing character of the sacred is evident. If one of the functions of defining something as sacred is increased social cohesion (Durkheim 1915) or societal integration (Parsons and Shils 1951), then what is selected to be regarded as sacred may be value-expressive for the social group, as well as self-expressive for the individual. This multivocality gives sacred objects much of their symbolic efficacy. Such objects are different from the purely instrumental objects of the profane world. They are not uniform commodities, but are individually singularized (Kopytoff 1986) and collectively expressive. Turner (1967, p. 108) views the central cluster of sacra as the "symbolic template of the whole system of beliefs and values in a given culture."

From the data presented thus far, we might speculate that handmade gifts uniformly express the values of craft and labor. But this is not completely borne out in the rest of the data. In fact, handmade gifts were considered profane by a woman in her sixties who recalled her youth in the rural Midwest.

> She talked about how things were when she was a child. . . . The others thought she was spoiled because she got things that they didn't get to have. She got to have a "boughten" doll and they only had rag dolls. She got to have some "boughten" dresses, although most of them were made at home. She remembers one dress that she had when she was about 4 or 5 years old. It was a "boughten" dress that was very light and had a very full skirt. Her mother put it on her one time and she remembers going out after it rained and playing in the water in it and that dress floated all around her and it felt very nice. She is not sure why she remembers that, but she does.

This would have been during the time when store-bought gifts began to supplant handmade gifts, aided by advertising supporting their appropriateness as gifts (Snyder 1985; Waits 1978). The handmade dresses were profane, while those that were "boughten" in a store were, at that time, considered sacred. The informant recalled a transcendent, magical experience that occurred while wearing the purchased dress. In light of our discussion of department stores as cathedrals of consumption, it is understandable that a "boughten" gift would engender just such an experience for a rural consumer. This experience also suggests that the cultural frames for goods employed by North American consumers (described as an evolutionary sequence by Leiss et al. 1986, p. 179--idolatry, iconology, narcissism, and totemism) may be regionally as well as temporally bounded. There is often a time lag in the diffusion of cultural frames from core to periphery, as well as in adaptation of these frames to local realities. Culture change occurs on a regional basis in such multicultural settings as the contemporary United States.

Gifts indicate the value-expressive nature of the sacred. Gifts handcrafted by the giver allow the giver and recipient to celebrate the values of friendship and singularizing labor. However, when "handmade" represents everyday toil expended to meet profane needs, manufactured goods may become glorified, in part because they represent the belief that technology provides a more comfortable life for consumers. Hand labor is appreciated for specially crafted items, but is superfluous for most of our needs. Technology is valued for providing the advances that give us "boughten" goods. We observed tourists riding in air-conditioned buses arrive at a large swap meet in Amish country, ready to "visit" the land of farmers who don't use contemporary technology, "sample" the foods prepared by the farm women, and buy these "simple folk's" crafts as handmade gifts to take back home. Yet, the tourists gladly boarded the air-conditioned buses at the end of a hot summer day of shopping out-of-doors to return to their everyday lives of technology and "boughten" goods. This dialectic between self and other drives much tourism. We found that both labor and laborsaving technology are more than just core values in our secular world. They are vehicles of hierophany, commitment, and flow. The sacred status of gifts derives from their multivocal ability to express these contrasting values as well as social connections.

Gifts are kratophanous in their ability to separate us from the material world and simultaneously bind us to it. The same woman who described the "boughten" dress discussed the changing role of gifts at Christmas:

She doesn't really remember Christmas gift giving. For her husband, a good Christmas was one when he would get 25 cents worth of candy. She thinks that perhaps Christmas was more of a family celebration then and not so much of a gift-giving time.

Gifts are not as sacred as the connections between people that they are used to signify.

They provide the contemporary material basis for kindred interaction once provided by other sources, such as the "kinship work" of writing letters and making phone calls, organizing gatherings, and communal labor formerly involved in the social reproduction of intimacy (Cheal 1987). For a younger generation, however, the affiliation with the material world is seen more positively. This is true even for an Amish boy growing up in an anti-materialistic religious community.

John's favorite toy is a wooden truck which is about 18 inches long and about 10 inches high. It was given to him as a Christmas present, but he doesn't know where it came from (whether it was bought or made). What John likes most about Christmas is getting gifts. (wm, 8)

The giving and getting, rather than the gift per se--although in our Amish case, the rustic simplicity of the gift itself is telling--are especially significant (Baudrillard 1981) of the sanctity of domestic affiliations.

So gifts acquire sacred status as expressions of deeply held cultural values. Sharing these values, givers and recipients are bound together in a ritual celebration creating and reinforcing social integration. Other gift-giving instances encountered confirm our understanding of this means by which objects attain sacred status. A boy (wm, 12) on vacation at a national historic site with his extended family bought a gift for a family member who did not come on the trip, using money he had earned doing odd jobs for neighbors:

"How does it make you feel to be in a place like this; kind of fun? old?

"Yeah, it makes me feel old; it makes me feel like going back into history. It makes you feel old. It makes you feel like you are in that time."

"What will it feel like when you wear your belt buckle?"

"I don't know. I guess it will feel (pause) make me feel like I'm a soldier or somethin' like that. Or it could give you some sort of, I can't explain. You know how you feel sort of proud? The Civil War makes you feel like you're a General or something like that; like you are in the army . . . ."

"So you will wear your belt buckle and that will kind of bring back what this place is like?"

"Well, the belt buckle's not for me."

"Oh, its not?"

"The belt buckle's for my uncle. So he gets the belt buckle. If I were to have it, I'd probably feel proud."

This gift selection episode creates a nostalgic image of a self-reliant and patriotic boy, proud of imagined military service, enmeshed in neighborhood and familial ties. Through the gift and his adolescent description of what it evokes, he celebrates the meaning of these cultural values using the object as a projectible field (Leiss et al. 1986).

Not all gifts are meaning-laden expressions of cultural values or love. Many are profane objects bought and given in an obligatory fashion. Many such gifts are soon forgotten, put aside, or discarded. Those who are in the business of producing objects to be sold as gifts are not unaware of these issues. One informant was in the business of making and selling dolls of St. Nicholas, Santa Claus, and Father Christmas. She used antique fabric to make the doll clothing as a means of recapturing the past.

> She began making these because she had always loved Christmas. She has had great success and can't keep up with the demand even though she claims to work 18 hours per day. She says she enjoys it. Despite the pressure, she has a representative and is trying to sell her work to gift stores through two major metropolitan merchandise marts. She is concerned that people won't see them as unique and handcrafted at a gift store the way they do at an antique sale (where she now sells them).

Some gift objects echo the values expressed by other kinds of sacred objects, such as the connection to the past of heirlooms, the sense of completion and mastery of collections, or the symbolism of true gifts of the self. This was often found to be the basis for the search for a gift to give on return from a trip. For this gift-giving occasion, the general expectation is that some object will be carried back from the sites visited during the pilgrimage. The ritual is a virtual reenactment of the archetypal monomyth of the heroic quest (Campbell 1949; Sherry 1987a). Buying a gift upon one's return would be inappropriate because it would not transfer any of the sacredness of the vacation to those who did not go. It would fail to allow others to participate in contamination by the sacred places and times that occurred during the vacation. Instead, it would offer them a profane commodity from their everyday world.

Sacralization Through Collecting. A fifth way objects are sacralized is by inclusion in a collection (Belk et al. 1988). Even though each item may not be unique, as with one informant's collection of Hummel figurines, together they are additionally singularized by formation into a collection. Taken as a whole,

collections are regarded by their owners as special, unique, and separate from the everyday items they have and use. The collection is revered and respected by collectors based on a series of superlatives most often involving its size and completeness and the energy and effort that went into assembling it.

Items that are offered for sale, even as collectibles, exist as profane commodities. Once included in a collection, an object acquires sacredness by adding to the completeness of the collection. It is ennobled by its connection to the other items and by adherence to the principles of No-Two-Alike and Unity-in-Diversity (Danet and Katriel 1987). It is also sacralized through the rituals of the hunt and enshrinement in an ordered display. The collection as a whole is sacred partially because it symbolizes attempted completeness and comprehensiveness, neither of which is ever attainable. The collector generally strives to have one perfect example of each kind of a particular item. In categories that are infinitely expansive, the collector gradually narrows the focus (e.g., all "retired" Precious Moments figurines).

Only those that objects somehow add to the completeness of the collection in the eyes of the collector are selected for this conversion. Search may assume proportions of a grail quest, indicating the scarcity of appropriate objects for inclusion. The informant who collects elephant replicas searches for them when he is on vacation, and at flea markets and garage sales, all situations with a possibility of treasure-finding. Once found for a collection, objects then take on meaning beyond their individual existence. They are now part of a set, an element in a larger scheme.

Items in collections may also attain sacred status by being bought in a state of disrepair and then transformed through labor into fine specimens. For example, one informant, an antique collector (wf, 40s), bought a table in disrepair for $3 at an auction. She planned to spend hours restoring it to its once fine condition. Through her investment of personal labor, it would be transformed into a part of a collection. Another collector did this by repairing pocket-watches. Sacredness in collections thus may derive not only from adding some completeness to the set, but also through the investment of oneself (Belk 1988b). This labor theory of value is an "elementary folk theory with deep existential roots" (Cheal 1987, p. 157).

Collectors often sacralize objects by finding and rescuing them from those who do not understand the objects' worth or value. For example, a collector of Mickey Mouse items (wm, 40s) found some original Disney display backdrops at a swap meet, where they were being used as tarps to cover and protect other merchandise that was considered valuable. He was proud to have rescued them and was now using them "appropriately" as backdrops to draw attention to the Disney items he sells. He priced the backdrops at $500 because he did not want to sell them. Folk narratives of such salvations from lucky finds are so common among collectors and swap meet habitués that the stories may be considered collectively as market mythology (Beards 1987) drawing from the theme of religious salvation and conversion.

Rather than being purchased or received in trade, some items in collections are received as gifts. This was true of all of the Hummel figurines of one collector and for some of the items owned by the elephant collector mentioned earlier. Here the object has already entered the realm of the sacred through gift-giving and remains in that realm by joining a collection. Significantly, for the elephant collector, some items were received as gifts from friends and others who had visited the museum, giving the collection a broader social significance for him. He said that he got "mushy and misty-eyed" as he thought about these gifts from museum visitors, some of whom previously had been strangers and one of whom was a movie star. The sacredness of this collection and its signification of his connection to others is enhanced by enshrinement of the gifts in the elephant museum he runs. Visitors to the museum and its related gift shop participate in further sacralization by stopping to pay homage to the significance of elephants, and by their purchases and comments. In the museum, each piece given by someone as a gift is marked with a hand-lettered sign commemorating its origin, as with donations and loans to art collections displayed in art museums. The sacralization of a collection is intensified also by drawing from the sacredness of gift-giving and museums.

Collections are often begun with objects that were given to the collector as a gift. The following excerpt from fieldnotes illustrates the way in which an object is sacralized through gift exchange:

> I talked to one woman (wf,20s) and her mother (wf, 50s) who are looking for a particular "collectible" figurine in the Precious Moments series. She bought one last year when she was here on vacation and now is having the salesclerk see if they have a particular one in stock. She has all of the "retired" figurines (a total of about 20). She got started collecting them when her brother gave her the first one. He also started a collection for his girlfriend. As

> a gift, he pays for her to buy the "Club selections." Sometimes she gives this type of figurine to him as a gift.

This collection began with connections to mystery, since the nature of a gift is initially not know, and ritual, since the role prescriptions incumbent on a gift recipient are observed (Caplow 1984; Sherry 1983). The starter gift nature of this collection is not unlike the friendship symbolized by starter recipes (e.g., sourdough bread, yogurt, brandied fruit) in which the original gift grows to produce more.

However, despite the sacred status of gifts and the sacredness of collections, collectors are not always pleased to receive gifts of the items they collect, as illustrated by the sentiments of a 13-year-old girl who collects Mickey Mouse figures as well as keychains:

> Her collection of Mickey Mouse items was started by someone who returned from Disneyland and brought her a gift. She can't remember who it was who gave it to her (later, off camera, her father tells her it was him). Often people will give her gifts of key chains or Mickey Mouse items. Although she appreciates the gifts, she would prefer to pick out the things for her collection herself. That way she can pick out the things that she likes. She doesn't know how to explain which ones she likes, but does know them when she sees them.

Collections may also be sacred because they are an expression of self. The personal acquisition of collectibles is an investment of self as well as a demonstration of one's hunting ability and persistence in searching for items for the collection. Since vacation travel takes people to new locales, it is often a time to search for additions to collections. Receiving items as gifts for a collection can deny one the opportunity to demonstrate hunting ability and self-expressiveness, and so such gifts may not be desired.

Some collections may be further sacralized because they are based on a more explicit expression of self, as with an informant nicknamed Bunny (wf, 30s), who also collects bunny replicas. This collection serves as a totemic representation of her individual (rather than tribal) identity. It connects the natural category of bunnies to the cultural element of an individual (Levi-Strauss 1962; Sahlins 1976). Through her collection, she simultaneously celebrates herself and nature. Similarly, other informants, women whose husbands are policemen, bought humorous-looking pig doorstops, which served to connect their husbands to a profession and to the animal kingdom. In both cases, the collection serves as a totemic expression of identity.

Finally, collectors sacralize collections by systematically labeling, arranging, and displaying the collection. This quasi-scientific or quasi-artistic activity sacralizes and legitimizes what might otherwise be seen as mere acquisitiveness by giving it a more noble apparent purpose.

Sacralization Through Inheritance. Objects may achieve sacred status through inheritance as family heirlooms (Shammas, Salmon, and Dahlin 1987). Removed from the world of commerce and increasingly singularized, in part by their age, these objects gain uniqueness and contaminating sacredness by their sentimental associations with the owner's past history. Such artifacts are repositories of family continuity (Csikszentmihalyi and Rochberg-Halton 1981; Rochberg-Halton 1986). Their history helps define who the inheritors are, where they came from, and where they are going.

Heirlooms that were handmade, that were worn close to the body (such as jewelry), or that denoted ties to a native land were frequently mentioned by Odyssey informants. In the case of items worn close to the body, there is more contamination and symbolization of the self. Preservation of these closely worn items partakes of positive sacred contamination. Similarly, items from one's native land are from a sacred place, if not a sacred time as well (Belk 1988b). Thus, heirlooms move from the profane realm in which they (or their materials) were purchased into the sacred realm through connection to deceased (primarily same-sex) family members. This sacralization intensifies if accompanied by meanings connecting it to the person's physical body or the symbolic body of the person's native land, as with one informant's cameos from her mother's homeland.

Like collections, heirlooms represent completeness. They indicate that family ties have not been broken by death. In this sense, heirlooms are gifts to the living from the dead and represent the continuity of one generation to the other. Characteristic of the short histories and the nuclear family orientation of Americans, few heirlooms linked to the family longer than from the prior two generations were mentioned by informants. It is not history and long lineage that is being celebrated by heirlooms, but rather the completeness and continuation of the family-- the formal celebration of which is particularly important to upper class families (Bossard and Boll 1950). Even so, as McCracken (1988) speculates, caring for family heirlooms may be decreasingly common as societies become

more mobile and materialistic. The logistics of maintenance, storage, display, and dispersal may dictate less curatorial forms of familial ritual.

Sacralization Through External Sanction. An object may be sacralized through sanction by an external authority. The enshrinement of a piece in a museum is one indicator of such recognition and the most common encountered during the Odyssey. That tourists bowed to the external authority of museums was evident in their quiet, reverential tones and formal conversations concerning the importance of relics on display--whether farm implements of the nineteenth century, possessions of Ellis Island immigrants, artworks and mansions of turn-of-the century robber barons, or even elephant replicas.

In mansions of the nouveaux riches, such as those at Newport, Rhode Island, preserved furnishings showed that the former owners had sought the blessing of famous architects and artists. Often rooms and furnishings had been moved en masse from castles and chateaux. Treasures of European cathedrals and royalty had been purchased to sacralize and cleanse the often ruthlessly attained wealth of the nouveaux riches. During the owners' lives, some art treasures were further sacralized by external authorities through loans to museums and world expositions. When the mansions became public museums, heirs received the additional blessing of historical societies, art curators, and guides, who interpret these wonders for tourists.

Summary of Ways of Achieving Sacredness. In summary, sacredness adheres in certain aspects of consumption through seven different processes: ritual, pilgrimage, quintessence, gift-giving, collecting, inheritance, and external sanction. With the exceptions of quintessence and external sanction, these sacralizing processes are enacted purposely by consumers in an effort to create sacred meaning in their lives. Whether social or individual in nature, each sacralizing process separates objects, people, and experiences from the world of the profane and imbues them with precious, positive sacredness. Other processes then serve to maintain the sacred status and prevent the encroachment of the profane.

Perpetuating Sacredness

Ecstatic as one might feel upon having contact with the sacred through an object, person, place, or experience, sacred status may be lost through habituation, forgetting, or encroachment of the profane. To prevent this loss, ongoing efforts are required to maintain sacredness. Four means for maintaining sacredness in consumption that emerged from analysis of our data are separation of the sacred from the profane, performance of sustaining rituals, continuation through inheritance, and tangibilized contamination. For each, there is a related avenue of desacralization that these maintenance activities are designed to prevent.

Separation of Sacred from Profane. Often we found the sacred separated, either temporally or spatially, from the profane to minimize the likelihood of unwanted contamination. Collections were separated from other objects to reinforce their sacred, non-utilitarian status and to prevent their entrance into the profane world where they might be consumed or used. The elephant collection was in a museum joining a gift shop filled with elephant replicas for sale. This separation prevented any confusion that items in the collection might be for sale. As a test of this notion, we asked the collector if he ever moves anything out of the museum collection and places it for sale in the gift shop. He responded:

"Never."

"Why not?"

"I wouldn't want to do that. I just don't want to do that. It would be, like, I don't know, like it would be *wrong*. It would seem wrong to me. It really would."

"What would that do? What would that do to the collection; what would that do to you?"

"I think it would lose some of its grandeur or something. It would not be as important if I was able to just put this elephant out in the store and sell it. People would say, "Well, my heavens, he just sells what he wants to whenever he wants to.' But I don't want to do that. When I buy a piece, it's because I really want it for the collection. I have had people offer me some nice sums for pieces in here, I mean, at times when I really could have used a nice sum, and it was difficult to say, 'No.' But I said, 'No'; if I liked it that well and I bought it, then it must be important to the collection, so I am going to keep it there."

"So once a piece joins the collection, then it stays with the collection?"

" . . . it becomes the collection. It's part of it. It's going to stay there, *period.*"

This collector's behavior may be somewhat extreme, but it gives bold relief to similar separations that other people employed to preserve the sacred status of certain possessions. When an item is sacred to someone, it is regarded as beyond price and will not be sold under any circumstances (Stewart 1984). Compliance with the self-imposed rule of "never sell" applied so absolutely to sacred objects that informants were surprised we would even ask if they would consider selling them. This logic explains the behavior of a Mickey Mouse collector/dealer and an antique collector/dealer who found it unthinkable that they would use items from their collections at home as merchandise. The only collector/dealers who mixed their merchandise with their own collections were two novice dealers who each had a mental understanding, if not a spatial representation, of things that were not for sale.

Artists selling their work separated the sacred creation from the profane sale in several ways. The male sculptor mentioned in the opening vignettes did not discuss the price or sale of his work; instead, his sister handled the business end of things. The woman at a swap meet selling handcrafted dolls, which she called her "babies," used different inflection and voice tone to refer to the dolls as commodities versus the dolls as babies. She kissed the "baby" as she sold the doll (one object with two communicative voices) and personified the transaction as sending her children into the world to bring happiness to someone who would love the "baby." In so doing, she emotionally, if not physically, separated the sacred from the profane.

Similarly, a painter/sculptor (wf, 50s) was willing to sell some of her works, but regarded other pieces as part of a serial collection in which she possessed items sequentially rather than simultaneously. She didn't want to part with her work until she had enjoyed it sufficiently. To prevent premature sale, she posted prohibitive prices on certain works and raised the price if she received serious inquiries. The collector/dealer of Mickey Mouse memorabilia followed the same tactic, and each time someone showed an interest in buying one of his favorite pieces, he raised the price. This pricing structure protects the sacred by preventing its entry into the profane world of commerce. Exorbitantly high prices confirm the sacred value of these artifacts, and the sacrifice of not accepting a high price offer is a further means by which the collector/dealer pays reverence to the sacredness of these objects.

Breen (1988) shows how rituals of non-consumption in the mass consumer boycotts of English goods were instrumental both in giving America colonists a sense of nation and in precipitating the American Revolution. Boycotts serve to avoid sacralizing profane consumption objects by mixing them with sacred objects in the home. By refusing to continue to enshrine English goods in their homes and in their lives, boycotting colonists refused to accept the authority of the British

Crown as either divine or legitimate to rule over them.

Home is a sacred space that provides separation from the profane everyday world, although certain areas within the home are viewed as more sacred than others (Altman and Chemers 1984). Societies differ with respect to whether communal public space or individual private space is more sacred (Tuan 1982). In contemporary Western society, the sacredness of the individual and of privacy or separation from others have gained dominance. Rochberg-Halton (1984) found that the room regarded as most special differed among three generations. About half of the children ages nine to 14 cited their bedrooms, whereas adults were likely to cite the living room where social life is enacted. Older adults (70+) cited their bedrooms, presumably because they increasingly lived their lives there. What is sacred, then, in home life is not necessarily a family gathered around the radio or hearth, as in a Norman Rockwell painting. Instead, the oldest and youngest generations in the United States are likely to harbor private treasures in their individual rooms.

Sacred possessions were separated from more functional (but similar appearing) profane objects in informants' homes. Some heirloom spoons in one home were hanging on the wall to indicate that these spoons were for viewing, not use. In another home with a bunny collection, ceramic bunny soup tureens were displayed to indicate they were not used for serving soup, at least not on ordinary occasions. Similarly, a woman who collected functional but fragile black amethyst glassware stored it on a plate rail above the kitchen cabinets, where she kept dishes that were used everyday. A grocery store owner who collected antique product packages kept them in display cases in his office, locked away from the salable grocery products that filled the shelves of the store. Collectors who sometimes used items from their collections were careful to do so only on special occasions. For example, car collectors showed these sacred possessions only at car shows or drove them in special parades and car club outings. All of these strategies maintain sacredness by separating the sacred from the profane.

Another way of maintaining object sacredness is to separate it from the profane by designating a particular space for it, creating, in effect, an enshrinement. This is evident in the elephant collection housed in a museum created for this purpose. Another informant (wf, mid-30s) preferred a separate place of honor on her bedroom wall for a sampler made by her grandmother, while non-family-made samplers could be decoratively clustered together. Fragile collections are often stored behind glass-doored cabinets in living and dining rooms that are often treated as tabernacles by adults. The items are ritually enshrined and placed in prominent areas of the house to be revered and to cast their spells on the inhabitants, while also being separated from the profane. The collector/dealer of Mickey Mouse items used to keep his collection in its own room at home, but his seven-year-old son was frightened to go into "the Mickey room," illustrating the kratophany of the sacred and acknowledging its potentially destructive power. This collector also acknowledged the "ruin and destruction" that occurs when collecting overpowers the collector and becomes addictive. By keeping the collection locked away, this kratophanous power is kept under control and separated from everyday life.

When people move from one home to another, they often become concerned about the safety of their sacred objects, which are used as vessels to transfer sacredness from one home to another. Their concern emerges, in part, because the sacredness housed in these objects must pass successfully through the profane, everyday world before reestablishment in the new home. This is reminiscent of Aeneas's flight form his home with his household gods on his back (*Aeneid,* III: 15-19). The items moved may be valuable or breakable, as with ceramic figurines and a fragile heirloom doll, or ordinary-appearing, such as an old washboard. Sometimes, people live for an interim period in a liminal house before moving into the home destination. This was the case with one couple moving out of a farmhouse to live in a small summer kitchen building for a year while a new dwelling, a reconstructed log house, was completed. The interim house was not imbued with sacredness. In fact, like another couple interviewed, they planned to keep many possessions in storage during the interim time. However, the sacred assemblage will later be brought together to transform and sacralize the newly built space. The couple was preparing for this interim period by sorting and reconsidering the status of the wide variety of objects they had acquired in their life together.

In a number of informants' homes, sacred objects were assembled together in decorative shrines, often on the mantle above the hearth, as with one young couple who noticed during the interview that all of the items displayed on the mantle had been wedding gifts. In homes without a hearth, such assemblages may be displayed in the front room on the television set. For example, one collector of native American replicas clustered an American Indian whirligig gift, a crocheted afghan, and a crying Christ head together in the front room. Likewise, an informant who is a passionate writer/researcher and jazz collector has a room in his home that contains his jazz records, his Steinway baby grand piano, and his current writing work. Similarly, a woman who had moved across the country for a one-year period described her preservation strategy.

> "Did you ship the watermelon collection out here?"
> No. Those kind of things I was kind of afraid to. That's the kind of stuff that *means* (touches heart) something to me: things we've collected, like on our honeymoon, or whatever. I would be real upset. I'd rather live without them for a year than risk having it all get busted." (wf, late 20s)

As with people who do not use sacred items for fear of breakage, this couple lived without some special things for a year rather than risk profaning them through breakage or loss. Their fears were realistic because some expensive but profane possessions, such as a microwave oven, were broken in the move.

In summary, spatial and temporal separation of the profane from the sacred was evident across contexts. There was no evidence that the sacred and profane can mix with impunity and maintain sacredness. The boundaries are permeable, but well guarded. Nevertheless, there were some instances of deliberate termination of sacred status, accomplished through mixing the sacred with the profane.

Somewhat ironically, given the elevated place of money in contemporary society, the most general way the sacred is desacralized is to turn it into a salable commodity, and thus desingularize it. This explains the exuberance of one informant upon selling her ex-husband's left-handed golf clubs at a swap meet. She had desingularized the last remaining object that symbolized him, and converted it into a commodity. Entrance into the world of commerce through conversion to cash commodifies what was previously sacred.

Our language in referring to dwellings makes this separation between (profane) housing--"a commodity . . . produced primarily for profit"--and (sacred) dwelling--which is "without economic value in any direct sense" (Saegert 1985, p. 295). Dovey (1985, pp. 53-54) also separates the profane house and the sacred home on the basis of the consideration of money:

> In the modern world, the house is a commodity involving substantial economic commitment. It is an investment of economic resources that yields profit and power. As such, the house has become increasingly similar to other products--being bought and sold, used and discarded like a car or washing machine. Home, on the other hand, involves a commitment not of money, but of time and emotion. It is the place where we invest dreams, hopes, and care. Although we can buy the props and freedom that make such an investment possible and secure, the phenomenon of home itself cannot be commoditized . . . . Yet the increasing commoditization of the house engenders a confusion between house and home because it is the image of home that is bought and sold in the marketplace.

Kopytoff (1986), like Marx (1972/orig. 1867), sees a general "drive to commoditization" in capitalist society. It is disturbing to many that everything can be bought and sold, leaving little that is sacred. However, informants were quick to point out what they would not sell. A show horse owner (wf, 20s) explained to us that her horse is "not a business," meaning that it was removed from the profane world of commerce.

Yet the language of commoditization is pervasive. Fromm (1947) argued that even people are commoditized when we market ourselves and take on "market personalities." Hyde (1983) cautions that when artists and scholars turn from presenting their work as a gift, and instead make profit a primary goal, they sow the seeds of destruction of their own creativity because no sacred soul remains in the work. Haug (1986) is among the many Marxist writers who see marketing as appropriating the sacred for selling purposes, leaving little that remains sacred after such appropriation.

The controversy attending the recent "Baby M" case, which has prompted a consideration of the propriety of commercial surrogate motherhood, illustrates the concern over commoditization (Kingsley 1987). It is difficult for many to accept that the sacred concept of motherhood is not above money. Believing that sacredness is a situational rather than absolute attribute whose boundary is inherently dangerous, van Gennep (1909) viewed *rites de passage* as protective rituals that define entrance to a new status. In a world in which surrogate mothers can be hired to bear one's children, the notion of such sacralizing and desacralizing rites is all but lost.

Although money can desacralize, this is not always the case in contemporary society. As Real (1975, p. 40) notes:

> When Duke Snider, center-fielder for the Brooklyn Dodgers, published an article in the *Saturday Evening Post* in the middle 1950s admitting "I Play Baseball

for Money," there was a tremor of scandal that ran through the American public, as if a clergyman had said he did not much care for God but he liked the amenities of clerical life. But when Mercury Morris was asked on national television after the Dolphins' one-sided Super Bowl VIII victory, "Was it fun?" he replied, "It was work," and no one batted an eye.

A possible interpretation here is that the focus on money has desacralized sports. However, it appears that, like quintessential objects in the marketplace and artworks that are sacralized by a high purchase price, sports stars are no longer desacralized by high salaries and may even be sacralized by them. If players were interchangeable robots, commoditization would result and fans would no longer view them as sacred heroes.

So money is not a sufficient indicant of commoditization in contemporary Western culture. Desmonde (1962) traces the flow of sacred symbols from religious to secular contexts by showing how traditional religious symbols were transferred to one essential component of a consumption-venerating society: money. In consumer culture, "mammon" retains its etymological denotation of "that in which one places one's trust," as well as its biblical connotation of "disorder" (Haughey 1986). Money is so strongly symbolic that it presents an intriguing dialectic between good-sacred and evil-sacred. In contemporary society, money is never merely profane or ordinary; it has a kratophanous power that at alternate times serves both beneficent and evil ends. Money can singularize as well as commoditize.

Because mixing the sacred with the profane threatens to destroy the sacred, advertising is often seen as a threat, having the potential to trivialize the sacred by its copresence. For example, on commercial TV in Great Britain, the juxtaposition of advertising with broadcasts of royalty and religion are two such threats (Laski 1959). Legislation enacted in 1954 prohibits advertising within two minutes before and after any broadcast of royal occasions. With religion, as with art, advertising threatens to banish the ecstasy achieved in formerly sacred contexts. The other threat is that commodities seek to appropriate the sacredness of royalty, art, or religion through contamination. This appears to be the concern of critics such as Berger (1972), Hudson (1987), and Williamson (1986), who find it offensive that advertising should feature art masterpieces or religious figures. Outrage at the use of Beatles music in television commercials for Nike shoes echoes this concern.

Experiencing what was previously considered sacred as now mixed with the profane produces emotional reactions of loss. For example, certain actors and actresses have their names imprinted on stars on a Hollywood sidewalk, but one informant was disappointed by recent choices.

"I was amazed at the Walk of Fame that they give stars to anyone. They had a star, I mean like Peter Frampton. I mean he was famous for like fifteen minutes. Now he's got a star for all eternity. You know, that's like real strange." (wm, late 20s)

He was disturbed because the inclusion of these supposed stars profaned what he had considered a sacred context. He lamented the loss of this illusion.

Desacralization by mixing the sacred and the profane occurs through two related phenomena: kitsch and decontextualization. Kitsch refers to decorative objects of bad taste that are popular with the masses, as with one informant's whimsical decorative pink flamingo. Discussions of kitsch imply that such objects are an offense to something sacred (e.g., Highet 1972); however, the precise nature of this offense is seldom agreed upon. In the case of religious kitsch, such as a sentimental rendering of Christ or a picture of the Virgin Mary painted on a seashell, the offense seems to be an inappropriate mixing of the sacred and the profane. Dorfles (1969) and Pawek (1969) worry that religious kitsch lead the faithful away from religion rather than toward it. In other cases, the offense seems to an inappropriate mixing of these pieces that makes them disposable rather than timeless (Schroeder 1977). In the case of kitsch souvenirs, the offense has been characterized as taking an object out of context inappropriately and turning it into a mere commodity (Gregotti 1969). This reflects both the commoditization discussed previously and decontextualization discussed next. Given the proprietary attitude of the upper class toward fine arts as a class marker (Lynes 1980), kitsch may represent to them a threat to desacralize fine art and may elicit an elitist fear of disenfranchisement.

Perhaps the most telling interpretation of the offense entailed in kitsch is the argument that it is inauthentic (Stewart 1984). Kitsch is charged with dealing with superficiality rather than substance (Brown 1975), with being turned out mechanically (Greenberg 1946), and with offering spurious value (Giesz 1969). The charge of inauthenticity is similar to charges of forgery or reproduction in art (see Belk 1987b) and to MacCannell's (1976) arguments concerning the "staged authenticity" experienced by the tourist. Inauthenticity charges that kitsch lacks the magic and power of the truly sacred, but pretends to sacredness through its associative representations and use.

A related desacralizing mixture of the sacred and the profane is decontextualization. This offense against the sacred involves removing it from its context or place of origin. Arnheim (1987) speaks of sculptures and paintings being "kidnapped" by museums and "torn from (their) moorings in space and time" (Arnheim 1987, p. 682). What seems to be threatened here is the sacredness of the time and place in which the art originated rather than the sacredness of the art object per se. Putting the London Bridge in Arizona may or may not lessen the sacredness of the bridge itself, but it does threaten to lessen the sacredness of old London. The outpouring of emotion, much of it outrage, in connection with the restorative cleaning of the Sistine Chapel ceiling, which is literally shedding new light on Michelangelo's paintings (Pope-Hennessy 1987), is another example of the power of decontextualization.

Sustaining Rituals to Prevent Rationalization and Habituation. Because sacred objects may begin to seem ordinary and profane over time, ritual maintenance is sometimes needed to preserve and revivify their sacred status. Meals, holidays, vacations, and other such family rituals not only sacralize the objects they involve, they do much to maintain the sacred status of the family.

The elephant replicas collector has performed a number of rituals to preserve the sacred status of his collection. Each time he has moved, he has packed the whole collection carefully. Before he started the Elephant Museum, he kept some things in boxes, rather than risk breaking them in the unpacking. He has been through three floods and has unpacked and repacked all of the items each time with no losses. It was this packing and unpacking that convinced him to open the museum, where he could share the collection with others. He feels that he preserves the sacred status of his collection through sharing it with those who visit the museum. He mentioned that elephant families stay together for life. In a sense it is a form of eternal life that he is trying to ensure for the collection and, by extension, for himself, through these rituals.

For an informant with some monogrammed heirloom silver spoons, sacredness-maintaining rituals include cleaning, repair, and display. The soft, silver spoons had some dents that she had removed after receiving the spoons from their mother-in-law. She then had the spoons mounted and framed to hang in her dining room. Another

informant had restored an heirloom quilt from her mother, as described in this fieldnote excerpt.

> The woman selling raffle tickets . . . had restored her mother's patchwork quilt and uses it in her home. It is draped over a quilt rack and used on a bed when it is needed. It had been mildewed from being packed away and a number of pieces had to be replaced. She anticipates that her daughter will take this quilt and keep it in the family.

Through her investment of labor and care in the object, she prevented it from becoming profane junk and restored its sacred status, which will be preserved by passing it on to her daughter. This fetishistic investment of labor in an object recompenses its neglect over the years. Once its sacred status is restored, it must then be preserved, having come dangerously close to vanishing. Similar levels of attention to a sacred heirloom in disrepair were reported by other informants who stripped furniture, sewed dolls back together, and oiled tools. These are not sacralizing actions, but rather are rituals that restore and maintain sacredness.

This type of restoration was described by an informant who has an heirloom that she had refinished to allow its sacred nature to shine through:

> "I have a tea wagon . . . in the dining room, . . . a little teacart that my coffee service is on, that belonged to my grandmother, that I just had refinished. It had been painted when that antiquing look was in that you painted furniture, and then you rubbed that sort of black paint over it to make it look old. And it had several layers of paint on it. I did not do the refinishing, but I decided that it is a pretty enough piece that I'd have it refinished. So that's kind of a special piece." (wf, early 30s)

Through a cleansing ritual, the once-sacred heirloom was restored. It is as if through this act of duty, the cart's glory can now shine through, as it could not when the black paint was profaning it. Oddly, for the relative who chose to put the black antiquing paint on, this was probably seen as a way of making an ugly piece more attractive. It seems odd that someone would "antique" an antique, but this too was probably done to try to resingularize the piece. This woman's refinishing of the piece restores its sacred status for her.

However, preserving sacred status in heirlooms does not always mean restoring items to their original condition. It may involve maintaining the imperfect condition of an object when imperfections serve as sacred marks of use by family members. One woman explained the logic of this approach, as noted in this fieldnote excerpt:

> Rene had a commode at home that was passed down to her by her mother who got it from her mother (Rene's grandmother). It has been used by each of her children as a dresser in their rooms. Her husband refinished it and took nine coats of paint off of it. He was trying to take off the cigarette stains from when her brother had it, but she told him not to take those off because "those make it even more precious." (wf, 40s)

Maintenance of an heirloom's sacredness then does not always mean preservation in the way that a museum or seller might approach the object. Unlike the marks of a famous person, these do not increase the object's economic value. However, preserving the cigarette marks makes the object more sentimentally valuable and sacred by preserving the extended self of a family member.

The sacredness of other heirlooms is maintained by ritual prohibitions against use. To use these objects would desacralize them by making them mere utilitarian commodities. During one interview, a woman in her mid-thirties corrected the interviewer who mentioned some toys in the living room.

> "I noticed a number of toys around. In the family room, there were toys, and in the library you called it, there were some toys. But in the *living room* there were some toys. There were some dolls . . ."
> "Oh (eyebrows raised and knowing smile comes to face--emphatically), there are not. They're not toys! There should not be toys in there. They're just sort of collectibles I guess . . . There's an old piece in there; a bed in there that was his grandmother's that has a doll; a chaise bed of sorts. So that's in there, and its got some dolls on it, but they're not for play. And there are some stuffed animals in there that used to be my husbands's when he was a child. So they're kind of fond favorites, I guess." (wf, mid-30s)

The items are, in fact, antique toys, but are now viewed by the informant as decorative objects removed from the profane world in which they might be used in play. Here the owners ritually comply with the self-imposed rule of "Never Use."

Some heirlooms are used, but only on ritual occasions. That is, they are separated temporally from the profane and are employed ritually. One informant (wf, mid-30s) has a lace tablecloth that was passed on to her by her grandmother. She uses it on holidays (sacred times when the family is brought together for ritual behavior) and on other "special occasions," but never for everyday use. The continuation of tradition in this way sustains the sacred status of the tablecloth as it further enhances it.

The sacredness of a place is also maintained by adherence to ritual behaviors. For example, informants at a weight loss resort were concerned about how they would be able to transfer their rituals at the resort to their home life. Many thought they would try, but would probably not be successful. They in essence admitted that the magic resides in the place and all that occurs there. They were not hopeful that they would be able to recreate this magic at home. The magical transformation that they hoped would occur was a result of their ritualistic exercise, dieting, and massages during their stay. Their daily regimen involved the abundant use of water (drinking it, swimming in it) making them feel cleansed in the transformation and intensifying their regard for the resort as a sacred place and their stay as a sacred time. For one woman, the resort "feels like home" because she has the same room each year and over time has come to know many of the others who come here. To her, the place exemplifies the American dread of achievement of one's goals, the importance of physical perfection, and stability over time. It is a place of baptism and rebirth, sacrifice and salvation. Through ritual, it maintains sacredness that is too fragile to transfer to the everyday world.

Gift-giving is a ritual that may be used not only to sacralize, as discussed earlier, but also to maintain the sacredness of personal goods, as with some informants' gifts to us intended to preserve our close connections to them. When we sometimes offered reciprocal gifts, they were refused, as they would have commoditized the interaction. We were given gifts of postcards to use as interview stimuli, candy, a handcrafted leather flyswatter, rides to get gasoline when we had run out, and dinners prepared in our honor.

The informants traveling by covered wagon had grown accustomed to being photographed by curious tourists, and a sign beside their wagon read, "Donations Appreciated for your Photos." As we had stopped, photographed them, conducted a video interview and come to know them rather well, it was unclear whether they would expect payment from us. When we mentioned that we would like to give them something for the rich insights they had given us, they refused the cash offer saying, "You don't have to do that!" When we responded by saying, "We know we don't *have* to do it, we just want to," the interaction returned to the sphere of gift-giving. The verbal exchange was a desanctifying and reconsecrating ritual to preserve the friendship while still permitting economic transfer. Under other circumstances, no amount of ritualistic framing can excuse irreverence. Clearly, for example, one should not accept a dinner invitation from friends and then leave a cash payment. The only acceptable "payment" is a reciprocal social offering that keeps the interaction in the sacred social realm rather than in the profane, commercial realm.

Despite numerous rituals designed to maintain sacredness, habituation and rationalization constantly threaten to desacralize the sacred. In habituation, movement from the sacred to the profane occurs in a way that is gradual enough to be little noticed as some objects become worn and familiar. But time may also restore objects to a sacred status, as was explained in this fieldnote excerpt by one antique dealer/collector:

> What is interesting to her is that the nice pie safes, which are popular as living room cupboards now, used to be kitchen pieces, but many of them are now found out in chicken coops. Her business brings them back into the house.

Initially, the object loses its sacredness and is relegated to more profane areas of the home. But then, when it is old enough to become appealing to antique collectors, it moved through the world of commerce into a more sacred position than that which it initially held (Thompson 1979). We observed the same movement with other old, functional pieces, such as carpet beaters now hung on the wall as decorative items and a tramp's cupboard that hung above one informant's desk. While newness may initially sacralize an object as being quintessential, irreverence creeps in with time. Later, someone again sees the object's potential for sacredness and saves it from obscurity.

Rituals also attempt to prevent rationalization, which may desacralize the sacred in two ways. The first is that to bring rational argument to bear on the sacred is to rob it of its essential mystery and hierophanous power. For example, this was seen by Weber (1958/orig. 1904) to have occurred when science split from art, producing the "disenchantment of the world." It occurs when the scientist dissipates the beauty of the rainbow by dismissing it as light reflected and refracted in air-suspended water droplets (Belk 1986). It is the same diminution of magic thought to occur when the Santa Claus myth is exploded for the child. Such rationalized views are seldom capable of

retaining the mystery, ritual, and power of former understanding and, thus, are likely to diminish sacredness.

A second way rationalization desacralizes is by offering principled excuses for ignoring, discarding, or otherwise failing to treat something with the "proper" respect. One of our informants, who raises mice to sell to pet stores or give to "good homes," rationalizes that she takes only "the mice with lousy dispositions or poor personalities" to feed to her snakes. Several small-scale pet breeders we interviewed rationalized the sale of their beloved animals by assuring us that they made sure that the animals were going only to good homes. There was undoubtedly some sincerity in this desire, but there was also an element of rationalization in turning these living beings into salable commodities. They avoided acknowledging this transformation by viewing the sale as a ritual to continue the love and affection given to the animal.

Similarly, informants discarding or selling sacred heirloom furniture or memory-laden baby clothes often suggested that someone else would make better use of them. There was an element of truth in this claim, but the need to offer such explanations suggests an element of rationalization as well. Explaining that something is the "logical thing to do under the circumstances" demystifies behavior and moves the object out of the realm of the sacred. Similarly, while the collection as a whole is sacred, some collectors are willing to convert particular items from the collection into profane, salable commodities, provided that they first find a replacement item that is "better" (e.g., a plate from a manufactured collectors' series to replace a similar, chipped plate already in the collection).

Sacred consumption may be profaned when consumers are not sufficiently reverential and do not follow prescribed rituals. MacCannell (1976, p. 43) describes tourist crowding at natural wonders as "profaning the place" in the eyes of other (presumably more serious) tourists. The burning or dragging of a flag through the streets is an act of intentional desecration of a sacred symbol, just as an overly stylized performance of the national anthem may be seen as irreverent (Rook 1984). Several informants mentioned that children weren't allowed in particular areas of their houses for fear certain items might be damaged or marred by fingerprints.

Rituals existed for some intentional desacralizations we observed. These transformation rituals are used to redefine the object's status with respect to the sacred/profane dimension. Because these rituals often preceded the disposition of formerly sacred items, they may be seen as the divestment rituals that McCracken (1986) speculated might exist. For example, a woman mentioned earlier gladly sold her ex-husbands' golf clubs at a swap meet as a ritualistic way of cleansing herself of his presence in her life. By moving the golf clubs into the realm of the profane, she cleared him out of her life. She was quite cognizant of this, and she and her women friends did a little dance of joy after the sale, saying "That's the end of him."

In summary, ritual maintains the separation between sacred and profane, ensuring that what is to remain in the sacred realm does not slip away. Other rituals transform that which was previously sacred into its now appropriate profane state, ensuring that only that which is marked by the ritual passes through the transformation.

Bequests. Bequests are a third mechanism found for preserving the sacred status of certain consumption objects and experiences. Some collectors attempt to ensure the continued sacred status of their collections after their death by planning to will them to descendants as heirlooms. For example, the collector of elephant replicas plans to leave his collection to his granddaughter, who was only a year old at the time of our interview. He wants to preserve "the grandeur" of the collection by bequeathing it in such a way that it will become an heirloom. If the collection remains intact, he "imagines history will stand in awe of what he did." Through his will, he hopes to invoke wider compliance to the "Never Sell" rule mentioned earlier.

A woman in a quilt-making group believes there are bequest "rules" that protect a family's heirlooms, as mentioned in this fieldnote excerpt:

> She says that the rule is to give sons property and money and to give daughters possessions and heirlooms, because they will stay in the family and be passed on to granddaughters that way; otherwise the son's wife may get a hold of them and this is not desirable, presumably because in case of divorce they might take them, and the family tradition would stop.

We can interpret this statement as implying that heirlooms will be passed matrilineally, whereas wealth will be passed patrilineally, an interesting hypothesis, particularly in light of the complexity of contemporary family structures. This rule also suggests that women nurture relationships and the heirlooms that symbolize these relationships, as has been found in other research (e.g., Wallendorf and Arnould 1988). It also suggests the converse, namely that women, in the image of a termagant, have the power to willfully destroy family traditions through appropriation of its symbols. Thus, when sacred heirlooms are prevented from entering the profane world by keeping them in the family, the family is nurtured and preserved.

There was wide understanding and acceptance of such rules among informants. The woman whose mother had furniture made for her from walnut trees cut down at their horse farm has placed that furniture only in certain rooms of her house. A piece inscribed with her initials is in the living room, a space reserved only for adults. A set of four-poster beds is used in her four-year-old daughter's room, but not in the room used by her stepdaughter when she visits. Even by their placement in the house, these objects speak of "real" family connections.

We also encountered heirloom preservation by males. When the heirloom furniture handcrafted by an informant's deceased father was damaged in a flood, he chose to work on restoring these pieces and his father's tools before reclaiming anything else in the house. An antique collector (bm, early 40s) who was also becoming a dealer, had some pieces that were heirlooms. Although he was anxious to get his business started, he said he would never sell the family heirlooms. And a man with three garages full of accumulated, usable objects to share with neighbors also had some heirloom tools that had belonged to his father. These were substantially more significant to him and would be passed on to his male heirs. Although not universal, there does appear to be a general pattern of maintaining the sacredness of connection to same-sex parents and family members through heirlooms.

The counterpart to maintaining sacredness through inheritance is losing sacred reverence for objects through lack of an appreciative heir. This was a frequent concern of collectors. The collector of elephant replicas does not want to leave his collection to his wife or daughter because he doesn't expect that either of them would carry on the museum after he dies. His fear is that the collection would be sold piece by piece on an auction block. Therefore, although the granddaughter is very young, he thinks she already enjoys elephants and hopes to bequeath the collection to her.

Why should heirs reject the responsibility of caring for the collection of a close family member? More than disinterest seems to be involved. Because collections are almost always the focus of intense attention in accumulating, classifying, maintaining, and displaying the assembled items, they normally take a great deal of the collector's time. Family members who do not share an interest in the collection may come to see it as a rival in winning their loved one's time, devotion, and attention. Resentment, perhaps unspoken, is to be expected under such conditions. Thus, to care for a deceased collector's objects of devotion may be seen as tantamount to caring for a spouse's or parent's mistress or lover.

Tangibilized Contamination. Besides rituals that allow objects to become associated with the owners and their histories, the sacredness of fleeting experiences and once-encountered places is preserved, it is hoped, through souvenirs and photographs. This is a process of tangibilizing contamination through an object. When places visited are regarded as sacred, the time spent there is also sacred (MacCannell 1976). In addition, items overtly intended as souvenirs, as well as more idiosyncratic mementos, may be regarded as sacred. They hold the contagious property of the sacred (Steward 1984). Gordon (1986) notes five types of sacred souvenir icons:

1. Pictorial images (e.g., photographs, postcards);

2. Pieces-of-the-rock (e.g., seashells, pinecones);

3. Symbolic shorthand (e.g., miniature Eiffel Tower, toy Loch Ness monster);

4. Markers (e.g., "Grand Canyon" t-shirt, restaurant matchbook cover); and

5. Local product (e.g., olive oil from Greece, local clothing).

In each case, some logical or symbolic reminder is sought in order that the memories attached to the visit will remain vivid and "real." Evidently there is also a status motive, since such souvenirs often visibly proclaim the visit to others. We may also include in the category of tangibilized contamination the personal memento, such as pressed flowers from a suitor, wine bottle labels from a significant meal, and ticket stubs from a concert attended. Souvenirs may also represent sacred persons who touched, autographed, or owned the item. This is illuminated by home buyers in Beverly Hills who are willing to pay more for houses that formerly belonged to prominent stars, an indication that used goods are sometimes worth more than new goods and that sacredness may be reflected in price.

The experience of being in a special place, such as a vacation site, is preserved through mementoes, souvenirs, and photographs for later savoring and enjoyment. Tourists do not seem to mind that their photographs will be exactly like those of all other tourists. In fact, this duplication is viewed as a mark of authenticity, confirming the validity of the tourist's experience (MacCannell 1976). At some sites, tourists gleefully cluster with their cameras around places designated as photo opportunities.

Since we travelled to a number of tourist sites on the Odyssey, the use of photography in preserving the sacred became a recurring theme. The role of photographs in sustaining sacred experiences and relationships also was evident in photographs people carried with them or enshrined in their homes. Some consumers' houses and vehicles were so sacred to them that they carried photos of these things with them on their travels. Often photos of loved family members, pets, and favorite objects and places were enshrined in the home on mantles, bureaus, and other places of reverent display. Photos of the past were also given prominent status in historical museums, where they were a tangible link with the past these museums were sacralizing.

Two professional photographers we interviewed differed in the extent to which they see their works as preserving the sacred. One photographer sees the work in which he helped preserve others' sacred moments-- wedding and bar mitzvah photos--as totally unrewarding work. He prefers taking pictures of stars like Perry Como because the subject is sacred to him and allows him to preserve the memory of his contact with such entertainment gods. The other photographer specializes in anthropological travel and nature photos, and sells prints at art shows. He has somewhat mixed feelings about selling these photographs to the public. He was pleased by one purchaser who was also photographer and who promised that the purchased print would be hung "in a place of honor." In general the photos themselves (i.e., his negatives) are clearly sacred to him and help preserve memories of meaningful experiences.

At a Renaissance Festival, we observed that people were able to experience the magical aspects of time travel and the romantic fantasy of being a part of another world. Through souvenir dragon-slaying swords and flowered wreaths for the hair, people attempted to transport an element of this experience back to their everyday lives. The tangible sacredness of such sites was often preserved in artifacts acquired there in the form of gifts, souvenirs, and photographs. One woman bought charms for a seldom-worn, but still cherished charm bracelet memorializing each vacation. She has a charm from Niagara Falls (from her current vacation) and one from Yellowstone Park (last year's vacation). She does not have one from her hometown. Although her own home is sacred, she feels no need symbolically to bring the hometown with her, since she is usually there. Similarly, a beauty queen representing a particular city, who is therefore herself an incarnation of that place, recalled as she looked over some souvenir pins on her sash the ethnic festival where she bought each pin, rather than the country which is supposedly symbolized by each of them. Through souvenirs and photographs, consumers tangibilize contamination of their contact with sacred consumption.

Just as the sacred can be made manifest and preserved in tangible objects, the loss of such objects threatens to desacralize. For example, collections sometimes irreverently move form the world of the sacred into the world of the profane in ways that deeply disturb people. An informant who moved across the country had a little watermelon dish broken in the move. This bothered her because she collects watermelon replicas and because her collection represents preservation and continuity, elements that are tenuous in her life at present. A man interviewed lost a $10,000 collection of books and records in a flood. A worker at a Small Business Administration Disaster Field Office talked with us about the effect of losing collections. It was her sense that young people bounce back faster than older people. Probably this is because the old have collected more and have more memories to lose.

Of course, the loss of collections or possessions in a disaster pales compared to the loss of life. The loss of a decedent's physical remains, a particularly wrenching casualty in the flood described by one informant, is more devastating still. But the loss of a collection or possessions can be unsettling nonetheless. The man who lost the books and records sustained other extensive property loss as well. He was deeply angered by these losses, even though we interviewed him six weeks after the flood. Such an occasion is disturbing because it destroys the possibility of eternal life for possessions that are closely connected to self. More important than the destruction of the items in collections is the destruction of the value that was being invested and expressed, namely continued existence of the self through the collection.

Losing a gift is another irreverent way of profaning it. Such an incident was described to us by a customer at a swap meet jewelry stand. The operators of this stand had been informants, and two of us had become close enough with them to help out with customers at their stall. As the customer looked over the wares, she explained that she once had a heart necklace that her father had given her, but its clasp broke, and she lost it. The loss was a source of great anxiety. Through such objects, one has the sacred experience of joy and connection. To lose a keepsake is irreverent and shows insufficient ritual care.

Summary of Ways of Maintaining Sacredness. Four distinct ways of preserving or maintaining the sacred status of times, places, people, things, and experiences were encountered. These were the separation of the sacred from the profane, ritual, bequests, and tangibilized contamination. In each case, we found corresponding ways that desacralization can occur. Lack of separation of the sacred from the profane, especially through commoditization, results in desacralization, and when rationalization and routinization supplant ritual, another form of desacralization occurs. Sometimes intentional divestment rituals are employed to desacralize items. And when sacred objects are lost or cannot find caring heirs, again desacralization occurs.

Interpretive Summary of Processes Involving the Sacred

We have explored the consumer behavior processes through which sacralization, preservation of sanctity, and sometimes deconsecration occur. Such rituals as contamination, gift-giving, and collecting, and various sacra such as souvenirs and heirlooms were explored in ethnographic detail to provide the reader with a feel for the many consumption settings in which sacred/profane transformations occur. Our remaining task is to provide some closure for our thesis, and to speculate upon its further significance for the field of consumer behavior research.

CONCLUSION

We have documented the properties of sacredness that consumers invest in material and experiential consumption, and have examined the ways the boundary between sacred and profane is strategically manipulated. Specifically, we have tracked the ways sacralization is initiated, sustained, and terminated. Using literatures from the social sciences and humanities, we have explored the personal, social and cultural significance of the transformations consumers effect between sacred and profane domains of experience.

In Berman's (1984) opinion, mind or spirit has been evacuated gradually from our relationships with phenomena. The transformation of Western epistemology from participating consciousness (knowledge acquisition via merger with nature) to nonparticipating consciousness (knowledge acquisition via separation and distance from nature)--that is, from dialectical to Cartesian rationality (Wallendorf 1987a)--has deprived consumer researchers of a potentially valuable perspective. We have sought to restore some semblance of balance by employing naturalistic, interdisciplinary team research to examine a fundamental yet heretofore inaccessible consumption phenomenon.

Consumers accord sacred status to a variety of objects, places, and times that are value expressive. By expressing these values through their consumption, they participate in a celebration of their connection to the society as a whole and to particular individuals. For society, defining as sacred certain artifacts that are value-expressive provides social cohesion and societal integration. For the individual, participating in these expressions provides meaning in life and a mechanism for experiencing stability, joy, and occasionally ecstasy through connection.

There are apparent benefits to the individual from participating in the sacred as a means of giving one's life purpose. Partly for these psychological reasons, it is generally societally approved that someone should collect something, or treasure historical sites, or avidly follow sports, for such activities focus one's life and seemingly make one happy. But there are other reasons why pursuing sacred consumption is generally societally approved.

Just as Karl Marx once proclaimed that religion is the opium of the masses, sacred consumption also has the ability to channel consumer energies into a focus that may preclude revolutionary thought and action. This channeling may be dialectically cast. Homeownership has long been seen as a commitment to the community, but it may also be seen as the confinement of women to the realm of consumption to maximize economic growth in an industrialized society (Galbraith 1973). Sports fanaticism can be seen to promote community identification and spirit, but also to separate family members with differing tastes. Just as sports fans see themselves as a unified community during sacred sports moments, so do gift exchangers, heirloom-passing generations, and collectors. Acquirers of quintessential objects and souvenirs may feel a sense of community in admiring one another's consumption objects, but may be viewed as materialistic or acquisitive by others. Pet ownership may promote good citizenship by kindling emotions that allow for greater empathy with others and decrease the probability of vandalism or other antisocial behaviors. However, pet ownership also allows and fosters the expression of domination (Tuan 1984). Although we recognize the potential pathologies of self-absorption, miserliness, and narrowness that may occur within sacred consumption, we generally believe that participation in sacredness in some area of consumption is superior to a complete lack of contact with the sacred. Singularizing the self

so one is not treated as a mere commodity, even if through one's possessions, involves consumers with the sacred, especially in collecting and experiences recalled through some tangible artifact.

What remains unanswered is the cultural consequence of the sacralizing processes we have examined. Sacredness exists at a cultural level to ensure the ongoing integrity of the culture itself. Through definitions of sacredness, culture hallows itself, working to compel belief. Intimations of this consequence are latent in theories of fetishism, especially in Baudrillard's (1981) critique of the "paleo-Marxist dramaturgy" that interprets commodity fetishism as mere object sanctification. Instead, the significance of fetishism is ultimately semiotic and consists in the reinforcement of cultural ideology. Through fetishism, the "closed perfection" of the system is celebrated and preserved (Baudrillard, 1981, p. 93). Through such ritualization, an individual becomes preferentially imprinted by an object while a culture simultaneously reproduces its critical structural categories. This is accomplished in large part by the sacralizing processes we have recounted in detail here.

We have chosen to adopt a clinical rather than critical perspective in describing he ways in which profane consumption is transfigured and made sacred. Divining the teleological and moral implications of secular sacralization is left to additional work adopting a theological or cultural criticism perspective. We hope such efforts will be aided by our clinical analysis. What is apparent is the capacity of consumer culture to facilitate expression of the sacred as it reproduces itself.

The behavioral complex we have described as sacralizing and desacralizing various dimensions of human experience is the ritual substratum of much consumer behavior. We have adopted the idiom of ritual to counter the "tyranny of paradigms" and the "constraining nature" of metaphors (Arndt 1985a, 1985b). By merging the phenomenological approach to consumer experience of the former paradigm with the criticistic or constructivistic orientation of the latter, a rich conceptual vocabulary for describing consumer behavior has been created.

Consider two of the metaphors that shape and reflect much inquiry in consumer research: involvement and loyalty. These two conditions or experiences suggest something of the talismanic relationship consumers form with that which is consumed. Yet, researchers have restricted their discussion of these constructs to the narrowly cognitive. Involvement has been glossed as focused activation (Cohen 1983), whether its duration is situational or enduring (Bloch and Richins 1983). Even when it has been considered as more than merely repeat purchase, loyalty is reduced to a function of decision-making, utilitarian, evaluative processes (Jacoby and Kyner 1973). Combined, these constructs deal with the arousal associated with personal meaningfulness, yet neither contends with the process of meaning investment or the cultural matrix from which that process ultimately emanates. We have described the sacred and the profane as conceptual categories that animate certain consumer behaviors. We have incorporated the spirit of these constructs into a more inclusive and culturally grounded process in which consumers routinely harness the forces of material and mental culture to achieve transcendent experience.

In his discussion of the political essence of the contemporary crisis of spirit in the Judeo-Christian tradition, Harrington (1983, p. 197) asks:

> Can Western society create transcendental common values in its everyday experience? Values which are not based upon--yet not counterposed to--the supernatural?

While the integrating consciousness affirmed by Harrington to be a potential solution to this question--namely, democratic socialism--may not appeal to many consumer researchers, certainly the question and corollary propositions he poses are of special interest. According to Harrington (1983), Western society *needs* transcendence. Like it or not, to our benefit or peril, consumption has become such a transcendental vehicle for many.

The processes used by marketers to attempt to singularize, and occasionally sacralize, a commodity so it becomes a differentiated, branded product have been described (Gardner and Levy 1955; Levitt 1984; Levy 1978). Processes that allow brands to function in unison on the social level as a constellation (Solomon and Assael 1987) to communicate status or on the cultural level as a brandscape (Sherry 1986b) to form a significant part of the built environment (Rapaport 1982) have been explored only recently.

Often quite apart from marketer efforts and considerations of brand, consumers themselves sacralize consumption objects and thereby create transcendent meaning in their lives. However, the processes used by consumers to remove an object or experience from a principally economic orbit and insert it into a personal pantheon, so that the object or experience becomes so highly infused with significance (*orenda, wakan, mana*) that it becomes a transcendental vehicle, have gone surprisingly undocumented given their

frequent occurrence. While this oversight is partially a function of the impoverished technical vocabulary of traditional consumer research, it is also largely due to methodological preferences, which make the direct encounter of researcher with consumer in a naturalistic setting a rare occurrence. Participant observation and situationally appropriate depth interviews permit less restricted access to the consumer's moral economy. By laying the foundation for an understanding of the sacred in consumption, we hope we have demonstrated how rich such a direct approach can be.

REFERENCES

Acquaviva, Sabinos. (1979), *The Decline of the Sacred in Industrial Society*, Oxford, England: Basic Blackwell.

Adler, Patricia A. and Peter Adler (1987), *Membership Roles in Field Research*, Qualitative Research Methods, Vol. 6, Beverly Hills, CA: Sage.

Altman, Irwin and Martin M. Chemers (1984), *Culture and Environment*, Cambridge, England: Cambridge University Press.

Appadurai, Arjun (1986), "Introduction: Commodities and the Politics of Value," in *The Social Life of Things: Commodities in Cultural Perspective*, ed. Arjun Appadurai, Cambridge, England: Cambridge University Press, 3-63.

Armstrong, Robert P. (1971), *The Affecting Presence*, Urbana: University of Illinois Press.

Arndt, Johan (1985a), "The Tyranny of Paradigms: The Case for Paradigmatic Pluralism in Marketing," in *Changing the Course of Marketing: Alternative Paradigms for Widening Marketing Theory*, eds. Nikhilesh Dholakia and Johan Arndt, Greenwich, CT: JAI, 1-25.

_____ (1985b), "On Making Marketing More Scientific: The Role of Orientations, Paradigms, Metaphors, and Puzzle Solving," *Journal of Marketing*, 49 (Summer), 11-23.

Arnheim, Rudolf (1987), "Art Among the Objects," *Critical Inquiry*, 13 (Summer), 677-685.

Bateson, Gregory and Mary C. Bateson (1987), *Angels Fear: Toward and Epistemology of the Sacred*, New York: Macmillan.

_____ and Margaret Mead (1942), *Balinese Character: A Photographic Analysis*, New York: New York Academy of Sciences.

Baudrillard, Jean (1981), *For A Critique of the Political Economy of the Sign*, trans. Charles Levin, St. Louis, MO: Telos.

Beards, Dick (1987), "Antique Shop Narratives--Lost Treasure Found--and Lost," paper presented at the Popular Culture Association Annual Conference, Montreal, Canada.

Beaglehole, Ernest (1932), *Property: A Study in Social Psychology*, New York: Macmillan.

Beane, Wendell C. and William C. Doty, eds. (1975), *Myths, Rites, and Symbols: A Mircea Eliade Reader*, Vol. 1, New York: Harper Colophon.

Becker, Howard P. (1957), "Current Sacred-Secular Theory and Its Development," in *Modern Sociological Theory*, eds. Howard Becker and Alvin Boskoff, New York: Holt, Rinehart & Winston, 133-185.

Becker, Howard S. (1978), "Arts and Crafts," *American Journal of Sociology*, 83 (4), 862-889.

_____ (1982), *Art Worlds*, Berkeley: University of California Press.

_____ (1986), *Doing Things Together*, Evanston, IL: Northwestern University Press.

Belk, Russell W. (1979), "Gift Giving Behavior," in *Research in Marketing*, Vol. 2, ed. Jagdish Sheth, Greenwich, CT: JAI, 95-126.

_____ (1983), "Worldly Possessions: Issues and Criticisms," in *Advances in Consumer Research*, Vol. 10, eds. Richard P. Bagozzi and Alice M. Tybout, Ann Arbor, MI: Association for Consumer Research, 514-519.

_____ (1986), "Art Versus Science as Ways of Generating Knowledge About Materialism," in *Perspectives on Methodology in Consumer Research*, eds. David Brinberg and Richard Lutz, New York: Springer-Verlag, 3-36.

_____ (1987a), "A Child's Christmas in America: Santa Claus as Deity, Consumption as Religion," *Journal of American Culture*, 10 (Spring), 87-100.

_____ (1987b), "Symbolic Consumption of Art and Culture," in *Artists and Cultural Consumers*, eds. Douglas V. Shaw et al., Akron, OH: Association for Cultural Economics, 168-178.

_____ (1987c), "The Role of the Odyssey in Consumer Behavior and in Consumer Research," in *Advances in Consumer Research*, Vol. 14, eds. Melanie Wallendorf and Paul Anderson, Provo, UT: Association for Consumer Research, 357-361.

_____ (1988a), "Qualitative Analysis of Data from the Consumer Behavior Odyssey: The Role of the Computer and the Role of the Researcher," in *Proceedings of the Division of Consumer Psychology*, ed. Linda Alwitt, Washington, D.C.: American Psychological Association, 7-11.

_____ (1988b), "Possessions and the Extended Self," *Journal of Consumer Research*, 15 (September), 139-168.

_____ , John F. Sherry, Jr., and Melanie Wallendorf (1988), "A Naturalistic Inquiry into Buyer and Seller Behavior at a Swap Meet," *Journal of Consumer Research*, 14 (March), 449-470.

_____ , Melanie Wallendorf, John Sherry, Morris Holbrook, and Scott Roberts (1988), "Collectors and Collections," in *Advances in Consumer Research*, Vol. 15, ed. Michael Houston, Provo, UT: Association for Consumer Research, 548-553.

Bellah, Robert N. (1967), "Civil Religion in America," *Daedalus*, 96 (1), 1-21.

_____ , Richard Madsen, William Sullivan, Ann Swidler, and Steven Tipton (1985), *Habits of the Heart: Individualism and Commitment in American Life*, Berkeley: University of California Press.

Benedict, Burton, ed. (1983), "Introduction," in *The Anthropology of World's Fairs*, Berkeley, CA: Scolar, 1-65.

Berger, John (1972), *Ways of Seeing*, London: British Broadcasting Corporation and Penguin.

Berger, Peter L. (1967), *The Sacred Canopy: Elements of a Sociological Theory of Religion*, Garden City, NY: Anchor.

Berman, Morris (1984), *The Reenchantment of the World*, Toronto, Canada: Bantam.

Birrell, Susan (1981), "Sports and Ritual: Interpretations from Durkheim to Goffman," *Social Forces*, 60 (2), 354-376.

Bloch, Peter H. (1981), "An Exploration into the Scaling of Consumers' Involvement with a Product Class," in *Advances in Consumer Research*, Vol. 8, ed. Kent B. Monroe, Ann Arbor, MI: Association for Consumer Research, 61-65.

_____ and Marsha Richins (1983), "A Theoretical Model of the Study of Product Importance Perceptions," *Journal of Marketing*, 47 (Summer), 69-81.

Bock, E. Wilbur (1972), "The Transformation of Religious Symbols: A Case Study of St. Nicholas," *Social Compass*, 19 (4), 537-548.

Boorstin, Daniel (1973), *The Americans: The Democratic Experience*, New York: Random House.

Bossard, James H. S. and Eleanor S. Boll (1950), *Ritual in Family Living: A Contemporary Study*, Philadelphia: University of Pennsylvania Press.

Bowlby, Rachel (1985), *Just Looking: Consumer Culture in Dreiser, Gissing and Zola*, New York: Methuen.

Breen, T. H. (1988), "'Baubles of Britain': The American and Consumer Revolutions of the Eighteenth Century," *Past and Present*, 119 (May), 73-104.

Brereton, Joel P. (1987), "Sacred Space," in *Encyclopedia of Religion*, Vol. 12, ed. Mircea Eliade, New York: Collier-MacMillan, 526-535.

Briggs, Charles (1986), *Learning How to Ask*, Cambridge, England: Cambridge University Press.

Brown, Curtis F. (1975), *Star Spangled Kitsch*, New York: Universe Books.

Calder, Bobby J. and Alice M. Tybout (1987), "What Consumer Research Is . . . ," *Journal of Consumer Research*, 14 (June), 136-140.

Campbell, Colin (1983), "Romanticism and the Consumer Ethic: Intimations of a Weber-style Thesis," *Sociological Analysis*, 44 (4), 279-296.

———— (1987), *The Romantic Ethic and the Spirit of Modern Consumerism*, London: Basil Blackwell.

Campbell, Joseph (1949), *The Hero With a Thousand Faces*, Princeton, NJ: Princeton University Press.

Caplow, Theodore (1984), "Rule Enforcement Without Visible Means: Christmas Gift-Giving in Middle-town," *American Journal of Sociology*, 89 (6), 1306-1323.

Capra, Fritjof (1975), *The Tao of Physics*, Toronto, Canada: Bantam.

Chaucer, Geoffrey (1948), *The Canterbury Tales*, New York: Simon and Schuster.

Cheal, David (1987), "'Showing Them You Love Them': Gift Giving and the Dialectic of Intimacy," *The Sociological Review*, 35 (February), 151-169.

Clark, Grahame (1986), *Symbols of Excellence: Precious Materials as Expressions of Status*, Cambridge, England: Cambridge University Press.

Clifford, James (1985), "Objects and Selves--An Afterword," in *Objects and Others: Essays on Museums and Material Culture*, Vol. 3, ed. George W. Stocking, Madison: University of Wisconsin Press, 236-246.

Clodd, Edward (1920), *Magic in Names and in Other Things*, London: Chapman and Hall.

Cohen, Erik (1979), "A Phenomenology of Tourist Experiences," *Sociology*, 13 (2), 179-201.

Cohen, Joel (1983), "Involvement and You: 1000 Great Ideas," in *Advances in Consumer Research*, Vol. 10, eds. Richard P. Bagozzi and Alice M. Tybout, Ann Arbor, MI: Association for Consumer Research, 325-328.

Coleman, Richard (1983), "The Continuing Significance of Social Class to Marketing," *Journal of Consumer Research*, 10 (December), 265-280.

Collier, John, Jr. and Malcolm Collier (1986), *Visual Anthropology: Photography as a Research Tool*, Albuquerque: University of New Mexico Press.

Colpe, Carsten (1987), "The Sacred and the Profane," *Encyclopedia of Religion*, Vol. 12, ed. Mircea Eliade, New York: Collier-MacMillan, 511-526.

Connolly, Robert and Robin Anderson (1987), *First Contact: New Guinea's Highlanders Encounter the Outside World*, New York: Viking.

Cornfeld, Betty and Owen Edwards (1983), *Quintessence: The Quality of Having It*, New York: Crown Publishers.

Csikszentmihalyi, Mihaly (1975), *Beyond Boredom and Anxiety*, San Francisco: Jossey-Bass.

———— and Eugene Rochberg-Halton (1981), *The Meaning of Things: Domestic Symbols and the Self*, New York: Cambridge University Press.

Culler, Jonathan (1981), "Semiotics of Tourism," *American Journal of Semiotics*, 1 (1-2), 127-140.

Cummings, Ronald (1972), "The Superbowl Society," in *Heroes of Popular Culture*, eds. Ray B. Browne et al., Bowling Green, OH: Bowling Green University Popular Press, 101-111.

Curry, Pamela M. and Robert M. Jiobu (1980), "Big Mac and *Caneton A L'Orange*: Eating, Icons and Rituals," in *Rituals and Ceremonies in Popular Culture*, ed. Ray B. Browne, Bowling Green, OH: Bowling Green University Popular Press, 248-257.

Danet, Brenda and Tamara Katriel (1987), "No Two Alike: The Aesthetics of Collecting," working paper, Communications Institute, Hebrew University of Jerusalem, Mount Scopus, Israel (02)883046.

Deffontaines, Pierre (1953), "The Place of Believing," *Landscape*, 2 (Spring), 22-28.

Demerath, N. J., III (1974), *A Tottering Transcendence: Civil vs. Cultic Aspects of the Sacred*, Indianapolis, IN: Bobbs-Merrill.

Desmonde, William H. (1962), *Magic, Myth, and Money: The Origin of Money in Religious Ritual*, Glencoe, IL: Free Press of Glencoe.

Dorfles, Gillo (1969), "Religious Trappings," in *Kitsch: The World of Bad Taste*, ed. Gillo Dorfles, New York: Universe Books, 141-142.

d'Ormesson, Jean (1984), *Grand Hotel: The Golden Age of Palace Hotels in Architectural and Social History*, New York: Vendome.

Dovey, Kimberly (1985), "Home and Homelessness," in *Home Environments*, eds. Irwin Altman and Carol Werner, New York: Plenum, 33-63.

Ducey, Michael H. (1977), *Sunday Morning: Aspects of Urban Ritual*, New York: Free Press.

Duncan, James S. (1985), "The House as Symbol of Social Structure: Notes on the Language of Objects Among Collectivistic Groups," in *Home Environments*, eds. Irwin Altman and Carol M. Werner, New York: Plenum, 133-151.

Durkheim, Emile (1915), *The Elementary Forms of the Religious Life*, London: Allen & Unwin.

———— (1953), *Sociology and Philosophy*, trans. D. F. Pockock, London: Cohen & West.

_____ (1960), The Division of Labor in Society, trans. George Simpson, Glencoe, IL: Free Press of Glencoe.

_____ (1975), Durkheim on Religion: A Selection of Readings with Bibliographies and Introductory Remarks, trans. J. Redding and W.S.F. Pickering, London: Routledge & Kegan Paul.

Eliade, Mircea (1958), Patterns in Comparative Religion, London: Sheed & Ward.

_____ (1959), The Sacred and the Profane: The Nature of Religion, trans. Willard R. Trask, New York: Harper & Row.

_____ (1964), Shamanism, New York: Pantheon.

Fabien, Johannes (1983), Time and the Other: How Anthropology Makes Its Object, New York: Columbia University Press.

Farb, Peter and George Armelagos (1980), Consuming Passions: The Anthropology of Eating, Boston: Houghton Mifflin.

Fenn, Richard (1986), Toward a Theory of Secularization, Society for the Scientific Study of Religion Monograph Series No. 1, Orono, ME: University of Maine.

Fernandez, James (1986), Persuasions and Performances: The Play of Tropes in Culture, Bloomington: Indiana University Press.

Ferrarotti, Franco (1979), "The Destiny of Reason and the Paradox of the Sacred," Social Research, 46 (4), 648-681.

Frankl, Razelle (1987), Televangelism: The Marketing of Popular Religion, Carbondale: Southern Illinois University Press.

Fromm, Erich (1947), Man for Himself: An Inquiry into the Psychology of Ethics, New York: Holt, Rinehart & Winston.

Galbraith, John Kenneth (1973), Economics and the Public Purpose, New York: New American Library.

Gardner, Burleigh and Sidney J. Levy (1955), "The Product and the Brand," Harvard Business Review, 33 (2), 33-39.

Geary, Patrick (1986), "Sacred Commodities: The Circulation of Medieval Relics," in The Social Life of Things: Commodities in Cultural Perspective, ed. Arjun Appardurai, Cambridge, England: Cambridge University Press, 169-191.

Geertz, Clifford (1973), The Interpretation of Cultures, New York: Basic Books.

Geist, Christopher D. (1978), "Historic Sites and Monuments as Icons," Icons of America, eds. Ray B. Browne and Marshall Fishwick, Bowling Green, OH: Bowling Green University Popular Press, 57-66.

Giesz, Ludwig (1969), "Kitsch-man as Tourist," in Kitsch: The World of Bad Taste, ed. Gillo Dorfles, New York: Universe Books, 157-174.

Glaser, Barney G. and Anselm L. Strauss (1967), The Discovery of Grounded Theory: Strategies for Qualitative Research, Chicago: Aldine.

Goodman, Paul (1960), Growing Up Absurd, New York: Vintage.

Gordon, Beverly (1986), "The Souvenir: Messenger of the Extraordinary," Journal of Popular Culture, 20 (3), 135-146.

Gould, Leroy C., Andrew L. Walker, Lansing E. Crane, and Charles W. Lidz (1974), Connections: Notes from the Heroin World, New Haven, CT: Yale University Press.

Graburn, Nelson H. H. (1977), "Tourism: The Sacred Journey," in Hosts and Guests: The Anthropology of Tourism, ed. Valene Smith, 17-31, Philadelphia: University of Pennsylvania Press.

Greeley, Andrew M. (1985), Unsecular Man: The Persistence of Religion, New York: Schocken.

Greenberg, Clement (1946), The Partisan Reader, New York: Dial Press.

Gregotti, Vittorio (1969), "Kitsch and Architecture," Kitsch: The World of Bad Taste, ed. Gillo Dorfles, New York: Universe Books, 255-276.

Guttman, Allen (1978), From Ritual to Record: The Nature of Modern Sports, New York: Columbia University Press.

Hardy, Alister (1979), The Spiritual Nature of Man: A Study of Contemporary Religious Experience, Oxford, England: Clarendon.

Harrington, Michael (1983), The Politics at God's Funeral: The Spiritual Crisis of Western Civilization, New York: Penguin.

Harris, Marvin (1985), The Sacred Cow and the Abominable Pig: Riddles of Food and Culture, New York: Simon & Schuster.

Haug, Wolfgang F. (1986), Critique of Commodity Aesthetics: Appearance, Sexuality and Advertising in Capitalist Society, trans. Robert Bock, Minneapolis: University of Minnesota Press.

Haughey, John (1986), The Sacred Use of Money: Personal Finance in Light of Christian Faith, Garden City, NY: Doubleday.

Hayden, Ilse (1987), Symbol and Privilege: The Ritual Context of British Royalty, Tucson: University of Arizona Press.

Highet, Gilbert (1972), "Kitsch," in The Popular Arts in America: A Reader, ed. William M. Hammel, New York: Harcourt Brace Jovanovich, 33-41.

Highwater, Jamake (1981), The Primal Mind: Vision and Reality in Indian America, New York: New American Library.

Hirschman, Elizabeth C. (1986), "Humanistic Inquiry in Marketing Research: Philosophy, Method, and Criteria," Journal of Marketing Research, 23 (August), 237-249.

_____ and Morris Holbrook (1982), "Hedonic Consumption: Emerging Concepts, Methods, and Propositions," *Journal of Marketing*, 46 (Summer), 92-101.

Hobsbawm, Eric and Terrence Ranger (1983), *The Invention of Tradition*, Cambridge, England: Cambridge University Press.

Holbrook, Morris B. (1987), "From the Log of a Consumer Researcher: Reflections on the Odyssey," in *Advances in Consumer Research*, Vol. 14. eds. Melanie Wallendorf and Paul Anderson, Provo, UT: Association for Consumer Research, 365-369.

_____ and Elizabeth Hirschman (1982), "The Experiential Aspects of Consumption: Consumer Fantasies, Feelings, and Fun," *Journal of Consumer Research*, 9 (September), 132-140.

Homer, n.f.n. (1963), *The Odyssey*, trans. Robert Fitzgerald, Garden City: Anchor.

Hope, Christine A. (1980), "American Beauty Rituals," in *Rituals and Ceremonies in Popular Culture*, ed. Ray B. Browne, Bowling Green, OH: Bowling Green University Popular Press, 226-237.

Houghton, A. T. (1955), "Animism," in *The World's Religions*, ed. J. N. Anderson, Grand Rapids, MI: William B. Eerdmans, 9-24.

Houston, Michael J. and Michael L. Rothschild (1978), "Conceptual and Methodological Perspectives on Involvement," in *1978 Educators' Proceedings*, ed. Subhash C. Jain, Chicago: American Marketing Association, 184-187.

Hubert, Henri and Marcel Mauss (1964), *Sacrifice: Its Nature and Function*, London: Cohen & West.

Hudson, Michael D. (1987), "An Appeal from Above: The Use of Religious Figures in Advertisements," paper presented at the Popular Culture Association Annual Meeting, Montreal, Canada.

Hyde, Lewis (1983), *The Gift: Imagination and the Erotic Life of Property*, New York: Random House.

Inkeles, Alex (1983), *Exploring Individual Modernity*, New York: Columbia University Press.

Ives, Edward D. (1974), *The Tape-Recorded Interview*, Knoxville: University of Tennessee Press.

Jackson, J. B. (1953), "The Place of Believing," *Landscape*, 2 (Spring), 22-28.

Jacoby, Jacob and David Kyner (1973), "Brand Loyalty vs. Repeat Purchase Behavior," *Journal of Marketing Research*, 10 (February), 1-9.

James, E. O. (1962), *Sacrifice and Sacrament*, New York: Barnes & Noble.

James, William (1961), *The Varieties of Religious Experience: A Study of Human Nature*, New York: Collier.

Jones, Lethonee (1982), "Fetishes and Fetishism in Foods and Eating," in *Objects of Special Devotion: Fetishism in Popular Culture*, ed. Ray B. Browne, Bowling Green, OH: Bowling Green University Popular Press, 238-256.

Kassarjian, Harold H. (1987), "How We Spent Our Summer Vacation: A Preliminary Report on the 1986 Consumer Behavior Odyssey," in *Advances in Consumer Research*, Vol. 14, eds. Melanie Wallendorf and Paul Anderson, Provo, UT: Association for Consumer Research, 376-377.

Keller, Evelyn Fox (1985), *Reflections on Gender and Science*, New Haven, CT: Yale University Press.

Kelley, Robert F. (1987), "Museums as Status Symbols: Attaining a State of Having Been," in *Advances in Nonprofit Marketing*, Vol. 2, ed. Russell W. Belk, Greenwich, CT: JAI, 1-38.

Kingsley, Michael (1987), "Baby M and the Moral Logic of Capitalism," *Wall Street Journal*, (April 16), 27.

Kirk, G. S. (1970), *Myth*, Cambridge, England: Cambridge University Press.

Koenig, Frederick (1985), *Rumor in the Marketplace: The Social Psychology of Commercial Heresay*, Dover, MA: Auburn House.

Kopytoff, Igor (1986), "The Cultural Biography of Things: Commoditization as Process," in *The Social Life of Things: Commodities in Cultural Perspective*, ed. Arjun Appadurai, Cambridge, England: Cambridge University Press, 64-91.

Kottak, Conrad P. (1981), "Rituals at McDonald's, in *The American Dimension: Cultural Myths and Social Realities*, eds. W. Arens and Susan P. Montague, Sherman Oaks, CA: Alfred, 129-136.

Kowinski, William S. (1985), *The Malling of America*, New York: Atheneum.

Kron, Joan (1983), *Home Psych: The Social Psychology of Home and Decoration*, New York: Clarkson N. Potter.

Lakoff, George and Mark Johnson (1980), *Metaphors We Live By*, Chicago: University of Chicago Press.

Laski, Marghanita (1959), "Sacred and Profane," *Twentieth Century*, 165 (February), 118-129.

_____ (1962), *Ecstasy: A Study of Some Secular and Religious Experiences*, Bloomington: Indiana University Press.

Leach, Edmund R. (1961), *Rethinking Anthropology*, London: Athlone.

Leiss, William, Stephen Kline, and Sut Jhally (1986), *Social Communication in Advertising: Persons, Products, and Images of Well-Being*, New York: Methuen.

Levinson, Daniel J. (1987). "The Stages of a Woman's Life," presentation at the 1987 American Psychological Association Convention, New York.

Levi-Strauss, Claude (1962), *Totemism*, trans. Rodney Needham, Boston: Beacon.

_____ (1965), "The Principle of Reciprocity," in *Sociological Theory*, eds. Lewis A. Coser and Bernard Rosenberg, New York: Macmillan.

Lincoln, Yvonna S. and Egon G. Guba (1985), *Naturalistic Inquiry*, Beverly Hills, CA: Sage.

Lipsey, Roger (1984), "Participators of Sacred Things," *Parabola*, 9 (1), 16-21.

Lopes, Sal (1987), *The Wall: Images and Offerings from the Vietnam Veterans Memorial*, New York: Collins.

Luschen, Gunter, Zaharj Staikof, Veronica Stolte Heiskanen, and Conor Ward (1972), "Family, Ritual, and Secularization: A Cross-National Study Conducted in Bulgaria, Finland, Germany and Ireland," *Social Compass*, 19 (4), 519-536.

Lynes, Russell (1980), *The Tastemakers: The Shaping of American Popular Taste*, New York: Dover.

MacAloon, John (1984), "Olympic Games and the Theory of Spectacle in Modern Socictics," in *Rite, Drama, Festival, Spectacle. Rehearsals Toward a Theory of Cultural Performance*, ed. John MacAloon, Philadelphia, PA: Institute for the Study of Human Issues, 241-280.

MacCannell, Dean (1976), *The Tourist: A New Theory of the Leisure Class*, New York: Schocken.

McCracken, Grant (1986), "Culture and Consumption: A Theoretical Account of the Structure and Movement of the Cultural Meaning of Consumer Goods," *Journal of Consumer Research*, 13 (June), 71-84.

_____ (1988), "Lois Roget: Curatorial Consumer in a Modern World," in *Culture and Consumption: New Approaches to the Symbolic Character of Consumer Goods and Activities*, Bloomington: Indiana University Press, 44-53.

Malinowski, Bronisilaw (1922), *Argonauts of the Western Pacific*, London: Goerge Routledge & Sons.

_____ (1954), *Magic, Science, and Religion, and Other Essays*, Garden City, NY: Doubleday.

Mann, Dennis A. (1980), "Ritual in Architecture: The Celebration of Life," in *Rituals and Ceremonies in Popular Culture*, ed. Ray B. Browne, Bowling Green, OH: Bowling Green University Popular Press, 61-80.

Marsh, Peter and Peter Collet (1986), *Driving Passion: The Psychology of the Car*, London: Jonathan Cape.

Martin, Bernice (1979), "The Sacralization of Disorder: Symbolism in Rock Music," *Sociological Analysis*, 40 (2), 87-124.

Marx, Karl (1972), "Capital: Selections," in *The Marx-Engels Reader*, ed. Robert C. Tucker, New York: W. W. Norton, 191-318.

Maslow, Abraham (1964), *Religion, Values, and Peak-experiences*, Columbus: Ohio State University Press.

Mauss, Marcel (1925), *The Gift*, London: Cohen & West.

May, Lary (1980), *Screening Out the Past: The Birth of Mass Culture and the Motion Picture Industry*, New York: Oxford University Press.

Miles, Matthew B. and A. Michael Huberman (1984), *Qualitative Data Analysis: A Sourcebook of New Methods*, Beverly Hills, CA: Sage.

Miner, Horace (1956), "Body Ritual Among the Nacirema," *American Anthropologist*, 58 (3), 503-507.

Mol, Hans (1976), *Identity and the Sacred: A Sketch for a New Socio-Scientific Theory of Religion*, New York: Free Press.

_____ (1983), *Meaning and Place: An Introduction to the Social Scientific Study of Religion*, New York: Pilgrim.

Moore, Alexander (1980), "Walt Disney World: Bounded Ritual Space and the Playful Pilgrimage Center," *Anthropological Quarterly*, 53 (4), 207-218.

Morris, Wright (1948), *The Home Place*, New York: Charles Scribner's Sons.

Nash, Jeffrey E. (1977), "Decoding the Runner's Wardrobe," in *Conformity and Conflict*, eds. James P. Spradley and David W. McCurdy, Boston: Little, Brown, 172-185.

Naylor, David (1981), *American Picture Palaces: The Architecture of FAntasy*, New York: Van Nostrand Reinhold.

Neal, Arthur G. (1985), "Animism and Totemism in Popular Culture," *Journal of Popular Culture*, 19 (2), 15-23.

Nisbet, Robert A. (1966), "The Sacred," in *The Sociological Tradition*, New York: Basic Books, 221-263.

O'Guinn, Thomas C. (1987), "Touching Greatness: Some Aspects of Star Worship in Contemporary Consumption," paper presented at the American Psychological Association Convention, New York.

_____ and Russell W. Belk (1989), "Heaven on Earth: Consumption at Heritage Village, USA" *Journal of Consumer Research*, 16 (September), 227-238.

Oliver, Paul (1987), *Dwellings: The House Across the World*, Austin: University of Texas Press.

Parsons, Talcott and Edward Shils (1951), *Toward a General Theory of Action*, Cambridge, MA: Harvard University Press.

Pawek, Karl (1969), "Christian Kitsch," in *Kitsch: The World of Bad Taste*, ed. Grillo Dorfles, New York: Universe Books, 143-150.

Pickering, W.S.F. (1984), *Durkheim's Sociology of Religion: Themes and Theories*, London: Routledge & Kegan Paul.

Pirsig, Robert M. (1974), *Zen and the Art of Motorcycle Maintenance*, London: Bodleyhead.

Plato, n.f.n. (1955), *The Symposium*, trans, Walter Hamilton, Harmondsworth, England: Penguin.

Pope-Hennessy, John (1987), "Storm over the Sistine Ceiling," *New York Review of Books*, (October 8), 16-19.

Punch, Maurice (1986), *The Politics and Ethics of Fieldwork*, Qualitative Research Methods Series, Vol. 3, Beverly Hills, CA: Sage.

Rapoport, Amos (1981), "Identity and Environment: A Cross-Cultural Perspective," in *Housing and Identity: Cross-Cultural Perspectives*, ed. James S. Duncan, London: Croom Helm, 6-35.

_____ (1982), "Sacred Places, Sacred Occasions and Sacred Environments," *Architectural Design*, 52 (9/10), 75-82.

Real, Michael R. (1975), "Super Bowl: Mythic Spectacle," *Journal of Communication*, 25 (Winter), 31-43.

Rheims, Maurice (1961), *The Strange Life of Objects: 35 Centuries of Art Collecting and Collectors*, trans. David Pryce-Jones, New York: Atheneum.

Richins, Marsha L. and Peter H. Bloch (1986), "After the New Wears Off: The Temporal Context of Product Involvement," *Journal of Consumer Research*, 13 (September), 280-285.

Roberts, Keith A. (1984), *Religion in Sociological Perspective*, Homewood, IL: Dorsey.

Rochberg-Halton, Eugene (1984), "Object Relations, Role Models, and the Cultivation of the Self," *Environment and Behavior*, 16 (3), 335-368.

_____ (1986), *Meaning and Modernity*, Chicago: University of Chicago Press.

Rook, Dennis W. (1984), "Ritual Behavior and Consumer Symbolism," in *Advances in Consumer Research*, Vol. 11, ed. Thomas C. Kinnear, Provo, UT: Association for Consumer Research, 279-284.

_____ (1985), "The Ritual Dimension of Consumer Behavior," *Journal of Consumer Research*, 12 (December), 251-264.

_____ (1987), "Modern Hex Signs and Symbols of security," in *Marketing and Semiotics: New Directions in the Study of Signs for Sale*, ed. Jean Umiker-Sebeok, Berlin: Mouton de Gruyter, 239-246.

Rydell, Robert W. (1984), *All the World's a Fair: Visions of Empire at American International Expositions, 1876-1916*, Chicago: University of Chicago Press.

Saegert, Susan (1985), "The Role of Housing in the experience of Dwelling," in *Home Environments*, eds. Irwin Altman and Carol M. Wener, New York: Plenum, 287-309.

Sahlins, Marshall (1976), *Culture and Practical Reason*, Chicago: University of Chicago Press.

Sanders, Clinton (1985), "Tattoo Consumption: Risk and Regret in the Purchase of a Socially Marginal Service," in *Advances in Consumer Research*, Vol. 12, eds. Elizabeth C. Hirschman and Morris B. Holbrook, Provo, UT: Association for Consumer Research, 17-22.

Scarry, Elaine (1985), *The Body in Pain: The Making and Unmaking of the World*, New York: Oxford University Press.

Schroeder, Fred E. (1977), *Outlaw Aesthetics: Arts and the Public Mind*, Bowling Green, OH: Bowling Green University Popular Press.

Scudder, Thayer (1982), *No Place to Go: Effects of Compulsory Relocation on Navajos*, Philadelphia, PA: Institute for the Study of Human Issues.

Serpell, James (1986), *In the Company of Animals*, Oxford, England; Basil Blackwell.

Shammas, Carole, Marilynn Salmon, and Michael Dahlin (1987), *Inheritance in America: From Colonial Times to the Present*, New Brunswick, NJ: Rutgers University Press.

Sharp, Dennis (1969), *The Picture Palace and Other Buildings for the Movies*, London: Hugh Evelyn.

Sherry, John F., Jr. (1983), "Gift-Giving in Anthropological Perspective," *Journal of Consumer Research*, 10 (September), 157-168.

_____ (1984), "Some Implications of Consumer Oral Tradition for Reactive Marketing," in *Advances in Consumer Research*, Vol. 11, ed. Thomas C. Kinnear, Provo, UT: Association for Consumer Research, 741-747.

_____ (1986a), "Interpreting Data From the Field," paper presented a the Annual Conference of the Association for Consumer Research, Toronto, Canada.

_____ (1986b), "Cereal Monogamy: Brand Loyalty as Secular Ritual in Consumer Culture," paper presented a the Annual Conference of the Association for Consumer Research, Toronto, Canada.

_____ (1987a), "Keeping the Monkeys Away From the Typewriters: An Anthropologist's View of the Consumer Behavior Odyssey," in *Advances in Consumer Research*, Vol. 14, eds. Melanie Wallendorf and Paul Anderson, Provo, UT: Association for Consumer Research, 370-373.

_____ (1987b), "Advertising as a Cultural System," in *Marketing and Semiotics: New Directions in the Study of Signs for Sale*, ed. Jean Umiker-Sebeok, Berlin: Mouton de Gruyter, 441-461.

_____ (1987c), "Heresy and the Useful Miracle; Rethinking Anthropology's Contribution to Marketing," in *Research in Marketing*, Vol. 9, ed. Jagdish Sheth, Greenwich, CT: JAI, 285-306.

_____ (1988), "Market Pitching and the Ethnography of Speaking," in *Advances in Consumer Research*, Vol. 15. ed. Michael Houston, Provo, UT: Association for Consumer Research, 543-547.

Shils, Edward and Michael Young (1953), "the Meaning of the Coronation," *Sociological Review*, 1 (2), 63-81.

Shiner, Larry E. (1972), "Sacred Space, Profane Space, Human Space," *Journal of the Academy of Religion*, 40 (4), 425-436.

Slesin, Suzanne, Stafford Cliff, and Daniel Rozensztroch (1987), *Japanese Style*, New York: Clarkson Potter.

Snow, David A. and Leon Anderson (1987), "Identity Work Among the Homeless: The Verbal Construction and Avowal of Personal Identities," *American Journal of Sociology*, 92 (May), 1336-1371.

Snyder, C. R. and Howard Fromkin (1980), *Uniqueness: The Human Pursuit of Difference*, New York: Plenum.

Solomon, Michael (1986), "Deep-Seated Materialism: The Case of Levi's 501 Jeans," in *Advances in Consumer Research*, Vol. 13, ed. Richard J. Lutz, Provo, UT: Association for Consumer Research, 619-622.

_____ and Henry Assael (1987), "the Forest or the Trees? A Gestalt Approach to Symbolic Consumption," in *Marketing and Semiotics: New Directions in the Study of Signs for Sale*, ed. Jean Umiker-Sebeok, Berlin: Mouton de Gruyter, 189-217.

Sontag, Susan (1973), *On Photography*, New York: Farrar, Strauss, and Giroux.

Stein, Michael (1977), "Cult and Sport: The Case of Big Red," *Mid-American Review of Sociology*, 2 (2), 29-42.

Stewart, Susan (1984), *On Longing: Narratives of the Miniature, the Gigantic, and Souvenir, the Collection*, Baltimore, MD: Johns Hopkins University press.

Stirrat, R. L. (1984), "Sacred Models," *Man*, 19 (2), 199-215.

Sudjic, Deyan (1985), *Cult Objects*, London: Paladin Books.

Sussman, Marvin B., ed (1985), *Pets and The Family*, New York: Haworth.

Thompson, Michael (1979), *Rubbish Theory: The Creation and Destruction of Value*, Oxford, England: Oxford University Press.

Titcomb, Margaret (1969), *Dog and Man in the Ancient Pacific*, Honolulu: Bernice P. Bishop Museum Special Publication No. 59.

Tuan, Yi-Fu (1978), *Space and Place: The Perspective of Experience*, Minneapolis: University of Minnesota Press.

_____ (1982), *Segmented Worlds and Self: Group Life and Individualism*, Minneapolis: University of Minnesota Press.

_____ (1984), *Dominance and Affection: The Making of Pets*, New Haven, CT: Yale University Press.

Turner, Terence S. (1977), "Cosmetics: The Language of Body Adornment," in *Conformity and Conflict: Readings in Cultural Anthropology*, eds. James P. Spradley and David W. McCurdy, Boston: Little Brown, 162-171.

Turner, Victor (1967), *The Forest of Symbols*, Ithaca, NY: Cornell University Press.

_____ (1969), *The Ritual Process*, London: Routledge & Kegan Paul.

_____ (1972), "Passages, Margins, and Poverty: Religious Communitas," *Worship*, 46 (7), 390-412.

_____ (1977), "Variations on a Theme of Liminality," in *Secular Ritual*, eds. Sally F. Moore and Barbara G. Myerhoff, Amsterdam, The Netherlands: Van Gorcum, 36-52.

_____ and Edith Turner (1978), *Image and Pilgrimage in Christian Culture: Anthropological Perspectives*, Oxford, England: Basil Blackwell.

van Gennep, Arnold (1909), *Les Rites de Passage*, Paris: E. Nourry.

van Imwagen, Peter (forthcoming), *Material Beings*, Ithaca, NY: Cornell University Press.

Voigt, David Q. (1980), "American Sporting Rituals," in *Rituals and Ceremonies in Popular Culture*, ed. Ray B. Browne, Bowling Green, OH: Bowling Green University Popular Press, 125-140.

Waits, William B., Jr. (1978), "The Many-Faced Custom: Christmas Gift-Giving in America, 1900-1940," published dissertation, History Department, Rutgers University, New Brunswick, NJ 08903.

Wallendorf, Melanie (1987a), "On Intimacy," paper presented at the American Marketing Association Winter Educators' Conference, San Antonio, TX.

_____ (1987b), "'On the Road Again': The Nature of Qualitative Research on the Consumer Behavior Odyssey," in *Advances in Consumer Research*, Vol. 14, eds. Melanie Wallendorf and Paul Anderson, Provo, UT: Association for Consumer Research, 374-375.

_____ and Eric Arnould (1988), "'My Favorite Things': A Cross-Cultural Inquiry into Object Attachment, Possessiveness, and Social Linkage," *Journal of Consumer Research*, 14 (March), 531-547.

_____ and Russell W. Belk (1987), "Deep Meaning in Possessions: Qualitative Research from the Consumer Behavior Odyssey," video distributed by Marketing Science Institute, Cambridge, MA.

_____ and Daniel Nelson (1987), "An Archaeological Examination of Ethnic Differences in Body Care Rituals," *Psychology and Marketing*, 3 (January), 273-289.

Warner, W. Lloyd (1959), *The Living and the Dead: A Study of the Symbolic Life of Americans*, New Haven, CT: Yale University Press.

Weber, Max (1958), *The Protestant Ethic and the Spirit of Capitalism*, New York: Charles Scribner's Sons.

_____ (1962), *The Sociology of Religion*, Boston: Beacon Press.

_____ (1968), *On Charisma and Institution Building*, ed. S. N. Eisenstadt, Chicago: University of Chicago Press.

Werner, Oswald and G. Mark Schoepfle (1987), *Systematic Fieldwork: Ethnographic Analysis and Data Management*, Vol. 1, Beverly Hills, CA: Sage.

Whetmore, Edward and Don J. Hibbard (1978), "Paradox in Paradise: The Icons of Waikiki," in *Icons of America*, eds. Ray B. Browne and Marshall Fishwick, Bowling Green, OH: Bowling Green University Popular Press, 241-252.

Williams, Rosalind (1981), *Dream Worlds: Mass Consumption in Late Nineteenth Century France*, Berkeley, Ca: University of California Press.

Williamson, Judith (1986), "Royalty and Representation," in *Consuming Passions: The Dynamics of Popular Culture*, ed. Judith Williamson, London: Marion Boyars, 75-89.

Wolowelsky, Joel B. (1977), "The Human Mean," *Judaism*, 26 (101), 92-96.

Zepp, Ira G., Jr. (1986), *The New Religious Image of Urban America: The Shopping Mall as Ceremonial Center*, Westminster, MD: Christian Classics.

Zerubavel, Eviatar (1981), *Hidden Rhythms: Schedules and Calendars in Social Life*, Chicago: University of Chicago Press.

Touching Greatness: The Central Midwest Barry Manilow Fan Club

Thomas C. O'Guinn[1]

PREFACE

The editor of this book wanted a photo-essay involving naturalistic research from the Consumer Behavior Odyssey. What I gave him is qualitative, but not strictly naturalistic.[2] It doesn't depend on photos, and I would not characterize it as an essay. Further, only some of the data reported were actually collected on the Odyssey. Yet, despite the qualifications, the Touching Greatness idea took initial empirical form on the Odyssey.

INTRODUCTION

During my month with the Consumer Behavior Odyssey, I collected the initial data involving what I now refer to as the "Touching Greatness" phenomenon. The essential research idea was to gain a better understanding of the constellation of behaviors in which consumers attempt to gain closer contact with those public figures whom they perceive as great. To gain this closer proximity, consumers engage in all sorts of consumption activities ranging from the truly excessive fan club member who buys and collects everything even remotely related to a celebrity, to the far more subtle and much more common behavior of asking for an autograph.

Traveling roadside America with a group of colleagues seemed a perfect way to see the Touching Greatness phenomenon in a variety of forms, and with an economy of time and money. When Russ Belk told me of the proposed Consumer Behavior Odyssey, I made my initial foray into a project which was solely qualitative.

The a priori model with which I entered the field was a religious one. I believed we had celebrities because we first had gods. The form of celebrity worship is substantially borrowed from religion, perhaps so too is its substance. Fan clubs seem like congregations, and stars a bit like gods.

MODERN CELEBRITY

Christianity will go. We're more popular than Jesus now.
 ‑John Lennon (1966)

It seemed to me then, as it does now, that one of the undeniable hallmarks of American consumer culture is a fascination with celebrity. Each week approximately 3.3 million Americans read *People* (Simmons Market Research Bureau 1990). Anyone who reads newspapers or magazines or watches television, will have no doubt noted that a great deal of air time and print space is devoted to covering celebrities. This interest and attention is not restricted to a certain social class; all have their celebrities, although each class tends to think the other misguided or too unsophisticated to appreciate the truly great. Some read of their admired ones in tabloids, others in the chic magazine of the "intelligentsia."

At the center of all this attention is a great deal of consumption. At least one million Americans belong to a fan club (Dornay 1989). Approximately five million tourists have visited Graceland since being opened to the public in 1982, 60,000 alone during "Elvis Week"[3] marking the tenth anniversary of Mr. Presley's death. Tourists throng to celebrity graveyards in Los Angeles; the most famous of them, Forest Lawn is often referred to as the Disneyland of cemeteries. Others take drive-by bus tours of the homes of the stars. "Meet-a-Celebrity" tie ins and other promotions are becoming routine. The production and marketing of celebrity could reasonably be called one of America's largest industries.

Yet, the question of why remains. Why do we devote so much attention to celebrities? Why do "we live in a society bound together by the talk of fame (Braudy 1986, p. vii)?" Why do celebrities matter so much to us; and from the perspective of consumer research, why do they sit at the center of so much buying and consuming?

Apparently no one is really even sure how long the celebrity has been with us.[4]

---

[1]The author would like to thank Mark Michicich, L.J. Shrum, Lisa Kay Slabon, Lisa Braddock, Ian Malbon and Connie O'Guinn who participated in this research. Further thanks go to Bill Wallendorf, Molly Ziske, Kim Rotzoll, Russell Belk, and the staff of the Overland Cafe, Los Angeles.

[2] Of course, a precise and consensual definition of naturalistic has proven elusive. Data were collected in natural settings, but a generally specified a priori model existed and was "tested".

---

[3]An Elvis week consists of nine days.

[4]While there are many reasonable definitions of celebrity, and related terms such as "fame," "star," and "renown," I choose to simply define a celebrity as one who is known by many, but knows far fewer, and the object of considerable attention.

Braudy (1986) traces the notion back to Homeric legends and early concepts of gods. Another frequently applied model is the traditional hero within the context of myth, probably best described by Campbell in his classic, *Hero With a Thousand Faces* (1949). Heros and their associated myths help us make sense of our lives, better understand our connections to each other, and our culture. There is also something special about heros in a techno-science culture where the concept of god is so fundamentally threatened. The need for magic may be at its greatest in such a world. This is the modern "crisis of heroism" put forth by Becker (1973) in *The Denial of Death.* When heros and gods are reasoned away, a vacuum of anxiety remains. Amplifying Becker (1973), Rollin (1983; 38) says:

> the therapy for the Age of Anxiety is apotheosis, the transformation of a human being into a heavenly being, a star, a hero, a god, a symbol of human potential realized.

Others (i.e. Klapp 1969; Lowenthal 1961) have argued that celebrities exist to give the individual identity in a modern mass culture. In this notion's most recent incarnation, Reeves (1988) presents an intriguing thesis on stardom, casting it as a cultural agent of personality development and social identification. Even though his specific focus is television stardom, the idea that stardom is a "cultural ritual of typification and individuation" extends well beyond that particular medium. Drawing on the work of Carey (1975), Geertz (1973), Bakhtin (1981) and Dyer (1979), Reeves (p. 150) argues that television stars help the individual connect who he or she is with "appropriate modes of being in American culture," or cultural "types," while at the same time providing just enough quirks against type to believe that we, like the stars, are actually unique individuals.
One of the more influential thoughts in conceptualizations of celebrity is Max Weber's (1968, v. 1, 241.) concept of "charisma:"

> to be endowed with powers and properties which are supernatural and superhuman, or at least exceptional even where accessible to others; or again as sent by God, or as if adorned with exemplary value and thus worthy to be a leader.

However, as impactful as this concept has been, few suggest a wholesale application of the "charismatic leader" (Weber 1968) concept to modern celebrity. The reasons are generally because the sociologist-cum-economist Weber's formulation requires a purposeful leader, a stable social system, and a clearly discernable power relationship. Two of these almost never exist in the case of modern celebrity, and the other, a stable social system, is a matter of some debate and interpretation (see Dyer 1979 and Alberoni 1972). Edward Shils (1965) also takes Weber to task for his narrow institutional conceptualization of charisma, and offers a much broader view of the concept. Still, it is Italian sociologist Francesco Alberoni who proposes an purely apolitical and modern model of celebrity..
Alberoni (1972) argues that the modern "star" does not and cannot possess generalized "charisma" in the true Weberian sense. Modern societies are too specialized to allow stars the kind of institutionalized power that Weber's charismatic leader demands. However, he does believe that they are perceived by their adoring masses as possessing some demi-divine characteristics that makes them "elite" rather than charismatic. They are seen as spiritually special, but lacking any type of political power. Alberoni thus terms stars the "powerless elite."
In fact, it could be that ritual is the central element in the Touching Greatness phenomenon. Rituals linger well beyond their substance. They can still be comforting even though their spiritual basis is long gone. Prayers said to a god not truly believed in may still benefit the supplicant. So too may be visiting the place of rituals, the church--even though the gods have gone away. Touching greatness may be a form that is substantially vestigial. The practice satisfies even though it is absent of much contemporary meaning. This could help explain why we seem to have such a need for celebrities which Boorstin (1962), saw as nothing more than "human pseudo-events," and people famous for being famous.

TOUCHING GREATNESS

The Touching Greatness project began at Mann's Theater in Los Angeles. We (Belk, O'Guinn, Sherry, Wallendorf) interviewed several people engaged in what seemed a particularly interesting form of consumer behavior. People spent from a few minutes to a few hours milling about looking at the hand and foot prints of movie stars. Some, such as the individuals in photo 1, chose to bend down, often while being photographed by family member or friend, and place their own hands or feet in the impressions left by the stars. Some bought Hollywood and celebrity related souvenirs, signed up for tours of the stars' homes, and otherwise participated in the celebrity centered consumption experience. Interviews then and during a return trip by Belk and O'Guinn two years later revealed that

PHOTO 1

to many it was merely something to do, just situationally normative behavior and curiosity. For others, it meant something more: a chance to remember and pay homage, to explain to their children who these men and women were and why they were important in their lives. Touching Greatness is more about the latter, or "true fans," but is not wholly without connection to the former appreciative masses. It remains an interesting and legitimate question why behaviors such as those observed at Mann's Theater are norms within our culture, and why such popular shrines exist at all.

The Central Midwest Barry Manilow Fan Club (CMBMFC) data are offered here as a case within the larger phenomenon and not as complete ethnography. These data will not allow the reader the depth necessary to fully appreciate the unique character of this particular club, for they were not collected for that purpose. Rather, they illustrate some of the themes observed across locale and fans,.

CENTRAL MIDWEST BARRY MANILOW FAN CLUB

Barry Manilow[5] is a celebrity. I talked to some of his fans. At the time the data were collected several themes had emerged from work at other Touching Greatness sites. The data collected here and at subsequent locales were used to expand upon what had already been learned, and to test the evolving model with new data. What follows are some of these findings, along with illustrative text and photos.

The findings being reported here are based on thirty hours of interviews with eighteen members of the CMBMFC. The

---

[5]Barry Manilow is a popular contemporary song stylist.

informants were all women. Most were in their mid thirties to mid forties. Socio-economic-status varied, but was typically observed to be lower middle class. We saw no men, but were told that there were a few male members.[6] Interviews were conducted in three places: a small restaurant, the home of the CMBMFC president, Bobbie, six hours prior to a Barry Manilow concert, and in a backstage press area secured exclusively for our use before and after the show. Besides the author, five graduate assistants, three men and two women, participated in the fieldwork.

THEMATIC FINDINGS

The Touching Greatness phenomenon has a broad cultural foundation. Apart from aspects of religion, I observed evidence of the fan club as surrogate family, and what could reasonably be viewed as a socialization outcome of life in a society in which the average family watches over seven hours of television a day (Condry 1989). Yet, the single best organizing structure is the first of these: religion. Perhaps it is because it is such a primal structure. Humans have been using it as a conceptual framework for explaining their existence, plight, and just about everything else for centuries. It is a very convenient and familiar source for interpretation and attribution. Religion has so many points of contact with so many aspects of believers' lives, that it is sometimes hard to see where it starts and stops. With this caveat in mind, a discussion of some of the uncovered themes follows. They are not exclusively religious, but are not inconsistent with a religious interpretation.

Barry is Everything:

"He's a husband, he's a lover, he's a friend, he's everything."

Barry Manilow pervades the lives of the members of the CMBMFC. In a very real sense, he is "everything." Evidence of this comes in several forms. First, there is the more concrete, such as the expenditure of time and money. It is not uncommon for the members to attend five shows a year, often traveling considerable distances. There is also the purchase and creation of Barry Manilow paraphernalia. These include hundreds of photographs, extensive album and video collections, clipping files and other memorabilia. Large phone bills from calling other Barry Manilow members are common. Vacations are scheduled around tour dates. Life revolves around Barry. In terms of time

and money, Barry is a primary beneficiary of these typically scarce resources.

Invoking Barry's name and spirit also makes important rituals and life events even more special, or sacred (Belk, Sherry and Wallendorf 1991). A particularly palpable example was when Bobbie and her husband were married. The couple had a number of Barry's songs played at the wedding, and the sheet music to a particular song, "Who Needs To Dream," was superimposed over the couple's wedding photograph (photo 2). Many religions place a god or other important personage (i.e., saint, martyr, prophet, etc.) at the center of celebrations and rituals marking important life events, such as weddings, which thereby come to be regarded as sacred institutions.

Barry's pervasiveness in the lives of the CMBMFC members was also apparent in that they often referred to him in terms of a significant other, most typically as lover, husband or friend. This love was, however, rarely sexual. It was rather more spiritual love, though often with an idealized romantic pallor. For example, one woman who describes herself as a very faithful wife, says she takes off her wedding ring on only one occasion: to attend Barry Manilow concerts. She does this although she and Barry Manilow have no personal relationship in any traditional sense; yet, she sees important symbolism in the act. This is an important thing for her to do. It would, after all, be wrong to be married to two men at once. Extending the religious metaphor, some nuns wear wedding bans to symbolize their marriage to Christ.

Perhaps most significantly, informants explain that Barry is able to provide the emotional support and understanding they need, like no one else in their lives. I was told that he "never lets them down." CMBMFC members frequently describe him as "all" of these important roles or personages "rolled into one," someone who can be all, provide all.

I believe in God, and I kind of think God sent Barry to help me. I think a lot of people feel that way, he's got a special gift and he kind of reaches out to a lot of people.

Barry's specialness occasionally borders on the miraculous. Bobbie tells of a time when a group of CMBMFC members were camping out for tickets in cold and wet weather. They had been out all night in rain and cold when sandwiches and coffee arrived "from nowhere." Bobbie was amazed that what initially seemed like a meager amount of food

---

[6]Most males mentioned were Barry impersonators.

PHOTO 2

had "fed everyone." We also spoke to a woman who told us that Barry had "somehow" heard of her child who had cancer, picked him up in his limousine and visited with he and his mother at their home. On another occasion, the CMBMFC members were waiting for Barry's plane to land. The weather was bad, but when Barry's plane approached, the sky cleared and it was able to land. When he was safely inside the terminal, it started raining again.

Barry's Work:
Like most religions, this church has a mission; there is work to be done. Among the

important duties are taking care of Barry, protecting him from bad fans, recruiting new followers, and always being there for him. These are all seen as important functions for members of the CMBMFC. Perhaps chief among them is the idea of providing emotional support to Barry and otherwise taking care of him. Sometimes, we think of gods taking care of their followers, and not vice versa. But in fact, in many religions that is precisely the purpose of human existence, to serve god. Christians, for example, are told that the path to heaven and happiness is through serving the Lord, doing His work. Sometimes "His work" is in the form of altruism, serving god by serving others. Such behavior is very consistent with that observed among CMBMFC members. They are quick to point out that Barry and his fans do a great deal of charity work.

It is here that the role of wife/mother becomes most intermingled with that of religious follower. The women of the CMBMFC seem to derive a very important benefit from taking care of Barry, giving of themselves. They believe he needs and appreciates this effort, his appreciation being very significant. In preparation for the show we attended, four different fan clubs competed to decorate Barry's dressing room. The members of the CMBMFC explained that decorations let Barry know they care, and are "there for him." They also wanted to make him as "comfortable as possible."

Some members have very personal ideas and aspirations about serving Barry. The president of the CMBMFC, herself a professional secretary, says that if she could be anything at all in relation to Barry she would be his secretary:

> I would like to just spend a day following him around with my little clipboard or whatever saying "you've gotta be here, you've gotta be here, you've got a meeting with so and so" and just do that for a day. That's all I want.

Serving Barry even extends to cleaning for Barry. After one show a group of CMBMFC members waited for Barry to leave his dressing room. When he did, he looked at the arena and commented on how dirty it was. They then explained that this was true except for the rows in which they had sat. Those were clean:

> He [Barry] said something like "what went on here today, looks like they had a circus, popcorn all over the floor" and I said "yes, but the first three rows are clean." He turns to Mark and he says "you're right..where they sat, those rows are clean."

Churches must be kept clean. True believers respect the sacred space, whereas infidels defile it. Members of the CMBMFC are true believers.

Still, after telling the researchers so much about what they did for Barry, the opposite question was posed.

> Researcher: And what does he give you?
>
> Bobbie: Just knowing that he's there and he cares, you know, like I told her (my friend) tonight going to the mall, I said "this man, the fact that he does realize what he puts us through."

Appreciation, particularly from a male, seemed very important. Further, it doesn't seem entirely coincidental that when asked to explain what makes Barry so good, informants very frequently mention that Barry is very good to his mother. Here is where the devoted religious follower and the role of the long suffering and nurturing woman intertwine. The fan's object of devotion is a person to whom they ascribe the attributes of specialness, extending to religious proportions. They serve him, and are happy in their work. It is not, however, insignificant that this minor deity or religiously imbued person is male. It is also important that this paradoxical relationship to suffering and pleasure seems so central to the gratifications derived by these women. It is also entirely consistent with the happy sufferer paradox of many religious experiences.

Suffering for Barry:

> "Our day will come."
>
> "Mostly they just sit and shake their heads at us."
>
> "I mean he cares for us too. In fact, he even told us ...; "I know you put up with a lot of grief and I've heard every name in the book just like you've heard every name in the book and you put with a lot," and he said "I want you to know I'm here" and he did everything he could do to make sure it doesn't happen but it's always gonna happen and he feels terrible about it because we're considered his ladies and he takes care of us... "
>
> "he realizes what he puts you through."

The members of the CMBMFC speak of the ridicule and oppression they must face for their beliefs. Their families, particularly their husbands, do not understand their devotion and love for Barry. People make fun of them. Yet, it is suffering not entirely without reward; there is a bit of martyrdom related satisfaction apparent in some informants.

Shrines and Relics

Many fans have collections of Barry Manilow things. Some have special "Barry Rooms" set aside for the display of their collections. Others have only parts of rooms, some just closets. Almost all attribute lack of room for Barry to unsympathetic husbands. Consistent with other research on collections (Belk, Wallendorf and Sherry 1989), the job is never done, collections are never complete. There's always more Barry stuff. Few would sell even a single piece of their collections, and they rank their contents as their most prized and meaningful possessions.

I'd kill just about anybody if they just go in the room and try to walk out of the room with a poster, a record, just a clipping out of a newspaper, scraps of tickets, you name it. A lot of us have rooms devoted to just that, in fact, few of us have understanding husbands. I'm about one of the only ones in the entire Central Midwest Club that lets me do all of that.

Bobbie's room is featured in two photographs (Photos 3 and 4). She devotes one of the bedrooms of her house to this pursuit.   The room is covered in posters, photographs, clippings, letters, autographs, etc. These things have a great deal of meaning for Bobbie. These are special because they involve Barry, and form an important emotional conduit to networks of friends, memories and an important sense of self.

The highest status things in the collections are the things actually touched by Barry. This somehow proves that Barry exists for them, through this person-to-object to-person connection (McCracken 1986). It is physical evidence of a personal relationship. A good example was a Perrier bottle from which Barry had drank. This bottle occupies a prominent place on Bobbie's shelf. The smaller bottles belong to members of Barry's entourage.

This collecting of things actually touched by the admired one is a particularly interesting aspect of the Touching Greatness phenomenon. It was observed consistently across venues and celebrities, and is very consistent with a liturgical interpretation, going as far as the levels of sacredness assigned to religious relics (Geary 1986) depending on how "near" they were once to the sacred being. It also draws us back full circle to the behavior observed at Mann's Theater, of wanting to actually touch the concrete images

left by the stars. It wouldn't be the same consumption experience if plexiglass covered the concrete impressions.

Yet another important distinction concerning collections should be noted. Apparently, "real fans" don't sell Barry things at a profit. This helps distinguish the infidel from the true believer. One of the most common behaviors at a Manilow concert is taking photographs of Barry, lots of them. Bobbie, for example, will take four to eight 24 exposure rolls per show, and see several shows per year. The photos taken of Barry are sold at cost or traded with other fans, but "it would be wrong" to sell them.

'The only thing I ever charge is if they want copies and they send me just for the print. Barry doesn't like when you make a profit."

This is very reminiscent of the parable of Christ driving the merchants from the temple. Apparently, putting a price on something that is seen as without price would seem profane or vulgar and would move something sacred into a the secular domain, and thus cheapen it (Belk, Sherry and Wallendorf 1989).

Fellowship:

Fellowship seemed to be the greatest of all the benefits of CMBMFC membership. Respondents talked at length of how much getting together with one another meant to them. Many said that relationships started via membership have become some of the most important in their lives. The behavior we observed supports this assertion. The members of the CMBMFC seemed very close and legitimately interested in each others' well being. The greatest thing they have in common is the love for and devotion to Barry Manilow. They get together and talk and reminisce, and share one another's joys and sorrows. There was a clear bond between them. This may be the strongest evidence for a Church of Barry interpretation, the centrality of fellowship. They gather in his name, but for each other.

Touching Greatness also provides other social benefits. When at Mann's Theater it seemed that the concrete shrines facilitated communication among visitors, much of it inter-generational. Why Jimmy Stewart or Marilyn Monroe were important to father was explained to son. For others, the stars were known-in-common referents. Their films marked time, set events in context, and seemed to provide meaning in a non-trivial way. There was something important underneath this, a connection to culture and the individual within it, with consumption being an important part of the link. Buying, giving and collecting things within the

PHOTO 3

touching greatness phenenonlogical frame is common and important to those involved. It concertizes the experiences and facilitates social interaction.

DISCUSSION

Religion is one of the oldest of culture's creations. Yet, "dead are all the gods" (Nietzsche 1893). Science and the ascendancy of the individual has either killed them or made of them vestigial forms which only vaguely resemble their ancestors. As the traditional social structures are challenged, evolve or succumb, contemporary cultures recast old into new. What were god-centered religions may be easily converted social structures for celebrity worship. Even though few if any CMBMFC members actually believe Barry Manilow to be a god, they do attribute the qualities of the religiously blessed to him. They certainly believe him to be closer to god than they are. Clouds part when his plane lands; he supplies food in mysterious ways; and he possess a special sense of knowing about his followers' lives that is clearly beyond mortal. This is a religious system. By any standards Barry Manilow is worshipped by his fans. He is someone more than a priest and

someone less than son of God in a traditional Protestant Christian model. In contrast, data from Elvis Presley fan clubs show his fans as seeing him closer to truly divine; whereas data from Johnny Cash fan clubs show a very fallible mortal, but still spiritually special.

The Touching Greatness data provide support for the thesis that celebrities perform some of the functions of gods, or god-sent beings. Yet, also clear is support for the idea that the fan club serves some of the social function churches once did. There, people who share a deep devotion or admiration for a special individual, meet and form important bonds, and fulfill important social needs once facilitated by the church. Maybe these fan clubs have taken on such a liturgical feel because the religious form was simply the most familiar, the most easily borrowed and transformed. The church is replaced in form, if not substance because it has the best, most familiar and most comfortable bundle of social uses, gratifications and shared meanings. We may miss God less than we miss each other.

While it is sometimes argued that extreme or marginal forms of behavior such as fanaticism are both qualitatively and quantitatively distinct from their more

PHOTO 4

"normal" expression, it seems difficult to explain one without the other. The very fact that Craceland and Mann's Theater exist and flourish means something apart from fanaticism. Likewise, the significance of the Touching Greatness phenomenon exists beyond the dispositional properties of individuals. It says something about the stage of a society's development (Alberoni 1972), our collective needs, motivations and values, and how these are expressed through consumption.

There's a great deal of consumption in the Touching Greatness phenomenon. Yet as a field, we have chosen not to give this and other aspects of popular culture much attention. Perhaps that is precisely the reason; it is too popular. Academics can be the worst snobs of all in their refusal to consider the popular (see Lewis 1988; Bellah et al. 1985). This seems odd, since by definition, it is where so much of life occurs.

REFERENCES

Alberoni, Francesco (1972), "The Powerless Elite: Theory and Sociological Research on the Phenomenon of Stars," in D. McQuail (ed.), *Sociology of Mass Communication*, Baltimore: Penguin, 75-98.

Bakhtin, M.M. (1981), *The Dialogic Imagination: Four Essays*, M. Holquist (ed.), C. Emerson and M. Holquist (trans.), Austin: University of Texas Press.

Becker, Ernest (1973), *The Denial of Death*, New York: The Free Press.

Belk, Russell W., Melanie Wallendorf and John F. Sherry, Jr. (1989), "The Sacred and the Profane in Consumer Behavior: Theodicy on the Odyssey," *Journal of Consumer Research*, (16;1), 1-38.

Belk, Russell W., Melanie Wallendorf, John Sherry, Jr. and Morris B. Holbrook (1991), "Collecting in a Consumer Culture," in Russell W. Belk (ed.), *Highways and Buyways: Naturalistic Research from the Consumer Behavior Odyssey*, Provo, UT: Association for Consumer Research.

Bellah, Robert N., Richard Madsen, William M. Sullivan, Ann Swindle, and Steven M. Tipton (1985), *Habits of the Heart: Individualism and Commitment in American Life*, Berkeley: University of California Press.

Boorstin, Daniel (1962), *The Image: Or What Happened to the American Dream*, New York: Atheneum.

Braudy, Leo (1986), *The Frenzy of Renown: Fame and Its History*, New York: Oxford University Press.

Campbell, Joseph (1949), *The Hero With A Thousand Faces*, New York: Pantheon.

Carey, James (1975), "A Cultural Approach to Communication," *Communication*, 2, 1-22.

Condry, John (1989), *The Psychology of Television*, Hillsdale, New Jersey: Lawrence Erlbaum.

Darnay, Brigitte T. (ed.) (1989), *Encyclopedia of Associations 1990*, v1. pt. 2, sections 7-18, Detroit: Gale Research.

Dyer, R. (1979), *Stars*, London: British Film Institute.

Geertz, Clifford (1973), *The Interpretation of Cultures*, New York: Basic Books.

Geary, Patrick (1986), "Sacred Commodities: the Circulation of Medieval Relics," in Arjun Appadurai (ed.), *The Social Life of Things: Commodities in Cultural Perspective*, New York: Cambridge University Press, 169-191.

Klapp, Orrin E. (1969), *Collective Search for Identity*, New York: Holt, Rinehart and Winston.

Lennon, John (1966), *New York Times*, "Comment on Jesus Spurs a Radio Ban," Aug 5, 1966., page 20, column 3.

Lewis, George H. (1988), "Dramatic Conversations: The Relationship Between Sociology and Popular Culture," in Ray B. Browne and Marshall W. Fishwick (eds.), *Symbiosis: Popular Culture and Other Fields*, Bowling Green, Ohio: Bowling Green State University Popular Press, 70-84.

Lincoln, Yvonna S. and Egon G. Guba (1985), *Naturalistic Inquiry*, Beverly Hills, CA: Sage.

Lowenthal, Lowel (1961), "The Triumph of Mass Idols," in Lowel Lowenthal (ed.), *Literature, Popular Culture and Society*, Englewood Cliffs, NJ, Prentice Hall, pp. 109-140.

McCracken Grant (1986), "Culture and Consumption: A Theoretical Account of the Structure and Movement of the Cultural Meaning of Consumer Goods," *Journal of Consumer Research*, 13;1 (June), 71-84.

Nietzsche, Friedrich (1893), *Also Sprach Zarathustra*, Leipzig: C. G. Naumann.

Reeves, Jimmy L. (1988), "Television Stardom: A Ritual of Social Typification" in James W. Carey (ed.), *Media, Myths and Narratives: Television and the Press*, Newbury Park, CA: Sage, 146-160.

Rollin, Roger R. (1983), "The Lone Ranger and Lenny Skutnik: The Hero as Popular Culture," in Ray B. Browne and Marshall W. Fishwick (eds.), *The Hero in Transition*, Bowling Green, Ohio: Bowling Green University Popular Press, 14-45.

Shills, Edward (1965), "Charisma, Order and Status," *American Sociological Review*, 199-233.

Simmons Market Research Bureau (1990), "Study of Media and Markets", New York: Simmons Media Research Bureau.

Weber, Max (1968), *Economy and Society*, v-13, New York: Bedminster.

Sorting
John Schouten

We move again,
this time cross-country, so we spend
a day in the basement
deciding what to save, what to throw away.

Certain things we keep --
a cast iron skillet,
some silver pieces from our wedding
wrapped in tissue --

other things, old parkas,
boots and the like go into a box
for Goodwill, it's little enough.
Then I come to the deep stuff.

Stuff from my youth.
A microscope my father gave me
when I was six or seven
I keep for my own sons

now seven, five and three.
I picture them marvelling
at the same prepared slides I stared at as a child,
wishing for one more step in magnification,

one step closer to that secret world . . . .
Other things I do not pass down.
A shoe box crammed with letters
from old girlfriends:

I pull one out of its envelope
and start to read. The words seem to fade
to nothing in my hands. I imagine
the rest as blank sheets

folded neatly in their envelopes.
I throw them away.
And a box of black and white photos:
one or two, a wheelbarrow,

a gash in a tree, pique my imagination.
Others have lost their meaning.
I throw them away.
One I find belongs to my mother.

It is my father at nineteen
or twenty in a sailor's uniform
with thick, curly hair
and eyes that shine forty years later

like the eyes of a twenty-year-old.
God, he was handsome.
Just yesterday we sat over Cokes
in an airport lounge, rattling the ice in our cups,

when he told me of a weakness they had found
in his heart. He described it in medical terms
and laughed it off. He said
it would make the end come quick and painless.

Possessions and the Sense of Past
Russell W. Belk[1]

ABSTRACT

Objects that stir our memories include souvenirs, photographs, heirlooms, antiques, monuments, and gifts. Such possessions are used mnemonically to create, store, and retrieve a sense of past that is instrumental in managing our identities. It would be a fundamental mistake however to assume that the processes involved are those of cognitive information storage and retrieval. For mementos evoke nostalgic, affective, and often fanciful links to the past rather than more documentary cognitive linkages. Material memory processes operate intentionally as well as unintentionally, at both individual and aggregate levels of identity, with systematic differences over the life course. Although they appear to be pervasive and inescapable, such processes have been the subject of very little prior research. The present chapter offers some redress to this fundamental omission.

When to the sessions of sweet silent
  thought
I summon up remembrance of things
  past,
I sigh the lack of many a thing I sought,
And with old woes new wail my dear
  time's waste:
Then can I drown an eye, unused to flow,
For precious friends hid in death's
  dateless night,
And weep afresh love's long since
  cancell'd woe,
And moan the expense of many a vanish'd
  sight:
Then can I grieve at grievances foregone,
And heavily from woe to woe tell o'er
The sad account of fore-bemoaned moan,
Which I new pay as if not paid before.
    But if the while I think on thee, dear
    friend,
    All losses are restored and sorrows end.
(Shakespeare 1609/1961).

In his thirtieth sonnet, Shakespeare foreshadows much of what I shall say about possessions and sense of past. From the opening courtroom metaphor until the final couplet, the mood is one of wistful recollection of former friends, lost loves, departed places, and unattained ambitions. But the final couplet, appropriately, closes the sonnet on a joyful note. Such is the bittersweet, sad but

longing, nature of nostalgia (Belk 1990, Davis 1979, Starobinski 1966, Stewart 1984). And it is nostalgia that provides the initial key to understanding the use of possessions in providing a sense of past.

NOSTALGIA AND MEMORY

Before the development of photography in the mid-nineteenth century, intergenerational legacies in the form of family heirlooms and portraits were restricted to the upper class (Ames and Ayres 1985). In contemporary societies, the most pervasive possessions used to establish a sense of past are snapshots. Snapshots have democratized self images and from the start of photography they have been available to nearly all social classes. They also ostensibly offer the possibility of accuracy in these images (Belk 1989). Quite unlike the veridical representations and documentary precision sought in scientific photographs however, the snapshot aims at another sort of truth that is more akin to poetry (Tibbetts 1981) or magic (Kaufmann 1980). The snapshots that fill our drawers, slide trays, and family albums do not present an honest portrait of our everyday lives. They are heavily biased selections of important moments involving family gatherings, holiday celebrations, vacation trips, new possessions, and such rites of passage as weddings, birthdays, anniversaries, and graduations. Our snapshots of these selected and posed gatherings are then further edited before entering our wallets, purses, picture frames, and family albums. It is these selective repositories that portray the selves we wish to preserve for the future -- our own and that of our descendants (Boerdam and Martinius 1980, Chalfen 1987, Milgram 1977, Sontag 1977).

In reflecting on these repositories filled with pictures of ourselves and loved ones, we are guided to the staged impression that the times depicted were always totally happy ones. Not only do the people appear happy, but the cars were new, the houses were clean and gaily decorated, and the places visited were only the most scenic or historic landmarks. Only occasionally, as in the damage photos that residents of a recently flooded community showed me, are the momentous times inherently sad ones. Rather, it is the realization that these happy times lie in the past, that the people are older and perhaps dead or departed, that produces the nostalgic wistfulness captured in the opening sonnet. The associations and memories themselves are joyous, thanks

---

[1]I would like to thank Jeff Durgee and Morris Holbrook for their comments on an earlier version of this chapter.

largely to judicious editing. It is the fact that things past *are* past that tempers this joy and produces the bittersweet emotion of nostalgia.

Among the photographs that were found to produce nostalgia for informants were such themes as my first car, the cars we left at home (for a traveling family), a truck we used to own, the children, our wedding, my parents, a dog that I used to have, our old house, and when we lived in Africa. These photos have in common, besides their pastness, their focus on persons, places, and objects as things experienced or possessed. That is, they share a tendency to make of the past a possession that can be savored, handled, treasured, and kept safe from loss. For the most part, this is done knowingly, so that these photographs can produce and reproduce the bittersweet emotion of nostalgia.

That photographs, as well as other mementos, tend to provoke nostalgia-laden memories is both inescapable as well as largely invisible within the vast psychological literature on human memory. The major reason for this neglect is that the overwhelming majority of memory research has been conducted in laboratory contexts with memory tasks divorced from daily life, friends, and family (see Neisser 1982). Ignored by all but a few (e.g., Neisser 1989) are those rare exceptions like Korosec-Serfaty's field study (1974) which found that French attics acted as a family memory box, Bachelard's (1964) analysis of the wardrobe as an intimate place for secret memories, and G. Stanley Hall's (1899) early study of his visits to the farms and houses of his childhood in order to examine the memories these places and their various artifacts might bring to mind:

> ...through every room of which I slowly went alone, note book in hand, memories crowded very thickly with the opening of every new door, and seemed almost to affect the vividness of sense impressions. The old parlor paint never looked so white, the castellated stove, almost never used except on Thanksgiving Day, was still there; on this side lay my grandfather and here my aunt in their coffins; the old mirror with its wide mahogany frame still had the little crack in the corner, which was even better remembered than the mirror itself; the smaller long narrow one with its gilt and black frame and the gaudy flowers painted in the glass of the upper part; the red table which still showed my ink spot on it; the old daguerreotypes; the carpet; wall paper; mahogany sofa; the same old black books ... were well remembered images in this room unvisited for at least thirty years (p. 498).

> ...several dress and bed quilt patterns; the little red and lettered cup; my penny banks; a curious old firkin; -- of a good many of these I could write a brief treatise were I to characterize all the incidents and especially the feelings which they brought to mind (p. 506).

While Hall has turned much of his nostalgic experience into words, it is not words but emotion-laden images which are the direct product of such memento-cued memory (Bartlett 1932). Such images are not necessarily visual, as Agee and Evans (1941) found:

> All these odors as I have said are so combined into one that they are all and always present in balance, not at all heavy, yet so searching that all fabrics of bedding and clothes are saturated with them, and so clinging that they stand softly out of the fibers of newly laundered clothes. Some of their components are extremely 'pleasant,' some are 'unpleasant'; their sum total has great nostalgic power (p. 155).

Even the recent more ecological studies of memory have not considered such topics as souvenirs, snapshots, and heirlooms (Neisser 1988). The external memory aids that have been examined are those that aid prospective memory (e.g., shopping lists, memos, alarm clocks) -- reminders for what Casey (1987) calls "remembering-to" -- rather than retrospective memory (Harris 1978/1982). No doubt many of us would prefer to think of ourselves in the rational utilitarian way in which most memory research portrays us. One woman (WF 60) first insisted that she had no strong attachments to sentimental possessions and that everything she owned could be replaced if it were lost. But later in the interview she lamented the recent breakage of clay handprints made by her children in kindergarten, calling it a "casualty" and "a sentimental thing." She again retreated to a utilitarian posture in saying that she is unconcerned with what happens to her things after she is dead. Except, she went on, she would want her children to keep her china and silver heirlooms, the walnut furniture she had custom-made, and all the family photographs. She also recalled that she is preparing a genealogical photo record of her family and that she has saved all of her children's toys for the past 40 years.

If traditional research and discourse misses the nostalgic nature of object-induced memories, art does not. As Holbrook (1989) notes of the 1935 song "These Foolish Things" (Remind Me of You), the relevant memory cues for this lost love include such diverse objects as an airline ticket, a piano, silk stockings, dance invitations, and perfume. In a more recent song Crystal Gayle laments:

> Though I very seldom think of him,
> Nevertheless sometimes a mannequin's
> Blue silver dress can make a window like a dream;
> Ah, but now those dreams belong to someone else,
> Now they talk in their sleep in a drawer where I keep
> All my old boyfriends (Gayle 1982).

One informant (WF 40) made a point of keeping photos of her old boyfriends and encouraged her daughter to do the same. A Swedish woman (WF 35) interviewed by the SAMDOK homes project (Nyström and Cedrenius 1982, Stavenow-Hidemark 1985), displayed gifts from old suitors in a wall display that also included souvenirs and gifts from others (Tyrfelt 1988). As found by others (e.g., Csikszentmihalyi and Rochberg-Halton 1981, Mehta and Belk 1991, Wallendorf and Arnold 1988), many of our dearest possessions are those that represent linkages to other people. As with wooden staff images and knotted cords with which the Polynesians formerly remembered their ancestry (Volland 1987), these mnemonic linkages are generally intentionally forged, as when we take a photo knowing that it will memorialize the occasion and those present. However, it may be the unintended associations represented in mementos that produce the deepest meanings. This contention rests on a second theme that helps us understand the role of possessions in sense of past: possessions tend to evoke richly textured webs of personal memories.

POSSESSIONS, WEBS OF MEANING, AND EMOTION

The best example of the webs of meaning that may be evoked by possessions from the past is Marcel Proust's three-volume autobiographical novel *Remembrance of Things Past* (1913-1917/1981). Initially spurred by the long-forgotten taste of lime blossom tea and madeleine pastries he remembered from childhood, and later prodded by photographs, clothing, and other everyday objects that had quietly absorbed parts of his past, Proust (actually the novel's Marcel) floods the reader with rich details and stories from his autobiography. These memories came rushing back to him largely unbidden and unsought -- they are "passive memories" (Spence 1988) -- and this makes them all the more magical or sacred (Salaman 1970/1982). They are memories of sights, people, moods, scents, events, conversations, and numerous other details. But more than that, they are part of an interwoven web that

can hold and sustain both writer and reader in a period of Proust's past. Rather than being evoked in a documentary or even iconographic fashion where the stimulus objects "stand for" certain events and people, these memory nets are evoked in a revivifying web in which each object and memory "leads to" numerous other associations in an invisible labyrinth that makes the past come to life (see Caughey 1984, pp. 126-128). Such objects are able to create an almost *déjà vu* feeling of having deeply experienced the object previously, except that unlike true *déjà vu*, the feeling is warranted. They may actually evoke in the body a visceral feeling of what it was like (Casey 1987). We say such memories transport us back in time and space because they help us feel as though we are there once again. It is this transcendence of the here and now that characterizes the sacred experience (Belk, Wallendorf, and Sherry 1989).

The difference between these two types of memory parallels and reflects differences between two types of knowledge. The more documentary type of knowledge is **propositional knowledge** or knowledge *that* a thing happened or *that* a person existed at a particular time and place. The associative web type of knowledge is **experiential knowledge** or knowledge *of* what some thing, time, place, and/or person was like (Belk 1986, Langer 1963). It is an image into which we are able to project ourselves. This distinction in types of knowledge is the same one that distinguishes the experiment from the ethnography and cognitive understanding from emotional understanding (Denzin 1989, 120-124).

Besides evoking webs of associations, objects that stimulate memories of our personal past also stimulate emotions. As Wright Morris (1978/1989) observes:

> When we say "How well I remember!" invariably we remember poorly. It is the emotion that is strong, not the details. The elusive details are incidental, since the emotion is what matters. In this deficiency of memory do we have the origins of the imagination....Artifacts mystically quickened with sentiment await their reappearance in the imagination, a reenactment and a confirmation. Each time these tokens are handled they give off sparks (pp. 75-77).

If it is the emotion that matters to our most cherished memories, it is not surprising that memory and fiction share much in common. Just as Stone (1988) finds to be true of family stories, the images of self and family that are constructed, rehearsed, and retained in our possessions (either intentionally or unintentionally) are essentially personal and family heroic fantasies rather than veridical documentaries. Nevertheless, they help define who we are, what we value, and how we got to be as we are. Such effects on sense of self form a third theme involving possessions and our sense of past.

SENSE OF PAST AND SENSE OF SELF

Just as our sense of self is extended physically through possessions that make us symbolically larger (Belk 1988), our sense of self can also be extended temporally when possessions connect us to the past. While the same is true of possessions that connect us to the future (Belk 1990, Olson 1985), such connections are not within the scope of the present chapter. By adding the dimension of time to the spatial dimension of self extension, we become richer characters; we are both literally and figuratively more multi-dimensional. This occurs in several ways, now considered.

Possessions and Ancestor Worship

Many of our possessions engage us in a contemporary western form of ancestor worship. While ancestor worship in a formal religious context is associated with traditional societies (e.g., Houghton 1955, Howells 1954, Lévi-Strauss 1962/1963) and Eastern religions (e.g., Baker 1955, Takizawa 1927), in a less religious sense of sacredness ancestor worship is much more pervasive (Belk, Wallendorf, and Sherry 1989, Hirschman 1985, Marcus 1988, Wiggins 1974). Although one function of all forms of ancestor worship is to extend the identities of these ancestors (Maines 1978), another function is to invoke the spirit of these ancestors as protectors of their descendants (Tuan 1976). While it was once popular to use locks of hair from ancestors to invoke their memories (Miller 1982), other possessions are currently more popular memorials. For instance, one woman (WF 35) interviewed treasured the last photograph of her mother and her great grandmother's teacart. Another woman (WF 35) kept a doll that had belonged to her mother in a place of honor. A third woman's (WF 40) favorite possession was the jewelry that had been her mother's. And a fourth woman (WF 35) displayed her grandmother's pewter plates on the "altar" of the fireplace mantle. It was common to find pianos, fireplace mantles, and televisions used as shrines on which to display photographs of the ancestors along with those of current generations. Sometimes special wall groupings of ancestor photos or ancestor possessions (e.g., the shoe lasts of a cobbler grandfather) were employed to the same end (see Coster and Belk 1990, Milspaw 1986, Pocius 1979).

While female linkages to female ancestors were those most commonly celebrated in revered possessions (not surprisingly in light of stereotypical female roles in preserving social linkages -- Cheal 1988), male linkages to male relatives were not uncommon. The artifacts revered in these cases included automobiles, swords, tools, books, homemade furniture, and photographs. Preserving the possessions of cross-sex relatives was also observed, but not as frequently as preserving possessions of same-sex ancestors. This is consistent with the identity implications of these possessions, since the traits of same-sex relatives are generally most salient to sense of self (Stone 1988).

The importance of such objects was evident in interviews with the flood victims in a recently flooded eastern community and with a disaster relief worker who was helping these people to rebuild their lives. Aside from loss of a loved one in the flood, the possessions that were missed the most were family photographs, family heirlooms, and such memorabilia as gifts connecting the victims to ancestors. The loss of these possessions resulted in a grief process that was virtually the same as that experienced at the death of a loved one.

When death does occur, cemeteries, monuments and funerary urns show our persistent desire for tangible reminders of our ancestors (Dethlefsen 1981, George and Nelson 1982, Grolnick 1978, Pike 1984). It may be significant that India is a cremating culture rather than a burying culture. As Vaidyanathan (1989) notes, India also has done little to create historic monuments and the history of India is an elusive one. Our attitude toward the dead may well parallel our attitude toward the past in general.

Romanyshyn (1989) distinguishes the totally de-personified corpse from the personified dead body and argues that we bury the latter rather than the former:

> The dead body is a memory. It is a memory of the person and of the relations of that person to us who now say farewell to his or her body. This is the body that we bury, and the grave that is prepared to receive this body is the place of remembrance. Indeed the grave may very well be the first instance of memory in the transition to the human species, for we are the only species who bury the dead in a fashion which marks it as a ritual. We mark a site in a special way and we prepare in one way or another the dead body which we lay in the grave for a journey. In doing so, we acknowledge a continuing kinship with the person of this body (p. 124).

This is an intentional act of remembrance; an act intended to provoke the active memory. Still it is passive memories, unintentionally cued by accidentally encountered possessions of the deceased, that are likely to be the most powerful:

> ...things are often the most poignant and painful reminders of someone's death. Even after a long time, the absence through death of someone you have loved can be brought home sharply upon discovery of one of their things. The pipe he smoked in the evening found now beneath the chair, or the necklace which was always her favorite, attest in their patient waiting to the depth of the loss. At such times it is as if the dumb faithfulness of things intensifies our emotions and through them we enter more profoundly into our grief (Romanyshyn 1989, p. 194).

In order to avoid such associations and to reestablish life without the one who has died, many societies have death rituals which involve the destroying, giving away, or putting aside the property of the deceased, including their possessions, name, room, dwelling, and land (see Rosenblatt, Walsh, and Jackson 1976). Still, ancestor worship persists and is aided by a variety of icons and images. (Freedberg 1989).

Antiques and Sense of Past

While it is evident that objects linking us to ancestors help to temporally expand our sense of self, it is perhaps less clear that antiques originally owned by strangers can also help provide a sense of past. In some cases antiques are used as surrogates for objects owned by ancestors or associated with personal history. Thus, one woman (WF 70) collected stickpins that were like the one she remembers her father wearing. Another woman (WF 45) bought her husband a wooden wagon like the one he used to deliver newspapers as a child. Several dealers in used military goods described a common type of customer who is trying to recreate the medals that a loved one had once earned. In other cases, the antique is used to evoke a time, place, or person that the owner admires. For instance, a baseball fan (WM 40) collects baseball cards and owns a sign reading "Entrance to the Lower Grandstand" from the stadium of the old Washington Senators. Another man (WM 45) enjoys knowing that an elaborate music box he owns once belonged to Winston Churchill. The extent to which antiques may evoke a sense of past is shown in statements by three different antique collectors that they feel a kinship toward certain antiques because they were somehow

associated with these objects or others like them in a former life (see also Cherry 1989). Others feel they are guarding a sacred heritage by preserving antiques. Even among several dealers, there was concern expressed that the antiques they sell go to "good homes" (i.e., to people who will appreciate and care for them properly).

The music box once owned by Winston Churchill does not physically announce this linkage. While it is vital for the sacred aura of Churchill to be imparted that this linkage be regarded as authentic (Belk 1990, Handler 1986, Trilling 1971), the association is made via stories rather than being directly conveyed by the object. The expression "if it could only speak" must be made manifest through these stories. One antique dealer (WF 40) noted that it is much easier to sell an antique if she has some information about its origins and history. Others suggested that the price can be higher if there is a story that can be told about the previous owners of the antique. Such incidents suggest that an important element of the antique trade is the intangible sense of past that is conveyed through such objects. Hillier (1981) notes that in this sense the antique acts as a talisman or fetish object used to conjure up the past. Reproductions are clearly inferior due to their inability to evoke such a past with anything resembling the special magic of the genuine antique (i.e., one that participated in the past).

Souvenirs and Sense of Past

Another type of possession instrumental to sense of past is the souvenir. When we think of souvenirs we commonly think of objects acquired during trips or visits to famous sites in order to remember and proclaim these places and our experiences there (Cybart 1988, Gordon 1986, Stewart 1984). This type of souvenir was indeed prevalent in the Odyssey research and in some cases was enshrined in a special display case, as with a Japanese souvenir cabinet set up by one family to memorialize their trip to Japan. Informants like these hope they can share the memories represented by such souvenirs by answering visitor questions about these objects with stories about the travel experiences they represent.

An equally important category of souvenir memorializes personal experiences not involving travel. Objects in this category included musical instruments that the informant once played, vehicles once driven, wedding dresses, love letters, gifts, jewelry, trophies and awards, imprinted t-shirts that encode places and events, toys, dolls, comic books, ticket stubs, and wine bottles. One man (WM 35) preserved a Subaru sedan he once drove because it reminded him of the dates he had in it. Another man (WM 35) kept the wine bottles associated with prior sexual adventures. And a third man (WM 30) assembled his miscellaneous childhood memorabilia into a memory box that hangs on his wall. As with souvenirs and photos from a trip, such personal souvenirs act as mementos that evoke and perpetuate the myth of a golden age of childhood or youth (McCracken 1988).

Besides childhood memories, memories of lost loves are the other significant category of non-travel souvenirs. The combination of nostalgic emotions contained in these two dominant categories of souvenirs is captured by John Prine's (1972) song "Souvenirs":

> All the snow has turned to water,
> Christmas Days have come and gone.
> Broken toys and faded colors
> Are all that's left to linger on.
>
> I hate graveyards and old pawn shops;
> Boy they always bring me tears.
> I can't forgive the way they rob me
> of my childhood souvenirs.

[Chorus]
> Memories, they can't be boughten;
> They can't be won at carnivals for free.
> Well it took me years
> To get those souvenirs,
> And I don't know how they slipped away
>   from me.
>
> Broken hearts and dirty windows
> Make life difficult to see;
> That's why last night and this morning
> Always looked the same to me.
>
> I hate reading old love letters;
> Boy they always bring me tears.
> Can't forgive the way they rob me
> Of my sweetheart souvenirs.
[Chorus Repeats]

Variations Over the Life Cycle

The importance and nature of possessions signaling the past appears to vary over the human life cycle. Immanuel Kant (1798/translated in Starobinski 1966) insightfully postulated that nostalgia is a longing for our lost childhoods. While childhood is a common focus of nostalgia, it is appears to be an uncommon age period in which to experience nostalgic longings. In my fieldwork I have encountered little active memorialization of personal experience before adolescence (although objects from pre-adolescence may be treasured later in life). Younger children, like the eleven- and twelve-year-olds encountered visiting Gettysburg, may be interested in a sense of national past, but they see the meaningful times in their personal lives as lying more in the future than the past. Csikszentmihalyi

and Rochberg-Halton (1981) also found that while parents and grandparents were likely to choose favorite objects based on the memories they evoked, children were much less likely to do so. Nevertheless, Rue (1990) found that by high school, students save memorabilia with an eye to the future, citing justifications that "what I've done and where I've been is who I am" (F), "you can depend on the past" (M), and "it helps remind me of where I come from" (M).

In old age, two opposing processes affect our use of possessions in remembering the past. On one hand there is a tendency to assemble the objects of our lives, and especially memory-cuing objects like photographs, in order to perform a life review (Gygi and Powell 1989). In addition, like paralyzed accident victims (Brickman, Coates, and Janoff-Bulman 1978), there is a tendency in old age of the old to believe that life was better for them in earlier stages of their life cycle and to cherish objects from this past (Kastenbaum 1977). On the other hand, there is a tendency (usually, but not always, voluntary) to begin to ready ourselves for death by disposing of material possessions (Unruh 1983). When we can bequeath meaningful items and heirlooms that we ourselves have received, we do so, hoping that perhaps the recipient will remember us. Becker (1975) explains this motivation:

> What man [sic] really fears is not so much extinction, but extinction with insignificance. Man wants to know that his life somehow counted, if not for himself, then at least in the larger scheme of things, that it has left a trace, a trace that has meaning (p. 4).

Sussman, Cates, and Smith (1970) found that of 1102 people interviewed (heirs, contingent beneficiaries, and disinherited persons), 170 mentioned receiving something of sentimental value from an estate. They also found that in cases of extreme attachment, possessions may remain with a person after death:

> It sometimes happens that the object is so inextricably linked to the decedent that the memento is buried with him. "His lodge pins are buried with him." "We buried her with rings and rosary." "His best cuff links and tie pin were put on him in the casket." (Sussman, Cates, and Smith 1970, p. 158)

When there is no willing heir for possessions from which we would like to detach ourselves, we must dispose of these possessions in other ways. In several follow-up visits with a man (WM 70s) who had accumulated three garages full of potentially useful possessions, he described his somewhat reluctant disposition of this hoard to strangers. But he was emphatic that the photographs, family swords, trophies, and souvenirs he had accumulated were being retained for heirs he hoped to convince to take them. The importance of such tangiblized connections to him was shown when an older neighbor (WM 85) for whom he was caring recently died; he was that he had acquired several of this man's possessions "to remember him by".

Somewhat similarly, due to failing physical health an otherwise spry woman (WF 85) in an expensive retirement home recently had to abandon her apartment and move into one of the home's infirmary rooms. In the process her furnishings have been reduced to a single dresser. She was able to find heirs for her other furnishings, but she has 20 cardboard boxes filled with the miscellaneous mementos of her life that she has had placed in storage. These mementos include old love letters, greeting cards, cancelled checks, photographs, souvenirs, maps, travel diaries, newspaper clippings, books, yearbooks from her years as a teacher, and a number of documents from her husband's business that was sold when he died. The boxes, she says, contain her life. She won't discard them because, "It would be like throwing away my life." She hopes these things will mean something to someone and imagines that when heirs finally go through them they will appreciate what an interesting life she has had. Neal (1985) tells a similar tale of how her 89-year-old grandmother became a bag lady after having her possessions stripped away as she moved into a nursing home. Her bag and purse, attached to her walker, became her world. They grew overstuffed with possessions which she feared others would steal. Dignity during old age in a materialistic culture may mean retaining control of the things from our past.

COLLECTIVE SENSE OF PAST

Collective Memory and Aggregate Sense of Self

The use of possessions in creating a sense of past is not limited to individuals and individual identity. As Lowenthal (1975) realized, "The collective past is no less precious than the personal; indeed, the one is an extension of the other" (p. 12). For memories are often shared and jointly enacted (Lynch 1972, Madden 1964). Even though it is uncommon to think of memory at anything except the individual level, societies too remember with a collective memory that differs from one generation to the next (Halbwachs 1950; Connerton 1989, pp. 1-3; Schuman and Scott 1989). Due to collective memory, for instance, different generations have different preferences in music (Holbrook and Schindler 1989) and have different favorite classic automobiles (Belk, Wallendorf, Sherry, and Holbrook, 1990). Generations also have different sports heroes, film stars, and favorite movies, as well as preferences for movies with different nostalgic images of the past (Rosaldo 1989). To the extent there are generation gaps, they are partly due to differing collective memories (Holbrook 1990).

This is not to say that the collective memory is necessarily fixed and invariant within a generation. Kavanagh (1989) notes with physical and social changes, a tiger that is shot, stuffed, and put in a museum may go from being an animal to an economic commodity (to the taxidermist) to a trophy to a symbol of class (for the donor) to a museum object to a "symbol of imperialists at play, disrupting and wasting wild life and natural resources" to evidence of wildlife in other lands to a nuisance and symbol of folly in acquisition to a convenient device in multi-cultural museum teaching. Such a progression perhaps reflects a greater malleability in collective memory than in the individual sense of self which is anchored by the experiences of a single individual rather than those of an entire society or generation.

Closely aligned to collective memory (a societal phenomenon) is the individual experience of aggregate levels of self (Belk 1988). Consider for example the phenomenon of Christmas memories for a member of a particular nuclear family. A part of the individual's family sense of self is tied to memories of the times, places, events, and people involved in past Christmas celebrations and is reified and cued by photographs, gift objects, and the sights, sounds, and smells that the are associated with these family Christmas experiences. A part of individual identity, thus, involves identifying with the family and derives from recollection of these shared experiences. For Christmas rituals to be repeated in a familiar way by the members of a given family, requires certain props (e.g., a Christmas tree, the old ornaments, traditional decorations and foods) as surely as it does the presence of these members of the family. Those things that can be inserted in the claim "Christmas just wouldn't be Christmas without ___," are essential props which assure that Christmas will be able to be performed as a series of familiar rituals. And just as a part of individual sense of self derives from identifying with a family that enacts Christmas celebrations in just this way, the family itself is reinforced and partly defined through the performance of these rituals.

At the broader level of the nation, specific individuals and props are less important for ritual performances than individual roles and types of symbolic props. While a divorce or a fire that destroys familiar Christmas props can disrupt a single family's Christmas, it should have no effect on the American Christmas celebration more broadly. Thus, as the scope of sense of self increases from individual to family to neighborhood to region to nation, the security and stability of our sense of past and sense of aggregate self also increases. There is still a burden on the individuals who form the aggregate to remember the meanings of the relevant props and the uses of these artifacts in group rituals (e.g., McCracken 1988, "Lois Roget: Curatorial Consumer," pp. 44-53), but the more people who share this knowledge, the safer it becomes.

At the national level, hero worship is the counterpart of individual level ancestor worship and the religious veneration of saints and prophets (Wecter 1941). An example of such hero worship is found in the numerous artifacts produced in the eighteenth and nineteenth century to support the mythical national cult of George Washington (Ames and Ayers 1985, Fishwick 1985, Rabinowitz 1978, Schwartz 1987). The popular household objects that carried Washington's heroic portrait during this era included cups, pitchers, spoons, clocks, prints, jugs, knives, watches, mirrors, snuff boxes, and plates. This same iconography was depicted and remains in such aggregate possessions as portraits, statues, busts, documents, monuments, Mount Vernon, currency, coins, and architectural friezes. Even without the Washington stories, namesakes, slogans, and birthday celebration, these tangible reminders assure that George Washington will remain first in the hearts of his countrymen [sic]. As Geist (1978) argues, we seek (or if necessary create) in the past that which is missing in the present.

Monuments are especially important in preserving aggregate memory, as Vygotsky (1978) posits:

> It has been remarked that the very essence of civilization consists of purposively building monuments so as not to forget. In both the knot and the monument we have manifestations of the most fundamental and characteristic feature distinguishing human from animal memory (p. 51).

Hubbard (1984) concludes that whereas books help us know previously unknown things, monuments help us re-know known things with deepened emotion. Casey (1987) also notes the function of "commemorabilia" in intensifying our remembering, especially when aided by rituals such as the American Memorial Day observances (see Warner 1959).

Informants interviewed during their visits to the Gettysburg battlefield, recognized that their pilgrimage helped them relive national history. Children were actively instructed by parents during these visits and encouraged to buy souvenirs to carry a piece of this history home with them. For visitors to the Statue of Liberty and Ellis Island, there was also a sense of pilgrimage to a national historical site. In this case however, family sense of past was also celebrated for some visitors whose parents and grandparents had entered America here. Other informants celebrated another sort of national history in visiting historical homes such as those of the Vanderbilts, William Randolf Hearst, Thomas Edison, and John Ringling. Although they are lesser deities than George Washington, these people, through their artifacts, also provide a self-enlarging sense of heritage and national pride to the majority of these visitors. More local and regional counterparts to this claiming of aggregate self are found in the tendency to show visiting friends and relatives local historical landmarks. The sense of identity and pride in these places was evident in the hosts' recoil if visiting guests disparaged such a landmark. It was as if they themselves had been criticized. Such feelings of place identity appear more strongly among older residents of an area (Belk 1987).

Another sort of aggregate possession yielding a sense of past is seen in various national treasures such as crown jewels. It is essential in order for emotions of national pride and sense of past to emerge that these treasures be owned by the country rather than the ruler, as Goldstein (1987) explains:

> That which must be passed on belongs, ultimately, to the group, to the office, to history -- and not to any one ruler. Crown jewels are an example of a collective inheritance, of something that belongs to a dynasty, and is but used by an individual (pp. 236-237).

> By and large, dictators lack Crown Jewels -- that is, objects with a history, with a pedigree -- and so they try to build monuments to themselves instead....Ferdinand Marcos, a man in some sense in business for himself, built statues of [himself], put [his] pictures on currency, and placed [his] portraits in every public building and on the front page of every newspaper. When they fell, their statues were pulled down, their pictures clipped out of the bills, and their portraits smashed....Kings and shahs allow access to the Crown Jewels and doubtless assume that the displays of wealth, and of the genealogy of both themselves and their objects,

contributes to their legitimization. Democratically elected leaders also invite the people to tour the seats of government. But the self-made tyrant, like Marcos, makes private that which should be public (p. 239).

However, our collective markers of the past are not composed solely of intentional monuments, national treasures, and designated historical landmarks. Just as such everyday personal possessions as tables and chairs can absorb a part of our lives through contagion, ordinary community objects like factory buildings, department stores, and street lamps can form important links to the past. Bommes and Wright (1982) term such objects a part of our "micro heritage." Although such objects may lack the ritual recognition of monuments, they may well be capable of evoking strong emotional meanings and feelings of community identity. Dominant social classes may have hegemonic control of the monuments, media, and museums conveying our "macro heritage" (Radley 1990, Lipsitz 1990), but control over everyday collective objects is unlikely. Rowles (1980) studied older residents of an Appalachian community and found that over time community artifacts also merge with personal identity:

> Each [resident] has created an environment richly differentiated as an array of places laden with personal meaning in relation to a life history. Over the years each one of them has become more a part of the place to the point where it becomes an autobiography -- literally an extension of the self (p. 162).

This is why we feel a sense of loss when the buildings of our familiar landscape are destroyed, especially if we return after an absence to find that our familiar landmarks are no longer there.

Hyperreality

According to one interpretation, as we are increasingly alienated from our postmodern environment, we seek missing feelings of authenticity in the past (e.g., Berger 1973). Just as antiques originally owned by strangers can provide a focus for an individual or family sense of past, there are also national and regional sites that attempt to create a sense of past out of ersatz artifacts. A prominent example is Disney World, although many other theme parks and some religious centers offer similar pseudo-histories (O'Guinn and Belk 1989). In Disneyland (as well as Disney World and Heritage Village, U.S.A.), a key feature of the theme park is "Main Street, U.S.A." which evokes a nostalgic, if entirely imaginary, image of small town midwestern America circa 1900 (see Francaviglia 1981 and Wallace 1989). The effect is achieved by romanticized architecture, 5/8- to 7/8-scale buildings, horse-drawn trolleys, patriotic flags, and pristine cleanliness. Nevertheless, parents join their children in actively participating in this imaginary historicism. To refuse to do so would be like telling these children there is no Santa Claus; it would rupture the sacred myth of this "magic kingdom" (Belk, Wallendorf, and Sherry 1989).

Disneyland and Heritage Village were not the only sites studied where the creation of a false sense of past through purified presentations was observed. Other sites using more genuine artifacts but equally sanitized presentations included a midwestern historical museum; an eastern location called Memoryville, consisting of a set of period buildings (now housing various souvenir shops and pubs); Williamsburg; and Henry Ford's Greenfield Village. Even though the midwestern historical museum studied involves a recreated village assembled from formerly far-flung buildings and a train that now travels in a circle, a family of four sisters (WF 60s with spouses) had come for a family reunion because the place evoked the era of their childhood and helped "bring back memories." This is clearly the museum's intent. Such museums hope to create "the human side of the past" (Vanderstel 1989). At this museum a slide presentation narrated by Henry Fonda, with appropriately romantic period music, tells the visitor that "the choke of nostalgia grips us at every turn," "everything is completely authentic," and this is "a true historical museum where there is no compromise with commercialism." While there may be less commercialism in this museum than at Disneyland, the authenticity is of a particular staged type. The houses and period household furnishings (e.g., a baroque piano, golf clubs, a stained glass dome) shown in the museum are those that belonged to the elite of society rather than the average citizen. Any hint of hardship has been carefully expunged. The sorting process here is an amplified version of the sorting applied to family snapshots before they enter the photo album. It is the same at "living history museums." "Williamsburg's order flows from the top down. It is a corporate world: planned, orderly, tidy, with no dirt, no smell, no visible signs of exploitation" (Wallace 1988, pp. 148-149). Even Gettysburg has been substantially altered by surrounding commercial establishments (Patterson 1989). In fact any such presentation of history is necessarily a re-presentation that nostalgically plunders the past to give meaning to the present (MacCannell 1976, Horne 1984).

The feeling achieved in such places is one of postmodern hyperreality (Baudrillard 1975, Eco 1983, Stewart, 1988). In hyperreality the sign has become conflated with its referent. Thus, the American gothic frame house with its gingerbread trim, picket fence, and porch, comes to mean simpler times, friendlier people, and a slower pace of life, but not long hours of toil, oppressive sex roles, and racial prejudice. It is not that we cannot discern the difference between the real and the hyperreal, but we have learned to prefer the sanitized image to the real thing. An example of hyperreality is found in Henry James' (1893) story, "The Real Thing." The narrator has been commissioned to do a drawing of a gentleman and lady for a book and is fortunate enough to encounter a real gentleman and lady who are willing to pose. However, try as he might, there is no way he can make the drawing come out "right." But when he dismisses the couple and substitutes an Italian street vendor and a cockney woman, he finally gets a more believable effect. Another good example of this preference for the sanitized image is depicted in Brian Moore's (1976) novel, *The Great Victorian Collection*. In the story a young history professor is attending a conference in San Francisco after completing his doctoral thesis on Victorian furnishings. Following the conference he drives to Carmel and rents a motel room next to a vacant lot. Miraculously, the next morning the empty lot is filled with authentic but new Victorian buildings, furnishings, and other artifacts that he has somehow dreamed into existence. The press and public alike flock to see these wonders and talk to their resident creator. This lasts for several months until Great Victorian Village is started several miles away, complete with three hundred motel units, two shopping plazas, the Florence Nightingale Tea Room, the Oscar Wilde Way Out men's shop, topless can-can dancers, and the Olde Curiosity Shoppe. The thousands of tourists who came to Carmel to see the Collection, spend their time in the Village and most no longer visit the collection itself at all.

Nor is this preference for the hyperreal limited to amusement parks and shopping malls. Museum curators I have talked with recently, worry about the "Disneyfication" of their museums. Eco (1983) reflected on the jumble of sacred, royal, and secular artifacts in Hearst's San Simeon castle:

> It is like making love in a confessional with a prostitute dressed in a prelate's liturgical robes reciting Baudelaire while ten electronic organs reproduce the *Well-Tempered Clavier* played by Scriabin (p. 22).

Others worry about the "touristification of cities and nations in order to market their history to international tourists (Leong 1989). While some of this criticism can be dismissed as elitism, the appetite of the public for the hyperreal shows how plastic our sense of past can be (Lowenthal 1985). As George Herbert Mead (1929) observed, the past is as hypothetical as the future. While objects may allow us to rehearse and remember the past, our predilection toward nostalgia and hyperreality also assure that these memories are shaped and cultivated in highly selective and often fanciful ways. In Orwell's (1949) *1984*, an authoritarian control of the past was imposed because "Who controls the past controls the future; who controls the present controls the past." No such authority is needed for the hyperreal; only our own nostalgia.

The loss that our slide toward hyperreality, even in our personal possessions, may entail is described by Romanyshyn (1989) and Berman (1989) as an anonymous alienation from ourselves. As Rilke (1939) forecast:

> Even for our grandparents a "House," a "well", a familiar tower, their very dress, their cloak, was infinitely more, infinitely more intimate: almost everything a vessel in which they found and stored humanity. Now come crowding over from America empty, indifferent things, pseudo-things, DUMMY LIFE.... The animated, experienced things that SHARE OUR LIVES are coming to an end and cannot be replaced. WE ARE PERHAPS THE LAST TO HAVE STILL KNOWN SUCH THINGS. On us rests the responsibility of preserving, not merely their memory (that would be little and unreliable), but their human and laral worth. ("Laral" in the sense of household-gods.) (p. 129)

What is at stake here is what we take to be authentic. As more of our lives are given over to mass production, mass media, mass marketing, and mass consumption, it should come as no surprise that the past is also becoming a commodity that is produced and consumed on a mass scale with standardization, pre-packaging, and advertising. What we lose are precisely those objects Morris (1978/1989) characterizes as "*saturated* artifacts." Instead of objects saturated with meanings inscribed by time and contagious proximity, we are increasingly willing to accept objects with a thin, if shiny, veneer of meaning painted on by others.

SOME CONCLUSIONS

Why Seek a Sense of Past Through Objects?

Aside from the mnemonic value of mementos and their ability to act as projective stimuli for our recollections of the past we would *like* to remember, several deeper motivations appear to underlie our preservationist attitudes toward possessions. Perhaps the major reason that we save and seek possessions that evoke a sense of past is that these objects provide a sense of security. Most, if not all, of the possessions I have been discussing are what Laughlin (1956) calls sotorial objects. These are objects that provide a "magical kind of love, protection, and security," via "a reaction through which security and protection which are apparently out of proportion to the stimulus, come to be experienced as coming from an external object" (Laughlin 1956, 198). A familiar type of sotorial object is the transitional object (e.g., teddy bear, blanket, pacifier) that helps the child reduce separation anxiety when first learning to be away from mother and home (Bowlby 1969, Furby and Wilke 1982, Winnicott 1953). While some of the objects discussed in this paper may serve as transitional objects for adults, the type of sotorial object that is more generally implicated in these adult attachments is the set that Laughlin (1956, 199) illustrates by photographs, mementos, and souvenirs. Such objects provide security through the magical belief that we are anchored in the world and are not floating about, unattached to the experiences of other people and our own past.

Another motive sometimes underlying the accumulation and preservation of objects involving a sense of past, is status. Especially in the case of antiques, prestige may be derived from material links to famous persons (e.g., Winston Churchill's music box), events (e.g., it came over on the Mayflower), and personal history (e.g., it has been in the family for over 300 years). Even in America older is better, and tangible links to famous or aristocratic ancestors are best of all. Given the right audience, more recent historical objects such as an invitation to a recent presidential inauguration, souvenirs from visits to exotic lands, or a movie star's autograph, can also provide prestige. The prestige in all of these instances derives from demonstrating personal attachment to a prominent person, place, or event in history. We can at least imagine ourselves, as we contemplate these possessions, before a rapt audience which is anxious to know just what it was like for us to have been there.

But perhaps the most general underlying motive for acquiring and possessing objects that provide a sense of

past is that such possessions are instrumental to knowing who we are. Without a demonstrable past, without the ability to remember where we've been, without some proof of our history, we don't know who we are and cannot forecast or plan where we're going. We are likely to feel at least a little like those amnesiacs or victims of Alzheimer's disease who have been alienated from life by being alienated from their pasts (e.g., Sacks 1985, Fontana and Smith 1989). Rousseau argued that memory is essential for interpreting and benefitting from our experience:

> I have studied men, and I think I am a fairly good observer. But all the same I do not know how to see what is before my eyes; I can only see clearly in retrospect, it is only in my memories that my mind can work (quoted in Di Piero 1989, p. 118).

The essential role of possessions in contributing a sense of past to the memory of self is shown in the trauma often experienced when the elderly are separated from their home and belongings (e.g., Sherman and Newman 1977).

Where Have All the Flowers Gone?

It does not follow from the ability of certain past-signalling objects to preserve a sense of self-worth, that the more such possessions we have the better we will feel. In the present materialistic age it is imperative that we dispose of a great many of our possessions during our lifetime and hope only that a few may be claimed as reminders of us after we die. For objects that have become highly cathected and laden with memories, it may be necessary to store these things for a while so that these memories can "cool" to the point that we can dispose of them (McCracken 1988). Young and Wallendorf (1989) find that even so, there is often a mourning process that accompanies the disposition of an object that had once been an important part of us. Sometimes however we may try to rid ourselves of things that recall parts of our past we would rather forget (La Branche 1973). For one woman (WF 40) at a swap meet selling the last of her ex-husband's possessions left with her, the last sale -- that of his left-handed golf clubs -- was a cause for celebration.

As illustrated by the desirability of an impressive provenance for an antique, the associations believed to inhere in an object may not entirely disappear when we dispose of it. Some of the antique dealers interviewed said they feel slightly uneasy in handling what could otherwise be some family's heirlooms. They rationalized this behavior or dissipated their uneasiness by assuring themselves that the new owners would more properly care for and appreciate these antiques. Nevertheless, one dealer who had experienced some anxiety in handling others' possessions at estate sales, said that when he dies he hopes his own antique collection is never opened to the public this way. In these attitudes we may not be very different from our prehistoric forebearers who commonly buried grave goods with the dead because these objects were seen to belong to them and because there was fear that the spirit of the dead still clung to their possessions (Belk 1982).

Appreciative owners of an antique, however, are unable to preserve the same sense of past that the object had for its original, but now anonymous, owner. Therefore, even at bargain rates, the market for other families' photograph albums is minuscule. When a buyer is found, the photographs are generally admired only for their artistic or general historical interest. In this case, the events and people in these photos become types or characters whose meanings and lives remain a mystery. The particular past becomes the general past and much significance is lost in the process. When the antique stays within the family as an heirloom there is a better chance of preserving its particular past, but even here something is bound to be lost. One informant (WF 50) who is a collector of nutcrackers carefully labeled each one to tell the daughter she hoped would inherit the collection when and where each piece was acquired and the price paid. But she herself neither needs to look at these labels nor restricts her memories of each nutcracker to such demographic data. Asked at random about one piece among the hundreds in her collection she replied:

> I got that one in San Diego. I remember the store and I remember how excited I was when I saw it, because I'd never seen it before. And now it was mine. There are a lot of memories in my collection. Its not just the things themselves.

More poignant still were the memories of those who had suffered involuntary losses of possessions. For one man (WM 40) whose house had been badly damaged by a flood 6-weeks earlier, the most significant losses were the furniture and rooms constructed by his recently deceased father and the carpentry tools that once had belonged to his father. While others in the community had moved far enough in the grief process for some tearful acceptance of their losses, he was still beside himself with anger. It was not just things he lost in the flood; he had symbolically lost his father all over again. It was as if he had been barred from achieving the closure of Shakespeare's final couplet:

> But if the while I think on thee, dear friend,
> All losses are restored and sorrows end.

In closing, it is useful to consider briefly whether the tangible preservation of memories in possessions is a good thing. This evaluation must be contingent upon the degree to which such a focus on past is central to our lives. Certainly a person, family, or nation without a sense of past has lost something important (e.g., Haley 1976). The sense of security, identity, and continuity which possessions that signal our past can provide is clearly beneficial. But when the past becomes so central to our lives that it begins to crowd out the present and the future, there is cause for concern. An excessive focus on the past can also make us resistent to any change (McCracken 1988). As Rochberg-Halton (1986) suggests:

> When remembrance becomes an end unto itself, mere nostalgia, it degenerates into a terminal bubble of the past that both closes one off from the living spontaneity of the present and denies the possibility of a future. [But] Without remembrance, a life is subject to all the transient social fashions of the day, a leaf in the flux of a stream, incapable of calling anything truly its own, without its own conditioned history and ground for self-control (p. 188).

While this conclusion perhaps makes too much of a virtue of western notions of mastery and self-control, it appropriately suggests that within limits, the tangible remembrance of things past can be a good thing. Reified reminders are not the only way of transcending our present time and place, but they are one of the most meaningful and reliable ways. Without these objects our memories may be as ephemeral as flowers. But through our treasure troves of mementos and souvenirs, these flowers can bloom again and again.

REFERENCES

Agee, James and Walker Evans (1941), *Let Us Now Praise Famous Men: Three Tenant Families*, Cambridge, MA: Riverside Press.

Ames, Kenneth L. and William S. Ayres (1985), "Memory and the American Home," slides and tape, Unit 7 from *The Material Culture of American Homes*, Winterthur, DL: Henry Francis du Pont Winterthur Museum.

Bachelard, Gaston (1964), *The Poetics of Space*, Maria Jolas, trans., New York: Orion Press.

Baker, Norman (1955), "Confucianism," *The World's Religions*, 3rd ed., J. N. Anderson, ed., Grand Rapids, MI: Wm. B. Eerdmans, 161-189.

Bartlett, Frederic C. (1932), *Remembering: A Study in Experimental and Social Psychology*, Cambridge: Macmillan

Baudrillard, Jean (1975), *The Mirror of Production*, St. Louis, MO: Telos Press.

Becker, Ernest (1975), *Escape from Evil*, New York: Free Press.

Belk, Russell W. (1982), "Acquiring, Possessing, and Collecting: Fundamental Processes in Consumer Behavior," *Marketing Theory: Philosophy of Science Perspectives*, Ronald F. Bush and Shelby D. Hunt, eds., Chicago: American Marketing Association, 185-190.

Belk, Russell W. (1986), "Art Versus Science as Ways of Generating Knowledge About Materialism," *Perspectives on Methodology in Consumer Research*, David Brinberg and Richard Lutz, eds., New York: Springer-Verlag, 3-36.

Belk, Russell W. (1987), "Identity and the Relevance of Market, Personal, and Community Objects," *Marketing and Semiotics: New Directions in the Study of Signs for Sale*, Jean Umiker-Sebeok, ed., Berlin: Mouton de Gruyter, 151-164.

Belk, Russell W. (1988), "Possessions and the Extended Self," *Journal of Consumer Research*, 15 (September), 139-168.

Belk, Russell W. (1989), "Visual Images of Consumption: What You See and What You Get," *Proceedings of the American Marketing Association Winter Educators' Conference*, J. Paul Peter, ed., Chicago: American Marketing Association.

Belk, Russell W. (1990), "The Role of Possessions in Constructing and Maintaining a Sense of Past," *Advances in Consumer Research*, Vol. 17, Marvin Goldberg, Gerry Gorn, and Richard Pollay, eds., Provo, UT: Association for Consumer Research, 669-676.

Belk, Russell W., Melanie Wallendorf, and John Sherry (1989), "The Sacred and the Profane in Consumer Behavior: Theodicy on the Odyssey," *Journal of Consumer Research*, 16 (June), 1-38.

Belk, Russell W., Melanie Wallendorf, John Sherry, and Morris Holbrook (1990), "Collecting in a Consumer Culture," this volume.

Berger, Peter L. (1973), "'Sincerity' and 'Authenticity' in Modern Society." *The Public Interest*, 31 (Spring), 81-90.

Berman, Morris (1989), *Coming to Our Senses: Body and Spirit in the Hidden History of the West*, New York: Simon and Schuster.

Boerdam, Jaap and Warna O. Martinius (1980), "Family Photographs -- A Sociological Approach," *The Netherlands' Journal of Sociology*, 16 (October), 95-119.

Bommes, Michael and Patrick Wright (1982), "'Charms of Residence': The Public and the Past," *Making Histories: Studies in History-Writing and Politics*, Richard Johnson, Gregor McLennan, Bill Schwarz, and David Sutton, eds., London: Hutchinson, 253-301.

Bowlby, John (1969), *Attachment and Loss*, Vol. 1, London: Hogarth.

Brickman, Philip, Dan Coates, and Ronnie Janoff-Bulman (1978), "Lottery Winners and Accident Victims: Is Happiness Relative?," *Journal of Personality and Social Psychology*, 36 (8), 917-927.

Casey, Edward S. (1987), *Remembering: A Phenomenological Study*, Bloomington, IN: Indiana University Popular Press.

Caughey, John L. (1984), *Imaginary Social Worlds: A Cultural Approach*, Lincoln, NE: University of Nebraska Press.

Chalfen, Richard (1988), *Snapshot Versions of Life*, Bowling Green, OH: Bowling Green State University Popular Press.

Cheal, David (1988), *The Gift Economy*, London: Routledge.

Cherry, Christopher (1989), "How Can We Seize the Past?," *Philosophy*, 64 (January), 67-78.

Connerton, Paul (1989), *How Societies Remember*, Cambridge: Cambridge University Press.

Costa, Janeen A. and Russell W. Belk (1990), "Nouveaux Riches as Quintessential Americans: Case Studies of Consumption in An Extended Family," *Advances in Nonprofit Marketing*, Vol. 3, Russell W. Belk, ed., Greenwich, CT: JAI Press, 83-140.

Csikszentmihalyi, Mihaly and Eugene Rochberg-Halton (1981), *The Meaning of Things: Domestic Symbols and the Self*, Chicago: University of Chicago Press.

Cybart, Sharon (1988), "Souvenirs: Memories for Sale," 5-part radio series, Madison, WI: WORT.

Davis, Fred (1979), *Yearning for Yesterday: A Sociology of Nostalgia*, New York: Free Press.

Denzin, Norman K. (1989), *Interpretive Interactionism*, Newbury Park, CA: Sage.

Dethlefsen, Edwin S. (1981), "The Cemetery and Culture Change: Archaeological Focus and Ethnographic Perspective," *Modern Material Culture: The Archaeology of Us*, Richard A. Gould and Michael B. Schiffer, eds., New York: Academic Press, 137-159.

Di Piero, W. S. (1989), *Memory and Enthusiasm: Essays, 1975-1985*, Princeton, NJ: Princeton University Press, 117-143.

Eco, Umberto (1983), *Travels in Hyper Reality: Essays*, William Weaver, trans., San Diego: Harcourt Brace Jovanovich.

Fishwick, Marshall (1985), *Seven Pillars of Popular Culture*, Westport, CT: Greenwood Press.

Fontana, Andrea and Ronald W. Smith (1989), "Alzheimer's Disease Victims: The 'Unbecoming' of Self the the Normalization of Competence," *Sociological Perspective*, 32 (Spring), 35-46.

Francaviglia, Richard V. (1981), "'Main Street U.S.A.' A Comparison/Contrast of Streetscapes in Disneyland and Walt Disney World," *Journal of Popular Culture*, 15 (Summer), 141-156.

Freedberg, David (1989), *The Power of Images: Studies in the History and Theory of Response*, Chicago: University of Chicago Press.

Furby, Lita and Mary Wilke (1982), "Some Characteristics of Infants' Preferred Toys," *Journal of Genetic Psychology*, 140 (July), 207-219.

Gayle, Crystal (1982), "Old Boyfriends," written by Tom Waits, *One From the Heart: The Original Motion Picture Soundtrack of Francis Coppola's Movie*, New York: Columbia Records.

Geist, Christopher D. (1978), "Historic Sites and Monuments As Icons," *Icons of America*, Ray B. Browne and Marshall Fishwick, eds., Bowling Green, OH: Bowling Green State University Popular Press, 57-66.

George, Diana H. and Malcolm A. Nelson (1982), "Man's Infinite Concern: Graveyards as Fetishes," *Objects of Special Devotion: Fetishism in Popular Culture*, Ray B. Browne, ed., Bowling Green, OH: Bowling Green University Popular Press, 136-152.

Goldstein, Judith L. (1987), "Lifestyles of the Rich and Tyrannical," *American Scholar*, 56 (Spring), 235-247.

Gordon, Beverly (1986), "Souvenirs: Messengers of the Extraordinary," *Journal of Popular Culture*, 20 (3), 135-146.

Grolnick, Simon A. (1978), "Etruscan Burial Symbols and the Transitional Process," *Between Reality and Fantasy: Transitional Objects and Phenomena*, Simon A. Grolnick and Leonard Barkin, eds., New York: Jason Aronson, 381-410.

Gygi, Janice and Sandra Powell (1989), "Disposition of Goods by the Elderly in Transition: A Case Study," paper presented at American Marketing Association Winter Educators' Conference, February, St. Petersburg, FL.

Halbwachs, Maurice (1950), *The Collective Memory*, New York: Harper.

Haley, Alex (1976), *Roots*, Garden City, NY: Doubleday.

Hall, G. Stanley (1899), "Notes on Early Memory," *Pedagogical Seminary*, 6 (October), 485-512.

Handler, Richard (1986), "Authenticity," *Anthropology Today*, 2 (February), 2-4.

Harris, John E. (1978/1982), "External Memory Aids," *Practical Aspects of Memory*, M. M. Gruneberg, P. E. Morris, and R. N. Sykes, eds, London: Academic Press, reprinted in *Memory Observed: Remembering in Natural Contexts*, Ulric Neisser, ed., San Francisco, CA: W. H. Freeman and Company, 337-342.

Hillier, Bevis (1981), "Why Do We Collect Antiques?," *Our Pasts Before Us: Why Do We Save It?*, David Lowenthal and Marcus Binney, eds., London: Temple Smith, 70-82.

Hirschman, Elizabeth (1985), "Primitive Aspects of Consumption in Modern American Society," *Journal of Consumer Research*, 12 (September), 142-154.

Holbrook, Morris (1989), "'These Foolish Things,' 'The Dear Departed Past,' and the Songs of David Frishberg: A Commentary and Critique," *ACR Newsletter*, (June), Provo, UT: Association for Consumer Research, 1-8.

Holbrook, Morris (1990), "Nostalgic Consumption: On the Reliability and Validity of a New Nostalgia Index," working paper, Graduate School of Business, Columbia University, New York, NY.

Holbrook, Morris and Robert M. Schindler (1989), "Some Exploratory Findings on the Development of Musical Tastes," *Journal of Consumer Research*, 16 (June), 119-124.

Horne, Donald (1984), *The Great Museum: The Re-presentation of History*, London: Pluto Press.

Houghton, A. T. (1955), "Animism," *The World's Religions*, 3rd ed., J. N. Anderson, ed., Grand Rapids, MI: Wm. B. Eerdmans, 9-24.

Howells, William (1954), *The Back of History: The Story of Our Own Origins*, Garden City, NY: Doubleday.

Hubbard, William (1984), "The Meaning of Monuments," *The Public Interest*, 74 (Winter), 17-30.

James, Henry (1893), *The Real Thing and Other Tales*, New York: Macmillan.

Kant, Immanuel (1798), *Anthropologie in Pragmatisher Hinsicht*, I.XXXII., Köningsberg: F. Nicolovins.

Kastenbaum, Robert (1977), "Memories of Tomorrow: On the Interpenetrations of Time in Later Life," *The Personal Experience of Time*, Bernard S. Gorman and Alden E. Wessman, eds., New York: Plenum Press, 193-213.

Kaufmann, James C. A. (1980), "Learning from the Fotomat," *American Scholar*, 49 (Spring), 244-246.

Kavahagh, Gaynor (1989), "Objects as Evidence, or Not?," *Museum Studies in Material Culture*, Susan M. Pearce, ed., London: Leicester University Press, 125-137.

Korosec-Serfaty, Perla (1984), "The Home From Attic to Cellar," *Journal of Environmental Psychology*, 4, 303-321.

La Branche, Anthony (1971), "Neglected and Unused Things: Narrative Encounter," *Review of Existential Psychology and Psychiatry*, 12 (2), 163-168.

Langer, Susanne K. (1963), *Philosophy in a New Key: A Study in the Symbolism of Reason, Rite, and Art*, 3rd ed., Cambridge, MA: MIT Press.

Laughlin, Henry P. (1956), *The Neuroses in Clinical Practice*, Philadelphia, PA: W. B. Saunders.

Leong, Wai-Teng (1989), "Culture and the State: Manufacturing Traditions for Tourism," *Critical Studies in Mass Communication*, 6 (December), 355-375.

Lévi-Strauss, Claude (1962/1963), *Totemism*, Rodney Needham, translator, Boston: Beacon Press.

Lipsitz, George (1990), *Time Passages: Collective Memory and American Popular Culture*, Minneapolis, MN: University of Minnesota Press.

Lowenthal, David (1985), "Past Time, Present Place: Landscape and Memory," *Geographical Review*, 65 (January), 1-36.

Lowenthal, David (1985), *The Past is a Foreign Country*, Cambridge: Cambridge University Press.

Lynch, Kevin (1972), *What Time Is This Place?*, Cambridge, MA: MIT Press.

MacCannell, Dean (1976), *The Tourist: A New Theory of the Leisure Class*, New York: Schocken Books.

McCracken, Grant (1988), *Culture and Consumption: New Approaches to the Symbolic Character of Consumer Goods and Activities*, Bloomington, IN: Indiana University Press.

Madden, David (1964), *Wright Morris*, New York: Twayne Publishers.

Maines, David M. (1978), "Bodies and Selves: Notes on a Fundamental Dilemma in Demography," *Studies in Symbolic Interaction*, Vol. 1, Norman K. Denzen, ed., Greenwich, CT: JAI Press, 241-265.

Marcus, George (1988), "The Making of Pious Persons Within Contemporary American Notable Families," paper presented at American Anthropology Association Annual Meeting, November, Phoenix, AZ.

Mead, George H. (1929), "The Nature of the Past," *Essays in Honor of John Dewey*, John Coss, eds., New York: Henry Holt, 235-242.

Mehta, Raj and Russell W. Belk (1991), "Artifacts, Identity, and Transition: Favorite Possessions of Indians and Indian Immigrants to the U.S.," *Journal of Consumer Research*, 17 (March).

Milgram, Stanley (1977), "The Image-Freezing Machine," *Psychology Today*, (January), 50-54, 108.

Miller, Pamela (1982), "Hair Jewelry as Fetish," *Objects of Special Devotion: Fetishism in Popular Culture*, Ray B. Browne, ed., Bowling Green, OH: Bowling Green University Popular Press, 89-106.

Milspaw, Yvonne J. (1986), "Protestant Home Shrines: Icon and Image," *New York Folklore*, 12 (3-4), 119-136.

Moore, Brian (1976), *The Great Victorian Collection*, New York: Farrar, Straus, Giroux.

Morris, Wright (1978/1989), "On Memory, Emotion, and Imagination," and "Origins," from Wright Morris, *Earthly Delights, Heavenly Adornments*, New York: Harper & Row, reprinted in Wright Morris, *Time Pieces: Photographs, Writing, and Memory*, New York: Aperture Foundation, 33-36, 75-82.

Neal, Patsy (1985), "My Grandmother, the Bag Lady," *Newsweek*, February 11, 14.

Neisser, Ulric (1982), "Memory: What are the Important Questions?," *Memory Observed: Remembering in Natural Contexts*, Ulric Neisser, ed., San Francisco, CA: W. H. Freeman, 3-19.

Neisser, Ulric (1988), "New Vistas in the Study of Memory," *Remembering Reconsidered: Ecological and Traditional Approaches to the Study of Memory*, Ulric Neisser and Eugene Winograd, eds., Cambridge: Cambridge University Press, 1-10.

Neisser, Ulric (1989), "Domains of Memory," *Memory: Interdisciplinary Approaches*, Paul R. Solomon, George R. Goethals, Colleen M. Kelley, and Benjamine R. Stephens, eds., New York: Springer-Verlag, 67-83.

Nyström, Bengt and Gunilla Cedenius (1982), *Spreading the Responsibility for Museum Documentation--A Program for Contemporary Documentation at Swedish Museums of Cultural History*, Stockholm: Nordiska Museet.

O'Guinn, Thomas and Russell W. Belk (1989), "Heaven on Earth: Consumption at Heritage Village, U.S.A.," *Journal of Consumer Research*, 16 (September), 227-238.

Olson, Clark D. (1985), "Materialism in the Home: The Impact of Artifacts on Dyadic Communication," *Advances in Consumer Research*, Vol. 12, Elizabeth Hirschman and Morris Holbrook, eds., Provo, UT: Association for Consumer Research, 388-393.

Orwell, George (1949), *1984*, New York: Harcourt, Brace and Company.

Patterson, John S. (1989), "From Battle Ground to Pleasure Ground: Gettysburg as a Historic Site," *History Museums in the United States: A Critical Assessment*, Warren Leon and Roy Rosenzweig, eds., Urbana, IL: University of Illinois Press, 128-157.

Pike, Martha (1984), "In Memory of: Artifacts Relating to Mourning in Nineteenth Century America," *American Material Culture: The Shape of Things Around Us*, Edith Mayo, ed., Bowling Green, OH: Bowling Green State University Popular Press, 48-65.

Pocius, Gerald L. (1979), "Holy Pictures in Newfoundland Houses: Visual Codes for Secular and Supernatural Relationships," *Laurentian University Review*, 12 (1), 101-125.

Prine, John (1972), "Souvenirs," *Diamonds in the Rough*, Atlantic Recording Corporation.

Proust, Marcel (1913-1917/1981), *Remembrance of Things Past*, Vols. 1-3, C. K. Scott Moncrieff and Terence Kilmartin, translators, New York: Random House.

Rabinowitz, Howard N. (1978), "George Washington as Icon, 1865-1900," *Icons of America*, Ray B. Browne and Marshall Fishwick, eds., Bowling Green, OH: Bowling Green State University Popular Press, 67-86.

Radley, Alan (1990), "Artefacts, Memory and a Sense of the Past," *Collective Remembering*, David Middleton and Derek Edwards, eds., London: Sage, 46-59.

Rilke, Rainer M. (1939), *Duino Elegies*, J. Leishman and S. Spender, translators, New York: W. W. Norton.

Rochberg-Halton, Eugene (1986), *Meaning and Modernity: Social Theory in the Pragmatic Attitude*, Chicago: University of Chicago Press.

Romanyshyn, Robert D. (1989), *Technology as Symptom & Dream*, London: Routledge.

Rosaldo, Renato (1989), "Imperialist Nostalgia," *Representations*, 26 (Spring), 107-122.

Rosenblatt, Paul C., R. Patricia Walsh, and Douglas A. Jackson (1976), *Grief and Mourning in Cross-Cultural Perspective*, New Haven, CT: Human Relations Area Files.

Rowles, Graham D. (1980), "Growing Old 'Inside': Aging and Attachment to Place in an Appalachian Community," *Transition of Aging*, N. Datan and N. Lohmann, eds., New York: Academic Press, 153-172.

Rue, Nancy N. (1990), "These Things Remind Me of...," *Current Consumer and Lifestudies*, (November).

Sacks, Oliver (1985), *The Man Who Mistook His Wife for a Hat, and Other Clinical Tales*, New York: Harper and Row.

Salaman, Esther (1970/1982), *A Collection of Moments: A Study of Involuntary Memories*, London: Longman, reprinted (in part) in *Memory Observed: Remembering in Natural Contexts*, Ulric Neisser, ed., San Francisco, CA: W. H. Freeman and Company, 49-63.

Schuman, Howard and Jacqueline Scott (1989), "Generations and Collective Memories," *American Sociological Review*, 54 (June), 359-381.

Schwartz, George (1987), *George Washington: The Making of an American Symbol*, New York: Free Press.

Shakespeare, William (1609/1961), "Sonnet XXX," *The Complete Works of Shakespeare*, Hardin Craig, ed., Chicago: Scott Foresman, 476.

Sherman, Edmund and Evelyn S. Newman (1977), "The Meaning of Cherished Personal Possessions for the Elderly," *International Journal of Aging and Human Development*, 8 (2), 181-192.

Sontag, Susan (1977), *On Photography*, New York: Farrar, Straus & Giroux.

Spence, Donald P. (1988), "Passive Remembering," *Remembering Reconsidered: Ecological and Traditional Approaches to the Study of Memory*, Ulric Neisser and Eugene Winograd, eds., Cambridge: Cambridge University Press, 311-325.

Starobinski, Jean (1966), "The Idea of Nostalgia," *Diogenes*, 54 (Summer), 81-103.

Stavenow-Hidemark, Elisabet (1985), *Home Thoughts From Abroad: An Evaluation of the SAMDOK Homes Pool*, Stockholm: Nordiska Museet.

Stewart, Kathleen (1988), "Nostalgia--A Polemic," *Cultural Anthropology*, 3 (3), 227-241.

Stewart, Susan (1984), *On Longing: Narratives of the Miniature, the Gigantic, the Souvenir, the Collection*, Baltimore, MD: Johns Hopkins University Press.

Stone, Elizabeth (1988), *Black Sheep and Kissing Cousins: How Our Family Stories Shape Us*, New York: Viking Penguin.

Sussman, Marvin B., Judith N. Cates, and David I. Smith (1970), *The Family and Inheritance*, New York: Russell Sage Foundation.

Takizawa, Matsuyo (1927), *The Disintegration of the Old Family System*, New York: Columbia University Press, 108-131.

Tibbetts, John (1981), "Arguments Between Art and Science in the Work of P. H. Emerson and H. P. Robinson," *Journal of American Culture*, 4 (Spring), 149-172.

Trilling, Lionel (1971), *Sincerity and Authenticity*, Cambridge, MA: Harvard University Press.

Tuan, Yi-Fu (1976), "Geopiety: A Theme in Man's Attachment to Nature and to Place," *Geographies of the Mind: Essays in Historical Geography*, David Lowenthal and Martyn J. Bowden, eds., New York: Oxford University Press, 11-39.

Tyrfelt, Annika (1988), Interview (Curator at Nordiska Museet, Stockholm), January 11.

Unruh, David R. (1983), "Death and Personal History: Strategies of Identity Preservation," *Social Problems*, 30 (3), 340-351.

Vaidyanathan, T. G. (1989), "Authority and Identity in India," *Daedalus*, 118 (Fall), 147-169.

Vanderstel, David G. (1989), "Humanizing the Past: The Revitalization Of The History Museum," *Journal of American Culture*, 12 (Summer), 19-25.

Volland, Anita (1987), "Metaphors of Time: Symbolic Dimensions of Polynesian Self-Images," *Mirror and Metaphor: Material and Social Constructions of Reality*, Daniel W. Ingersoll, Jr. and Gordon Bronitsky, eds., Lanham, MD: University Press of America, 113-125.

Vygotsky, Lev S. (1978), *Mind in Society*, Cambridge, MA: Harvard University Press.

Wallace, Michael (1986), "Visiting the Past: History Museums in the United States," *Presenting the Past: Essays on History and the Public*, Susan P. Benson, Stephen Brier, and Roy Rosenzweig, eds., Philadelphia, PA: Temple University Press, 137-161.

Wallace, Michael (1989), "Mickey Mouse History: Portraying the Past in Disney World," *History Museums in the United States: A Critical Assessment*, Warren Leon and Roy Rosenzweig, eds., Urbana, IL: University of Illinois Press, 158-180.

Wallendorf, Melanie and Eric Arnould (1988), "My Favorite Things: A Cross-Cultural Inquiry into Object Attachment," *Journal of Consumer Research*, 14 (March), 531-547.

Warner, W. Lloyd (1959), *The Living and the Dead: A Study of the Symbolic Life of Americans*, New Haven, CT: Yale University Press.

Wecter, Dixon (1941), *The Hero in America: A Chronicle of Hero-Worship*, New York: Charles Scribner.

Wiggins, James W. (1974), "The Decline of Private Property and the Diminished Person," *Property in a Humane Economy*, Samuel L. Blumenfeld, ed., LaSalle, IL: Open Court, 71-84.

Winnicott, D. W. (1953), "Transitional Objects and Transitional Phenomena," *International Journal of Psychoanalysis*, 34 (2), 89-97.

Young, Melissa and Melanie Wallendorf (1989), "Ashes to Ashes, Dust to Dust: Conceptualizing Consumer Disposition of Possessions," *American Marketing Association Winter Educator's Conference Proceedings*, Chicago: American Marketing Association.

The Delivery and Consumption of Vacation Performances

Jeffrey F. Durgee
Morris B. Holbrook
John F. Sherry

INTRODUCTION

A defining characteristic of entertainment (with a small "e") as opposed to Art (with a capital "A") is that it belongs to the realm that sociologists refer to as "popular" as opposed to "high" culture. Sociologists like Gans (1974) have often looked askance at the implicit elitism entailed by drawing a potentially pejorative distinction between pop culture and high culture. Yet, at bottom, one cannot avoid the recognition--however grudging--that something can achieve mass popularity only by virtue of its ability to appeal to some fundamental substratum of esthetic, ludic, ceremonial or hedonic tastes. Mass acceptance depends on broad accessibility which, in turn, requires ease of comprehension, primal level of engagement, and communality of appreciation. As Herbie Mann (a commercially successful jazz-rock musician) once told a reporter, "Don't let your taste get in the way of reaching a broader audience." (*Newsweek* 4/2/79).

World Wrestling Federation wrestling matches are good examples of this insofar as they have a basic dramatic substratum which has wide appeal. Another example is what we call "vacation performances." This term refers to events staged for vacationers by professional and semi-proessional entertainers. These events, as encountered by researchers during their travels on the Consumer-Behavior Odyssey, constitute the theme of the present chapter.

Specifically, much of one month of the Odyssey was spent amidst summer vacationers in eastern Pennsylvania. These vacationers come from the New York City, New Jersey, and nearby Pennsylvania regions and consist mainly of middle and lower-middle income families. The area, a popular vacation spot for over forty years, offers miles of wooded foothills as well as resorts, health spas, craft shops, discount stores, amusement parks, sight-seeing spots, and special activities such as county fairs or historic festivals. For example, recreations of Civil War battles have become especially popular. While most of the vacationers come with immediate families, some of the resorts are targeted to special groups such as honeymooners, people who want to lose weight, and certain religious sects or cults.

Park owners and promoters in the area have found that in order to attract vacationers, they must stage special events. For example, owners of amusement parks feel pressure to design and build bigger and more exciting rides. Meanwhile, fair and resort promoters find that they draw bigger crowds if they provide special performances and stage shows. Thus, an amusement park seems to attract larger attendance if it stages a cowboy gunfight two times a day, while a revolutionary-war period theme park generates more interest if it features a brief show about some period-related event.

The present chapter focuses on these stage shows. In brief, we consider five shows: a small circus, a country-and-western music show, and comedy routine along with a medieval joust at a renaissance festival, and a newlywed game at a honeymoon resort. Each lasts approximately thirty minutes and is designed to appeal to all family members (with the exception of the honeymoon game). All give vacationers a chance to rest and be entertained passively-- as opposed to walking around the parks and being involved actively in rides and amusements. All punctuate the day-long experience of being at a park ("shows at 11:00, 2:00, and 4:00"). All bring the theme of the park to life (e.g., a battle display at a Civil War park). And all involve between five and six principal actors, acrobats, musicians, or comedians performing for audiences of from one to two hundred people.

These shows command our interest for at least three reasons.

First, they reflect a general trend toward vacation performances. This trend is occurring nation-wide and is interesting to consider from a mass consumption standpoint. For example, it is possible that much of the shows' popularity is due to television. Because of television, vacationers have become a ready market for holiday programs that are similar in format and content to standard network programs--i.e., thirty minutes long, with heavy action or comedy components, low intellectual content, and readily identified story lines. Another factor that might account for the trend toward vacation shows is the desire to collect show experiences. In this connection, vacationers were noted to boast that they had seen "the Renaissance show, the old time music show, and the western stuntman show."

Second, in its own right, each show has a peculiar type of magic, a unique way of involving people in its content, flow, and personalities. The shows therefore provide condensed versions of large-scale stage shows. This makes it possible to scrutinize them carefully so as to consider which show elements do or do not "work," which ones appeal to which audiences, which reactions are stirred by which elements, and which ways the audience and actors relate to each other.

Third, these shows represent collectively a genre of cultural performance that is reflexive in nature. Such performance serves to reveal people to themselves, and allows them to re-experience in significant measure the experiences of their progenitors and forerunners (Turner 1985, 187;207). These contemporary shows have their roots in the ritual process, and involve the communication of the sacred symbols of community, the ludic deconstruction and recombination of the culturally familiar, and the simplification of social structural relationships (Turner 1985, 293). According to Turner (1985, 295-296) these performances collectively are

"...one of the many inheritors of that great multifaceted system of preindustrial ritual which embraces ideas and images of cosmos and chaos, interdigitates clowns and their foolery with gods and their solemnity, and uses all the sensory codes, to produce symphonies in more than music: the intertwining of dance, body languages of many kinds, song, chant, architectural forms (temples, amphitheaters), incense, burnt offerings, ritualized feasting and drinking, painting, body painting, body marking of many kinds, including circumcision and scarification, the application of lotions and drinking of potions, the enacting of mythic and heroic plots drawn from oral traditions. And so much more."

The shows described in the following pages convey a constellation of meanings through which individuals, as actors and as spectators, conspire to reproduce the cosmos.

This is the purpose of the present chapter. First, to preview briefly, we describe the performances of interest in depth. We then use these to analyze themes and forces that might help us understand (1) the increasing popularity of vacation performances, (2) the sense of involvement or magic they produce in the audience, and (3) the cultural significance of performance.

DESCRIPTIONS OF PERFORMANCES

The Merrio Circus

On Saturday, August 2, the Odysseans visit the Green County Fair near Centertown, NY. In our eagerness to get off to an early start, we reach the gate at 10:00 a.m., only to learn that the main fair grounds do not open until noon. This allows ample opportunity, while waiting, to visit the goat show--an event

that, with its carefully calculated and complicated multiattribute scoring system (based on general appearance, straightness of back, slope of rump, and milk-giving capacity as indicated by largeness of udder) bears an undeniable resemblance to the Miss America Pageant (except that, in the case of goats, talent is irrelevant and the criterion of breast size is made somewhat more explicit). Owners of the caprine contestants include local farmers, but also some gentry from the surrounding community, such as the Madison Avenue advertising executive who becomes an informant and eloquently explains his positioning strategy for winning blue ribbons.

After a two-hour delay, during which we *more* than satisfy our curiosity about the standards for judging the relative merits of goats, the fair finally opens for business. We lug our camera, tape machine, and other gear through the front gate and wander past the little stalls, food shops, and other concession stands. In one undercover area, a man sells electric pianos. In another, a man runs a charity game in which children pay a small fee to fish for prizes. Everyone wins something, though usually not much. We pause to admire and photograph the tattoos of the barker who runs the electronic handwriting-analysis machine. Then we devote some serious time and energy to interviewing two pet salespeople--one who sells ferrets and another who specializes in parrots.

Besides the attractions already mentioned, the fair's square mile of grounds includes a two-lane midway, livestock exhibits, produce exhibits, horseshoe-throwing contests, rides, fortune tellers, beer tents, a petting zoo, and a large open dirt stadium area for horse races or, on occasions, major stage productions with big name entertainers. The racetrack sits in the middle of the fairgrounds, and the rides, exhibit halls, and midway booths are arranged around it.

The Merrio Circus is a short walk from the midway. It offers four shows a day, all under a large red-and-white tent. There is no charge because admission is covered as part of the price of the fair. The "cast" consists of a ringleader named Mr. Merrio, three women performers, two male clowns, and one older male roustabout. The single ring is surrounded on three sides by bleachers with three tiers. The audience, including standees, averages around 150 people and consists mainly of mothers, some fathers, and many, many children. There are four bright lights suspended from the tent roof. Taped music comes from some tinny-sounding speakers.

Before the Merrio show begins, one of the clowns comes out to warm the crowd. He says, "Let's have a little noise," and the many children yell, timidly at first but louder and louder as the clown asks for more.

The ringleader then comes out and introduces the first act, "Miss Neena and her trained pig Ralph." Ralph weighs over 300 pounds and is led on a leash. He runs out very fast, jumps two hurdles, and leaves. The hurdles are only six inches high; so the act draws a lot of laughter.

A second woman performer comes out, "Miss Keysa and her Canine Review." The review includes two king poodles dyed pink. The two dogs run around, jump over each other, and push a barrel. Miss Keysa then has one jump a jump rope. Afterward, the ringleader says, "What a mess of mutts that was."

A clown named "Big Mac" now enters. Mac boasts to the ringmaster that he can balance three small balls on the end of a broom handle. He does, but shows later that he has tricked the ringmaster by putting a wire through the the centers of the balls. The children howl.

Next, Miss Neena returns, this time on a two foot high ball. She manages to jump rope on it but falls when she tries to walk it up and down a seesaw. All the while, the tinny music plays a tense rock-and-roll theme. Miss Neena walks the ball up a long ramp, turns, then walks it back down.

A trained llama is next, jumping hurdles and crawling on her knees. She is "Calypso, the High Jumping Llama." "She is certainly graceful," says the ringmaster.

Big Mac returns and boasts to the ringmaster that he is the world's strongest clown. He invites children to pull on two ropes, one in each of his hands. About sixty children run into the ring. They pull very hard, but get nowhere because the two ropes are actually one rope that runs through the clown's sleeves. Big Mac steps out of his coat, and runs out of the ring.

The ringmaster then enters the ring astride an Appaloosa, "Apache Bandolero," and rides through a brief dressage routine. The horse prances to rock-and-roll music; gets on one knee, then two; and lies down while the ringmaster stands on its side.

Miss Keysa returns and climbs up the "Spanish Web," a long rope with a loop for her wrist. She hangs from the top of the tent, about 16 feet from the floor, and spins slowly to another rock-and-roll theme.

A new performer, Miss Wanda, comes out with a person in a very real-looking gorilla suit. The gorilla escapes from his cage and runs into the crowd, dragging a teenage male into the ring by his leg. Miss Wanda cracks her whip over him. She makes him jump on a pogo stick, but he gets away again and takes a purse from a woman in the audience. He climbs to the top of the cage and pulls from the purse a bra and panties, which he places on his head. The children scream. The woman goes after him, but he attacks her, pulling off her blond wig and skirt. At this, the children scream with laughter.

A grand finale featuring a man riding a motorcycle inside a steel cage globe, the "Globe of Death," is cancelled because it is rainy and the globe is slippery.

Later, driven by the rain to seek shelter in a crowded spot under a small overhanging roof, we pause to interview a man and his wife. They have driven here from Danbury, Connecticut, and are quite disappointed that the rain is so bad. They came mostly to see the circus. It had no jugglers nor big wild animals, but did have horses and dogs and a woman who walked on something (though they could not specify what). They did not feel disappointed, however, because it was free. The drive did not bother them because they do this all the time and it's no big deal. Almost every weekend they go to a fair or flea market or amusement park somewhere in the area (Connecticut or New York). This week, it is time for the Green County Fair, which they've visited before and always enjoy.

The Country-and-Western Show

At the same county fair is a large tented area that can seat one to two hundred people at long tables. At night, shows are held for the fair goers which they can watch while drinking beer and eating pizza. A popular show each evening is "Outlaw", a five-piece country-and-western band with a female vocalist.

All band members wear blue jeans and cowboy hats except the vocalist. She wears a print blouse, skirt, and cowboy boots. The show is about an hour long, broken into two sets.

The audience consists of middle-aged couples with a few children present. Many wear blue jeans. A couple near the front of the audience wears large cowboy hats, which they nod vigorously in time to the song rhythms. Half the audience is talking among themselves while the other half pays close attention to the show. Many couples seem to know each song and mouth the words along with the singers.

The lead singer directs the show. She says, "We'd like to start with a song from the Forrester Sisters titled `Just in Case'." Like many of the songs, "Just in Case" consists of a half dozen lyrics and a chorus which many in the audience join in singing. The chorus for "Just in Case" is "I saw you with another woman, what can I do? Just in case you ever change your mind and give me one try, just in case you ever change your mind."

The next song is "Your Cheatin' Heart" followed by a more upbeat "Playin' with the Queen of Hearts." One verse of "Queen of Hearts" is: "Midnight and I'm awaitin' the twelve oh five, hopin' it'll take me just a little farther down the line. Moonlight, you're just a heartache in disguise, won't you keep my heart from breakin' if it's only for a very short time." The chorus is: "Playin' with the queen of hearts, knowin' it ain't very smart. The joker is the only fool who'll do anything for you."

The lead singer says, "Pete Rose has got a little advice for you," and the entire band sings, "Mamas, don't let your babies grow up to be cowboys."

The next song is "Mama, He's Crazy Over Me," then the singer launches into a song called "It's Alright, It's Midnight, and I've Got Two More Bottles of Wine."

A song follows with the lyrics, "How can I be just your friend. You want me to act like we've never kissed. I've cried and cried. I fall to pieces each time someone speaks your name. Each time I go out with someone new, you walk by and I fall to pieces."

A guitar player steps up to sing the Johnny Cash song, "Folsom Prison." Then another song follows with the chorus, "Satin sheets to lie on, satin sheets to cry on, you've given me everything money can buy. But you didn't keep me satisfied."

The last two songs to end the set are "Wastin' Away in Margueritaville" and a happier, more upbeat "Good Old Mountain Dew".

Comedy Show at Renaissance Fair

The next day (Sunday, August 3), we visit the Renaissance Festival in Sherwood Forest Park, down near Buffern, NY. This festival is a three-day re-creation of life in a small medieval village. The village is set up in a valley surrounded by woods, and consists of tents and plywood buildings assembled to look like medieval street scenes. Admission is relatively high (ten dollars for adult). Yet the parking lot is filled with the cars of vacationing families.

The fair is intended to be an educational as well as a recreational experience. It includes over fifty people dressed in medieval costumes who work in shops, pubs, and craft centers. There are also entertainment centers which feature medieval music, Elizabethan drama, and jugglers.

On arrival, we spend some time at the gate of the Renaissance Festival persuading the manager to let us in free and to give us permission to tape the activities and people. After cautioning us against videotaping anything that is copyrighted or protected by Actor's Equity he lets us in with his blessings.

We head for the Mud Show. The Mud Show features five young "buffoons" in a sort of slapstick romp through a filthy pit filled with deep mud. We shoot quite a bit of footage of these clowns build audience excitement and hustle for coins. The audience responds enthusiastically and is especially receptive to the aspects of the performance that include

wallowing in the mud and putting it into the mouth. Dressed as medieval "street beggars," the five actors put on a twenty minute show four times a day. The beggars wear rags and are covered with dried mud. Several have beards and long hair which are also caked with mud. All speak loudly as they lie in the streets and then enter the pit: "Alms for a poah beggah, alms?"

The pit sits in a theater-in-the-round setting, the audience on benches which ring the elevated muddy stage. The audience, in light-colored summer clothes provides a sharp contrast to the dirty, brown entertainers.

One of the troupe yells, "What is mud spelled backwards?" The crowd, especially the children, roars back, "Dum!" The leader then announces that the troupe will do the five classical elements of Greek mythology: "water, earth, air, fire, and the void". He introduces the first character "Gonzo" as "the Black Sheep of the Medici family." "Gonzo," he says, "will gargle swill for your amusement and edification." Other members of the troupe pass among the audience asking for donations: "fifty cents to a dollar." The leader asks the audience for background music to the act, and it is decided to do the theme from a television show, "Gilligan's Island." While the troupe hums the theme, the audience sings along, and Gonzo gargles muddy water.

Next, the audience endures another request for money, this time for a troupe member who will do "*air*-obics." The request is for sixty cents. A few people donate money. Then, while the "Beggars Choir" sings a song ("The Summer Wind"), one of the members ("Half-brain Bernard") slips and does pratfalls into a puddle of thick mud. The audience laughs and groans, and the leader says, "You ain't seen nothin' yet."

The troupe members then go among the crowd to beg again-- this time, for a dollar. The theme for this stunt is "fire." A woman is brought on stage from the audience. A comedian stands on a stump above the stage with a foot-long strip of rag hanging from the front of his pants. The other members shout, "Only a fool would let a woman near his tools with fire." Led by a troupe member, the crowd counts backward, 3 - 2 - 1, and the woman lights the end of the strip with a lighter. The flame rises up a few inches, then the comedian dives stomach first into a large mud puddle.

The troupe then begs for a donation of three dollars but there are few donors. This act is "The Void." Gonzo, the star of the first act, lies on his back while the other members cover him in mud. The crowd howls as he is covered and left with a large mud phallus.

The last act calls for a donation of four dollars. The leader asks what is the most disgusting thing that can be done with mud, and the crowd answers, "*eating it!*" After another countdown, all members of the troupe take large handfuls of moist mud, and pretend to eat it. One says it is, "a touch too tart."*

After the show, we are pondering the possibility of interviewing the trio sitting behind us when one of the actors--a tall thin young man of about 22 or 23--comes over, takes an interest in the camera, and starts talking. We get the tape rolling, reposition the camera, and begin shooting the interview.

This fellow intends to pursue a career in comedy. He has graduated last year from Columbia University where he majored in Urban Sociology and worked with a comedy-improvisation group. He has been driving a cab, but got this opportunity for a comedic gig and grabbed it.

We ask our informant how it feels to commune so intimately with Mother Earth. In response, the buffoon minimizes the importance of his culinary actions. Before long, he begins clowning for the camera and occasionally lapses into what sound like canned routines. He does have a serious side, however, and makes some earnest statements about his career plans. He first realized he had a flair for comedy when he gave the valedictorian speech in high school. Everybody laughed in all the right places. Now he works on improvised comedy, something he illustrates at the end of the interview, indicating his phone number by holding up the appropriate number of fingers to represent each digit.

The Joust

After these two interviews, we all head for the joust. This is the festival's big spectacle and concludes the day on an appropriately festive note. The joust is held on a three-acre open field, and is attended by over two-hundred vacationers. It begins with some preliminary displays of horsemanship and knighthood. After a while, the Queen arrives. She is "played" by a very attractive middle-aged actress who converses with great conviction about the excellence of today's tournament. This Queen is accompanied by an enormous entourage of courtiers as well as a king, a princess, some knights, and assorted townspeople--all in period costumes. Two knights then ride in on horseback, one in red, the other in black.

The knights gallop at each other. The red knight clicks his lance off the black knight's shield. There's a second pass, and both miss. The crowd boos the black knight, and all laugh. Another pass, and the red knight's lance glances off the black's shield.

---

*Geophagy- the eating of earth- is a culturally significant behavior of ethnographic record.

Red is given a new lance and charges again. The lance, made of light wood, splinters into many pieces, and Red looks weakened. Black knocks him on the side of his helmet, and he falls to the ground. Black charges, but Red pulls him from his horse. Both draw broad swords and fight. Things begin to look bad for Red as Black's seconds join the battle against him.

Then, to laughter and cries of "oh no!" in the crowd, Robin Hood runs onto the field with his Merry Men and joins the fray. Red throws Black to the ground and is poised to kill him, but the crowd roars back, "no!" Red then charges around the field on Black's horse, picks up the princess, and gallops off into the trees.

The Honeymooners Game

On Monday, August 4, the Odysseans drive deep into the heartland of the Poconos' honeymoon heaven. We visit a memories-oriented tourist town called "Nostalgiaville" and a resort called "Breezy Peaks Lodge." Breezy Peaks' main building has 1940's furniture, rather dirty carpets, and crowds of guests. We shoot some photos of the activity board, some furnishings, and formal portraits of a couple in their heart-shaped tub.

There are many honeymoon resorts in the area. Some are for honeymooners only and prohibit non-honeymooners from using their restaurants, bars, or other facilities. Others cater to honeymooners and non-honeymooners alike.

Nero's Springvale is a club that caters to both groups. It was built recently by a Las Vegas holding company in anticipation that legalized gambling would be introduced into the area. There are separate cabins with dark-stained wood siding, abundant sports facilities, and a large, modern lodge with dining halls, video game rooms, and a nightclub which seats two hundred people.

We quickly find this nightclub. Its audience includes a few honeymooners but mainly consists of groups of friends or "old marrieds" sitting in groups of four, five, and six to a table. These patrons are listening half-heartedly to a loud lounge band (bass guitar, drums, electronic keyboards, reeds, and a female singer). People applaud only on cue.

The leader of the band, "Licentious Lou Sacci" emerges as the master of ceremonies for Nero's very own imitation of "The Newlywed Game." Wearing a black tuxedo and a large-brimmed, white fedora hat, Lou starts the show: "We know the honeymooners--they come in walking funny. Tomorrow is Tuesday. We have a softball game against Paradise Valley and then a volleyball game. Tomorrow night is Mardi Gras night. You'll each receive a mask. We'll have cajun food, then have horse races out at the pool with a dixieland band."

Lou speaks with a heavy put-on Brooklyn accent: "Da guys knows whats I means, da girls don't." He selects three couples from the floor to play the game. Two of the couples are newly married, the third has been married for a year. None of the other newlyweds in the audience want to participate.

Lou gets all three couples on the stage and begins teasing, "We find whips and chains in the rooms when you guys leave. Did you see the mirror over the bed? You didn't? You're only lookin' down!"

The women are sent from the room, and Lou asks the men the first question: "On your first date, would your wife say you were Gentle Ben, Sloppy Joe, or Horny Harry?" All reply "Gentle Ben." The next question is, "What part of a man's body would your wife look at first?" All reply, "chest." Next: "What type of guy would your wife like best, Robert Redford, O.J. Simpson, Tom Selleck, or Boy George?" The answers are "Redford," "Selleck" and "Simpson." Then, "What size banana would your wife like, the small, medium, or jumbo?" All say "jumbo."

The women come back, and the men are excused. Lou asks, "Will your husband say your breasts remind him of fuzzy peaches, warm apples, huge grapefruit, or dried up, sunken bananas?" All reply, "apples." Lou asks, "What is the first name of your last boyfriend?" and, "What is the weirdest place you ever made love?" The players are willing to give ex-boyfriends' names although one woman balks suddenly at the love-making question. She is visibly shaken and tells Lou "that's enough." Lou pries further, however, and she finally relents, "a park bench." Lou then asks, "Who is the moaner?" Then: "Since you've been here at Springvale, how many times have you made love?" To the last question, the woman who balked earlier balks again, "That's none of your business."

The men return, and Lou, upset by the lack of cooperation, says, "This is the worst game ever." He then asks the women the questions he asked the men, and vice versa. The one woman player is still upset, and looks down in her lap. Lou tells a joke, "I heard a guy through the wall last night. He must sell candy for a living because all night this girl is saying, `Oh Henry'."

One couples' answers are the closest, and Lou says to the other two (losing) couples: "I usually don't do this, but give these two couples bottles of champagne on me, you have been great players." (One couple includes the young woman, who is still obviously upset.) To the winning couple, he says, "I have no washer or TV. The prize is a book, `How to Honeymoon' and a small trophy (four inches high), and a bottle of champagne."

One of the Odysseans, who owns a summer house in the Poconos, found Lou Sacci's recreation of the "Newlywed Game" a difficult experience--not so much of Lou's vulgarity as because of the obvious discomfort of his victims. This Odyssean's log contained the following entry:

This newlywed rip-off proceeds with heavy hand through a series of questions that serve mostly to embarrass one black, one white, and one inter-racial couple (all in their 20's). As one might expect, none of the couples shows much inspiration or insight. Often, all three contestants simply repeat each other's answers verbatim. For example, all three men think that their wives like jumbo as opposed to small or medium bananas. The well-spoken young black man thinks that his wife's breasts are like rosy red apples; he thinks his wife would like to have an affair with O.J. Simpson. The extremely shy, even younger white newlyweds stare at the floor and hide behind their fingers while telling their connubial secrets; they have made love on a bench and in a truck but cannot agree on which was stranger. The white woman in the inter-racial couple would most like to have an affair with Robert Redford; this jibes with the independently expressed opinion of her tall, black husband.

THE TREND TOWARD VACATION PERFORMANCES

The trend toward vacation performances is ubiquitous. Large parks such as the Universal Cities Studios tour in Los Angeles have added so many stuntman performances that the tour mostly consists of shows rather than rides. Disneyland and Disney World run shows constantly throughout the day (e.g., rock 'n roll singing groups, night time parades), and specialty parks such as the Busch Bavarian Gardens in Virginia (a group of old European-styled villages) feature mainly stage shows. Nearly all historic parks (e.g., Gettysburg Civil War battlefield, Okracoke Plantation in North Carolina) offer recreations of historic events, and even smaller regional parks that are less well known (e.g., "Great Escape" in upstate New York, "Kennywood" in Pittsburgh) feature singing groups, circus-type acts, and stunt shows.

These shows serve many functions for park managers. They legitimize the parks as "big time" in the eyes of parkgoers and lend the park a special excitement (e.g., "Live bands!"). They help manage the flow of crowds insofar as they position them in time ("shows at 2:00 and 4:00") and place ("The western show is located in Frontier Land"). Also, they capitalize on special aspects of the physical setting--for example, the "son et lumiere" shows which are popular at historic spots in Europe.

It is interesting, however, to consider broader social forces that might help explain the growing popularity of these shows.

One force is television. It is possible that television has shaped peoples' expectations to the point that they now look for television-like entertainment values in all entertainment forms. Further, it can be argued that peoples' experience of such traditional forms as myth, ritual, and narrative has become so mass-mediated, and televiewing so ennobled in the bargain, that people wrest significance from performances in proportion to their ability to reposition their performances as TV shows (Carey 1988). If people watch an average of 6 to 7 hours of television a day, it is not implausible that leisure-related expectations are largely shaped by television. For example, the Honeymooners Game show is a direct copy of the popular television show from which it derives. (The added appeal of the resort show is that performers are more likely to confess explicit details of their sex lives than on national television). The joust is similar to storylines from "knights-of-the-round-table" television shows. The circus and comedy show reflect typical television comedy formats: broad slapstick, strong male orientation (men in charge, aggressive content and actions), and short bits of brief content (two to three-minute gags and actions versus longer, more sustained soliloquies and scenes). In fact, given the high action content of most television programs, vacationers might perceive historic park displays and exhibits to be relatively stiff and uninteresting without the more lively, action-oriented distractions. In this connection, the aggression in the vacation shows is especially apparent. Today, television seems to shape expectations in terms of more violent words and actions (e.g., Morton Downey). For example, audience interest was especially aroused in the Honeymooners Show when the master of ceremonies repeatedly pried into the sex life of the shy, withdrawn, embarrassed woman player.

A second factor driving the vacation-show trend is the move toward collecting experiences. Like other collecting-type behaviors (see the chapter by Belk et al.) people seem to perceive the vacation shows as challenges--that is, events that are somewhat difficult to endure, yet worth the effort to collect. Bumper-sticker advertisers recognize this, as people like to decorate automobiles with signs that proclaim the many different parks and shows they have seen. Park marketers also realize this and develop advertising that lists all the parks and spots vacationers might visit. As indicated earlier, some vacationers select parks and experiences to pursue their personal interests (history, thrill-seeking, nostalgia, antiques) while others "try to see as many as they can."

A third factor involves peoples' desire for "short-hand" experiences. For example, vacationers in Paris feel they have fully experienced the Louvre Museum if they see only the Mona Lisa and will stand in line for an hour to accomplish that without bothering to look at any of the other paintings. Vacationers at the Statue of Liberty are most satisfied if they can stand in the small crown atop the statue's head. Similarly, the vacation shows might be growing in popularity because they represent condensed versions of the total park experience. They express, in a more abbreviated form, the excitement and feeling of the whole park. In this, they are the leisure-related equivalents of convenience foods. Thus, the circus encapsulates the general excitement of the county fair, and the Country-and-Western Music Show best expresses the fair's "down home" feeling. The Honeymooners Game embodies all of the anxieties about being newlyweds, and the joust not only includes all of the day's performers in the renaissance park, but also encapsulates the excitement and interest in the middle ages.

VACATION SHOW MAGIC

Several of the shows are interesting because they are heavily cut-down versions of larger shows but still succeed in engaging and involving audience members. The circus, for example, is one-fourth the size of the average three-ring event, lasts only 30 minutes versus Ringling Brothers' four hours, and yet draws laughter, cheers, and a sense of awe from most of the audience nonetheless. The Country-and-Western Music Show features singers and instrumentalists with mediocre abilities at best; yet it succeeds in moving most of the crowd to clap hands, stamp feet, and sing along with the music. The earliest recorded "performances,"which pre-date Greek and Roman civilizations (Sumner 1940), began as religious ceremonies. Hence, it is not surprising that performances generally attempt to produce a special sense of magic, awe, or other-worldliness. In a sense, as most teachers know too well, this is the difference between a performance and a lecture or a presentation.

While much of the interest and excitement in the vacation-show audiences might reflect the fact that they are with close friends and families on holiday, most of the shows do succeed in getting audience members to "suspend disbelief" and to let themselves be drawn into the experience. Researchers who study the phenomenology of aesthetic behavior describe this as a loss of the self-other dichotomy so as to achieve a sense of "oneness" with the aesthetic object (Moncrieff 1978; McConville 1978).

In the case of the vacation performances, this sense seemed to be produced in several different ways. We shall provide six specific suggestions.

1. Physical Setting

Their physical settings give several of the shows a special feeling. The deafening noise of the children in the circus, the beer odors at the Country-and-Western Show, and the stage lighting at the Honeymooners Game --not to mention the ear-shattering loudness of the music at the latter two event--all give these shows an unreal quality (Nye 1981). This comes on top of the fact that vacationers are away from home--that is, in a liminal place away from the real, day to day environments. In fact, the physical juxtaposition of the shows within the parks is an interesting ploy. In the language of public relations strategists, this maneuver is called "creating an event within an event." Thus, baseball park public relations people provide not only baseball games but also "old timers" games, celebrities singing the National Anthem, sky divers, and clowns to heighten the excitement of the regular game. Here, the outcome resembles the effect on church-goers who are asked into the altar area of a church during a church service--that is, asked into the most sacred area of the general sacred area. Similarly, the vacation show legitimizes the general park atmosphere, and vice versa. The excitement of being on the Universal Studios' sunny California grounds is greatly intensified as one enters the pitch black studios for a stunt-man show.

2. Contents With High Emotional Significance

The shows are compelling and "draw people in" because they deal with subjects that are very sensitive. The most obvious example is the Honeymooners Game. In this game, overt topics include love making, genitalia, sex secrets, and marital spats. Writers who study entertainment (e.g., Goodlad 1971; Lazarsfeld and Merton 1956) refer to this as "expressing the unexpressible." Sensitive topics also abound in the Comedy Show (e.g., "setting the man's tools on fire") and, to a lesser extent, in the Merrio Circus (When a gorilla rips the clothes off a woman from the audience). In a similar light, the country-and-western songs all deal with a strong fear, the fear of rejection and loneliness. ("I saw you with another woman, what can I do?"). Other themes in the country-and-western music include deviant behaviors such as alcoholism, adultery, gambling, crime, and consequent punishments (e.g., "Folsom Prison"). Less overtly, the joust has deep but veiled sexual significance (e.g., as mating ritual for females

or intense competition among phallic projections), while also touching on emotionally-loaded subjects such as violence and death.

3. Suspension of Disbelief and Other Inhibitions

Vacations are a time when people are freed from normal, day-to-day roles and obligations. Hence, the popularity of shows dealing with subjects which are usually supressed is not surprising. The circus is a good example. Like medieval festivals, the circus turns normal role relationships upside-down. Just as masters become servants while servants become masters in medieval festivals such as Fasching, in the circus children make adults look funny while animals act out human behaviors (or vice versa for the fake gorilla).

4. Affirmation of Deep Convictions

In spite of role relationships, however, the vacation audience continues to represent middle class morality. And, often, this is what they continue to consume on holiday. Thus, curio shops do a heavy business in statues and T-shirts with pious, patriotic, and patronizing slogans (such as one shirt with a picture of a large bear carrying a rifle and captioned, "Support your right to arm bears"). Implicit messages in the vacation shows tending to reinforce conventional middle-class morality include the following:

- "The pretentious wind up looking stupid."
  This theme is evident in many shows. Circus clowns make pompous ringmasters look foolish; comedy show performers mimic important-looking people falling in the mud, and Licentious Lou makes fun of newlyweds' pretenses about their sex lives before marriage.

- "Men should be men, and women should be women."
  The sexism of lower middle-class morality is evident in many of the shows. In all of the country-and-western songs, women are represented as helpless and dependent ("I saw you with another woman, what can I do? I cried and cried"). In the Honeymooners Game, the master of ceremonies makes fun of the women ("You didn't see the mirror on the ceiling?") and asks only questions that treat women with inherent disrespect (e.g., "Would your husband say your breasts remind him of dried up bananas?")

- "What really counts in life is true love."

Country-and-western songs stress the value of love over all other things or considerations ("Satin sheets to lie on, but you don't keep me satisfied"). The most important moment in the joust comes at the end when the winning knight carries off the beautiful princess.

5. Sense of Some Other-Worldly, Instinctual Power at Work

Interestingly, many of the shows convey a notion that some other-worldly power or force is at work. Comedians in the Comedy Show act as if they are insane ("touched by the gods?"), and the joust scenario is based on the notion of some "good" force that overcomes evil. In the Weberian sense, circus performers are "charismatic" figures, gifted by the Gods with superhuman capabilities (Weber 1947). They look stronger, more beautiful (thanks, in part, to heavy makeup). They can perform impossible feats. In this connection, one of the circus performers backstage told a story about the animal acts:

It's eerie, but sometimes an old animal trainer will die and no one knows how to do his act. When that happens, the new trainer has to learn the act from the animals.

The implication here is that, once trained, the animals internalize some force which propels them to do their acts. This makes it possible for a new trainer to learn the acts from them. It also suggests some type of living presence of the dead trainer, who has passed away yet who still controls the animals. (In this sense, teachers--who are at least partly performers--cannot help but wonder if, through the expectations of their students, they are controlled by the ghosts of teachers past.)

6. Live Nature of Shows

The shows generate excitement because they are live. People seem to like live shows for several reasons. First, they feel that a live performance is much more personal, more intimate. Obviously, a television program broadcast to one hundred million people has difficulty generating this type of feeling. Second, live shows present the possibility of accidents. The Honeymooners audience is most aroused when the woman player balks at the host's questions. The country-and-western band builds excitement when they say, "We're going to *try* to do a number for you by Hank Williams now." Here, they imply that they *may* not be successful. Third, live performances bring the audience into personal contact with performers, thereby putting them closer to people with the

charismatic qualities referred to above. Audiences seek this quality of intimacy with the great. Thus, playbill programs in theaters list the major television, movie, and theatrical productions the actors have appeared in. When interviewed backstage after the show, one of the circus performers said, "People are in awe of us. They think we travel around a lot and have exciting lives."

7. Reaction of the Researchers

The performances described in this chapter achieve significance on two levels not yet explored. First, the shows may be considered as "metagenres," insofar as they link "differentiated forms of symbolic action into new wholes by means of a common spatiotemporal location, expressive theme, affective style, ideological intention, or social function" (MacAloon 1984, 250). Second, collectively, these performances comprise a "metacommentary, explicit or implicit, witting or unwitting, on the major social dramas of its social context (Turner 1985, 300-301). Through these performances, cultural meaning is negotiated in ceremonial and ritual fashion.

The performances occur in liminal time and liminal space, as critical incidents in what is readily construed as a pilgrimage (Belk 1987, Belk, Wallendorf and Sherry 1989; Sherry 1987). Core cultural values--the primacy of culture over nature, integrity, gender roles, fidelity, autonomy and competence, personal accountability, status equality, nostalgia, the uneasy dialectic of work and leisure, competitiveness, fair play, property, etc.--are performed, lampooned, and then re-enshrined through the vehicles of the shows. Participants are invited to meditate on the social order, to consider alternatives to the status quo, and to reaffirm tradition, in a highly charged ceremonial context. It is through such memorable and affecting experiences that the fundamental categories of cultural are continually reappraised and renewed. In an era when, increasingly, products are values for the experience they afford (McKenna 1988), the commoditization of ritual can be expected to have a growing impact on the (de-)formation of culture.

CONCLUSION

As indicated earlier, today's "performances" on television, stage, and movie screen descend ultimately from early religious festivals. People have always come together for expressive purposes, whether to bless harvests, to appease gods, or to celebrate victories. Interestingly, many religions still have strong performance components. Indeed, such components have gained increased impetus in recent charismatic movements. Thus, while the content of a fundamentalist preacher's sermon matters, equally important is his/her showmanship or ability to excite the crowd by gestures and other histrionic or rhetorical devices.

Note that the focus here is on *forms*. The performance component of the preacher's sermon lies in how he exaggerates basic forms in his motions, speech, and images. In the same manner, professional wrestlers exaggerate the basic forms of wrestling in order to achieve a dramatic effect, even though true sports fans label it fake.

In a nutshell, a "performance" (whether a vacation performance or some other type) takes some basic form from everyday life and modifies or exaggerates it to achieve some effect on an audience. This effect changes the emotional or intellectual state of the audience (or both). Circuses put people in happy moods; country-and-western music shows render them melancholy and reflective; jousts permit them to learn about and contemplate medieval festivals as well as to laugh at the antics of the villains and court jesters.

In other words, like all services, performances or other forms of entertainment intended to cause changes in the state or condition of the customer. A barber cuts people's hair, while a comedian makes them laugh and takes their mind off their problems. It makes sense, therefore, that to compete more effectively, many service marketers increasingly include more performance components in their offerings. Restaurants now place more emphasis on a flashy presentation of foods than on the quality of the foods themselves. Similarly, an airline on the West Coast has become famous for the jokes and banter by its captains and crews during flights. And, of course, some professors who specialize in teaching business programs to executives are as famous for their stories and delivery as for the content of their lectures.

If television-related forms continue to influence peoples' expectations regarding other entertainment services, one might expect that they will also shape more non-entertainment services in the future. In this sense, as Macluhan (1964) prophesied long ago, we may have found another case in which "the medium is the message."

REFERENCES

Belk, Russell (1987), "The Role of the Odyssey in Consumer Behavior & Consumer Research," *Advances in Consumer Research*, Paul Anderson and Melanie Wallendorf, eds., Provo, Utah: Association for Consumer Research.

Belk, R., M. Wallendorf and J. Sherry (1989), "The Sacred and the Profane in Consumer Behavior: Theodicy on the Odyssey," *Journal of Consumer Research*, 16 (June) pp. 1-38.

Carey, James, ed (1988), *Media, Myths and Narratives: Television and the Press*, Newbury Park, CA: Sage Publishing.

Gans, H. (1974) *Popular Culture and High Culture: An Analysis and Evaluation of Taste*, New York: Basic Books.

Goodlad, J. (1972), *A Sociology of Popular Drama*, New Jersey: Rowman and Littlefield.

Lazarsfeld, P. and R. Merton (1957), "Mass Communication, Popular Taste and Organized Social Action" in *Mass Culture*, ed. Rosenberg and White, New York: The Free Press.

MacAloon, John, ed. (1984), *Rite, Drama, Festival, Spectacle: Rehearsals Toward a Theory of Cultural Performance*, Philadelphia, PA: ISHI.

McConville, M. (1978), "The Phenomenological Approach to Perception," in Valle, R. and M. King, *Existential-Phenomenological Alternatives For Psychology*, ed. R. Valle and M. King, Oxford: Oxford University Press.

McKenna, Regis (1988), "Marketing in an Age of Diversity," *HBR* (Sept-Oct.) 88-95.

McLuhan, M. (1964) *Understanding Media: The Extension of Man*, New York: McGraw-Hill.

Moncrieff, D. (1978), "Aesthetic Consciousness" in *Existential-Phenomenological Alternatives For Psychology*, ed. Valle, R. and M. King, Oxford: Oxford University Press.

Nye, R.B. (1981), "Eight Ways of Looking at an Amusement Park," *Journal of Popular Culture*, Vol. 15, No. 1, pp. 63-75.

Sherry, John (1987), "Keeping the Monkeys Away From the Typewriters: An Anthropologist's View of the Consumer Behavior Odyssey" in *Advances in Consumer Research*, Paul Anderson and Melanie Wallendorf, eds., Provo, Utah: Association for Consumer Research.

Sumner, W. (1940), *Folkways*, Boston: Mentor Books.

Turner, Victor [ed. Edith Turner] (1985), *On the Edge of the Bush: Anthropology as Experience*, Tucson, AZ: University of Arizona Press.

Wallendorf, Melanie and John Sherry (1989), "Sacred and Profane...", *JCR*.

Weber, M. (1957), *The Theory of Social and Economic Organization*, ed. A. Henderson and T. Parsons, Glencoe: The Free Press.

"To Everything There Is a Season:" A Photoessay of a Farmers' Market

Deborah D. Heisley
Mary Ann McGrath
John F. Sherry, Jr.[1]

PHOTO #1
The Midville Farmers' Market

ABSTRACT

This photoessay documents the emergence of findings in an ethnographic field study of a midwestern farmers' market. It focuses on three cycles: the market day, the season, and a cycle of long term field immersion. Consumer segments are differentiated by the time of day they visit the market, giving a distinctive cadance to the selling day. The seasonal cycle is characterized by increasing complexity and abundance as the growing and selling season progresses for the farmer vendors. The third cycle is that of field habituation, through which the researchers gain trust and access to informants and acquire deeper holistic understanding of the market and its participants.

[1]The authors are listed in alphabetical order. The first two researchers spent every Saturday, with the exception of three, from June 28 through November 1, 1986, in attendance at the Midville Farmers' Market. The third author made occasional visits to the site, served as a resource and sounding board for the ideas of the other two authors, and audited the research process.

INTRODUCTION AND OBJECTIVE

On June 28, 1986, three researchers embarked upon a research odyssey along a two block strip in a midwestern city, as they spent the first Saturday of the selling season at the Midville Farmers' Market. This first day of the market was the first step in an ethnographic journey that would last nineteen weeks. They would witness the emergence of a variety of recurring themes, the reinforcement of several theoretic constructs specific to marketing, and the development of relationships with vendors, customers, and city representatives.

Using a variety of research methods and media - in particular participant observation, directive and nondirective interviews of customers and vendors, development of key informants, reflective journal entries, audio

PHOTO #2

A researcher, laden with goods from being a participant consumer at the market, conducts an interview under an umbrella during a rainstorm.

PHOTO #3

A researcher works at a vendor's booth as part of her participant observation.

recordings, photographs, and audio/video recordings - the researchers constructed a richly documented natural history of the market. In the course of the study, researchers participated in a variety of activities such as buying and selling products, as well as setting up and packing up produce and booths, in physical environments ranging from warm and sunny, through rainy accompanied by monsoon level winds, to snowy (photos 2 and 3).

THE USE OF PHOTOGRAPHY IN THE STUDY

One thousand two hundred and sixty-two photographs were made with a 35-mm single lens reflex camera using a standard (i.e., not a "zoom" lens), normal lens, and black and white film. A 50-mm lens is considered "normal" because it reproduces what we see most accurately. Photographs were printed full frame (i.e., nothing was "cropped" or removed from the original photographs while printing them in the darkroom). These consistencies in making the photographs and printing them unaltered facilitate visual comparisons between and within markets. The use of black and white photography allowed the photographer to develop and print the photos. Contact sheets were made for all the negatives. Contact sheets are made by placing all the negative strips for a roll of film in a transparent 8 by 10-inch sleeve and developing a picture from it. That is, one 8 by 10 inch contact sheet contains the information from an entire roll of film and each picture is the size of a 35-mm negative. More printing was done selectively from the contact sheets to 5 by 8-inch photographs. This close relationship with the development and printing processes adds control and helps intimately familiarize the researcher with the photographic data. Valuable insights are often gained during the printing process while the researcher examines photographs in detail. This core data base was supplemented by 16 other black and white photos and 99 color photos, for a total of 1377 photographs. All photographs in this essay are from the core black and white data base with the exception of #2, #29, and #46, which were originally made with color film.

VISUAL COMPARISONS OF DAY 1 WITH LATER MARKETS

The objective of this essay is to capture, through a combination of photographs and text, something of the significance of the opening day of the market. A deeper understanding of the events of this day is achieved by supplementing the materials collected on June 28 with notes and photographs from later dates.

As the market season matured, and the vendors' wares ripened and increased in bounty and variety, the relationships between the researchers and key informants developed from cautious exchanges to comfortable, sometimes humorous and teasing, interactions. While the researchers observed and recorded a myriad of happenings on June 28, true understanding and insight into these events came at a later date, as the intimate familiarity with the Midville market developed over the course of the season.

In this essay, the focus is upon the photographs and field notes from this first day of the market. Photographs of the first market day, June 28th, are used in the first part of this paper to illustrate and document interpretations of the market day and of customer and vendor behaviors. When photographs of later markets are compared with this first day's shots later in the essay, the dates are noted. The ability to compare and contrast findings on various days, and document findings over time, became a notable benefit of long term field immersion.

Using photographs and accompanying field notes from the first market day, the cycle of a market day can be illustrated and documented, as it proceeds from set up to close. The ethnographic present tense is used in the description.

THE CYCLE OF THE MARKET DAY

At 5:30 a.m. the streets of Midville are virtually devoid of cars and people. In the emerging light of dawn a single truck is parked at the market site. A mother and her two adult sons are unpacking tables and setting up produce for a display (photo 4). They evince a degree of pride in being the first to arrive today. As they work, they reminisce about their participation in the first Midville Farmers' Market in 1975.

"There were only three farmers there that day. We went home twice for refills."

At this first market of 1986 they are selling carrots, beets, green beans, and lettuce. They anticipate that they will "sell out early," prior to the 2:00 p.m. market closing time. They complain that they have been allowed to rent double spaces in previous years, but that this year they are restricted to a single 25 foot long space. For a rental fee of $110, payable to the city, vendors will occupy this space for the duration of the market season. A total of 40 spaces are marked off on both sides of a two block long section of street.

By 6:15 a.m. there are 15 vendors setting up in the market area (photos 5 and 6). The city police and tow trucks have cleared the street of four parked cars that were in violation

PHOTO 4
The first vendor to arrive, a mother with her two adult sons, begins to unpack and set up.

PHOTOS 5 AND 6
Early set up on the first market day.

of posted no parking signs. As the layout of the market has changed from the previous year, vendors are jockeying for space and there is discussion of the boundaries, most notably the appropriate width, of each booth. Since this is the first market of the season, the vendors seek to configure the equipment they have brought to display and protect their wares (tables, umbrellas, shelves) to the space available, and to prepare the produce for sale (photos 7 and 8).

As the farmers turn their booths into retail selling areas, they work continuously, yet this is a social time as well. Several of the farmers know each other and have worked side by side at this market and at others for years. The Midville Market last met eight months ago, so this first market becomes a setting for the renewal of friendships and for catching up on what has happened over the winter (photo 9). Farmers also cautiously and sadly note who is not present in a euphemistic, slightly superstitious reference to former colleagues who have lost their farms. On a more optimistic note, a conversation is overheard between a vendor and an early customer as they compare cruises they have taken the previous winter.

Customers begin arriving by 6:30 a.m., and the market is in full swing by 7 a.m., even though posters and signs posted by the city indicate that the market opens at 8 a.m. It is warm, sunny, and clear. Customers exchange greetings with vendors, whom they have not seen for eight months, and visit with acquaintances along the market midway (photo 10). A local nonprofit group sells coffee and baked goods at the south end of the street, and this area becomes a gathering place as customers consume refreshments while they socialize (photo 11).

By 10 a.m., the warm sun is engulfed by clouds, and the overcast morning becomes cooler. The crowd continues to grow, reaching its peak around 11:00 a.m.. The majority of customers are white, with an estimated 10% to 15% minority population made up of Asians, blacks, and hispanics. The distribution of ages is wide and varied, with all groups being represented except teenagers. The presence of children in the infant and toddler age group is evident to consumers trying to negotiate the midway because of the many strollers and wagons in the market area (photo 12).

After noon the market becomes quieter. The crowds have thinned, and several vendors have left early after either selling out or having their stock depleted to levels too low for what they perceive to be an adequate display. The afternoon becomes hot and clear, giving both the remaining produce and the vendors who have been standing for hours a wilted appearance (photo 13). At precisely 2 p.m., the

Market Master removes the barricades blocking traffic access to the street and formally ends the market (photo 14). At a later date the researchers learn about post-market, after-hours socializing. Several vendors have lunch together at a local restaurant.

CONSUMER BEHAVIOR AT THE MIDVILLE MARKET

Examination of the photographs of the June 28 market day and subsequent interviews with key informants at later market dates reinforced the researchers' sense of the cyclicality of the market day. On this first day all of those who would eventually become key informants were present and photographed at the market. On June 28, however, the researchers were not cognizant of the role that each customer or vendor would assume in the study. The photographs of this first market were a naive attempt to capture thoroughly the visual aspects of the market. There were no specific hypotheses or predispositions associated with this first day. An attempt was made to document the event through photographs and notes. Researchers did have an acute awareness of the transient nature of the market, its customers and the day itself, and it was with this awareness that photographs were made of vendors and customers present in the marketplace. The two researchers worked separately during a significant portion of the day, and several photographs made by one researcher were of persons who later became key informants of the other.

Later interviews with several key informants allowed the researchers to characterize the customers at the market by the time of day these customers chose to attend. The following is a chart of the etic segments.

6:00 to 7:30 a.m. *The Die-Hards* (photo 15). These people attend every market, regardless of the weather or selection of products available. They want the freshest and the best selection.

7:30 to 9:00 a.m. *The Sociable Die-Hards* (photo 16).This group is more social than the first. They want good selection, but they also want to visit with friends. They consider themselves "early birds".

9:00 to 11:00 a.m. *The Very Social* (photo 17). These consumers arrive when the midway of the market is most crowded. There is still fairly good product assortment, but "the best" has already been purchased.

11:00 a.m. to noon *The Late People* (photo 18). These people are of two types: those who complain that they are late, and those who do their market shopping after they have

PHOTO 7
Vendors decide how to display their wares.

PHOTO 8
Vendors prepare their wares for display.

PHOTO 9
Two vendors visit early on the first market day.

PHOTO 10
Customers and vendors renew their acquaintances.

PHOTO 11
Customers socialize at one of two bake sale booths.

PHOTO 12
Children in and with strollers and wagons fill the market midway.

PHOTO 13

As the end of the market day approaches, stock is depleted, and vendors and remaining produce
begin to wilt.

PHOTO 14

At 2:00 p.m., the market formally ends.

PHOTO 15
The Die-Hards.

PHOTO 16
The Sociable Die-Hards.

PHOTO 17
The Very Social.

PHOTO 18
The Late People.

PHOTO 19
The Bargain Hunters and Night People.

finished other errands. The socials have missed their friends. The purchase selections at this time period are poor and shoppers cannot be very picky.

12:00 to 2:00 p.m. *The Bargain Hunters and Night People* (photo 19). At this time of day more minority group members and college students are in evidence in comparison to the white, middle-aged, middle-class complexion of the previously detailed groups. This later group does little socializing and shops in a less crowded marketplace.

Certain customers note a preference to come to the market at a specific time of day.

"We come religiously at seven each Saturday."
"We're late today. I don't like the nine o'clock people. They're too pushy."
"I usually come late, around eleven, when my other errands are finished."

In general, consumers make mention of being late, rather than of being early or on-time. Their awareness of being late does not seem to alter their shopping or socializing behavior, however. Once at the market site, they will visit if they meet their friends, and there is no observable evidence of shoppers rushing to complete their shopping in order to leave the market site.

"Look at us. We were an hour late today, and now we've stood and talked for another hour. We had better start shopping soon, or we'll never leave."

The time sense of some consumers, and certainly that of the researchers, appears to correspond to the periodic nature of the farmer's market itself. Some sense of urgency and immediacy is produced by time compression. Consumers know that the freshness of the produce is a function of this periodicity; abundance and scarcity of individual items are daily and seasonal conditions. So, also, is the intensity and regularity of outdoor social relations governed by the seasons. Midville residents cherish the bounty of summer in the face of brutal midwestern winters; they know full well the market and its charm are evanescent. The researchers are acutely aware that they themselves must seize the day if they are to capture comprehensively the character of this periodic market.

Photographs of this first market meeting illustrate that the Midville Market is more than a place to shop for farmers' wares. Two musicians begin to play around 10 a.m., and open their instrument cases for donations (photo 20). A young man with a tricycle-type ice cream cart parks near the musicians. In the absence of customers, he begins to juggle three balls. Several photographs show customers taking a break from their shopping and visiting at the market while resting on the grass or in a shady spot nearby (photo 21). Consumers readily admit that they come to the market for reasons other than product assortment or to restock ingredients for physical sustenance.

"This is recreational shopping. I'm here to try to amuse the kids." (Comments of a father with children aged 3 and 1.)
"It's social, and people come for the gladiolus."

The cycle of this market day repeats itself on subsequent Saturdays (Photos 22 vs. 23 and 24 vs. 25).

In retrospect, it is this first Saturday that is exceptional in that customers and vendors appear to know and act out the script of the market without question after an eight month hiatus. It is the researchers who do not fully understand the plot and significance of the activities unfolding. After several weeks of building trust in relationships with informants, the researchers are able to document and interpret this script.

DIFFERING PERCEPTIONS OF ABUNDANCE AND COMPLEXITY

Photographs of the first market of the season document the transformation of an empty street into what may appear to be a cornucopia of abundance. A journal entry of June 28 notes that "the colors of the market were dominated by pinks, reds, bright greens and yellows, the colors of spring." Tables appear heaped with merchandise and consumers mention specific items they plan to purchase (asparagus, mushrooms, gladiolus, etc.). While researchers perceive bounty and abundance in the marketplace, the vendors speak of anticipated bounty nearer the late summer and fall harvest time. Vegetable farmer Mrs. Theopolis mentions that she will open a roadside stand at their farm in the fall. Fruit vendor Maggie Moran tries to recruit an employee to help at this market later in the season, "when we have bushels of apples." The researchers better understand the significance of these remarks through observation of the late summer and autumn markets.

A series of photographs visually documents increasing in assortment, abundance, and complexity of display. Photographs 26 and 27 allow a comparison of two-thirds of Blake's booth at the first (6/28) market with one-third of his booth at the

PHOTO 20
Entertainment at the Market.

PHOTO 21
Taking a break.

PHOTOS 22 VS. 23
Early and late photos of two vendors on this first day visually reveal the depletion of stock and consolidation that occurs over the course of a market day.

PHOTOS 24 VS. 25
Early and late photos of two vendors on this first day visually reveal the depletion of stock and consolidation that occurs over the course of a market day.

PHOTO 26 VS. 27
Blake's booth at the first (6/28) market and at the thirteenth (9/20) market.

PHOTO 28 VS. 29

A comparison of comprehensive photographs of the Wilcox booth on the second (7/5) and the fourteenth (9/27) markets.

thirteenth (9/20) market. Tables evolve into two tier displays, signs are in greater evidence and detail, and produce is of greater quantity and variety. Photographs 28 and 29 compare the Wilcox booth at the second (7/5) market and the fourteenth (9/27) market. Both photographs include the entire display. Like many vendors, Wilcox's display area spills over the boundaries of his designated area as the season progresses.

Photographs 30, 31, and 32, document the second and eleventh markets. In the photograph of the Theopolis booth on the second market day (7/5), several tables are lined up facing east. Mrs. Theopolis is waiting on a customer. On the eleventh market day (9/6) the two photographs show Mrs. Theopolis waiting on a customer on the southeast side of a booth which is now shaped like a horseshoe; her daughter is waiting on the same customer on the northeast side, and Homer Theopolis is facing east, working in the center of the booth. The increased abundance of produce, complexity of booth display, and number of signs is evident in this comparison.

Photographs 33, 34, and 35 are a series taken of Mrs. Blake's booth on the second market day (7/5), the fifth market day (7/26), and the last market day (11/1), respectively. The booth evolves from a straight line of tables facing east, to a much-expanded corner booth set-up with the tables facing east and north, and finally, on the last day of the market, to a free form style with produce piled wherever it can be placed.

The Jameson family often exhibits complex display configurations. On the second day of the market (7/5) the Jamesons mount a multi-level display effort (Photo 36). By the fifth market day (7/26) the booth has evolved into a horseshoe shape that, unlike other vendors' horseshoes, is open to the market and designed to entice customers to enter (Photo 37). Other vendors, as in photographs 31 and 34, enclose themselves with the horseshoe configuration, keeping customers on the "outside." By the seventh market day (8/9), the Jameson booth is the most complex of the market. It exhibits a horseshoe design around a central display area, and is open to the market. A sign invites the customers to "Walk on in" (Photo 38).

An impression gleaned from interviews is that the farmers make a perfunctory appearance at the early markets to establish their presence among their regular customers, but that they do not anticipate their busiest or most profitable market days until later in the season. Attendance figures are not as helpful in demonstrating this as they were anticipated to be. Attendance at the first market by vendors is 70%, with 28 of the 40 assigned spaces filled. At the height of the harvest season in September, attendance increases to 32 vendors, or 80% of the available spaces. Four additional farmers who participate in the market at the start of the season cease to attend due to flooding of their lands and also being "harvested out" of the crops they chose to grow, most notably corn. Consumer attendance estimates were not recorded.

HABITUATION OF KEY INFORMANTS TO RESEARCHERS' PRESENCE

Several vendors and customers became key informants during the course of the study. A picture of each of these key informants was made at the first meeting of the market, though at the time their subsequent significance to the study was not known to the researchers. Journal entries and photographs of these informants on the first day of the market are contrasted with photographs made near the conclusion of the study. The use of a standard lens and full-frame printing gives full and consistent information about the photographer's position in relation to the informant. Therefore, valid statements and comparisons about this relation can be made. The comparisons reflect the levels of trust that developed between participants and researchers, that in turn led to a negotiated or collaborative interpretation of marketplace behavior.

In the earlier pictures, the informants assume the posture of unknowingly being photographed, ignoring the photographer, or of suspicion toward the camera in particular or toward the researchers in general. In the later photographs, the friendly relationship with the photographer/researcher is evident. The informants in the later photographs are smiling and demonstrate a tolerance of the camera and a willingness to be photographed. Differences are evident in the facial expressions, the presence or absence of eye contact and posing of the body, and the angle of the bodies with respect to the camera. Several photographs demonstrate a notable contrast between the first and later markets. A photograph on the first market day is a photograph of strangers. Photographs of vendors are distant, removed shots. Photograph 39 is a first market day shot of a vendor who was later to become a valued informant. In the background of this photo, a man is looking with skeptical curiosity at the photographer. This man, we learned later, is the market manager, Tom McKensey. Tom became another of our most valued informants. The degree of rapport between the photographer and her informant, as well as that between another of the researchers and her informant, is evident in the spatial relationships demonstrated in photographs 40 and 41; the former was made

PHOTO 30 VS. 31 & 32

The Theopolis booth on the second market day (7/5) and two photographs of the eleventh market day (9/6).

PHOTOS 33, 34 & 35

Mrs. Blake's booth on the second market day (7/5), the fifth market day (7/26), and the last market day (11/1).

PHOTOS 36, 37, & 38

The evolution of the Jameson family booth on the second market (7/5), the fifth market (7/26), and the seventh market (8/9).

PHOTOS 39 VS. 40 & 41

The habituation of key informants to the presence of the researchers evolves from the first
market (6/28), and alters over the duration of the study (7/26 and 10/11).

on the fifth market day (7/26), the latter on the sixteenth market day (10/11).

Another visual demonstration of the relationship between researcher and informant is a comparison of photographs 42 and 43. The first is of Mr. and Mrs. Theopolis on the first day of the market. Mrs. Theopolis is looking at the camera in a detached, distant manner. Conversely, in the photograph on the sixteenth (10/11) market day she exudes warmth and friendship. She has clearly become involved in the research process. Note too, once again the photographer's position has changed. That a greater degree of intimacy has been achieved is evident in the photographer's ability to be physically close to her informant with a potentially intrusive and invasive object (i.e., the camera) without being perceived as a hostile aggressor.

Some concern has been voiced within marketing that researchers should be concerned about using audio and video recording tools because they are obtrusive, they call attention to the presence of the researcher, and they may alter behavior; and because there is an ethical issue if the recordings are made secretly, so as to be unobtrusive. However, visual researchers and audio/visual ethnographers believe that (1) certain patterns of behavior persist that will be informative, (2) a skillful audio or visual recorder will use the recording process to establish rapport between the researcher and the informants, not to spy on the informants, and (3) if the nature of the research calls for accurate on-site recording, then audio, visual, or written recording are the choices - audio and visual recording not being inherently more obtrusive than scribbling away in a notebook. In this study, a combination of visual recordings (the photographs) was supplemented with written notes and audio recordings. A limited amount of videotaping was undertaken on 7/26, the day a visiting team of researchers attended the market. In all cases the researchers explicitly revealed to informants the purpose of their study, freely answered questions, and shared photographs and notes with all involved in the study.

THE EMERGENCE OF INFORMED FIELD NOTES

Field notes of the first market may be described as naive and uninformed. An attempt is made to document as much as possible, but the commitment that the researchers have made to remain at the site for the duration of the market season reassures them that they will be able to supplement their observations or change their focus at a later date. Inventories of specific items and prices are started at the fourth market, when that information is deemed

relevant. The researchers engage in fewer, but longer, conversations at subsequent markets. As relationships with key informants develop, these informants consume more of the researchers' time each week. Informants frequently watch for the researchers at the market each Saturday. One consumer informant in particular thinks about the market each week, and comes to the farmers' market on Saturday prepared with insights and stories to share with the researchers.

Researchers become more involved with the vendors as the study progresses. On the last day of the market, vendors who are key informants are thanked and given photographs of themselves made by researchers. Many vendors give the researchers gifts as well. Relationships have developed, as can be seen in Photographs 44, 45, and 46. Photograph 44 was taken near the end of the first market day (6/28). The photographer makes an attempt to move closer to her subject and is waved away with a scowl. Photograph 45 was made of Otis Plato on the sixteenth market day (10/11). By now a friend and wonderful informant, he poses for the photographer with an unshucked pussywillow in his right hand and the finished product in his left hand. He has just patiently taught her his art of shucking. On the last day of the market, she gives Otis and his wife, Andrea, some photographs made of their booth over the season. In turn, he makes the photographer a grapevine wreath with which to remember them (Photo 46). The leave-taking is an emotional experience, as one researcher notes in a final journal entry:

"I had a lump in my throat as I said good-bye to everyone. I am grateful that I have gotten to know the farmers, and I value the trust they have demonstrated toward me....The market has changed me--the way I shop, the way I eat, and the way I do research. I will miss these people."

CONCLUSIONS

This essay illustrates how impressions formed early in an ethnographic study can, when viewed later in context, provide useful insights into the processes of interest to researchers. The changing relationships with key informants clarify and enhance several of the initial impressions formed by the researchers. These bonds help produce a negotiated interpretation of marketplace behavior. This essay demonstrates that ethnographic research is a labor intensive process that emerges over time. The incorporation of several, sometimes opposing, perspectives of a phenomenon over time yields a deeper understanding of the setting

PHOTO 42 VS. 43

The changing relationship between photographer and informant is illustrated in photographs of the Mr. and Mrs. Theopolis at the first (6/28) and the eleventh (10/11) markets.

PHOTOS 44, 45 & 46

Informant posture at the first market (6/28) contrasted with a pose for the camera at the sixteenth market (10/11) and a gift-exchange at the last market (11/1).

and its participants that is not evident on the first day of the market.

On day one, we caught a colorful, noisy, fleeting glimpse of the budding market. Had we not continued to attend and observe, we might have mistaken the market as being in full flower. Our view of the vendors was as romantic and idealistic, independent, self-sufficient Americans engaged in an archaic, but quaint lifestyle. We perceived shoppers as a homogeneous group. We witnessed the market spring up, akin to a mushroom; we had no understanding of the historical and structural compost that formed its basis and nurtured its eventual blossoming.

By the last day of this nineteen week study we had seen the market mature, ripen, and culminate with the onset of the killer frost and the winter chill. Our understanding of the market encompassed not only its flowers and its fruits, but also its roots, its chaff, its fodder, and its seeds. At the conclusion of the study we had greater understanding of the issues of complexity, cyclicality, and abundance. We saw the market as a complex system, interacting with the local city government, local retailers, and several market segments in the community. We learned about the farmers' business acumen; they were recognized as marketers, rather than merely producers. Their market planning was evident in what they chose to grow and where they chose to sell their goods, as well as their displays, layouts, pricing strategies, point-of-purchase advertising, and competitive analyses. It was over the long term that we appreciated the cyclicality of the market day and the seasonality of the market itself. By the end of the market we appreciated the relationships between vendors, customers and vendors, and between customers; we found ourselves caught up in the relationships themselves. We ended the experience having grown with and becoming part of the market itself.

PHOTO 47

"The Walking Plant." A customer leaves the market accompanied by a newly acquired companion.

The Wives of Woodville
Jeffrey F. Durgee
Morris B. Holbrook
Melanie Wallendorf

BACKGROUND
Several days of the Consumer Behavior Odyssey project were spent in Woodville, New York. Woodville is a suburb of an old, small manufacturing town in the New York countryside. It is large and quite wealthy, in spite of the small size and blue collar heritage of the town it adjoins. Like the Buena Vista suburb next to Winston-Salem, N. C. and the town of Saratoga near Albany, N.Y., it appears to be a place where wealthy people have chosen to live for many years, even though their money and financial holdings might be elsewhere. The homes are predominantly old (mainly built in the twenties and fifties), large, and bordered by lush grounds, trees, and broad boulevards. Although certainly its citizens have individual identities, nonetheless it is the type of suburb that has a relatively homogeneous population of well-educated homeowners who enjoy an upper-middle class lifestyle (Baumgartner 1988).

Woodville provided the Consumer Behavior Odyssey project an opportunity to explore the lives and lifestyles of a growing population segment, the female heads of households of upper-middle class families. These women are interesting for at least four reasons. 1) They make up what practioners call "New Traditionalists" (*Ad Age* 1989). Whether or not they are employed outside the home, they place primary importance on their children's welfare; their activities follow decisions about residential location that are based on their husbands' careers; and they tend to make many of their consumption decisions based on traditional criteria, e.g., classic furniture designs, joint husband-wife decision making, and careful planning for the future. 2) The wives of Woodville adhere to a narrowly defined consumption ethic, sometimes labeled "preppy", "WASP" (Baltzell 1964) or "old money", whether or not they actually attended prep schools or are of wealthy Anglo-Saxon Protestant backgrounds. This, then, is a consumption ethic that may or may not completely derive from demographic or socio-economic roots. This consumption ethic is interesting not only because it is so tightly defined, but also because it is widely imitated and adopted as evidenced by the success of dozens of catalogs and other marketers including Orvis, J. Crew, Izod, L.L. Bean, Ralph Lauren, Talbots, and Brooks Brothers. 3) To many people, the consumption lifestyle of the wives of Woodville represents the American dream: large homes that are carefully decorated, more than adequate financial resources, country clubs, late model cars, coastal vacations, prestigious neighborhoods, and a wide range of sports and arts lessons for their children. 4) Their location in Woodville constrains their lifestyles insofar as they are limited primarily to shopping in Woodville and to interacting with each other. Unlike the wealthy suburbs that serve Manhattan and Chicago, Woodville's location constrains its residents to spend the vast majority of their time and energies in Woodville. Despite exposure to mass media and travel, the result is a culture that is isolated and self-contained in ways that are important for consumption.

The Consumer Behavior Odyssey researchers interviewed five women who live in Woodville. All are married, and all were interviewed in their homes. Four are Baby-Boomers between the ages of 30 and 40, and one is in her seventies. All but one of the younger women were re-interviewed by the authors a year after the Consumer Behavior Odyssey in order to track changes and new developments in their lives. The women are not independent of each other. The oldest woman, Valerie was the mother of one of the younger informants, Martha. Martha, in turn, was a friend or fellow Junior League member of the three remaining informants, Cindy, Shirley, and Nan. Also, Martha had worked or otherwise consulted as an interior decorator for Cindy, Shirley, and Nan, as well as for her mother Valerie. Martha arranged the interviews with the other women and therefore was central to this research in several ways. Not only was she the carrier and embodiment of old Woodville values from her mother, she was also a key gatekeeper and prescriber of traditional decorator values to her friends. The chart below summarizes the women and their relationships to each other.

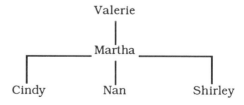

The following sections describe the lives and homes of each woman.

VALERIE

During the initial interview, Valerie sits on the flagstone patio in her back garden wearing a white dress and confines much of her talk to her house and family. She and her husband Al live in a large stone and wood house built in the 50's. The landscaping is lush and mature, and everything in and around the house is spotless. Valerie and her husband have added onto it many times. As she says, "it has been a constant doing". They changed a two-car garage into a three-car garage and enlarged the master bedroom suite and its bathroom. In 1957, they revamped the den by tearing out closets and building bookcases. Recently, Valerie says that they redid the upstairs so they could have a bigger closet for her husband, Al. Al was tired of moving his clothes from one closet to another each time the season changed. Now his clothes are all in his large, new, cedar-lined closet. The renovation was troublesome, Valerie says, but adds that the compensation is (to her) the big new bathroom they added to supplement the existing master suite bathroom. The new bathroom and closets are described in fieldnotes as follows:

A shock awaits in the form of an immense bathroom done in mauve with fabulous fixtures by Kohler including a bidet and sink counter stacked with big perfume bottles. I photograph the perfectly hung purple towels and jealously regard the arrays of storage space... Behind a mirrored door is Al's closet, which he has designed himself and which features a long double row of handing garments and ... tall, vertical columns of neatly stacked footwear... The whole place looks as if someone has spent two weeks scrubbing it.

The notes also describe a recent kitchen remodelling as well as changes in the master bedroom brought about by the bathroom remodelling.

I soon move into the spanking new kitchen. Here, everything matches in a festival of grey with white piping around the edges - including the refrigerator, dishwasher, and gigantic ice machine. ... I sneak upstairs .. (and)... immediately encounter a magnificent bedroom with everything put neatly away and hardly any signs of habitation except a stack of magazines topped by "Architectural Digest" and a copy of William F. Buckley's latest spy novel. ... (I find that)..symmetry greets me at every turn. The bed is flanked by two identical lamps and by two wallpaper-disguised doors on each side, with a double curve of

small pictures hung carefully above it and flowery bedspread that perfectly matches the wallpaper".

This domestic environment has been made possible by Al's success in the novelty chocolate candy company he started many years ago. Valerie sees him as an innovator in his creation of characters of bunnies and ducks. He developed new molds for making hollow chocolates and added character to the animals. She says, "If I may be so bold, my husband was a pacesetter". However, business and home are kept separate; the only overt indication of the family business in the house is a framed picture of the family ocean cruiser, "Easter Egg".

In addition to her daughter, Valerie has two grown sons. The eldest, who has now taken over his father's position in the candy business, lives nearby. He is divorced and has one daughter, age 11, who lives nearby with her mother. Valerie is saddened that she doesn't get to see her granddaughter now as often as she did prior to the divorce. She doesn't feel that she can just drop in for a visit at the house where her ex-daughter-in-law and granddaughter live. Now Valerie only gets to see her granddaughter when she visits her father.

Her second son lives in Texas and does not have any children. Martha, her daughter, lives nearby and has one daughter, age 3. This child, therefore, is the only grandchild with whom Valerie has frequent contact. Thus, although large enough for all of her children and their progeny, Valerie's home is seldom filled with the entire extended family.

Valerie's nurturant mothering extends to plants as well. Her backyard features flowers including marigolds to keep the rabbits away; her dining room contains some lush rubber plants that she prides herself on propagating.

Valerie and her husband also own a horse farm about 30 miles away. They have a large stone home there, as well as a small house for a caretaker who looks after their three horses. Valerie calls the youngest horses her "babies". Although she thinks it is good for them to ride, she is concerned when her children and grandchildren ride. She is especially protective of her grandchildren, and worries much more when the 11-year-old rides than when her daughter Martha used to ride as a child.

Al and Valerie also own a condominium in Florida where they spend the winter now that Al is retired. However, they only go there after Christmas, preferring to spend the holiday with as many children and grandchildren present as possible in the New York house that has served as their primary family home all of these years. Valerie acknowledges that she and Al do not need all of the space of this house, but she wants to keep it for the times when the children come home for the holidays.

While she enjoys planning and making changes to the house, she adds that there are some serious pitfalls to undertaking major changes. One accident during a recent project, she said, "bothered her to death". A box containing some framed clay pieces showing the children's hand prints when they were in kindergarten was lost. She calls it "a box of the children's hands," and clearly feels terrible about the loss. In contrast to her matter-of-fact description of the numerous display cases of valuable ceramics, crystal, and silver, she is almost in tears while describing these mementos, and says it "is a sentimental thing".

MARTHA KEELER

Valerie's daughter, Martha, is in her mid-thirties and lives in a large, colonial-style house with her husband who is a successful attorney and her 3-year-old daughter. At the time of the initial interview, she is pregnant with a second child. She formerly worked in New York City in sales for a large office equipment corporation, but decided that she didn't want to be in middle management all her life and would rather work for herself. Once, during a sales training program, she got to spend a day in a design center, and felt it was "the most exciting day of her life". In order to make a career change, she got a degree from Parsons in design, and established her own design business, initially in the city and then in Woodville after she was divorced from her first husband. She currently runs her design business out of an office in her basement. About half of her design work is commercial. She feels that commercial work is very different from residential interior design work, which she also does. She prefers commercial work because of the license given to her on such jobs. In doing residential interior design work, she often encounters women who think that they are natural decorators and just want her for a second opinion. However, those who hire her for commercial jobs are more likely to just turn the job over to her. She claims that what she says "goes nine times out of ten."

Both Martha and her husband were married previously. One of the primary reasons why Martha divorced her first husband was that he did not want children. Martha has a three-year old daughter by her current husband, and is expecting a second child at the time of the initial interview. In addition, Martha's husband's 10-year-old daughter from his former marriage lives in the area and visits weekly. The house is large enough for each child to have a bedroom of her own.

During the interview, Martha wears a white and pink-striped maternity sun dress, matching lipstick, necklace, earrings, silver headband, and blue eye makeup. The interview was held on the back deck of her house, where her outfit was a colorful complement to the late-summer deep-green lushness of the heavily fertilized and watered lawn and the pink-flowering planting beds and window boxes.

The house is a somewhat eclectic mixture of traditional and contemporary styles. Martha sees this as reflecting the house's as well as her own personality. As she says, the house is "schizophrenic. ... The front is formal, the back is contemporary, where we live. I have a split personality, so the house is that way". In fact, much of the front of the house is sparsely furnished. She says they moved much of the furniture from the living room to the family room. The television is in the family room, and she does not want the children in the living room. That way, she says, "it is presentable if I have an evening meeting or if someone stops by." She adds that toys - and even *children* - are not allowed in the living room: "It is nice to have one room that is not destroyed by your children."

In decorating her house, Martha has conformed to the wishes of others, especially her husband, who hates her favorite lavenders and purples and insists on blue and grey. In other respects, he has supported her decorating business (unlike her first husband), while her dad has also encouraged her entrepreneurial flair (which she learned from him). Her mother has served as a role model for many of her decorating activities. For example, Martha's living room features a coffee table modeled on one her mom owned, a highboy made from walnut grown on the family's farm, and the baby grand piano that she played as a child. These family heirlooms give the room a very special quality for her, in spite of its relative emptiness.

Both Martha and her husband love dogs, but he is allergic to them, so they have only a large stuffed dog in the family room. He is also allergic to horses, so she does not often take him to her parents' horse farm. She has some plants, but does not have time to take care of them. In her own home, therefore, and in the homes she designs, she uses a lot of artificial flowers and plants, chiefly made from silk. She loves real flowers, but can't afford them. She knew some people in New York who had fresh flowers delivered to them every week. She thought that was wonderfully luxurious, although expensive. She detests plastic flowers. Her love of flowers extends to the numerous floral patterns on sofas and draperies throughout the house.

She and her husband hope to move into a house they can design themselves. She says, however, that her parents would hate to see her move. Living near them, she is not as independent as she could be. Her mother sees any change she makes in her house. She tries to break away from being a good daughter, but she can't toss that aside because she wants to make her mother happy. She says that she is the kind of person who focuses on pleasing other people rather than pleasing herself. She said that she especially likes to entertain, and can cook and serve dinners in her home for forty people. This skill and interest was reflected in dinners she prepared for us on our interview trips, assembled despite her work and family obligations.

When Martha was re-interviewed a year later, some major changes had occurred. She had given birth to a second daughter, and her mother-in-law had died. Of the two changes, the birth of the new daughter seemed more impactful. She said that the effect of a second child was "crippling". For example, she had a difficult time taking both children to the grocery store, and had to hire a sitter on days when she drove her older daughter to her school.

Another change that had occurred in the year was that Martha and her husband had bought land for a new, modern house. During our second interview visit, they proudly showed us the plans and explained their dreams. The house was to be made of grey fieldstone and glass, because "that (combination) ties together the combination of traditional and modern furniture". The new house was also to have a toy room for the girls, and would be surrounded by a lot of open space.

CINDY SAWYER

Cindy is 39 and lives with her husband and two children (6-year-old boy and 10-year-old girl) in a large 3-story stone home built in the 1920's. She and her daughter wear white shorts and matching red Polo tennis shirts during the initial interview.

The family has lived in the house for only a year. Cindy notes that they are "renovating" it - as opposed to remodelling or redecorating (although she has had extensive help in decorating from Martha Keeler). She does not want to modernize it. She wants a traditional style, particularly on the first floor, with the possible exception of the family room. She isn't really sure what she is going to do with the bedrooms, because it will be several years before she gets to them.

While she prefers old houses, her husband does not. He is an engineer, and did not think it would be sensible to buy an old house. In some ways, he is correct, she says, because the house has become like the house in the movie, "The Money Pit"; that is, it has required a lot of time and money already. They do not do all the restoration work themselves. That would be "monumental". Neither of them

has that much time; her husband's job takes much of his time and she is very busy as a volunteer for a local women's health services clinic. While the initial interview was being conducted, two workmen were outside, painstakingly burning and scraping paint off the hundreds of small window mullions which a previous owner had wrongly painted with oil base paint.

Their first priority of areas to work on was the first floor. Most of the work so far has been cosmetic, such as wallpapering and paint. It used to be flashy and dark, but she changed it to be airy and open. As was also true in Martha's house, the living room is off-limits to toys and children. She would like to have Chinese rugs on the light-stained oak floors, but currently she only has one which is in the living room. It will be a while before they get any others. She thinks that many people would have wanted to redo the kitchen, but she loves it the way it is.

She speaks of the house in a deferential and solemn way. It is infrequent that one of these older mansions on a broad boulevard comes up for sale, so she feels "fortunate to have acquired the property". As she says, "the house commands elegance". She is "thrilled to have the honor to be living in this house. ... It is really grand". The other women also refer to this house as a "grand" house.

Her husband's engineering and electronic interests mean that they have a VCR and computer equipment. Because she doesn't like the way these things look, she would prefer in time to have them hidden away in nice built-in cabinets that go with the style of the house.

She and her husband moved into this house from a 15-year old split level. She has some old furniture from her grandmother which, she says, "looks much better in this house than the last one". She grew up, however, in a large three story house, which was older, but not as grand as this one. Her grandparents and uncle lived on the first floor, and her family had the top two floors. Her husband, in contrast, grew up in a very modern house.

At earlier points in her life, she liked a more rustic and country style. But that type of furniture does not suit a house of this "stature", so she got rid of those things. Fifteen years ago she would not have wanted wing chairs, but now she just loves them. She is not counting on this taste changing.

Later in the interview, while she was fixing lunch for the children, she talked about the house and all the children's activities - and realized that she had taken on quite a lot. Caring for the house, the gardens, the pool, the carriage house, and her husband, she says, is overwhelming. When the interviewer asked what she did for herself, she paused and appeared to be ready to start crying. She intends, however, to go back to school, and get a degree in social work.

By the time of the second interview, the exterior work of refinishing windows and painting shutters was complete. She discussed the difficulties she and her husband encountered in trying to decide on a color for the exterior trim. They simply could not agree, until one day she came up with a wonderful idea and phoned him at work to suggest a color (white). They were quite proud of the result and were pleased to be finished with the mess and invasiveness of workmen.

NAN SCHLINGER

Nan is also in her thirties and is married to an engineer. Her husband is president of a plastics company owned by his father. They live in a large, new (less than one year old) colonial home on a large, treeless lot in a development of similar new colonials. During the interview, Nan wears a blue and white maternity dress (she is six months pregnant), pearl necklace, and has a short, pageboy haircut similar to that of Valerie Parks. She has a two and one-half year old son, and would like one or possibly two more children. She was originally from Connecticut, although her husband was from Woodville. She taught elementary school French and then worked in college admissions, but is not currently employed. She does volunteer work at a shop (not to be called an outlet since that has a different meaning to her) which sells hand-crafted items on consignment for elderly people. She met her husband through mutual friends while they were both working in Boston. She plays golf as does her husband. His interest, she says, is much more on the golf course than at working on projects around the house. In decorating the house, she wanted to use a decorator, but decided against Martha Keeler. They were friends and are both members of Junior League, and she thought that hiring Martha as a decorator might impair the friendship. The decorator she chose, however, selected some patterns and colors that were too bold for her. A floral pattern recommended by the decorator for wallcovering in the first-floor powder room had bright colors and big patterns, and she felt that, "it was too much of a jolt". The pattern she finally selected was a Williamsburg pattern that was more subdued with smaller flowers. She says that dramatic style appeals to her but she wouldn't want to live with it.

She describes her house and interiors as "traditional", and explains that a traditional style is comfortable, homey, inviting, warm and safe. Some contemporary homes, in contrast, do not look inviting and warm. Her husband likes contemporary styles and, if given a choice, would opt for a contemporary interior.

As one researcher notes about the house and interior:

Everything in this house has the feeling of being new. Everything smells new, clean, and freshly painted. Doors stick because of the new paint whose odor permeates the house. This new smell contrasts with the visual impression of the traditional decor. The older objects - books, photos of family members - are lost in this ocean of newness.

The cleanliness in the house is even present in the fireplace, which shows no signs of ever having a fire.

Thus far, Nan and her husband have decorated only the first floor. For this reason, and in order to not disturb her son who is taking a nap, she asks that we not go upstairs. This was the only restriction on access we encountered in any of the homes. She says that she has a long way to go before the house will be done.

Her son's toys are mostly kept in the family room. He is not allowed in the living room. That way she can have figurines and other things sitting out in there and not have them broken. Many of her ceramics and other figurines are shaped like rabbits. She admits that her nickname is "Bunny", and that she has a large collection of bunny figures throughout the house. She got the nickname in college. She jokes that it was because of her teeth, but also joked that it might be because she looked like a "Playboy" bunny.

SHIRLEY CRUSADER

Shirley is 40 and lives with her husband and two boys in a development of large new homes. This development, like Nan's, lacks large trees, but aspires to reforestation as evidenced by the number of young saplings. The houses are much closer together, and suggest more of a mix of traditional and contemporary house styles. Her husband is a senior engineer with a local battery company.

For the interview, she wears a sun dress and has no makeup. She has short cropped hair and a dark sun tan. She has her summers free, she says, because she works as a speech pathologist in the school system. They have been in the home for four years, moving to Woodville from Illinois.

The house is wide open. Although it is a hot, muggy day, the air conditioning is not on, and it seems as though all the doors and windows are open. The interview is conducted on a deck next to the family room which also opens to the outside. Shirley says she loves the out-of-doors, and enjoys spending much of her time on the back deck.

The house is full of craft items and antiques. Shirley calls it a "country" look, and is very proud of it. Many items, including figurines, pot holders, and wall hangings repeat similar design motifs: hearts, ducks, flowers, wreaths, and alphabet letters. She says that country style seems more back to nature, more natural, informal, and more comfortable. Country style, she says, is a style she has adopted over time, having begun with a more traditional decorating style. The family room and kitchen are all "countrified", she says, and she is considering changing the living room to a more country style. She does not have the time to learn about antiques and how to refinish them, so she pretty much has to buy them in good shape.

Recently, she bought a pine tramp's cupboard and hung it over her desk in the kitchen. This is an unusual thing to do with it, but she likes it there. Most people would sit it on the floor. It is called this because tramps made it out of old pine boards which don't fit together well.

A large sampler, a special gift made and given to her by her grandmother, has been framed and hung in the dining room. It has this poem on it:

"Give me a house to call my own
Family and friends to make it a home
Love and kindness that ne'er will depart
Enough to fill a thankful heart"

When she was married, Shirley received china, silver and crystal as wedding gifts. But now she prefers a more informal entertaining style. They never use the living room, and when they eat in the dining room, it is usually casual, buffet style. She prefers eating and entertaining outside on the deck. She sees china, crystal and silver as things that just make work for you, "Why make all that work for yourself?" Although she grew up in a home which emphasized traditional, formal styles, she first saw antiques in the home of a girlfriend in elementary school. She always felt comfortable in that house. She is particularly fond of a recently-purchased braided rug: "It looks old, the colors look muted, it doesn't grab you." Her identification with this style is a close one. She says that antiques and country style have always been in her; she hasn't had to learn to like it or learn about it. It comes from *in* her. (At that moment in the interview she touches her hand over her left breast, over her heart).

In the initial interview - and later, in a second interview after a year - she describes that she is not very close with her neighbors. She says she has been snubbed because she is not interested in spending her time going to others' homes for coffee. She likes friends but doesn't want them in her house all the time.

She has too many other things she likes to do. She says that she has friends but that she doesn't need a lot of people.

Some changes have taken place in Shirley's house by the time of the second interview. Most notably, a new addition has been constructed on the back of the house, enlarging the family room. The enlarged family room (new and old spaces together) has been wallpapered in a pattern that continues Shirley's love of duck and heart patterns. The entire space has been "countrified" using primarily pieces that were purchased new and manufactured to incorporate a country style.

THEMES

As suggested earlier, all of these women employ roughly the same consumption ethic or style. Oddly, the *women* of Woodville seem to be the upholders and keepers of this style. Their husbands seem to prefer more modern styles, and generally seem more oriented toward contemporary homes and new technologies: home computers, VCR's, and compact disc players. While Martha obviously grew up in an affluent setting, Cindy, Bev and Nan appear to have grown up in more middle-class surroundings. To them, it might be that the Woodville lifestyle is a goal which, once achieved, is held onto tightly. While their husbands (who mainly grew up in Woodville), might want to "break away" to a more contemporary style, they do not.

Several themes were identified as part of the Woodville lifestyle. These themes are examined below.

1. RECONSTRUCT PAST IN PRESENT VERSUS PROJECTING LIVES INTO FUTURE

In spite of the multitude of women's lifestyles that have emerged in the last twenty years - including childfree, working single, parents without partners, professional career - these women of Woodville lead very conservative lifestyles. All of the women have children as well as husbands who work at full time jobs. All are the primary caretakers of their children and their homes. Despite their affluence, none of the women has live-in household help, a pattern true of at least 90% of Americans since 1940. Their work activities are also conservative: they either do volunteer work but are not gainfully employed outside the home (Valerie, Nan, and Cindy); work out of rather than outside of the home (as with Martha's design business); or are employed in a job that fits with their children's school schedules (Shirley's job as a school speech pathologist). Their volunteer work as well as their career fields preserve traditional roles for women, such as nurturer of children (school speech pathologist, elementary school French teacher), nest builder (interior decorator), protector of health (volunteer work for the women's health clinic), and caregiver for the elderly (Nan's volunteer work at the craft store). Like the volunteers studied by Daniels (1988), their primary energies and time are invested in their children and their homes, followed by their community-based caregiving through their volunteer work. They have the financial resources to live this way, and use home and interior planning to express drives and needs that otherwise might have been expressed in full-time careers. In crafting these roles for themselves, they can be viewed as reconstructing women's traditional roles from the past in new ways (that are not really so new) in the present.

In buying and selecting items for their homes, a key criterion is that the items look old, but not necessarily "used". For the most part they have not inherited many antiques or heirlooms, but rather buy things that look old. Whether "country" or "traditional" in style, their purchases reflect a nostalgic image of the past that they are reconstructing in the present (Davis 1979). They prefer that the new technologies in their homes must fit in context with the old; for instance, VCR's are best hidden behind traditional styled cabinets.

In part, this is an economic decision. Classic designs supposedly never go out of style and never have to be replaced. This decision, however, is largely emotional and rooted in early family background. Martha Keeler maintains a link with her parents by decorating with heirlooms and surrounding them with other traditional designs. In addition, however, she appears to "break away" via her interest in contemporary design and the use of it in her basement office. Cindy Sawyer lives in a house that has 3-stories like the house she grew up in. The pageboy hairdos of Valerie and Nan date back to a prosperous, happy time in contemporary US history, the 1950's. Shirley's use of a country style transplants her midwestern roots into this Eastern suburb. So a preference for something that looks "old" or "traditional" is a way of creating a feeling of being linked with one's past.

Interestingly, however, these women did not actively identify with or want to live in some previous historic period. Cindy Sawyer liked her house and the fact that it was built in the 20's, but she did not express any strong identification with that period. Nor did Shirley Crusader express much interest in Colonial times.

Rather, what seems to be important is what these old designs mean *today*. Older designs and styles symbolize "old money" and achievement. Like classical music, classical furniture and home designs have stood the test of time. One is confident that all will recognize that one can afford the best.

But these houses do more than construct an image of the past in the present; they also serve to represent opportunities for the future. Oddly, the major satisfaction derived from these homes and furnishings does not seem to be in owning them, but rather the expectation or anticipation of the joys of creating new room and furniture arrangements in the future. Their plans to replace furniture are never justified on the basis of need; instead they will redecorate or buy new furnishings to send a message to themselves and others about their identity and status as expressed in taste (Loyd 1976). As Valerie said, "this house is a constant doing". The homes, like the lives of the women who arrange and manage them, are never finished. Instead, they are always in a state of becoming or evolving. Although Valerie is in her 70's, she is in no way "done" with her house. Martha, Nan and Cindy have many rooms which are largely empty because they do not (yet) have the money to furnish them. At the same time, they also find considerable gratification in the act of planning and designing these future changes.

Belk (1985) defines materialism mainly in pathological terms: possessiveness, nongenerosity, and envy. Yet, if there is a positive side to materialism, it may exist in the happy anticipation of the future experienced by these women through their homes. Rooms, furniture and houses to these women are palettes and paints which they feel they use to express themselves. The joys of materialism to these women are the joys of planning and anticipating new decorating schemes. While the Martha, as a decorator, has made a profession out of her decorating and design skills, all of the women feel competent to select and decide what looks best. Unlike the anti-social tendencies in Belk's study of materialism, materialism here pulls people together, as wives and husbands negotiate and plan what to buy and how to decorate. Martha and her husband talk excitedly of the new home they are designing. Valerie's husband proudly shows his new closet. In other words, the thrill lies in the process of planning, rather than in the having. How one feels about items one has owned for a while is not an issue. Consciousness and hopes are invested in the ongoing process of the houses' "becoming", becoming more elegant, becoming more comfortable, becoming more impressive.

2. FORMAL VERSUS INFORMAL

The women want their homes to be striking and impressive - yet also comfortable, warm, and inviting.

On the one hand, this means a serious striving toward perfection. Houses are spotless. Every last detail concerning appearance is attended to. Everything has its place and is put away. Everything is chosen to "go together": make-up is right, earrings are right, wallpaper is right, forming the Diderot unities discussed by McCracken (1988). Arrangements of paintings and household artifacts follow classical concepts of balance, symmetry, and proportion (e.g., rugs become "focal points".)

On the other hand, these women sincerely want people to feel at home in their houses. They do not like interiors that "jolt" or unsettle people. They talk a lot about entertaining other people in their homes and how well they can accommodate large parties. A common word they use to describe their homes is "liveable".

This suggests an interesting conflict. How can one maintain a home that is always neat, clean, perfect and formal in appearance - yet also comfortable, liveable, warm and inviting? Four solutions were observed, and are discussed below.

Segregate children: Children are typically not allowed in living rooms or dining rooms. Children are not viewed as little adults, but are instead expected to behave in ways that may not be compatible with adult lives (Aries 1962/1960). Therefore, certain rooms are set aside as "children's rooms", and toys and other children's things are to remain there. This confines children's clutter to rooms that are the "lived in" rooms, for example, the family room. This is the liveable part of the house. Living rooms and dining rooms are typically reserved for adults invited into the household. This is the striking and impressive part of the house, where impressions can be staged (Duncan 1981). Interestingly, it appeared that it was these more formal areas that were decorated first in a newly acquired home.

Subtle prints and colors: There was a common resistance to bold, large prints and bold colors. Nan said she did not like interiors to "jolt" people. She likes floral prints, but chooses patterns with small flowers. Shirley likes muted colors and fabrics. Like the expected demeanor of the women themselves, homes are expected to have a gentler, more subtle impact. Valerie bragged a bit about her husband's career success, but softened the impact by saying "if I may be so bold," reflecting the self-effacing modesty Daniels (1988) found characterized women volunteer community leaders. Similarly, Nan indicated that others have told her she has good taste, after demurring "if I may be so immodest." The boldest decorating was the contemporary red and white furniture in Martha's basement office. Like her relative boldness in establishing her own business, these furnishings contrasted sharply with the more typical subtle prints and soft colors chosen for

decorating the remainder of her house and the entirety of the other houses.

Open to outdoors: Many of the homes feature large windows and doors in the formal spaces, and deck spaces opening off of the informal spaces. The flowers and garden views have a long tradition in formal architecture, yet are also warm and inviting. In the new homes, decks and open views are much more popular than dark, closed-in studies and libraries. The flowers of gardens are echoed in the floral prints typically chosen in decorating. In these ways, these women use culture to transform nature and re-present it to those who enter their homes. Their suburban life is thus able to blend the contact with nature enjoyed in agrarian communities with the tamed environments of the city. In so doing, the association of women with flowers and their system of meanings is heightened (Stilgoe 1988), allowing formality and casualness in the same home.

"Country Style": Of all the older styles of furniture and decorating, "country" style seems to connote the most warmth and naturalness. Items look handmade, although they may in fact be mass-produced, and are made from basic materials, such as wood and ceramic. While neocolonial styles revert back ultimately to English country homes and aristocratic lifestyles, country items symbolize the sincerity and authenticity of rural American lifestyles. One can fill one's home with these items - and create a warm atmosphere - yet still keep the home spotless and perfectly arranged, thereby accomplishing both formality and informality at once.

In the arrangement and decoration of these homes, then, both formality and informality are made available, reflecting a pattern of preferences that emerged in the Netherlands by 1650 (Rybczynski 1986). Like much of the rest of their lives, their homes allow them to encompass and alternate between opposites.

3. REAL VERSUS ARTIFICIAL

In the fieldnotes about Shirley, one researcher writes,

"..Most of what Shirley points out appears quite authentic. However, one striking exception greets me in the kitchen. On the stove, I find a beautiful freshly baked berry pie. At first, I am overwhelmed to think that this lovely lady got up early to cook something for us. Soon, however, I realize that the pie is artificial. Later, I ask Shirley about this and she tells me that the pie sits in an antique tin. It is strictly ersatz, but she feel that this is OK because it's only for decoration. Besides, it has a heart on top (Shirley collects heart-shaped objects)."

There were many such cases of women juxtaposing real items and artificial ones. Real flowers, real pearls, real paintings (versus prints) and real wrought iron fences are expensive. The women, therefore, draw interesting lines between items they feel should be real - versus items which can be artificial.

One frequently-chosen way to draw this line is to use items that are artificial but which can be made to look as real as possible. Martha likes silk flowers and plants because they look real and can be put in places that do not get much light. Also, she knows tricks such as placing dead (real) leaves in pots of artificial ficus trees to enhance the illusion. Artifice is used, but disguised to appear real.

4. INHERITED VERSUS ACHIEVED STATUS, OLD WOODVILLE RESIDENTS VERSUS NEW

As indicated earlier, these women live the American dream. The homes, cars, clubs and clothes represent success symbols to most Americans. This fact is not lost on the Woodville women. Nan is careful to point out, "We live in *Woodville, not Tyler*" (the industrial town Woodville adjoins).

Most of the cues and upper class design codes the women follow are learned from each other, from experts (e.g., Martha) and from magazines. Magazines such as "Colonial Homes", "Country Living", and "Architectural Digest" appear to be very popular with these women. On colorful, glossy pages, they hold out the dream world of homes that these women have bought into. Yet, it seems ironic that this dream world of elaborate lifestyles is made possible by such mundane industries: plastics manufacturers, battery companies, candy factories.

An interesting distinction relates to the recency of these women's financial situation. Valerie and Martha grew up in relatively affluent surroundings while Shirley, Nan, and Cindy came from more modest backgrounds. Also, Valerie and Martha are long-time residents of Woodville, while Shirley, Nan, and Cindy are relatively new.

Thus, Valerie and Martha speak of Woodville and neighbors in a casual way. They have been there a long time, have many friends and relatives, and feel at home in this setting.

In temporal and social terms, Shirley, Nan and Cindy seem more on the fringes of Woodville social life. Shirley admits she does not get along with neighbors, Nan is described (by Martha) as "a very private person", and Cindy says she is disappointed with the noise and bustle in her new neighborhood. It is possible that the perceived emphasis on

homes and things for the women who have more recently arrived interferes with opportunities to build social ties. Particularly with new wealth, consumption and materialism might be associated with the negative social characteristics that Belk (1985) describes. With old money, however, consumption behavior appears to have little negative impact on social relationships. If anything, Valerie and Martha appear to be most strongly oriented to nonconsummatory concerns: children, grandchildren, career, volunteer work. The tendancy for older, established groups (both high income and low income) to stress social ties over conspicuous household consumption has been noted in other U.S. cities (e.g., Boston, Gans 1962) as well as other cultures (India, Duncan and Duncan 1976).

5. SEPARATIONS

An overarching theme that runs through these homes and lives in one of separations. As mentioned previously, adults and children have separate areas in the home. Similarly, men's and women's worlds of activity have a high degree of separation, with the home being the place where men return from the male world of enterprise and industry to enter women's domain (Goldthorpe 1969). Men's world is that of industrial productions and women's is that of domestic production or consumption (Campbell 1987). Although master bedrooms are the territory of both husband and wife, these rooms are decorated in feminine florals with beds that in some cases wear ruffled skirts. Office and home are separated; not one of the men has a study or office designated for his use within the home. Despite the contemporary character of these lives, men have their place and women have theirs. Work and play are not mixed. In this regard, home takes on an important cultural meaning and function. Women's cultural task is broader than that of caring for children and husbands. Through the home environments they build, the moral order and its virtues are restored; home is haven for manners, sentiment, and values that are threatened in contemporary life (Forty 1986, Loyd 1976) as well as being the expression of individual personality (Halttunen 1989).

6. MATRIARCHY VERSUS TRAP

Most of the heroes and mythology in Woodville concern men. Valerie's husband founded the successful chocolate factory, Shirley's husband was just promoted to vice president of his battery company, and Cindy's husband, she relates, is a well-known area athlete.

At the same time, the women of Woodville have considerable influence and stature. All have at least an undergraduate college degree and are actively involved in community activities via the Junior League. All won out over their husbands who preferred to live in contemporary homes. All have husbands who work long hours, relinquishing home and childrearing decisions largely to them. All talk about connection to others in the community via entertaining in their homes. Martha in particular appears to identify with the role of the young "grande dame", saying she likes to throw dinner parties at her house for 40 people. However, they also place limits on their availability to others. Nan and Valerie are very firm about their homes and which rooms are open to whom; these two women either voiced concerns about the researchers seeing certain rooms or flatly forbid them to go in certain areas. All strongly identify with the role of mother. Each in her own way is deeply motivated by her connection to her children: Valerie almost cries at the loss of "the children's hands"; Martha divorced a husband who didn't want children; Nan wants the backdoor kept open while the interview is being done so that she might hear her sleeping son if he cries. It is clear that children hold superordinate importance for these women. Through their homes, they project and construct a strong sense of their maternal power (Bensman and Lilienfield 1979).

In spite of these powers and capabilities, however, several of the women reflected feelings of frustration. Cindy seemed trapped by the financial and physical energy costs of running a family while restoring a 1920's mansion and meeting the never-ending demands of extensive volunteer work. Martha acknowledges the difficulties of relating to her new step-daughter. She also seems torn between her mother's wishes and her desires to break out on her own and live farther away. Shirley is concerned about one son who is having trouble at school. All of the women voice the same regret: that they do not have enough money or time to do the things to their homes that they would like. Rooms remain empty of furniture. Children clamor and draw attention away from house projects. Despite their relative wealth and freedom from having to work, they nonetheless constantly experience the inadequacy of their time and money, just as do others who have so much less discretion in each category.

CONCLUSION

The wives of Woodville represent a surprising mixture of demographics and sociographics. They include baby boom women who are highly educated, career-minded, and urban in outlook. At the same time, they lead very traditional lifestyles in a semi-rural suburb of a small New York industrial town.

Their consumption of traditional-styled furniture, homes, clothing and other furnishings follows the growth in popularity of this style in the 70's and 80's (Birnbach 1980). While fads come and go, however, it is expected that Woodville wives will hold to this style for many years to come. Unlike suburbs in large cities, Woodville offers few other subcultures than itself for these women to identify with. Through their home-related consumption, these women construct familial bonds and class definitions that sustain them and the assumptions on which their world is built.

BIBLIOGRAPHY
Advertising Age (1989) "The New Traditionalist" (advertisement) Oct. 30, p 33.

Aries, Philippe (1962/orig. 1960), *Centuries of Childhood: A Social History of Family Life*, Robert Baldick, trans., New York: Vintage Books.

Baltzell, E. Digby (1964), *The Protestant Establishment: Aristocracy and Caste in America*, New York: Random House.

Baumgartner, M. P. (1988), *The Moral Order of the Suburb*, New York: Oxford University Press.

Belk, Russell W. (1985), "Materialism, Trait Aspects of Living in the Material World," *Journal of Consumer Research*, Vol. 12 (December), 265-280.

Bensman, Joseph and Robert Lilienfield (1979), *Between Public and Private: The Lost Boundaries of the Self.* New York: The Free Press.

Birnbach, Lisa, ed. (1980), *The Official Preppy Handbook*, New York: Workman Publishing.

Campbell, Colin (1987), *The Romantic Ethic and the Spirit of Modern Consumerism.* Oxford: Basil Blackwell.

Daniels, Arlene Kaplan (1988), *Invisible Careers: Women Civic Leaders from the Volunteer World*, Chicago: University of Chicago Press.

Davis, Fred (1979), *Yearning for Yesterday: A Sociology of Nostalgia.* New York: Free Press.

Duncan, Nancy G. (1981), "Home Ownership and Social Theory," in James S. Duncan, ed., *Housing and Identity: Cross Cultural Perspectives.* London: Croom Helm, 98-134.

Duncan, Nancy and James Duncan, "Housing as Presentation of Self and the Structure of Social Networks in

G. Moore and R. Golledge, eds. *Environmental Knowing*, Stroudsburg, Pa.: Dowden, Hutchinson and Ross.

Forty, Adrian (1986), *Objects of Desire: Design and Society from Wedgwood to IBM.* New York: Pantheon Books.

Gans, H.J. (1962) *The Urban Villagers: Group and Class in the Life of Italian Americans*, New York The Free Press.

Goldthorpe, J.H., D. Lockwood, F. Bechhofer, J. Platt (1969), *The Affluent Worker in the Class Structure*. Cambridge.

Halttunen, Karen (1989), "From Parlor to Living Room: Domestic Space, Interior Decoration, and the Culture of Personality," in Simon J. Bronner, ed., *Consuming Visions: Accumulation and Display of Goods in America 1880-1920*, Winterthur, DE: Henry Francis DuPont Winterthur Museum, 157-190.

Loyd, Bonnie (1976), "Women, Home, and Status," in James S. Duncan, ed., *Housing and Identity: Cross-Cultural Perspectives*. London: Croom Helm, 181-197.

McCracken, Grant (1988), *Culture and Consumption: New Approaches to the Symbolic Character of Consumer Goods and Activities*, Bloomington: Indiana University Press.

Rybczynski, Witold (1986), *Home: A Short History of an Idea*. New York: Viking.

Stilgoe, Michael H. (1988), *Borderland: The Origins of the American Suburb, 1820-1939*, New Haven: Yale University Press.

Collecting in a Consumer Culture
Russell W. Belk
Melanie Wallendorf
John F. Sherry, Jr.
Morris B. Holbrook[1]

ABSTRACT

In contemporary America, collecting has become a pervasive phenomenon that reflects many aspects of the modern consumer culture. In this chapter, we define collecting, review its history, and present a grounded theory of its meanings, motivations, moments, and modes before concluding with an assessment of its social desirability. Throughout, we draw on the relevant literature and on data supplied by informants both during and after the Consumer Behavior Odyssey. Thus, we move between empirical and conceptual approaches to the topic, as was true in the development of this research project over its five year history to date.

INTRODUCTION

Asked what things they would save in a fire, people we have interviewed commonly cite a number of "special" objects including photographs, keepsakes, heirlooms, and valuables. It is no coincidence that many of these objects constitute collections that have been purposively and systematically gathered and preserved. For, unlike ordinary objects of consumption, collections tend to take on an importance and character comparable in some respects to that of family members. Collected objects are often anthropomorphized, fetishized, and personified until they define and occupy the little world of an intimate family in which the collector reigns as an absolute sovereign.

Consider the case of Sigmund Freud -- certainly not a typical human being, but a reasonably representative collector whose example proves instructive. Although our knowledge of his collecting behavior is secondary -- based on written accounts and interviews with the curators of the Freud Museums on Hampstead Heath in London and at 19 Berggasse in Vienna -- we offer the following synopsis of Freud as collector. Starting two months after the death of his father in 1896, the then 40-year-old Freud began to amass a collection of Roman, Greek, Egyptian, Assyrian, and Chinese antiquities that eventually numbered approximately 2300 pieces. These objects crowded his desk and cabinets in the two rooms where he wrote and consulted with patients. When Edmund Engelman took secret photographs of this collection before Freud fled to England to escape the Nazi occupation of Vienna in 1938, he described the decor in this way:

> antiquities filled every available spot in the room. I was overwhelmed by the masses of figurines which overflowed every surface. To the left of the door was a large bookcase covered with tall ancient statuettes. In the corner, at the end of the wall facing these statuettes, was Freud's chair, almost hidden by the head of the couch.... To the left and right of the door were glass showcases filled with hundreds of antiquities. These were set up in several rows; every bit of cabinet space was filled.... I was amazed by the unbelievable number of art objects (Engelman 1976, pp. 137-138).

Similarly, Jobst (1978) suggests that Freud's office took on a museum-like appearance, and Peter Gay notes that:

> The first and overpowering impression that Freud's habitat makes on the visitor is the profusion of things.... The sculptures, finally, have their assigned shelves and their glass cases, but they intrusively invade surfaces intended for other purposes: bookshelves, tops of cabinets, writing tables, even Freud's much used desk. The whole is an embarrassment of objects (1976, p. 17).

The hundreds of statuettes in this collection are of animal and human figures that Freud arranged facing him at his desk (Gamwell 1989), "in close-packed ranks like soldiers on parade" (Gay 1976, p. 17). Friends and family noted that the fortunate transfer of Freud's collection from wartime Vienna made his adjustment to England far easier, as he was surrounded by familiar loved objects. In a perhaps overstated 1931 letter to his biographer, Stefan Zweig, Freud claimed that "despite my much vaunted frugality I have sacrificed a great deal for my collection of Greek, Roman and Egyptian antiquities, have actually read more archaeology than psychology" (quoted in Freud, Freud, and

[1]The authors would like to thank Tom O'Guinn and Dennis Rook for their very helpful comments on an earlier version of this paper. They would also like to thank Ginny Davis, Scott Roberts, John Schouten, Sherri Stevens, and Tiana Wimmer for post-Odyssey fieldwork and the entire Odyssey team for fieldwork during the Odyssey.

Grubrich-Simitis 1978, p. 234). Although he is far better known for his writings, clearly these objects played a major role in Freud's life. He personally scouted for antiquities during his travels and developed relationships with dealers who brought him objects they knew would be of interest. In *The Psychopathology of Everyday Life*, Freud described how, due to his preoccupation with collecting, he would often misread vaguely similar shop signs in foreign cities as proclaiming "antiquities" ; "this displays the questing spirit of the collector," he noted (Freud 1914, pp. 119-120).

Freud's student and colleague Ernest Jones (1955) describes how, after making a new acquisition, Freud would first bring the piece to the dining room table so that he could admire it during the meal. After placing the pieces in his study or consultation room, he frequently rearranged them. According to a long-time maid, before beginning work each day Sigmund Freud would bid "good morning" to a favorite Chinese figure on his desk (Spector 1975). He was also in the habit of holding, examining, and fondling the statuettes as he talked to patients (Spector 1975, p. 21; Sachs 1945, p. 101). As Gay (1989) concludes:

> Collecting stamps, or china--or Greek and Egyptian and Chinese statuettes, for that matter--partakes of, and preserves, early erotic pleasures; Freud, we are told, liked to gaze at the antiquities on his desk as he worked and, at times, moving from looking to touching, would stroke his favorites. But there is more passion to it still; collecting, as anyone who has ever collected can testify, gives power. To possess a complete collection of certain stamps or of one's reviews or letters to the editor is, in some intimate fashion, a way of controlling and commanding the world (p. 18).

Considering his extreme devotion to the clutter of little ancient icons with which he surrounded himself, Freud was remarkably silent on the subjects of collecting in general and his own collecting in particular. However, he did offer one brief interpretation of collecting activity:

> The core of paranoia is the detachment of the libido from objects. A reverse course is taken by the collector who directs his surplus libido onto an inanimate object: a love of things (Freud 1908, quoted in Gamwell 1988).

We shall return to this interpretation and to Freud's own collecting later in this paper. For the present, it is sufficient to note that Freud's collecting activity and his comments on collecting both support the observation that a key feature of collecting consists of elevating possessions in the collection to an extraordinary status not bestowed upon the vast majority of objects in the collector's life.

METHOD AND SAMPLE

Collection of primary data materials for this project began during the summer spent traveling on the Odyssey. However, reading of the literature on collection, some of which reports empirical findings, began prior to the Odyssey and guided the questions asked in interviews. Many of our data on collecting were gathered subsequent to the summer of travel. The data are primarily from unstructured interviews with people who are currently collectors. Some of these data are based on participant observation of action in context. In general, however, the data describe in detail collectors' perspectives on their action and are less rich with regard to perspectives in action (Gould, Walker, Crane, and Lidz 1974). Because of their pride in the collection, we encountered little resistance on the part of collectors to being interviewed; more difficult was shifting their focus from the objects themselves to the process of collecting. Most collectors in the sample were interviewed once, although a few were studied in sufficient depth over time to permit the construction of case study material (Yin 1990).

Most people included in the sample fall into the category of avid collectors, since a substantial portion of the sample was initially contacted through collector shows. Other members of the sample were identified through self-designation. Many interviews were conducted at collectors' homes, while others were conducted in the midst of collectors' shows. Purposive sampling was used to add fine art collectors and various demographic groups to the sample; however, this was not a technique employed throughout the project. The approach used was in part the grounded theory suggested by Glaser and Strauss (1967) and in part an attempt at the thick description and thick interpretation suggested by Denzin (1989). In total, over 190 collectors are included in the sample representing differing geographic regions within the U.S.. They also represent a broad spectrum of objects collected in terms of breadth of appeal, price, and availability. Talking to collectors of *anything* rather than limiting the sample to collectors of particular objects (as is prevalent in studies of collectors) shifted our focus from the objects themselves (often the focus for the collector) to the process and meaning of collecting as a consumption activity. We first use these data and the literature to construct and frame a definition of collecting.

DEFINITIONS AND DISTINCTIONS

Collecting

Collecting is a specialized form of consumer behavior (i.e., acquiring, using, and disposing of products). Collecting is inherently acquisitive because its primary focus is on gathering more of something (Brown 1988). In the most common contemporary form of collecting, the objects collected are acquired through marketplace purchase; used through maintenance, display, and related curatorial activities; and disposed of only at death. Rather than viewing shopping as a necessary or even odious task to be minimized or avoided, collectors commit to a constant and continual shopping trip in pursuit of objects for the collection. As Herrmann (1972, p. 22) notes, "the genuine collector...has stilled once and for all any inhibition against spending money on the...objects of his choice." Like Freud, the collector is ever vigilant for hidden treasures in the marketplace.

Lehrer (1990, p. 58) offers this view of the collector's quest:

> Envy us [collectors] because all our car trips down country lanes and "blue" highways are treasure hunts....Envy us because every mail delivery has the potential for having the note about or Polaroid shot of an item we have been looking for desperately....Envy the adventures we have while on The Hunt....But mostly envy us for the Thrill of The Find.

Collectors are engaged in a competition that, for some, becomes an heroic mission in an indifferent or scornful world. There are few other consumer activities that match the passion of collecting as a mode of consumer behavior. And collecting is perhaps the purest example of a consumption activity that is also a form of production. At its best, collecting creates and produces a unique, valuable, and lasting contribution to the world. For example, had not the writings of Plato, Aristotle, and Homer been collected and partially preserved, the world would be the poorer for their lack.

We take collecting to be the selective, active, and longitudinal acquisition, possession, and disposition of an interrelated set of differentiated objects (material things, ideas, beings, or experiences) that contribute to and derive extraordinary meaning from the entity (the collection) that this set is perceived to constitute. This definition coheres with that of Belk (1982) and Belk, Wallendorf, Sherry, Holbrook, and Roberts (1988). It is also generally consistent with prior definitions such as the following:

collection...[is] "an obsession organized." One of the distinctions between possessing and collecting is that the latter implies order, system, perhaps completion. The pure collector's interest is not bounded by the intrinsic worth of the objects of his desire; whatever they cost, he must have them (Aristides 1988, p. 330).

To collect is to gather objects belonging to a particular category the collector happens to fancy.... and a collection is what has been gathered (Alsop 1982, p. 70).

A collection is basically determined by the nature of the *value* assigned to the objects, or ideas possessed. If the *predominant* value of an object or idea for the person possessing it is intrinsic, i.e., if it is valued primarily for use, or purpose, or aesthetically pleasing quality, or other value inherent in the object or accruing to it by whatever circumstance of custom, training, or habit, it is not a collection. If the predominant value is representative or representational, i.e., if said object or idea is valued chiefly for the relation it bears to some other object or idea, or objects, or ideas, such as being one of a series, part of a whole, a specimen of a class, then it is the subject of a collection (Durost 1932, p. 10).

To qualify as a collection, the items collected must have some similarity and interrelationship. By being part of the collection each piece is transformed from its original function of toy, icon, bowl, picture, whatever, into an object with new meaning -- a member of an assemblage that is greater than the sum of its parts (Kron 1983, pp. 193-194).

Each of these definitions shares with ours the specification that the collector views the collection as an entity due to a perceived unity in its components. The basis for this unity is identified by labeling the set as "a collection of _____" and is further defined through the boundaries that the collector consciously or unconsciously heeds in adding to the collection.

While a collection remains a collection when additions stop, a collector ceases to be a collector under these conditions. Freud called such a collection "dead" (Freud, Freud, and Grubrich-Simitis 1976, pp. 313). Although the original collector may continue to preserve and display the dead collection, such curating activity is then separated from collecting activity. As the most recent collecting activity recedes into the past, the passive possessor becomes less and less of a collector. In specifying that the collector is an active agent in assembling the collection, we also eliminate the passive recipient of previously collected objects provided by others without personal choice or direction (Durost 1932).

Similarly, to acquire a number of potentially related objects without keeping them (in tangible or symbolic form) is to be acquisitive without collecting. The ingredient missing in this case is the possessive construction of a set. For instance, we have interviewed world travelers who do not perceive their travel destinations as a set, as well as other travelers who consciously collect an expanding set of travel destinations experienced within a specified domain (e.g., continents visited). As with travel experiences, a number of car collectors whom we have interviewed do not have all of their collection physically at hand. Rather, because of the expense of acquisition and storage, theirs are often *serial* collections involving ownership of only one or a few automobiles at one time. Nevertheless, because they view these sequential acquisitions as part of set, they qualify as collectors. Ownership (or at least a proprietary feeling) also appears to be essential to collecting. A number of our informants express sentiments similar to those of a stamp-collector interviewed by Danet and Katriel (1989):

> It's mine (the collection). I can do with it what I want. I can arrange it in the album the way I want. I can display it in exhibits (p. 263).

Since ownership or possession is required for collecting, a museum curator who uses other people's money to make acquisitions for the museum is not a collector unless he or she has strong proprietary feelings for the objects acquired. However, the museum itself may be regarded as an institutional collector if the other requirements for collecting are fulfilled. While groups, families, or even entire societies or whole cultures may engage in collecting behavior, it is not uncommon that it is individuals within these institutions who develop the strong proprietary feelings required to be considered individual collectors. Thus, a couple or family may refer to "our house," but the collection is usually "mine."

Another similarity between our definition of collecting and many of those just quoted is that they jointly note that once a thing, idea, or experience enters a collection it becomes non-ordinary, non-utilitarian (at least in the case of formerly utilitarian items), and somehow "special." In a term we will develop more thoroughly later in this chapter,

the collected item becomes *sacred* (Belk, Wallendorf, and Sherry 1989). While fine art items and some other aesthetic objects (such as books and recordings) may enter a collection without a major change in their extraordinary sacred character, other items are sacralized when they first enter a collection. This normally means that they stop serving their former functions as, for instance, advertisements, stones on a beach, stamps for paying postage charges, or dolls for ordinary play activity. Even those collected objects that retain their original uses (e.g., antique furniture, cars, jewelry, hats, recordings) are regarded as *more* than functional products, are treated with extreme care, and are often only employed ritually or on special ceremonial occasions. For example, someone who owns a rare recording might tape it for everyday listening and store the original for safe-keeping. If this is not the case and the objects are instead used routinely or casually without regard for their special significance, we do not consider them as parts of a collection.

Our definition is more expansive than the others mentioned above in going beyond material objects to include experiences, beings, and ideas as collectibles. We believe that the theoretical model developed in this paper applies equally well to collections of both tangibles and intangibles as well as both inanimate and animate objects. (Here, the latter refers to plants and animals, occasionally including the collections of persons -- as in the dwarfs who were once a part of royal collections, the wives of Henry VIII, or the husbands of Zsa Zsa Gabor. For comments on the opprobrium now attached to "collecting" people, see Danet and Katriel 1989).

Our view involves several further differences from some of the prior definitions. We do not insist that collecting is necessarily an act of formal classification, as do Phillips (1962) and Humphrey (1983), for instance. Rather, as will become evident, we believe that such classification defines one of two major types of collecting; one which epitomizes a common model of science, but which is not essential for another type of collecting involving connoisseurship. There must be some systematic pattern displayed (even if not consciously discerned) in adding items to any collection, but deciding selectively whether an item belongs in the collection (or how to display it) need not be a classificatory act any more than deciding whether to add an article of clothing to one's wardrobe (or deciding how to wear it) needs to be an act of classification.

We also do not view collecting as a necessarily obsessive act, as does Aristides (1988). While it may become obsessive, compulsive, or even addictive, this need not happen. Furthermore, as argued in a later evaluative section, these undesirable labels are at least as much social as clinical in nature. Love, for example, can sometimes be seen as involving an obsessive behavioral pattern as well. While collecting is often characterized less favorably than love, we did not prejudge it to be either a positive or negative phenomenon.

In summary then, we define collecting as a form of acquisition and possession that is selective, active, and longitudinal. A necessary condition is that the objects, ideas, beings, or experiences derive larger meaning by their assemblage into a set. We turn now to distinctions between collecting and other phenomena.

Accumulating, Hoarding, and Investing

Collecting must also be distinguished from several other phenomena with which it is sometimes confused. The simple accumulation of possessions, ideas, or experiences is excluded from our definition of collecting, first, because it lacks selectivity (Kron 1983, p. 193). Because of the lack of systematic selectivity in acquiring them, items in an accumulation also lack unity and defy categorical description. To the extent that the accumulation is merely a passive refusal to dispose of items that may have entered our possession, accumulation also lacks the agency needed for collecting. Unlike collected items that may bring pleasure and pride in possession -- and even though the underlying motive for accumulation is often security-seeking (Jensen 1963; Laughlin 1956; von Holst 1967, p. 3) -- accumulated items may tend to create clutter and to cause conflict, displeasure, or even shame (Phillips 1962; Novey and Novey 1987; Warren and Ostrom 1988). Thus, an informant in his seventies who had accumulated three garages full of miscellaneous possessions was succumbing to pressures from his family to begin discarding these things so that they were not faced with the burden of having to do so after his death.

If collections are distinct from human accumulations, they are even farther from animal accumulations, despite the attempt by some to suggest a basis for collecting in animal behavior (e.g., Humphrey 1979). We assume, first of all, that animals -- such as a squirrel piling up nuts for the winter -- lack the appreciation of any interactions within a set of interrelated objects (Stewart 1984, p. 183). Secondly, as an anonymous author notes:

A used postage stamp is to a man what a bone without flesh is to a dog: but the collector of postage stamps goes further than the dog, in that he prefers an old postage stamp to a new one, while no

dog, however ardent a collector of bones without flesh, would not rather have a bone with flesh on it. There is more method in the human collector, however, since he always has before him the ideal of a complete collection, whereas no dog, probably, ever dreamed of acquiring specimens of all the different kinds of bones that there are in the world (Johnston and Beddow 1986, pp. 13-15, quoting from an anonymous article in *The Times* [of London], August 12, 1910; also quoted in Rowed 1920, pp. 6-7).

Unlike accumulation, hoarding is selective and active. But it differs from collecting by focusing on utilitarian items in the expectation that they may be needed in the future (McKinnon, Smith, and Hunt 1985). Because the items hoarded are typically for common uses (e.g., fuel, food staples, cleaning supplies), they are unlikely to take on the sacred character of collected objects. Simmel (1907/1971) distinguishes the miser who hoards money from the numismatist who collects money, based on both the utilitarian character of the miser's hoard and its lack of sacredness. However both of these assumptions are challenged by the extreme case of a miser who starves or freezes to death in an effort to save still more money (Belk and Wallendorf 1990b; Michaels 1985; Schwartz and Wolf 1958). But a further distinction between collecting and hoarding is that collecting involves differentiated objects and tends to follow the rule "no two alike," while hoarders want many of the same thing (Danet and Katriel 1989). By this criterion we can still classify the self-sacrificing miser as a hoarder rather than a collector.

Further, we do not regard as collectors those who acquire a set of items solely as an investment (e.g., Duggleby 1978; Avery and Colonna 1987). Certainly a collection may ultimately be sold due to financial need or a change in taste (e.g., Christ 1965). However, when profit is the *sole* purpose for acquisition and possession, the items acquired are likely to lack the sacredness and unity found in a true collection. A collector who is also a dealer in the same collectible can remain a collector if the items in the collection and those that are merchandise are kept separate. We find that this is common and that such dealers generally have firm rules that objects cannot freely pass between the collection and the saleable stock of merchandise. The most prominent exception is that when the dealer upgrades a collection, the superseded items may then be sold. Another exception is when a dealer becomes disenchanted with an entire collection and sells it off, often in order to undertake a new and different collecting enterprise. For dealers who also collect, price is a much more salient criterion in the case of buying merchandise than in the case of acquiring items for the dealer's personal collection.

Care is needed in assessing investment motives however, since investment is sometimes given as an emic rationalization for collecting, especially when collectors fear they will be ridiculed if their love of the collection is instead offered as a rationale (Bloom 1989; Olmsted 1988a; Paton 1988). While collectors frequently recount lore concerning the fortunes amassed by other collectors, in fact many collections do not maintain their purchase prices, much less increase in value (Beards 1987). For this reason many collecting guides, including those in financial newspapers, advise that new collectors pursue a collection for its intrinsic pleasure and *not* for expected monetary gain (Cox 1985). Still, for a few collectors at least, positive investment consequences can derive from passionate advocacy of an area of collecting interest. One collector has managed not only to indulge his obsession for Rodin sculptures, but also to build both the scholarly and market infrastructure reinforcing the value of the pieces (Cox 1978).

HISTORICAL AND INSTITUTIONAL ASPECTS OF COLLECTING

The history of collecting that follows is necessarily a brief sketch drawn with a broad brush. For more detailed and individualized treatments, the reader might consult such excellent sources as Alsop (1982), Cabanne (1961), Caxton Publishing (1974), Cooper (1963), Impey and MacGregor (1985), Moulin (1967/1987), Rheims (1961), Rigby and Rigby (1944), Saarinen (1958), Stillinger (1980), Taylor (1948), and von Holst (1967). However, for the most part, these treatments limit their foci to fine art collecting. The reasons for this bias in favor of the history of the rich and elite collector are not difficult to discern. As Johnson (1986) notes:

> Demand for certain types of objects is linked to taste and fashion.... Ownership of art objects is a mark of personal status demonstrating wealth and discrimination. Possession of desirable objects confers prestige, gives aesthetic pleasure and is a form of investment. Collectors, dealers and institutions compete to obtain them.... Rich collectors can achieve renown merely by assembling collections of esteemed `works of art'. The philanthropic act of donating a collection to a museum confers fame in that the name of the previous owner is forever linked with the bequest and in some western countries

has the added benefit of tax concessions (p. 74).

In addition, it is art objects that most often are acquired through plunder, serving as trophies of conquest and visibly enriching collections of powerful nations and individuals (Chamberlin 1983). And it is collections of art objects, rather than more humble collectibles, that museums and other repositories have been inclined to preserve. Furthermore, published biographies and television treatments are most likely to focus on the rich and famous who are the collectors of such art. As a result, the extant history of collecting is strongly biased in favor of fine art collections.

History

The presence of unusual pebbles in 80,000-year-old Cro-Magnon caves in France suggests that collecting may have begun at the same time in human history as art (Neal 1980). The more widespread emergence of collections from hoards and accumulations may well have occurred with the growth of civilizations supporting art and science. Ancient Mesopotamian royal collections in Chaldea, Sumeria, Babylonia, and Assyria included gems, writings on clay tablets, birds, omens, and incantations (Taylor 1948, p. 7). It is clear from the intact riches of Tutankhamen's tomb that he collected walking sticks, staves, whips, mineral specimens, and toys (Rigby and Rigby 1944, pp. 94-102). His tomb also included relics of predecessor Egyptian collectors, including Amenhotep III's blue enamels and the botanical specimens and foreign art collected by Thutmose III. While these collections reflect individual tastes, their collectors benefitted from both royal and divine rights:

> Not men but gods, however, were the greatest of the early collectors. Through their servants, the priests and the priest-kings, it was they who took a toll of all the products of the land. The ancient temples, like the churches and monasteries of our own middle ages, were repositories for great accumulations of wealth, of art and literature; and the temple treasuries were the forerunners of our banks, our libraries, our museums. Even these divine collectors began, as nearly as we can judge, with the collection of food and wealth, graduating soon to the collecting of books and [written] records, of art objects and antiques, of curiosities and relics (Rigby and Rigby 1944, p. 96).

This was the case with the early religious sanctuaries of ancient Greece, which collected painted vases, furniture, weapons, gold and silver vessels, and votive statues (Taylor 1948, p. 11). On feast days, the faithful were invited to see these treasures in the underground chambers where the priests catalogued and guarded them (Caxton Publishing 1974, p. 9). Eventually, these temple collections grew to include the rare and exotic:

> Piles of ivory...barbarian costumes, Indian jewelry, snake skins, bear hides, elephant skulls, whale skeletons, gorilla skins (thought to be those of "hairy, savage women"), reeds as thick as tree trunks, coconuts, distorting mirrors, antique musical instruments, foreign weapons, curious vessels of all sorts (Rigby and Rigby 1944, p. 115).

By the time of Alexander the Great, Greek art and antiquity collections began to be used to proclaim political and military power in an effort to acquire and demonstrate a cultural heritage. At about the same time, the individual collector finally emerged in Greece.

Ancient Romans also sought to collect Greek antiquities and art, and by the second century B.C., the rage for collecting was widespread (Rheims 1961, pp. 8-9). Copies were suitable when the Greek originals were lacking and private collectors opened their collections to the public on certain days. Antique dealers were established, and connoisseurs shopped the streets of Rome where goldsmiths, cabinet-makers, and sculptors set up their businesses which occupied one-fourth of the city. Plunder was the major source of the foreign treasures that poured into Rome. Rivalries between collectors quickly developed. One unscrupulous collector, Gaius Verres, was eventually killed when he refused to relinquish his collection to Mark Antony (Caxton Publishing 1974, pp. 11-12). Petronius collected bowls that became the envy of Nero. When Nero sent poison to him, the saucy writer drank it from a prize bowl that he smashed upon completion (Rigby and Rigby 1944, p. 135). Collections sometimes proved esoteric and eccentric. In the third century A.D., Heliogabalus is reported to have had a collection of 10,000 pounds of cobwebs gathered (by his slaves) for his amusement (Tuan 1986).

At about the same time in China (the Han dynasty), manuscripts in literature, philosophy, mathematics, medicine, and war were collected in the Imperial Library, along with silk paintings, bronze vessels, and other relics (Rigby and Rigby 1944, p. 114). When the Han dynasty fell in 221 A.D., there followed a 500-year stagnation in collecting until prosperity revived interest in art, literature, and relics (Rigby and Rigby 1944, pp. 145-153).

When Rome was overrun in the fifth century A.D., the west was also plunged into the dark ages, and the center of collecting shifted to Constantinople where Byzantine art, manuscripts, jewels, and religious treasures were assembled by the court (Rheims 1961, pp. 9-10).

During the Middle Ages in Europe, wealth was concentrated among hereditary rulers and prelates of the Christian Church. Collecting was infrequent, even among the upper classes. Security was the predominant motivation for the limited collecting that did occur. Even kings were more concerned with the material value of their treasures than with their artistic or historical merit (Rigby and Rigby 1944, p. 138). Since numerous treasures were melted down for the monetary value of their gold, silver, or gems (Alsop 1982), we do not include such treasuries in our definition of a collection. The Church became the foremost repository of art, manuscripts, treasures, curiosities, and relics. Cathedrals, monasteries, and other religious centers developed a new collecting rivalry, as bones and bits of saints and sacred places became coveted (see Geary 1986; Sumption 1975). Pilgrims and crusaders returned with relics and curiosities that added to church collections as well. It was not until the twelfth century that individual collecting began to regain prominence.

With the Fourth Crusade's sacking of Constantinople in 1204, treasures and relics again began to appear in European collections. Within the thirteenth century, Marco Polo also introduced Europe to the art of the Orient, providing still more exotic objects for collecting. By the beginning of the fourteenth century, church power was declining, and newly wealthy European merchants were collecting an increasing variety of luxury items -- tapestries, stained glass, reliefs, antiquities, coins, and heraldic signs, as well as paintings (Rigby and Rigby 1944, pp. 154-155). Italy was in the forefront of such collecting, and the Medici collections were the most extravagant. By the fifteenth century, daily life was shaped by the "triumph of individualism" (Aries 1989, p. 7) which supported efforts to amass individual collections. With such encouragement, art collecting became an important enough focus of European society that the names of great painters were well known. By the sixteenth century, names of the famous collectors themselves were equally well known (Rheims 1961, p. 11). During the sixteenth and seventeenth centuries, starting in northern Germany, the *Wunderkammer* (cabinet of wonders) became a popular addition to the *Kunstkammer* (art cabinet) and *Schatzkammer* (treasury) among the royalty and wealthy (see Impey and MacGregor 1985;

Mullaney 1983). Eclecticism, the promise of magic, and curiosity were key elements in assembling the contents of a wunderkammer. Praz (1964, pp. 138-139) records that one such collection included: lamps and ink wells made of seashells, musical and mathematical instruments, stuffed serpents, Mexican curios, the rope with which Judas supposedly hanged himself, ostrich eggs, mosaics of hummingbirds' wings, portraits of famous jurists and beautiful women, carved cherry pits, automata, objects of ivory and coral, a peg used in King Solomon's temple, elephants' tusks, sharks' teeth, and a coconut mounted in silver. Such an assortment of objects could be found among royalty, as in the Hapsburg collections, as well in religious collections -- including those of the Popes and those at the Royal Abbey of Saint Denis (Taylor 1948, p. 49, pp. 122-123). In part, the ideal was to show one's breadth by such a collection, but the exploration of the New World also stimulated curiosity for the strange and unusual. Whereas the medieval ideal was the compendia or systematization of knowledge of the world, during the sixteenth to eighteenth centuries interest shifted to finding new knowledge and to "collecting the world" (Defert 1982). Along with various curios of the New World, Christopher Columbus returned to Lisbon with native Americans who were exhibited in the capitols of Europe (Hodgen 1964). That the collection of the world sometimes involved collecting written accounts and people (however objectionable to our current moral standards), as well as things brought back from various expeditions, exemplifies our definitional contention that collecting is not limited to material objects.

The scientific revolution that began in the late 17th century is characterized as Cartesian thinking after René Descartes. The same turning point has been described by Berman (1981), following Max Weber, as the "disenchantment of the world." The separation between art and science in this epoch was clearly manifested in collecting. By the eighteenth and nineteenth centuries, collections began to be specialized with artistic versus scientific foci being the first fundamental split (Belk 1986, pp. 11-12; Caxton Publishing 1974, pp. 41-42). The first public museums since the destruction of the Mouseion at Alexandria also formed along these two lines during the late seventeenth through nineteenth centuries (Alexander 1979). Royal and private collections were most often transformed into public institutions in order to initiate these museums, thus allowing the public to view and admire the formerly private treasures of the wealthy. The scientific zeal of the era gradually eliminated the more bizarre

curiosities, although the fascination with the curious remained longer in the United States.

It appears that a several hundred year trend toward the democratization of collecting has accelerated in the twentieth century, with more and more people collecting. This has been possible only partly though rising real incomes, since the control of fine art has remained concentrated in the hands of the wealthy and museums. The stronger impetuses for more widespread collecting have been the broadened conceptualization of things that are collectible, the accelerated production of identical objects in series or sets, and the reduced age at which old things are seen as worth preserving. Museums have aided this trend by displaying increasingly diverse material and by expanding the array of offerings, with more marketing-oriented merchandising strategies (Kelly 1986). The democratization of collecting has also been aided by the increasingly branded and differentiated set of products available in the marketplace, providing additional objects to be collected.

Contemporary Institutional Dimensions of Collecting

The commoditization/singularization dialectic (Kopytoff 1986) that drives much collecting behavior in consumer culture underlies the institution of collecting. The symbolic value of a singularized item is frequently reinforced by a high monetary value, whether or not the item ever circulates in exchange relationships after its acquisition. The symbiosis of symbolic and exchange value (or sacred and profane dimensions) is apparent in the following examples:

- Movie memorabilia is especially rewarding to collectors. A pair of "ruby slippers" worn in the *Wizard of Oz* fetched $165,000 from a collector. Another paid $12,000 for a uniform worn by Elvis Presley in *G.I. Blues*. A large poster for *Casablanca* goes for $17,500. A biweekly guide entitled *Movie Collector's World* already boasts 5,000 subscribers (Dunn 1988).
- The founder of the G.I. Joe Club of America, himself an owner of over 500 of the action figures, desires to build a national monument to the character. Early model versions of the toy now sell for more than $2,000 (Pereira 1989).
- A teddy bear was recently sold by Sotheby's for a record price of $85,000 (Millership 1989). The auction house also dispersed items from Andy Warhol's collection that commanded similarly astonishing

prices: 152 cookie jars went for $247,830; a Black Mackintosh table for $275,000; a Rolls Royce Silver Shadow for $77,000; and three Campbell's soup can banks for $7,150 (Cox 1988).

- Before the collapse of the junk bond barons at Drexel Burnham Lambert, the firm was able to reposition much of its material (coffee mugs, T-shirts, tennis balls and other office bric-a-brac) as collectibles, and dispose of it quite profitably (Herman 1990).

- Among the rapidly appreciating speculative investments some experts view as a hedge against conventional market downturns are Elvis memorabilia, presidential autographs, rare books, toy figurines and both classic (1930's - 1940's) and muscle (1950's - 1960's) cars produced by American manufacturers (Gottschalk 1988; Johnson 1990; Peers 1988).

- The profitability of collectibles has fueled a rise in such activity as the counterfeiting of baseball cards (Leptich 1989), the use of baseball cards as promotional premiums in such products as laundry detergents (n.a. 1988) and the manufacturing of hood ornament replicas (Wright 1989).

- Collecting behavior radiates to increasingly novel niches. With the rise of direct marketing activity, junk mail has become a collectible for some consumers (Crossen 1989). In Japan, prepaid magnetic cards intended to render service encounters more automatic and convenient have spawned a market of more than 200,000 collectors (Kilburn 1988). Socially responsible collecting has been promoted as a marketing vehicle to subsidize efforts such as documentary projects (n.a. 1990).

That collecting can be both passionate and profitable is a common observation (Crispell 1988; Klein 1990; Lynwander 1990; Read 1990; Trachtenberg 1990; Wartzman 1990). That a collecting "industry" and elaborate social network of voluntary associations of collectors supports the enterprise is less commonly acknowledged.

A number of discrete institutions comprises the collecting industry. Formal sector organizations such as auction houses like Christie's and Sotheby's, or the thousands of galleries which constitute the infrastructure of the art world, are perhaps the most widely known exemplars as a result of their importance to society's aesthetic domain of experience. Similarly, museums are widely recognized principally for their contribution to the preserving of a collectively constructed and valued version of a material cultural past. The rise of so-called "unusual" or unconventional museums (Jurnovoy and Jenness 1987) celebrating less hegemonic or elitist visions of cultural production is also linked to this conservation or preservationist ethos. The cultural significance of these organizations is explored in later pages of this chapter. Retail galleries for collectibles such as rare documents have begun to spring up in shopping malls, angering purists concerned about inflationary pricing, packaging, gimmickry, and forgery (Yoshihashi 1990). Vehicles such as *Rinker's Antiques and Collectibles Market Report*, and the Antiques and Collectibles Information Service, instruct consumers in all phases of the collecting enterprise. Informal or alternative sector organizations (Sherry 1990a; 1990b) such as flea markets and garage sales constitute another important conduit for the collecting industry.

Of particular importance to this chapter is the existence of specific institutions whose mission is the mass-merchandising of pre-singularized "collectibles" to consumers desiring to own special objects with perceived investment value. Firms such as the Bradford Exchange, the Franklin Mint, the Franklin Library, the New England Collectors Society, and the Danberry Mint, among others, offer just such portfolios to their clients. These firms provide important search and validation services to consumers for whom the joy of treasure-hunting is not so exhilarating as the certainty of authentication is comforting (Beckham and Brooks 1989). For many, the thrill of acquisition consists in the anticipation of the inevitable arrival of a pre-selected item, rather than in the discovery in which a personal grail quest might culminate. These commercial "societies" reinforce the social and economic significance of aspects of collecting behavior by prepackaging the experience for consumers. Firms such as Hummel, Lladro and Waterford, among others similarly encourage collecting by producing items whose principal value or point-of-difference resides in their collectibility. Thus the commercialization of a social activity - the commoditization of collecting - is at once a cooptation and a reinforcement of an important consumer behavior.

Collecting is institutionalized in a number of other commercial formats. For example, the magazine *Memories* is targeted to consumers for whom nostalgia -- a culture-bound syndrome discussed in later pages -- has become a salient experience. The magazine allows readers to collect a mass-mediated past which is promoted as an integral component of their extended selves. The Cable Value Network includes such shows as "Collectibles" and "The Doll Collector" among its programming fare. Many newspapers now run regular feature sections on "Collectibles" which read as commercial analogs to more traditional advice columns. Entire newspapers themselves are increasingly marketed as "collectibles", and sold to enshrine such "big events" as the Kennedy assassination, or such personal events as a reader's birthday; the edition for a particular date is often offered in an enshrining document case. Each of these vehicles serves to reinforce the significance of collecting -- whether it be the economic utility, the aesthetics of connoisseurship, or the fraternity/sorority of collectorhood -- for society at large.

Finally, the prevalence of voluntary societies of collectors is worthy of note. Such societies may be relatively informal and generalized. For example, many collectors are socialized into a family of orientation where collecting is a valued ethic, and in turn socialize their own families of procreation into the collecting ethic. Intergenerational transfer of collecting behavior, rather than of specific-object collecting, appears to be a common phenomenon. Participation in a shared hobby or communal ritual seems to be an important integrative mechanism in many families of collectors. Other voluntary societies are much more formally constituted, providing individuals with a reference group with which to identify and interact, based upon a particular passion. For instance, at the 10th National Sports Collectors' Convention held recently in Chicago, collectors could buy from and sell to a range of dealers and exhibitors, have items autographed by a host of attending sports heroes, attend seminars ranging from entrepreneurship through ethics to estate planning, obtain formal and informal advice on the craft of collecting (e.g. sourcing, authenticating, pricing), and engage in the kinds of after-hours socializing that pushes the mechanical solidarity of nominal affiliation forward into the organic solidarity characteristic of small group culture. There appear to be as many voluntary associations of collectors as there are categories of collectibles. These associations serve to reinforce the social and psychological significance of collecting in consumer culture. Perhaps ironically, such associations may mitigate some of the alienation that consumer culture seems to engender.

SIGNIFICANCE AND DISTRIBUTION OF COLLECTING

O'Brien (1981) estimated that one of every three Americans currently collects something. Another study found that 62.5 percent of households surveyed reported that they have at least one collection, with an average of 2.6 collections per household (Schiffer, Downing, and McCarthy 1981). Even if these figures are exaggerated, at least according to our definition of collecting, it is evident that in recent times collecting has diffused to a large portion of the population in affluent nations. Almost ten percent of American men collect coins, and about four percent of both men and women collect stamps (Crispell 1988). Thus, one reason to study the neglected phenomenon of collecting is the large number of people it involves and the large amount of time, talent, effort, and money they spend pursuing their collecting interests. Another reason is that collecting represents a striking form of consumption. Since, by definition, the objects in a collection are beyond ordinary everyday use, the passion, rivalry, and marketplace attention that these objects engender challenges rational models of behavior. Furthermore, collected objects often require considerable time and effort to maintain (Aristides 1988; Durham 1985) and are more likely to produce a financial loss than a profit, if indeed they can be sold at all (Cox 1985). Thus, while we shall delay our considered appraisal, at this point we note Singh's (1988) assessment that collecting celebrates ownership and that collectors are driven by "the obsessional greed of ownership" (p. 86). Even without celebration and obsession, collecting appears to be a quintessential form of acquisition and possession, involving extreme concentration and care lavished upon the collection by its collector. Perhaps a principal contribution to be made in future research on collecting would be a systematic collection of biographies and life histories of collectors (e.g., Carmichael 1971; Stillinger 1980) that would capture something of the richness of motivation driving this form of consumption.

The importance of collecting may also depend upon its distribution and symbolic significance in the population. To what extent does the phenomenon of collecting transcend boundaries of age, gender, and social class? Do collections act as signs of age, gender, and social status?

Age. Our interviews with young collectors suggest that they are encouraged and often started in collecting by parents and other relatives. Mechling (1989) finds that youth organizations have done much to encourage collecting by children. In some cases, a key adult acts as a mentor and guide. Several fathers encouraged their sons' baseball-card collecting and visited shops, card collectors meetings, and card conventions with them. Collections of natural materials like minerals and seashells often depend upon adults taking children to collecting sites. Adults nurture children's collecting activity; we have encountered no incidents of intentional discouragement by adults. Collecting is a cultural model "of" and model "for" reality, in Geertz's (1973) sense. Through collecting, the individual learns that "getting" and "having" are social cultural pursuits, and that activity should be directed toward becoming what you own. Danet and Katriel (1989) found that, even among the ultra-orthodox Jews of the Mea Shearim quarter of Jerusalem, children are encouraged to collect and trade cards with photos of various rabbis. A U. S. firm, Torah Personalities, Inc., markets trading cards of the world's most famous living and dead rabbis, complete with "statistics" on the card's obverse side (Time 1989).

During the first third of the twentieth century, there were a number of surveys of collecting activity among children. An early study reported that grade school children had an average of three to four active collections and that peak collecting years were between ages eight and eleven (Burk 1900). While a 1927 study reported a lower incidence of collecting and concluded that collecting was a fad whose time was passing (Lehman and Witty 1927), a 1929 study using different methods found an even higher incidence of collecting among children than had Burk (Whitley 1929). In follow-up studies Witty and Lehman (1930, 1931) found that, during peak collecting years, girls averaged twelve collections and boys eleven. Durost (1932) reported that boys' collecting activity peaked at age ten with an average of 12.7 collections, while girls' collecting peaked at age 11 with an average of 12.1 collections. A recent study in Israel found that, between first and seventh grade, at least 84 percent of both boys and girls collect something, although in eighth grade these figures drop to below 50 percent (Danet and Katriel 1988). From all these studies, it is clear that collecting is more common among children than among adults. Its peak coincides with the onset of adolescence and the desire to individuate through doing rather than having (Csikszentmihalyi and Rochberg-Halton 1981). Prior to this age, the collection may constitute the self, and the self may be seen as part of the collection. Even though collecting may offer the illusion of a return to childhood, one inhibition to collecting as an adult appears to be the fear that others will think that the collecting is a childish indulgence (Bloom 1989; Kozden 1989; Olmsted 1988a). Another inhibition, no doubt, is the amount of time involved. A third explanation may be the wider availability of other channels for attaining a sense of mastery and identity as an adult.

Although collections are sometimes liquidated for financial reasons during old age (Christ 1965), collections begun in youth may be continued over a lifetime (e.g., Dannefer 1981; Olmsted 1987b). Indeed, increased time resources after retirement are often devoted to collections (Dannefer 1980). The community of fellow collectors can also be an important source of satisfaction. However, given the specialized nature of most collections, they are not likely to produce integration among neighborhood friends (Unruh 1983, pp. 108-110).

Gender. The studies just reviewed consistently find that, among youthful collectors, girls are at least as likely as boys to collect. Among adults, however, the literature suggests that men are more likely to collect than are women (Danet and Katriel 1989; Olmsted 1988a, 1989; Belk and Wallendorf 1990a). Rigby and Rigby (1944, pp. 326-327) suggest that the economic requirements and the competitive nature of collecting have traditionally favored males. Danet and Katriel (1986, p. 48) argue that the proactive mastery involved in collecting is inconsistent with the more passive and familial social roles that have been encouraged for women. And Saisselin (1984, p. 68) contends that historically men's purchasing has been viewed as serious and purposeful collecting, while women's buying has been perceived as (and confined to) frivolous consumption. As Baekeland (1981) emphasizes:

> we rarely think of accumulations of dresses, shoes, perfumes, china and the like as collections.... Men's collections, however, be they of stamps, cars, guns or art, tend to have clear-cut thematic emphases and standards, external reference points in public or private collections. Thus women's collections tend to be personal and ahistorical, men's impersonal and historical (p. 47).

One need only look to the array of shoes assembled by Madame Marcos to find one inflated example of this distinction (see Goldstein 1987). However, it might be argued that women's collecting is transmuted into domestic production. That is, women both produce and reproduce "consumption" in their creation of the domestic economy. That economy might be regarded in part as a "living" collection. Furthermore, a more complete examination of collecting activity indicates its essentially androgynous qualities. While acquisition may require aggressive competition and mastery, preservation of a collection requires care, creativity, and nurturance (Belk and Wallendorf 1990a). Thus, collecting activity requires characteristics stereotypically associated with both genders.

A second question with regard to the connection between gender and collecting is whether males and females tend to collect different types of things. While not all objects are seen to be gendered (Allison, Golden, Mullet, and Coogan 1980; Golden, Allison, and Clee 1979), many objects are. Gender can be imparted through strong design differences as with motorcycles versus motor scooters (Hebdige 1988), or through more subtle features as with the size, shape, and ornamentation of hair brushes (Forty 1986). The historical studies of child collectors, cited previously, confirm that boys tend to collect different objects (e.g., marbles, nails, insects) than girls (e.g., dolls, jewelry, photographs).

Among adults in our sample of 192 collectors, some of the strongest gender differences we have found among collectors is in the overwhelming predominance of males among firearms collectors (cf. Olmsted 1987a, 1988b, forthcoming; Stenross 1987) and automobile collectors (cf. Dannefer 1980, 1981). We also find men to be conspicuously more likely to collect antiques, books, tatoos, and sports-related objects, while women are more likely to collect animal replicas, jewelry, and housewares such as dishes and silverware (cf. Belk and Wallendorf 1990a). Other studies have found men to be more likely to collect stamps and coins than are women (Christ 1965; Crispell 1988; Olmsted 1987b). Interestingly, Sigmund Freud's collection of antiquities includes a large number of phallic amulets and phalluses from statues. Similarly, the ubiquitous statuettes in his collection can be interpreted as phallic (Spitz 1989; cf. Holbrook 1988a, 1988b). It is almost as if Freud were acting out the satirical tale of Flaubert's naïve collectors, Bouvard & Pécuchet:

> At one time towers, pyramids, candles, mile-posts, and even trees had the significance of phalluses -- and for Bouvard and Pécuchet everything became a phallus. They collected the swing-bars of carriages, legs of armchairs, cellar bolts, chemists' pestles. When anyone came to see them, they asked: `What do you think that's like?' -- then confided the mystery; and if the visitor protested, they shrugged their shoulders pityingly (1880/1954, p. 131).

Again, the models of/models for reality analogy is apt. Collecting enables males to celebrate aggressive behaviors abetting commerce or the hunt, and ultimately shaping the realm of political economy. Collecting enables females to enact behaviors creating household nurturance, which shape domestic economy.

Our case studies of a husband and wife who both collected for most of their lives provide an informative contrast between male and female collecting. The woman, whose husband posthumously enshrined her collection in a museum called the Mouse Cottage, was a collector of mice replicas. The collection began during her childhood when she acquired the nickname "Mouse" because, according to the museum brochure, she was "so clever and charming in character and petite in stature." Her lifelong collection consists of toy mice of every description, displayed in homey pseudo-antique golden oak furniture, around a perennial Christmas tree, and in a dollhouse. Both the dominant pattern of Christmas as "woman's work" (Cheal 1987, 1988; Caplow 1982, 1984) and the association of the diminutive and miniaturized with women and children (Stewart 1984) reinforce the dominant theme of domestication in the Mouse Cottage. Another major feature of the collection is its Mickey Mouse replicas. In this regard it is instructive that when Mickey was initially introduced with a thinner appearance and masculine voice, he lacked his current popularity. Only by means of an emasculating voice change, a more babyish and androgynous appearance, and a concomitant social clumsiness with female mice, did Mickey gain popularity (Mollenhoff 1939, Gould 1979). The diminutive mouse (n.b. Mickey rather than Mike or Michael) is nevertheless the hero in Disney comics. He succeeds with the magical guile of a child in overcoming more adult-like villains, thus fulfilling a common childhood fantasy.

Mouse's husband also institutionalized his major collection (fire engines) by establishing the Fire Museum. In contrast to the diminutive Mouse Cottage, this museum of fire-fighting equipment (billed as the world's largest) is spacious, has a guide, and charges admission. The guide, display, and brochure all emphasize that this is a serious historical museum, in contrast to the entertainment rationale given for the Mouse Cottage. Two other collections of this collector have also been given display space: (1) his collection of paintings and bronzes of American cowboys and Indians and (2) his collection of African hunting trophies that began with a family hunting safari in the 1920s.

The collections of these two spouses present a graphic illustration of gender differences found in other collections studied as well. These differences were detected independently by the two authors who conducted research at these sites. Using the general equation, Mouse Cottage:Fire Museum::X:Y, we note these relevant pairs of X and Y --

Tiny : Gigantic
Weak : Strong
Home : World
Nature : Machine
Nurturing : Extinguishing
Art : Science
Playfulness : Seriousness
Decorative : Functional
Inconspicuous : Conspicuous
Animate : Inanimate

Belk and Wallendorf (1990a) also discuss further cases of gendered identity work including two collections of Barbie dolls. As with the mice and fire engines, these collectibles can provide a circumscribed arena in which a variety of gender and other identity issues are played out. In the Barbie doll cases studied however, the key gender identity issues center on the recent radical mastectomy undergone by one of the Barbie doll collectors and the homosexuality of the other. In both cases these collectors were able to express and work through these issues using their doll collections.

Social Class. A final issue in the distribution of collecting concerns its locus in the class structure of American society. To a certain degree, the poor are precluded from many collecting realms due to their low income. Although the wealth of the mouse replica and fire engine collectors just discussed belies the common assumption that the wealthy collect only fine art, it remains true that collectors of expensive fine art are almost always at least moderately wealthy (Moulin 1967/1987). Since virtually anything is collectible (Reid 1988), the contemporary collector can always find some affordable category of objects to collect. Therefore, income is not necessarily a barrier to collecting. One survey of subscribers to a general collecting magazine found that the sample had a median income about 30 percent above the U.S. population median and was over 70% white collar (Treas and Brannen 1976). Bossard and Boll (1950) found that the upper class were more likely to collect than the middle class, although more recent studies have found that the working and middle classes are well represented in such areas of collecting as baseball cards (Bloom 1989) and stamps (Bryant 1982; Olmsted 1987b). Rochberg-Halton (1979) reported that although visual art was cited as a favorite possession more frequently by members of the upper middle class in Chicago, other collectibles were cited more frequently by lower class informants. Our own data (based on the sample of 192 informants) suggest that, with the exception of fine art collecting, most collecting areas (including automobiles) appear to be dominated by the middle class. This may imply that firms specializing in sales

to collectors have successfully targeted the large middle class in the U.S. (e.g., Butsch 1984).

In sum, contemporary collecting is unevenly but broadly distributed across age, gender, and socioeconomic categories. It seems to reflect a heightened acquisitive and possessive orientation that epitomizes the modern consumer culture. The considerable inputs of time, money, skill, and energy devoted to collecting also help to make it a consumption activity eminently worthy of study. But most importantly, collecting is a passionate sphere of consumption from which collectors seem to derive significant meaning and fulfillment in their lives. It is, in Stebbins' (1982) terms, serious leisure (cf. Bloch and Bruce 1984). Smith and Apter (1977, p. 65), thus, observe of antique collectors:

> Finally, collecting antiques, like any hobby pursued with intensity and passion, helps to give life meaning and purpose. The goals of antique collecting may at first seem arbitrary and the activity may initially be taken up for excitement...but for many people the goals eventually become serious and building the collection would seem for some people to take on almost religious proportions.

This point is well illustrated in a recent play by Terrence McNally (1989) entitled *The Lisbon Traviata*. McNally's work offers what must be the first full-length theatrical production that takes record collecting as its central theme (but see Eisenberg 1987). On its surface, the play depicts a love quadrangle involving four homosexual men, two of whom (Mendy and Stephen) are held together emotionally by their shared devotion to opera in general and to the performances of Maria Callas in particular. Thus, much of the action and most of the humor in Act I revolve around Mendy's desperation to hear a new bootleg recording of Maria singing *La Traviata* in Lisbon. This scene contains lines guaranteed to move any compassionate record collector to the deepest commiseration. In this, it reflects the playwright's own avowed musical fanaticism and obsession with opera recordings and performances:

> In the first act of McNally's play, audiences are treated to an encounter between two rabid fans of Maria Callas.... Mendy goes into a frenzy when Stephen mentions a pirated recording he owns of a performance of *La Traviata* sung by Callas in Lisbon in 1958.... Most of the first act dwells on the two men's Callas obsession and their disdain for other great singers.... McNally, himself, admits

to having been an ardent Callas fan during the Golden Age of Opera (Botto 1989, p. 66).

In Act II, we find that Stephen's apartment features row upon row of vertical shelves that house literally thousands of lps and CDs carefully arranged in a well-organized order that permits him to pluck examples of interest from the filing system with barely a glance. In a touching comic thrust, Stephen recounts how he had to explain to his father why anyone would want more than one recording of the same piece of music. "For the same reason," he says, "that *you* need to watch the Super Bowl again every year." Thus does the collector notice subtle distinctions, even those among performances of the same composition by the same artists recorded on different occasions. Though McNally's play deals primarily with classical music in general and opera in particular, the same fanatic interest in different performances appears in the desire of jazz fans to hear alternate takes of pieces played -- sometimes only minutes or seconds apart -- by improvisers of the stature of (say) Lester Young or Charlie Parker. Similarly, "Deadhead" fans of the Grateful Dead strive to make, trade, and collect tapes of every concert by the group (Pearson 1987). In the case of McNally's comic hero, the obsession with hearing and owning *all* available performances by a favorite artist borders on the pathological. But, in general, the extent to which such subtle differences *matter* is the *essence* of the true collecting spirit.

A THEORY OF COLLECTING

What Collections Mean

Magic. One key to understanding the intensity with which collections are pursued is the finding that collections are often magic. In a related vocabulary, the items in a collection are frequently "sacred" (Belk, Wallendorf, and Sherry 1989). We have already noted that, by definition, the contents of a collection are usually set apart from the ordinary. Asked whether she ever eats using her collection of Lustreware dishes, a collector (WF 30) replied, "Never! I never use it. You know why? Its because they're completely non-functional." Once an item enters a collection, it does not leave, except in the case of serial collections and upgrading. A collector of nutcrackers (WF 50), after explaining that she never uses them to crack nuts, was asked if nutcrackers ever leave her collection: "No! *No way.* [laughs] They're *mine* and they're going to stay mine." A couple (WM 65/WF 65) who collect saltcellars was observed serving a holiday feast using salt and pepper shakers rather than objects from the sacred collection. Similarly, as previously noted, we find that collector/dealers generally

keep their sacred personal collections separated from profane saleable merchandise and do not tolerate traffic between the two. It is as if the magical power of the collected objects would be diminished if they were treated as market commodities and removed from the safe haven of eternal life in the collection.

The magical quality of objects in a collection is also revealed by the reverent care given to them. Fieldnotes from an automobile show reflect some of this fetishistic attention:

One man driving his car in the "parade" awaiting space assignment, jumped out of his car when the line stopped and polished the wheels a bit. One person used a paintbrush to get the dust out of his grill. Another man was doing finishing touches to the chrome around his headlights with a toothbrush.

In a similar vein, Dannefer reports a car collector's response to a woman who asked where she could put her Coke among the clutter: "Just anywhere except on the white car -- that's God" (1980, p. 393). For some, this concern for these metal objects of affection extends beyond life itself. One informant (WM 60s) has a will leaving his Model A Fords to his 14-year-old grandson, but the will also contains a provision stipulating that if the grandson violates them or doesn't care for them properly, they will be sold to a professional restorer who can appreciate them. Another owner of four restored cars (WM 60) has willed one to each of his four children: "They promised me to take good care of them. If they don't, I'll come back and haunt them." And a recently divorced shell collector (WM late 30s) laments that he kept the house and children but his ex-wife kept the shells that she refers to as "her babies." Such personification is an important element in fetishizing objects (Ellen 1988). While Stewart (1984) distinguishes collecting from fetishism based on the order that characterizes collecting, we disagree and see collecting as often fetishistic. In our view, the compulsive desire for order in the collection only serves to reinforce such fetishism.

Reverence for the power of the collected objects is also displayed in other ways. Clark (1963, p. 15) notes that "In a Rothschild collection I always found myself whispering, as if I were in church." Collectors of contemporary art, like the billionaires who once bought Renaissance art from Joseph Duveen (Behrman 1952), find themselves wondering "Am I good enough to own this painting?" (Greenspan 1988). Danet and Katriel (1986, p. 38) refer to such reverence as "thing magic." Laughlin (1956) calls collections -- along with talismans, amulets, religious tokens, relics, and charms -- "soterial objects," after the Greek *Soteria*, meaning "objects that deliver one from evil."

Besides delivering them from evil, collectors also hope that the extraordinary power of collected objects will deliver them from the ordinary world of everyday life into a magical world. This belief is evident in the treasure tales that surround most collecting arenas. These tales typically involve a discerning collector using a combination of cleverness and luck to acquire a rare and valuable collectible for little or nothing (e.g., Beards 1987). In one tale, shyly told but fervently believed, a car collector (WM late 30s) recalled searching for years for the pickup truck that he and his deceased father had once fixed up. As the fieldnotes record:

> He had looked for it for much of the 11 years since he got rid of it, but with no luck. They had lost a son and had some other difficulties, so they had despondently gone to his father's grave. He and his father had done a lot of racing together and were close. He told his father that if he was alright to give him a sign. Shortly after that, a friend told him about a Cameo, and they went to see it. When he saw the "R & R Racing" on it, he knew it was his old truck and bought it. Ron's wife said they weren't very religious, but that made believers of them.

It often seems that the collector is assembling a miniature world that he or she can control and rule over (Berger 1972, p. 86; Danet and Katriel 1989, p. 263; Stewart 1984, p. 162). If so, it is an enchanted world of magical objects not unlike the fairy tales of childhood (Bettelheim 1975).

Other Times, Other People, and Other Places. If collections evoke magical worlds, they are aided in this evocation by their linkage with a distant, exotic otherness (Mascia-Lees, Sharpe, and Cohen 1989) displaced in time or space from the here and now. The collected object is imbued with the aura of the time, place, and persons once associated with it; for instance, a collection of rocks and seashells from vacation trips (Appleyard 1979). In fact, Urry (1990, p. 32) has characterized contemporary tourists as "collectors of gazes," who are less interested in revisiting the same exotic sites than in capturing the "initial gaze" of the other. Because collecting is a longitudinal activity, even a collection of contemporary art acquires historical markers over the history of the collection. A common incentive to collect involves the desire to conserve, assemble, preserve, or rescue objects. More generally,

such activity is often part of a search for self-meaning.

The ability of a collection to evoke other places is seen among two informants who totally devote their houses to their collections of artifacts from particular places -- one from Bali and the other from Nigeria and nearby African countries. In each case, the collector previously lived in these countries, although the collections were acquired over a period of time and continue to grow with return visits. Each house is filled with furniture, wall decorations, masks, musical instruments, carvings, and other artwork from the foreign lands. In one collection, the material overflows numerous glass front cases and is stacked up to five items high in each room on all three floors of the house. And, in both houses, every piece recalls for the collector the story of its acquisition. The initial guided tour in one of these houses took five hours. In a less literal way, stamp collections and books provide means of tangibly acquiring other places. One of Olmsted's (1987b) collectors remarked, "Stamp collecting is also a way of traveling and getting acquainted with other countries" (p. 3). Although she no longer climbs, Janet Smith (1988) relives adventures of climbing in the Alps through her collection of Alpine climbing books and journals, and she notes, "I can't think of any keener invitation to take an ego-trip down Memory Lane" (p. 480).

Not only place, but also time is acquired and made manifest in a collection. Sigmund Freud's interest in collecting the antiquities of ancient Greece, Rome, and Egypt appears to have arisen in part from his fascination with the Egyptian illustrations in the Philippson Bible he read in his home as a child (Kuspit 1989). Some of his antiquities were acquired during his travels to the ruins of these ancient civilizations. When these pieces were brought home, they served as reminders, "promising him that after the long winter in Vienna he could return" (Bernfeld 1951, p. 109). In fact, Freud's travels were often shaped by his penchant for collecting, as Walter (1988) notes:

> During his visit to America in 1909 he showed no interest in the country, saying that all he wanted to see there was Niagara Falls. Refusing to read travel books before the trip, he studied a book on Cyprus instead and wanted to see the principal collection of Cyprian antiquities that was on exhibit in New York. In that city, the place that attracted him was the Metropolitan Museum, where he spent his time absorbed in the antiquities of Greece (pp. 102-103).

Not incidentally, Freud also used archeological metaphors in his work -- as in his references to psychoanalysis as the archaeology of the mind and his symbolic interpretations of key myths such as that of Oedipus. It has even been suggested that his crafting of the psychoanalytic enterprise was dominated by an object-oriented passion for archaeology (Walter 1988, p. 111). In Kuspit's view, it was Freud's hope "to have some of the heroic quality associated with archaeology rub off on psychoanalysis" (1989, pp. 133-134). The collector of antiquities, in Hillier's (1981) words, is "an archaeologist without a spade" (p. 71). As Rheims (1961) reflects:

> An object's date is of prime importance to a collector with an obsession for the past. He values it for its associations, that it once belonged to and was handled by a man he can visualize as himself. The object bears witness: its possession is an introduction to history. One of a collector's most entrancing day-dreams is the imaginary joy of uncovering the past in the guise of an archaeologist (p. 211).

In this daydream the collector also magically transcends time and travels to another era.

The desire to bask in the imagined glory of the past is also evident in the strong emotional attachment that many antique collectors have to the persons, eras, and places that their collections represent (e.g., Kaplan 1982; Stillinger 1980). Collections of family photographs (Hirsch 1981), autographs, locks of hair in Victorian hair wreaths (Miller 1982, Payne 1988), and contemporary baseball cards are all, in this sense, collections of people. The attraction is all the stronger when the contagious magic of a prominent provenance is attached to objects in the collection. Thus, one collector was especially attached to an antique music box because it once belonged to Winston Churchill. As Malinowski (1922) observed:

> When, after six years' absence in the South Seas and Australia, I returned to Europe and did my first bit of sight-seeing at Edinburgh Castle, I was shown the Crown Jewels. The keeper told many stories of how they were worn by this and that king or queen on such and such an occasion.... I had the feeling that something similar has been told to me.... And then arose before me the vision of a native village on coral soil...and naked men and one of them showing me thin red strings and big worn-out objects, clumsy to sight and greasy to touch. With reverence he also would name them and tell their story.... Both

heirlooms and *vaygu'a* are cherished because of the historical sentiment which surrounds them. However ugly, useless, and -- according to current standards -- valueless an object may be, if it has figured in historical scenes and passed through the hands of historic persons, and is therefore an unfailing vehicle of important sentimental associations, it cannot but be precious to us (pp. 88-89).

Sometimes this attachment even takes on metaphysical qualities. Three different antique collectors we have interviewed have explained their unaccountable attraction to and intuitive knowledge about particular antiques as being due to some association with their past lives. In a less mystical sense, many collectors strive after an image of their own childhood through their collections. As Frances Graham, editor of *Antiques & Collecting Hobbies* magazine explains:

> People want things from their childhood for two reasons. Either they had something as a child and have fond memories of it, or they wanted it and couldn't have it, so they're buying it for themselves now (Crispell 1988, p. 39).

Having objects from our past can provide a sense of stability in our lives (Forty 1986). Baseball-card collectors often begin their adult collections by trying to recreate a childhood collection that their mothers once discarded (Bloom 1989). There also appears to be some striving to regain love and security in these cases. The acquisition of objects desired earlier in life is evident among many car collectors who begin in mid-life by acquiring the car they had or wished they could have had as an adolescent. Like Dannefer's (1980) interviews, some car collectors we interviewed said they can predict the market price of cars by anticipating increased popularity of the "hot cars" when men now reaching 40 were in high school. Increased financial resources at this stage of life may facilitate this tendency, but the desire to reflect on earlier life at midlife and the more general nostalgic inclination to use collections of the past to give meaning to the present may be stronger motivating factors (Belk 1990, Davis 1979).

Because the collection takes the collector into a new realm of experience (baseball cards into the world of childhood heroes, dolls into the world of fashion models, stamps into exotic lands), it allows pleasurable expression of fantasy (Gotelli 1988, Rheims 1961, Travis 1988). Through such activity, the collector can potentially experiment with a fantasy life without suffering the consequences and disappointments of enacting it (Friday 1975).

Thus, for various reasons, collections signal other times and other places. As the preceding section emphasizes, collections also mean magic. These meanings are basic to all collectors and collections. The next section explores other meanings of collections that are relevant to the motivations for collecting.

Motivations for Collecting

Acquisitiveness Legitimized as Art or Science. While many motivations have been offered to explain collecting, two basic motivations that are useful in understanding the pervasiveness of collecting are legitimization and self-extension. Legitimization concerns the willingness of society to approve or condone behavior that might otherwise be construed as acquisitiveness, possessiveness, or greed, by applying the labels "collecting" and "collectors" to certain activities and people. The process of learning what defines legitimate collecting activity begins in childhood, as Clifford (1985) explains:

> Children's collections are revealing...a boy's accumulation of miniature cars, a girl's dolls, a summer vacation "nature museum" (with labeled stones and shells, a hummingbird in a bottle), a treasured bowl filled with the bright-colored shavings of crayons. In these small rituals we observe the channeling of obsession, an exercise in how to make the world one's own, to gather things around oneself tastefully, appropriately. The inclusions in all collections reflect wider cultural rules, of rational taxonomy, of gender, of aesthetics. *An excessive, sometimes even rapacious need to have is transformed into rule-governed, meaningful desire.* Thus the self which must *possess*, but cannot have it all, learns to select, order, classify in hierarchies -- to make "good" collections (p. 238, italics added).

Thus do we begin the process of channeling our materialistic desires into "meaningful" pursuits; to become collectors rather than hoarders or misers; to produce knowledge and beauty rather than displaying selfishness.

The general social sanction for collecting over hoarding and accumulating is sometimes aided by self-deception. A collector of all manner of elephant replicas told us he expected that history will some day stand in awe of what he has accomplished in building his collection. Specialized clubs (including one for elephant replica collectors), publications, shows, and meetings help foster this feeling that collecting is legitimate. Olmsted (1987a, p. 16) detects this legitimization process in the rhetoric of gun collectors at gun shows. Fine (1987) sees a similar process operating through the "community of [common] knowledge" and boundary-establishing stories among mushroom collectors. We observed a similar set of legitimizing activities at a meeting of a midwestern "sports [baseball card] collecting club." The meeting began with a quiz asking 20 questions such as: who has the highest batting average in baseball this year, who has the most American League strikeouts, and who is leading in stolen bases. The person with the most correct answers (after a tie breaker between the two who each had 17 correct) won tickets to an upcoming baseball game. At the same meeting, one of the several members who had attended a national baseball-card collectors show reported on what took place there. A debate on whether to spend $13,000 and first-class airfare from Seattle to bring Al Kaline (in the baseball Hall of Fame) to the local show was followed by a show-and-tell in which members appreciatively learned of each other's recent card acquisitions. Each of these activities, in addition to the large meeting turnout, helped club members feel that their collecting is justified, legitimate, and important.

The general legitimization of collections, coupled with tenuous price guides and rationalizations that collecting is a good investment, means that even a person who is not normally materialistic or self-indulgent can safely exercise these traits in the arena of collecting. Saarinen (1958, pp. 349-355) describes John D. Rockefeller, Jr. as such a man. Even though he was fond of jewels, collecting art was as close as he would allow himself to come to what he perceived as self-indulgence. He argued that since these works would eventually be willed to a museum, he could feel guilt-free in acquiring them and possessing them for a time. Meyer (1973) notes this legitimization of collecting through feelings of grandiosity:

> The great collector has a sense of destiny, a feeling that he is mankind's agent in gathering and preserving what might otherwise be heedlessly dispersed. And the collector is capable of collecting anything -- one has a complete cabinet of all varieties of Coca-Cola bottles, while another displays an array of Ford Radiators (p. 187).

Whether a collection is believed to be legitimized as contributing to art or to science depends in part upon what is collected. But it also depends upon the type of collector. For instance, Rubens kept an extensive art collection in his studio, but rather than serve as a source of aesthetic inspiration, it served a more scientific or technical purpose in providing examples for his assistants (Bellony-Rewald and Peppiatt 1982). The type A collector takes the taxonomic approach thought to characterize science, while the type B collector follows aesthetic criteria thought to predominate in the world of art (Danet and Katriel 1989). In both cases, the rigorous pursuit of these criteria gives collectors confidence in the acceptability and importance of their activity. And as others have observed, underlying the acquisitiveness sanctioned in these ways is a desire for security (Belk 1982; Beaglehole 1932; Danet and Katriel 1986; Rigby and Rigby 1944; Saarinen 1958; von Holst 1967).

Collections as Extensions of Self. Another general motive for collecting, at least in an individualistic and possessive culture, is to gain an expanded or improved sense of self through gathering and controlling meaningful objects or experiences. As John Dewey (1922) puts it:

> No unprejudiced observer will lightly deny the existence of an original tendency to assimilate objects and events to the self, to make them part of the "me." We may even admit that the "me" cannot exist without the "mine." The self gets solidity and form through an appropriation of things which identifies them with whatever we call myself.... "I own therefore I am" (p. 116).

Behind the desire to control and master the objects in a collection (Belk, et al. 1988; Bryant 1982; Danet and Katriel 1986; Rheims 1961; Stebbins 1982), it appears that there is an intention to build, restore, or alter the extended self (Alexander 1979; Beaglehole 1932; Belk 1988; Danet and Katriel 1986; Moulin 1967/1987; Stillinger 1980). For this reason, as noted earlier, collections are almost always *personal* possessions rather than group or family possessions, at least within the hedonistic and individualistic ethic of modern consumer culture (Campbell 1987). The tendency to connect the collection to other times, places, or people is also due to the individualistic desire to extend oneself through the collection. Moulin (1967/1987) found that such an outlook was much in evidence among French art collectors:

> Ultimately they identify with what they own, with the collection they have "created," which gives them a sense of accomplishment.... for collectors the attitude is, "I am my paintings."
> Identification with the painting gives

them a positive sense of themselves (p. 83).

We found this attitude expressed at a comic book show where visitors could bring their comic books to be appraised by the experts who had set up displays and sales booths. The hesitant and reluctant approach that the visitors made as they neared these experts, treasures in hand, reflected their fear of a negative judgment upon *them* if the comics turned out to be worthless or of minor significance. The feeling of dejection when such a judgment was received may not be so much a disappointment at the collection's lack of financial importance as a feeling of loss-of-self. But perhaps the most telling signal that collections are seen as extensions of self involves the involuntary loss of collections. One man (WM 40) who lost his lifelong collections of phonograph records and books in a flood felt profound despair and the sinking feeling that now his life was a failure rather than a positive contribution to the world.

Sense of self is also involved in the goal of the collector to complete the collection, for to complete the collection is symbolically to complete the self (Belk 1988, Wicklund and Gollwitzer 1982). While this tendency may be stronger among type A collectors (Danet and Katriel 1989), even those employing purely aesthetic criteria are interested in having a balanced or aesthetically pleasing whole that represents them as possessing parallel traits (Storr 1983). At the same time that collectors strive to complete their collections, there is a great fear should this ever be close to happening; for if a collector is through with a collection, who is he or she then? A finished collection, like a finished life, connotes death. Collectors can calm this fear of completion by upgrading the standards for the collection, branching out into related collecting areas, or starting entirely new types of collections. These strategies show too that the collector's joy lies in the process of collecting rather than in the outcome, reflecting a focus on what Maslow (1968) termed being needs. Collecting in multiple categories is an especially common strategy to forestall completion. Thus, one of our informants (WM 40) collected stamps, coins, baseball cards, football cards, sports-team t-shirts, jerseys and hats, vintage cars, big band 78 rpm records, and antique furniture. A husband and wife (WM 65, WF 65) collected (between them): dolls, saltcellars, purses, glassware, plates, jewelry, spoons, watches, several types of figurines, and antique furniture. While these collectors are extreme examples of maintaining multiple collections, the tendency eventually to begin a collection of collections is widespread among collectors. Along with the other strategies noted, multiple collections can indefinitely preclude a shift to non-collector status due to the completion of a collection.

Temporal Aspects of Collecting

Over the life of a collector and a collection, consistent patterns tend to emerge. These patterns involve the birth, life, and death or immortality of the collection. While collections can be of diverse types, they tend to follow a similar life cycle.

Collections Seldom Begin Purposefully. Ironically, in light of the seriousness and purposefulness that the collection generally attains, its start is seldom preplanned. The collector rarely consciously ponders what to collect or whether to collect. The elephant replica collector, mentioned previously, began when he received an elephant figurine as a wedding gift. In fact, gifts often act as the seeds around which a collection eventually forms. Alternatively, a collector may purchase an interesting curio, perhaps on a vacation, and become interested in pursuing the interest it stimulates. It may take the acquisition of several items before the collector sees the pattern, becomes committed, and begins to say "I collect _____." Once this occurs, others may begin to give the collector gifts of items for the collection, helping to reinforce this self-definition. In order to be regarded as a true collector, however, the owner must also actively participate in acquiring additional objects for the collection.

Olmsted (1988a) asked the owner of a used marine supply store if he was a collector:

> If you had asked that two months ago, I would have answered no, I am a dealer. When I buy for the shop I often buy knives. When I get a real nice one I throw it in a drawer in my bedroom dresser. One night my wife asked me when I would bring those knives to the store. I said there was only a few, I probably wouldn't bother. She said "I counted them last night. There are 75 pocket knives in that drawer." They still aren't in the shop, so I guess I am a collector now (p. 3).

Connell's (1974) *The Connoisseur* tells a similar story of a man slowly but inexorably drawn into avid collecting. He initially picks up an interesting piece of pottery at a curio shop in the American Southwest while there for a professional convention. Out of curiosity, he stops at a university anthropology department before leaving town to inquire if it might be a genuine Mayan piece. Learning that it probably is, he acquires several books about such pieces to read on the plane on the way home. Over the next several months he is slowly seduced -- first, by the remarkable collection of a former stranger who now welcomes him as a fellow collector and, later, through his efforts to authenticate a forgery he buys at an auction and through the ministrations of several dealers. He eventually becomes so immersed in his pursuit of Mayan pottery that he woefully neglects his family. Although collecting does not inevitably become destructive, it does commonly begin with such incidental purchases, finds, or gifts.

Tendency Toward Specialization. Like *The Connoisseur*, the collector almost always begins to concentrate on one or several specialties within a broader area of collecting. For instance one purse collector (WF 65) looks for French beaded purses, sterling silver mesh purses, and "miser's purses". The primary reason for such specialization is to set challenges that offer a realistic chance of success (completion and superiority over other collectors). Just as academics within any field tend to specialize in only a few topics within an already bounded field, so do collectors. In this way, they greatly enhance their chances of becoming authorities and having superior collections. This trend is a modern one that was not in fashion among the Renaissance collectors who assembled wunderkammern. Contemporary collectors we have encountered include a man who only wanted Mickey Mouse Replicas from the 1950s, a woman who only collected oyster plates from the Eastern U.S. (with indentations for 5 rather than 6 oysters), and a man who collects only Model A Ford Roadsters. Similarly, Olmsted (1987b) found that stamp collectors were most likely to switch from collecting stamps of the world to collecting only a few countries or specific issues, and Stenross (1987) found that gun collectors are likely to specialize by time period, country of production, and type of gun.

Unlike the decision to start collecting, the decision to specialize in a particular sub-area is made more deliberately. An art collector we interviewed decided to specialize in netsukes and Japanese block prints, partly because he spent time in Japan when in the military and later lived there for three years as an attorney. A collector of British Army ceramic medals was pursuing the grail of a Royal Order of the Garter medal ("like the one Winston Churchill was buried with"). And a comic book collector was concentrating on issues of Swamp Thing after number 20, when a writer he admires took over the scripts. In each of these cases of specialization, there was a more elaborated cognitive rationale than had been formulated to explain the initial interest in the general area of the collection. At a more societal level of analysis, undoubtedly structural variables such as family background and education also play a role in such choices (cf., DiMaggio 1987), but we think the incidental start of collections cuts across these structural variables.

Collection as Cumulative Experience. A collected object becomes a reminder of the story of its acquisition. The object is, thus, a cue for recalling and retelling this story (e.g., Benjamin 1955). The images that a collection conjures up may therefore be a part of the collector's personal history of times and places. Stewart (1984, p. 151) calls these associations "souvenirs" (because of their metonymic authentication of the past) and distinguishes them from collections (which she contends involve only a metaphoric derivation of authenticity from the past). However, we consider personal history to be an inescapable part of collections. "It is as if," says Abbas (1988), "the experience of possession could be transformed into the possession of experience" (p. 230).

A collection, therefore, is more than just a small museum of the objects collected. It is also the major museum of the life of the collector qua collector. The term "museum" is literally appropriate for more than half a dozen of our informants who have transformed their collections into public museums during their lifetimes. Another several dozen informants have had their collections temporarily enshrined in other exhibitions open to the public or have opened their homes to interested viewers at certain times of the year. And, in several cases, the collectors have received mass media attention to their collections. In each case, we find that these collectors share a pride in showing their particular proof of a life well-spent. Since those who patronize these displays are self-selected and generally find them interesting, the collector's feelings of accomplishment tend to be reinforced by the comments of these visitors. While some people may write autobiographies or consolidate their life experiences into photograph albums, for the collector, the collection is autobiography. It is both reified experience and the demonstration of an accomplishment. It is a monument to the self.

The Quest for Immortality. If the collection is an autobiography and a monument, it is not surprising that collectors are concerned with the fate that will befall their collections after they die. As Rigby and Rigby (1944) observe:

> because the collector has identified his creation so closely with himself (a very strengthening bond for some men), he sometimes feels that, like a strong boat, it will bear him through the centuries after his body has gone to the earth again (p. 47).

It is not necessarily the case that the collector wants the collection to perpetuate his or her identity; there may also be a concern for the immortality of the collection itself. The feeling is often one of seeking a way that the entity of the collection can be preserved and cared for; a caring heir is sought who will appreciate the collection.

Because suitable heirs in the immediate family are often hard to find (for reasons we shall later explore), an heir is frequently sought among grandchildren. Thus, the elephant replica collector hopes his two-year-old granddaughter will take over his collection and was preparing her by reading her elephant stories and giving her elephant gifts. A baseball-card collector had already willed his collection to his two-year-old grandson. A stamp collector is giving his grandchildren stamp books in hopes that one will "get the bug" and take over his collection.

Another way in which collectors attempt to gain immortality is by convincing a museum to preserve their collections. Behrman (1952) notes of Duveen's sales to wealthy collectors, "he was selling immortality. Since most of his protégés were aging men, the task of making them yearn for immortality was not hard" (p. 102). Their immortality was assured by buying high-quality pieces that museums would be anxious to accept. However, this is becoming increasingly difficult as the prices of fine art skyrocket and museums increasingly refuse gifts that will limit their flexibility in the future. When no heir and no museum acceptance is likely for the collection, the collector can only hope that the collection will go to "a good home." As Lord Kenyon contemplated the fate of his autograph collection, he reflected:

> No one will ever be as fond of my pets as I have been.... I look upon them almost as one might upon the children whom he must leave behind.... None the less dear to me are these relics of the leaders of life and of literature. Some one will preserve them, and perhaps fondle them as I have done. I trust that they may come under the protecting care of a true collector, a real antiquary -- no mere bargain-hunter, no `snapper up of unconsidered trifles,' but one endowed with the capacity to appreciate whatsoever things are worthy of the affection of the lover of letters and of history (Joline 1902, pp. 306-307).

In more contemporary times, another way for a collector to achieve immortality is to have their collection featured in a publication like *Architectural Digest* or *Connoisseur*. For example, a *Connoisseur* article featuring the collections of His Serene Highness Prince Johannes von Thurn und Taxis, quotes the self-congratulatory Prince as saying "I especially love the jewels of Marie Antoinette," "We have 480 clocks, 300 of which are prize pieces," "I can't begin to figure out how much we've got," and "What I have would fill the Metropolitan Museum" (Dradgadze 1988). The title of another article laments, "The Warhol Collection: Why Selling it is a Shame" (Kaylan 1988). And thus, the life cycle of the collector is completed: from a typically accidental start, through specialization and the accumulation of experience, to a final hope that the collector or at least the collection will achieve some measure of immortality.

IS COLLECTING DESIRABLE?

Collectors and Collections

A critical question about collecting concerns its desirability. While we have noted that collecting is generally a socially sanctioned form of acquisitiveness and possessiveness, we have not considered what beneficial and harmful effects collecting has on the individual who practices it and the society which sanctions it. We will first consider positive and negative aspects of collecting for the individual and then consider implications of collecting at the societal level.

Olmsted (1988a) contends that collecting is a form of deviance that largely escapes criticism because it is more prevalent among the upper than the lower classes of society. Nevertheless, most fictional portrayals of collecting depict collectors in negative ways, ranging from odd to pathological, that suggest opprobrium (e.g., Balzac 1848/1968; Chatwin 1989; Connell 1974; Dreiser 1925; Flaubert 1880/1954; Fowles 1963; Galsworthy 1906/1967; Williams 1945/1984). Based on our interviews with collectors, we detect both positive and negative aspects within collecting.

Positive Aspects for the Individual

Collecting and Meaning. While we have thus far presented collecting primarily as a consumption activity, it is also possible to consider it as a form of production. The production of a collection is a creative act that brings something new into existence: the entity of the collection of particular things selectively assembled. Depending on the type of collection and collector, the result of this assemblage may be the production of knowledge and/or beauty. From the perspective of the collector, these productions may be experienced as further producing enlightenment, learning, aesthetic joy, or feelings of mastery, meaningfulness, and accomplishment (Torgovnick 1990). In this sense, collecting (especially in an achievement-oriented society -- McClelland 1971) may provide a purpose in life and a degree of satisfaction that, when the collector is employed, exceeds that present on the job (Ackerman 1990). On a less grand scale, collecting focuses activity, or as some collectors say, "It keeps me busy" (Soroka 1988; Travis 1988).

In addition to creativity, a second source of meaning derived from collecting is that it can be a form of play. It can be serious instructive play, joyful releasing play, or passionate escapist play. In the latter cases, especially, collecting may provide sources of satisfaction not often available in the workplace, where play is often frowned upon. It may offer the adult a chance to engage in a generally approved behavior that would otherwise be disparaged as childish and immature. Given the presumed human need for play, this opportunity may be quite healthy:

> There is nothing rational about collecting; but this personal expression is reassuring -- it shows that there are still among us, in this doggedly materialistic society, many poets and dreamers, prepared to indulge their fantasies (Caxton Publishing 1974, p. 185).

As with games and many other forms of play, collecting is a structured rule-governed activity. There are rules to be learned in any collecting area, and participation in these shared rules helps the collector feel justified, secure, and appropriate in the pursuit of the collection. Further, one's ability to follow rules provides an all-important sense of mastery or competence (White 1959). This play-related aspect of mastery hinges on the ability to achieve closure or order and serves as one key source of motivation for collecting behavior (Danet and Katriel 1989).

Thus, a third source of meaning in collecting involves wresting personalized control from an alienated marketplace. Miller (1988) finds that residents in a council housing estate have created inalienable culture from alienable goods through the personalized redecoration of their rented kitchens:

> the collector is engaged exactly in a struggle *against* universal commodification. His possession of objects strips things of their commodity character (p. 220).

By reassembling the things of the world in a newly meaningful way, the collector decommoditizes and sacralizes consumer goods in a manner that can transcend the standard package of commodities in a consumer culture.

Finally, a fourth source of meaning in collecting concerns the extent to which collections permit their owners to achieve a sense of uniqueness. Fromkin and Snyder (1980; Snyder and Fromkin 1980) have documented the American need for uniqueness. Collecting can provide a basis for identity formation (Erikson 1959) for many collectors, allowing them to feel more fully individuated (Jung 1921/1971) and different from others. The collection is tangible evidence that the collector is unique (Kline 1988). This is because, almost by definition, each collection tends to be unique, the one-of-a-kind creation of its owner. Thus, collections confer a heightened sense of individuality, autonomy, and specialness upon those who possess them. Along these lines, Rigby and Rigby (1944) repeat the collecting story about an Englishman who pays a fortune for the only known duplicate of a rare book in his collection and then triumphantly throws it into the fire so that he can enjoy the satisfaction of owning the only extant copy.

Collecting Creates Comrades and Sustains Social Ties. A second set of individual benefits that may result from collecting is the establishment and maintenance of a social network comprised of fellow collectors as well as dealers and other experts. Just as their common interest in a sports team may bring together disparate fans in a common cause, so does collecting. Personal friendships may result, especially among more avid collectors who regularly attend auctions, shows, club meetings, and other gatherings. In fact, one large scale survey of collectors attending an auction found that friendship was the primary reason given for collecting (Soroka 1988). Although it is the exception rather than the rule, we find that sometimes those brought together through collecting are members of the same family -- husband with wife or children with parents. When this is the case, collecting not only creates new social networks but integrates existing ones (Parsons 1951).

A collection may also serve to connect the collector to others by potentiating more appropriate gift-giving, since gift-givers are able to clearly identify the collector's interests (Gotelli 1988). However, as noted previously, such gifts are often perceived by collectors as robbing them of the joys of participating in the process of search and the application of personal taste and knowledge.

Collecting may also be an attempt to fill the void left by the loss of loved ones. Freud was not the only collector who started collecting after the death of a same-sex parent. We have found this among several other collectors as well. "Empty nest" households are also prone to start or increase collecting activity (Christ 1965). In such cases

it appears that the objects collected may be acting as a surrogate family for the collector. Emic references to these objects as part of the family are not uncommon among our informants. In the same way that pets may sometimes be regarded as part of the family, so may the objects collected (Baekeland 1981) -- with pets themselves sometimes being part of such collections. Freud's good morning greeting to a Chinese statue is one example of this personification and anthropomorphism.

Collecting Captures Cherished Memories. Besides its role in social bonding, collecting may permit an individual to capture and preserve certain cherished memories of past experiences and precious human relationships with people and places which are now distant in time and space, if they remain at all. In some cases, this sort of nostalgic meaning may help to compensate to some extent for the loss of a loved one or partially to assuage an otherwise unbearable sorrow. Certainly, family photo albums play this role for many of us.

A touching evocation of this aspect of collecting appears in the recent movie written by Stu Silver (1987) called "Throw Momma from the Train," in which Owen (Danny DeVito) tries to persuade Larry (Billy Crystal) to murder his unbearably harridan-like mother (Anne Ramsey). The resulting black comedy (heavy with satiric overtones that parody Hitchcock's "Strangers on a Train") eventually takes Larry to Owen's house, where he meets the shrew herself and where Owen shows Larry his prized collection of coins.

Owen: You want to see my coin collection?
Larry: No!
O: I collect coins. I got a dandy collection.
L: I don't want to see it, Owen.
O: But it's my *collection.*
L: I don't care. Look, Owen; I'm just not in the mood. OK?
O: [Removing a box from under the floor boards, lying on his belly like a small child at play, and beginning to extract the coins from their envelopes] I never showed it to anyone before.
L: [Impatiently] All *right,* I'll look at it.
O: No, it's OK.
L: Show me the collection.
O: No, you don't mean it.
L: [With exasperation] Show me the damned *coins!*
O: [Happily] All right. This is a nickel. And this one, *also,* is a nickel. And here's a quarter. And *another* quarter. And a *penny.* See? Nickel, nickel, quarter, quarter, penny.... And *here* is another nickel.

L: [Bewildered] Why do you *have* them?

O: What do you mean?

L: Well, the purpose of a coin collection is that the coins are *worth* something, Owen.

O: Oh, but they *are*. This one, here, I got in change when my Dad took me to see Peter, Paul, and Mary. And this one I got in change when I bought a hot dog at the Circus. My Daddy let me keep the change. He *always* let me keep the change. Uh, this one is my *favorite*. This is Martin and Lewis at the Hollywood Palladium. Look at that. See the way it shines, that little eagle? I loved my Dad a lot.

L: [Realizing...] So this whole collection is, uh....?

O: Change my Daddy let me keep.

L: [Tenderly] What was his name?

O: Ned. He used to call me his "Little Ned." That's why Momma named me "Owen." I really miss him.

L: [Gently] That's a real nice collection, Owen.

O: Thank you, Larry.

The economy with which the creators of "Throw Mama from the Train" have evoked the collecting spirit in this scene strikes us as a masterpiece of compactness. The relevant moral is articulated by Larry: "The purpose of a coin collection is that the coins are *worth* something.... That's a real nice collection, Owen." In sum, the point that should not be missed -- in the present chapter as well as in the scene with Larry and Owen -- is that collections are one type of consumption that can draw forth powerful feelings of tremendous significance (in this case, loving memory of a lost father). Collecting is a consumption experience that engenders and reflects deep and profound meanings in people's lives.

Collecting Evokes Deep Emotional Involvement. As this episode from the movie clearly illustrates, collections tend to be strongly cathected as vehicles for arousing, expressing, and even embodying powerful emotions and deep involvement. Danet and Katriel (1989) point out that "collectors of all ages share [t]his intense emotional involvement" (p. 1). Bloch and his colleagues have written insightfully about related phenomena, which they call "product" as opposed to "purchase" involvement:

enduring involvement with a product derives from the product's relatedness to a consumer's needs, values, or self-concept.... At very high levels, enduring involvement may be termed product enthusiasm and is characteristic of product enthusiasts such as car buffs, wine connoisseurs, or avid video gamers. Product enthusiasm entails a strong, abiding, hobby-like interest in the product class in question which transcends the temporary purchase process arousal investigated in most involvement research (Bloch and Bruce 1984, p. 197).

The transcendent qualities of collecting have been characterized earlier in this chapter as magical or sacred. When this sacredness reaches the highest level, the accompanying emotion is that of ecstasy. We count this kind of emotional commitment as a social advantage. It seems to encourage and to channel the expression of undeniably powerful feelings that touch the core of the human condition.

Negative Aspects for the Individual

The advantages just discussed all serve to encourage people to participate in collecting. However, collecting also has a number of disadvantages. Interestingly, many of these are closely connected to the advantages. That is, the same phenomena that produce positive consequences for the collector can also produce negative consequences in people's lives. Although collecting provides a basis for identity formation, it may simultaneously limit identity development to one arena. That is, it may encourage depth at the expense of breadth. While collecting provides tangible social expression of a facet of the self, it often houses that identity in tangible objects that can be lost, damaged, or destroyed. In tangibilizing the self, the collector runs the risk that this tangible evidence will be destroyed (Jones 1986). Although gift-givers may welcome others' collections because they provide a ready guideline for deciding what to give, this encourages a shallow understanding of the collector by these givers. They may see the collector in terms of what he or she has, rather than who he or she is. Such gift-giving commoditizes the identity of the collector, and denies him or her the pleasures associated with hunting for appropriate additions to the collection. It misunderstands the pleasure of collecting as resulting from having rather than doing.

In focusing talents and energies on the collection, the collector restricts his or her range of experience and the people with whom he or she interacts. For many, collecting means lessened contact with other people because increasingly the focus of attention is narrowed to the objects of the collection (Travis 1988). Collecting for such people begins to reflect an obsessive interest in perfection (Rheims 1961; Woodman 1982). Focusing attention so totally on a collection may, however, be seen as trivial by others (cf., Reid 1988). Collections which permit some fantasy enactment can illuminate the disappointing ways that reality fails to match fantasies. And in the hunt for additions to a collection, limited funds may result in a feeling of frustration and incompetence.

Addictive Aspects of Collecting. In examining literary and social science treatments of collecting, and in reviewing the emic constructs captured in our fieldnotes, it is apparent that collecting is a highly cathected activity for many consumers. Some regard it as a passion, others as a disease. It is frequently described as a pleasurable activity that can have some unpleasant consequences. In its pleasurable aspect, collecting embodies the characteristics of flow as described by Csikszentmihalyi (1975) and reported by Belk, Wallendorf and Sherry (1989). It is an optimal experience (Csikszentmihalyi and Csikszentmihalyi 1988) that is psychologically integrating and socially beneficial. In its darker aspect, collecting is an activity over which many consumers fear losing control. In Chatwin's (1989) chilling phrase, the collection can hold the collector prisoner. Whether likened to idolatry or illness, collectors acknowledge the very real possibility that collecting can become addictive. Danet and Katriel (1990) suggest that the seemingly self-deprecating admission of addiction to one's collection can be a way of disclaiming responsibility for uninhibited collecting. At the same time they recognize that "serious" collectors relish their ability to freely express passion in their collecting activity. What apparently is being negotiated in the area between passion and addiction is the definition of whether the collector controls or is controlled by the activity of collecting.

We use the metaphor of addiction in full awareness of the highly charged socio-clinical political arena in which the term exists. Peele (1985, p. xii) notes that the idea of addiction " has always expressed central cultural conceptions about motivation and behavior." This is especially true when the focus of the addiction itself embodies such quintessentially central cultural preoccupations -- work and play, production and consumption, mastery and control -- as does collecting. Here the line between a prosocial, life-enhancing "positive addiction" (Glasser 1976) and a more conventionally construed dysfunctional addiction is much more difficult to draw. Certainly, the tendency to pursue an altered state of consciousness of the kind produced by any ritual activity, whether behaviorally via collecting, or pharmacologically via chemical use, is a cross-cultural universal. Some theorists have elevated (or reduced) the tendency to the level

of a drive (Seigel 1989). The means by which the tendency is implemented are valued differentially across time and space. That these means are subject to abuse is widely recognized. Thus, what follows is a culturally constructed account of some of the difficulties encountered by collectors who have become addicted to collecting.

Although addictive collecting is not present among all collectors, there is compelling evidence of its pervasiveness in the observations of others (Rheims 1961), self-reports in surveys (Travis 1988), and the emic self-labels used by our informants (e.g., "magazineaholic", "getting a Mickey (Mouse) fix", "print junkie"). In the words of one of Danet and Katriel's (1990) informants, "Its a disease." A colleague of Freud reported that he described his collecting passion as "an addiction second in intensity only to his nicotine addiction" (Gay 1976, p. 18). Before pursuing this diagnosis, we must define what we mean by addiction, and how it is evidenced.

Addiction Defined. Most commonly, addiction implies a substance upon which a person is physiologically, as well as psychologically, dependent, such as alcohol or cocaine. However, according to some authors, it is possible to be addicted to behaviors as well as substances (Schaef 1987). This is a non-physiological type of addiction. Although this is a position not accepted by many researchers, there is no consensus definition of addiction (cf. Jenike 1056; King 1981; Lang 1983; Marlatt, Baer, Donovan, and Kivlahan 1988; Money 1980; Nathan 1980; Salzman 1980; Smith 1986; Sutker and Allain 1988; Winston 1980; Yates, Leebey, and Shisslak 1983). In our analysis we employ a broad functional definition that is best formulated by Peele (1975):

> An addiction exists when a person's attachment to a sensation, an object, or another person is such as to lessen his [sic] appreciation of and ability to deal with other things in his environment, or in himself, so that he has become increasingly dependent on that experience as his only source of gratification.

Addiction to a behavior can then be assessed by looking at the consequences of attachment to this behavior as a source of gratification. A person might be addicted to a love relationship (Peele 1975), shopping (O'Guinn and Faber 1989), television viewing (Smith 1986), working, running (Yates, Leebey, and Shisslak 1983), eating, or dieting (Bruch 1968, Spignesi 1983). That is, even activities which are included in a normal, healthy lifestyle for most people can become the focus of addictive tendencies for others who become dependent on this behavior as their primary source of gratification. The question then becomes whether the clinically addictive behavior is seen as undesirable enough to be culturally labeled as an addiction (Walker and Lidz 1983).

Addictions that escape society's condemnation may be evidenced by noting the person's limited interaction with the environment. Addicts exhibit an intense focus of behavior in a single direction, performing the same behavior repeatedly to fill their time (Travis 1988). Crucial to the addiction pattern in many definitions is a lack of satiety with an increasing rather than decreasing desire to engage in this behavior. In other words, addicts do not adhere to the law of diminishing marginal returns, but rather seek ritualistic and repeated use of a behavior pattern for gratification (Peele 1975). The ritual provides a sameness of stimulation, rather than variety and growth. Addiction gives into the human tendency to become fixated on something in a way that resists both change and growth (de Dampierre 1987).

A widespread clinical perspective on addiction places the genesis of the addictive cycle in feelings of low self-esteem and a sense that the world is unpredictable, which produce anxiety in the individual. The person attempts to control these feelings of anxiety and unpredictability by using the addictive pattern of behavior to block experience of the variable world. By contrast, the predictable routine and pattern of the addiction feels comforting and reassuring. However, the addicted individual may eventually experience problems (e.g., physical, familial, financial) resulting from this behavior. These problems produce feelings of lower self-esteem and gender anxiety. Because the person continually reverts to the addiction to block these feelings, clinicians refer to this as the addictive cycle. This cycle is extremely difficult to break. Even recovering addicts may find that a craving for the addictive substance or process can be induced visually, as with cocaine addicts who sometimes experience such cravings merely by seeing drug paraphernalia or driving by the place where they used to buy drugs (Barnes 1988).

It is equally important to define what addiction is not. Addiction is not merely absorption in a behavioral process which is used to intensify (rather than block or avoid) novelty and stimulation (de Dampierre 1987). This is often a difficult assessment for a researcher to make, but certainly an important one. It is also useful to note that addiction is not the same as a habit, which may be performed to enable the conduct of other aspects of life. Habitual behavior patterns may help the person better cope with the rest of life, while addictions do not.

Similarly, something cannot be labelled an addiction merely because it is time-consuming; what is crucial is whether for the time spent, one experiences an enhanced and abiding feeling of mastery and self-esteem. Failing this, the time-consuming habit becomes a limitation or restriction and, ultimately, a self-defeating confinement.

There are other concepts used in the literature on addiction that are useful in understanding collecting addictions. The term "cross-addiction" is used to refer to the tendency of a person who is addicted to one substance to substitute other substances in a generalized pattern of addiction. This perspective sees addiction as a pattern residing primarily in the person, not in the interaction of the person with a particular environment or a particular substance. The term "co-dependency" is used to refer to the tendency for entire families to develop behaviors that foster the continuance of the addict's addictive cycle. That is, the structure and pattern of life in a particular family may actually perpetuate one family member's addiction, despite the fact that the non-addicted family members find the addiction troubling. The addictive pattern of one family member structures family expectations about what can be expected of the addict. As a way of handling their own anxieties about their worth and the predictability of the world, other family members may become dependent on the predictability of the addicted family member's addictive behavior. The addiction allows various family members to play either the role of the patient, the helpful caregiver, or the wronged party. Co-dependents are addicted to someone else's being the one with "the problem" (Schaef 1987). Continuance of the addiction enables other family members to continue relationship patterns to which they have grown accustomed, allowing them to remain the same rather than challenging them to change. With these definitions and terminology in mind, we can now begin to assess the addictive patterns of behavior present in collecting.

Addiction in Collecting. Although almost any behavior can become addictive, the pattern of behavior characteristic of collectors makes it especially prone to addiction. Most collectors interviewed mentioned the search for additions to a collection as the central activity of their collecting behavior. Rather than spend time examining or organizing items that are already in the collection, collectors prefer to search or shop for additions to the collection. Search behavior may be compulsively and ritualistically enacted (cf., Reid 1988). Acquiring rather than possessing provides the temporary fix for the addict. A sense of longing and desire (Johnson 1983; Campbell 1987) -- a feeling that something is missing in life -- is temporarily met by adding to the collection. But this is a temporary fix, a staving off of withdrawal, followed by a feeling of emptiness and anxiety that is addressed by searching for more. Shopping and searching are the ritualized means by which the collector obtains a sense of competence and mastery in life. These activities are the bittersweet consequences of experiencing longing in the arena of the marketplace.

Emic descriptions of shopping for additions to a collection highlight this ritual aspect of search behavior. It is patterned, repetitive, and carries with it particular liturgical rules concerning appropriate sequence. For example, one Barbie doll collector (GWM 35) who spends considerable time at doll shows explained particular rules that guided his doll buying pattern, such as having the dealer completely undress then redress the doll to allow him to see if any part of the body is damaged. Only when carried out in this ritualized way does the addict feel "right". Objects found in the search are often seen as having irresistible power over the person, as with a collector of antique bronzes (WF 45) who recounted, "I just had to have it. It had to be mine."

By placing the source of such power outside of themselves, addicts reinforce their belief that it is impossible for them to resist the temptation (Sandor 1987). They are possessed by the collection as much as they possess it. Through believing that this mysterious power is beyond them, they begin to construct a first-order lie -- a lie to the self -- that negates the possibility of taking control of the addictive behavior pattern (Schaef 1987).

But searching for additions to a collection, although of central importance, is not the only addictive focus for collectors. Compulsive attention to and control over the objects in the collection provides an additional source of feelings of control and mastery (Danet and Katriel 1988, 1990) -- important feelings to an addict (Kisly 1987). For example, one interpretation of the propensity of collectors to will their collections to museums is that, by doing so, they retain a certain sense of control of the collection by insuring that it will not fall into the hands of another collector (Rheims 1961).

Collecting activity allows a collector to avoid other aspects of life. It is a form of withdrawal from other aspects of life that is nevertheless often positively sanctioned, as evidenced by media attention featuring collectors as heros. Rather than widening our scope, an addiction narrows and deepens it (Kisly 1987). This is an observation that many collectors object to; they counter that through their collections they have met many interesting people and have learned many things. For some, this may be correct, but for others the strength of this objection may be a first-order lie to themselves, as is commonly noted among addicts (Schaef 1987). On the whole, collecting, particularly for the addict, involves the individual in a repetitive, predictable pattern of behavior which can provide a form of solace for someone who is troubled by living in an unpredictable world. This is acknowledged indirectly by the more than 2/3 of a sample of 1200 collectors who agreed that the label of addict was appropriate to describe their involvement in collecting (Travis 1988).

Some collectors exhibit cross-addictions to other substances and processes. Several informants are especially notable in this regard. One couple (WM 65/WF 65) is so addicted to collecting that they collect flow blue plates, beaded purses, silver spoons, open salt dishes (both glass and crystal), first-day-of-issue Franklin Mint coins, stamps, deer replicas, Cupid Awake and Cupid Asleep pictures, mother of pearl opera glasses, leather bound books by James Whitcomb Riley, numerous kinds of figurines of women, and perfume bottles, to mention just a few of their collections. Another man (WM 45), a collector of Mickey Mouse memorabilia, had previously been addicted to heroin as well as alcohol. He quit both of these substance addictions, but admitted that he later became psychologically addicted to collecting the Mickey toys. Thus, cross-addictions to other behaviors as well as other substances are evident in some people who are addicted to collecting.

A phenomenon of considerable interest in the mental health literature in the last few years has been the recognition that children of addicts may often manifest addictions of their own as adults. Having grown up in families where co-dependency on the addiction of another family member was present, they may later in life become the addict in their own families. We often found inter-generational transfer (both downward and upward -- Soroka 1988) of collecting, but generally in a different specialty area. The son (WM 35) of a collector of porcelain dolls grew up to become a Barbie doll collector. The collectors of multiple types of items mentioned previously started one son collecting open salt dishes, and began to work with a granddaughter on a stamp collection. A father who collects baseball cards (WM 35) reported that he is teaching his children some important values by helping them become baseball card collectors. He believes this is a way for his son and daughter to learn to take care of things. He credits his own maternal grandfather with instilling certain values in him through the baseball games they watched together --

standing in the living room with their hands over their hearts when the national anthem was played at the beginning of the games. We also found evidence of a complex web of addictive co-dependency among family members who may not be addicted themselves. Collecting, while probably due more to social enculturation (nurture) than to genetic determination (nature), does appear to run in families (Olmstead 1988; Rheims 1961).

But unlike most other areas where addictions are formed, collecting is culturally sanctioned, rather than disapproved or scorned as a character flaw. Collecting represents immersion in acquisitiveness, individualism, competitiveness, and display of personal accomplishments through material objects -- all central values in American culture. By contrast, collecting does not represent asceticism, collectivism, cooperation, or introspective learning and spiritual growth. Instead the collector says, through the collection, "See what I have, and you don't." Rather than being viewed as unhealthy, addiction to collecting is regarded positively in our consumer culture and is often treated as an achievement to be admired (cf., Owen 1988). In its core assumption of exclusive possession, collecting celebrates private property as a societal value. Further tribute is paid to this addiction by the enshrinement (Belk, Wallendorf, and Sherry 1989) of collections in museums, which often devote as much attention to the collectors as to the artists or creators of the collected item (Berger 1972). One writer has called museums the "churches of collectors" (Rheims 1961), implying the utmost regard given to this activity in contemporary Western culture. Our field data on collecting support the notion that contemporary U.S. culture is an Addictive System (Schaef 1987) in its encouragement of individual addictions to collecting behavior.

Rivalry with Spouses and Children. While collections can sometimes create surrogate companionship through personification and anthropomorphism, this same tendency can also alienate living members of the family. We were at first perplexed by the tendency of children and spouses to deny the collector's fervent wish that they adopt and care for the collection when the collector grows old or dies. The explanation for this puzzle, we believe, is that the collection is regarded by these children and spouses as a rival. It has occupied a considerable portion of their loved one's time and attention and therefore is now resented for having alienated the collector's affections from them. It has become an enemy -- a target for derogation rather than an object of reverence.

Here, it is instructive to further consider Sigmund Freud's collection. Two dominant themes in the collection, not surprisingly, are sex and death (Ransohoff 1975; Spector 1975). We have previously noted Freud's tendency to fondle objects from his collection while talking to patients and his observation that collecting represents a libidinal transference. He also expressed a wish to be buried with his antiquities, and his ashes were accordingly interred in one of his Egyptian urns (Spector 1975). But it is the sexual theme in collecting that makes collections potential rivals for a loved one's affections. Thus, Olmsted (1988a) suggests that collections may be an increasing cause of divorces. As Baekeland (1981) notes of his art-collector patients:

> To a man, they report that they usually know immediately whether or not a piece really appeals to them and whether they want to possess it. They often compare their feeling of longing for it to sexual desire. This suggests that art objects are confused in the unconscious with ordinary sexual objects, an idea that gets some confirmation from the fact that many collectors like to fondle or stroke the objects they own or to look at them over and over from every angle.... The only other context in which looking, fondling and caressing loom so large is sexual foreplay (p. 51).

In this connection, we are reminded that Freud (who so easily saw beneath the surface of things) was either unable or unwilling to apply his own theoretical perspectives on sex, death, and anal retentiveness to collecting activity in general or to his own fetishisms in particular (Fenichel 1954; Menninger 1942).

Post-Mortem Distribution Problems. As noted in the preceding section, one major problem in bequeathing collections is finding willing heirs (McCracken 1988a). While commercial dealers and museums compete with each other and with individual heirs in a climate of market growth for some collectibles (Nason 1987), there is often no accounting for any one particular collector's taste. What is supremely important to the avid collector is often unimportant to most others. Other problems are created in alternative forms of disposition. Because collections represent the distilled effort of the collector, they may also come to represent the distilled essence of the collector. Reluctant heirs may therefore feel ambivalent about possessing, selling, or, worse, junking the collection. In anticipation of this problem, collectors may seek to make arrangements for the disposition of their collections or even to dispose of them themselves in preparation for death. In some extreme instances, collectors want their collections buried with them or destroyed at their deaths (Baekeland 1981; Rigby and Rigby

1944). Hence, ironically, toward the end of the collector's life the collection can shift from being a source of great satisfaction to being a burdensome problem.

Sociocultural Importance of Collecting

Apart from individual benefits and problems of collecting, why do contemporary western societies seem to approve of collecting? What benefits and problems does collecting create at a societal level? Clearly, collecting creates problems to the extent that it channels labor, love, and money into activities not generally considered to be productive. Similarly, the collecting passion has occasionally led to robbery, pillage, murder, colonialistic exploitation of Third World cultures, and in some cases, the wholesale destruction of indigenous cultures (e.g., Chase, Chase, and Topsey 1988; Clifford 1988; Cole 1985, Nichols, Klesert, and Anyon 1989). To the extent that the collection is regarded as a rival for the collector's affections, it weakens the family as a social institution. Unless Olmsted (1988a) is correct that collecting is positively sanctioned because it is more prevalent among the upper than the lower classes, for societies to tolerate and generally sanction collecting, there must be some benefits to counter these formidable problems which threaten the social order.

A material argument, often given by collectors themselves, is that the artistic and scientific legacy of collections benefits current and future generations. However, this argument seems to be more of a rationalization than an explanation for the societal acceptance of collecting, particularly in light of the content of many collections (e.g., beer cans, Franklin Mint figurines, elephant replicas) and the problems of disposition mentioned earlier. One alternative reason that the possessiveness involved in collecting may be sanctioned is that, like home ownership, ownership of an extensive collection may create responsible law-abiding citizens with a stake in the stability of the nation and community. Competitive rivalry between collectors, like many sports competitions, also serves as a channeled release of aggressions and a visible reinforcement of what remains of the Protestant work ethic. Even though the achievement does little to increase national productivity, the intense individualistic competition engendered by collecting symbolically endorses the social Darwinism of capitalism. Collecting may stabilize and solidify class boundaries by allowing successful competition within narrow collecting categories that members of a social class have the money, support, and knowledge to pursue. In this way, competition is deflected laterally rather than vertically in the class structure. Further, the acquisitiveness

involved in collecting both symbolically and materially supports a profit-based capitalist system dependent on escalating consumer desires. In fact, collecting epitomizes and reifies consumer desire for ever more and better material things. Just as consumers learn to enact the economic myth of insatiable needs, collectors learn to push the horizons and boundaries of their collections past the possibility of completion. Collecting codifies the current credo that the one who dies with most toys wins. Even in toy collecting, however, this is usually modified to "most and best." Increasingly, selectivity -- based either on symbolic or exchange value -- rather than mere quantity, may be the guiding principle behind contemporary collecting (Landis 1990a). Whether this potentially elitist trend becomes a brake to the otherwise democratic trend in remains to be seen.

Thus, although collecting creates some social problems, it also enacts the values that provide impetus and momentum to consumer culture. Appetitive behaviors such as collecting are the constituting essence of consumer culture and of the identities forged in its crucible. Collecting is at once the process by which such a culture evolves and the diagnostic product of the culture itself. It permits the formation both of a "proper" (that is, "rule-governed") relation of people with objects and a "deviant" (whether "idolatry" or "erotic fixation") one as well (Clifford 1988, p. 219). Whether it aspires to aesthetic redemption (Clifford 1988) or decays to personal fetishism (Stewart 1984), collecting shapes and reflects the identity of the culture and the individual. In McCracken's (1988b, p. 133) view, collecting is a bridge to displaced meaning: the elusive nature of collectibles allows collectors to invest them with idealized values realizable in their pursuit. Collecting is a vehicle by which authentic experience is sought. The nature of authenticity is negotiated through collection.

Authenticity may take a number of forms. Collectors may harness and tame the cultural imperatives of acquisition, ownership, and display -- canalizing these forces in a way that minimizes the social consequences of their abuse and maximizes the individual's sense of competence and mastery. Here, both society and individuality are affirmed; desire is transmuted to everyone's gain. To the extent that nostalgia is encouraged by collection, authenticity assumes the form of a selectively recollected and reconstituted past. For those susceptible to nostalgia, collecting may be both a vehicle of alienation and salvation from contemporary culture. Whether such consciousness is viewed as "false" or "expanded", the collector is able to access a cultural vision that is personally meaningful. At any rate, the ritual or ceremonial celebration of authentic U.S. experience -- the probing of the tension between work and play, production and consumption, order and disorder, spurious and genuine -- is a principal sociocultural function of collecting.

As a reaction against cultural imperatives, authentic experience may be intimately entwined with counterculture. It may also be embodied in the recontextualizing of a stigmatized past, which may provoke a number of ethical concerns. Collectors of such "uneasy pieces" (Landis 1990b) as Nazi war memorabilia or racist black Americana on the order of Little Black Sambo cookie jars preserve a haunting heritage that could be rekindled as easily as reviled. When blacks collect these racist memorabilia, the intent is either to preclude forgetting the horrors of racism (as with Jewish preservation of the memory of the Holocaust), or to appropriate these symbols and thereby to rob them of their power through another sort of recontextualization (Adler 1988).

Collecting resists the forces of homogenization in a commoditized world. Stewart (1984) regards collecting as the total aestheticization of use-value. Pushed to the limits of commodity fetishism, collecting is the eroticization of use-value. It is a way of re-enchanting the world, of reanimating our relationship with objects. It is a form of play that may permit a relearning or realigning of priorities in the world of goods.

CONCLUSION

If collecting began in prehistory, it shows no signs of abating in our hyper-industrial post-modern era. If a certain abundance and surplus is necessary to support the non-utilitarian use of things in collections, then only severe economic hardship or a significant reorientation of consumer culture could curtail collecting. Short term hardships, such as changes in laws eliminating tax breaks for donations to museums, may actually accelerate the pace of collecting, as collectors auction their wares, and as museums sell portions of their collections to finance new acquisitions (Stout, 1990). Collecting is a paramount feature of consumer behavior that deserves far more attention than it has received. Quite conceivably, the study of collecting could become the cornerstone upon which an ecology of artifacts (Krippendorff 1989), essential to understanding the nature of contemporary consumer culture, is ultimately founded. The mythology governing such an ecology is discernable in microcosm in the collector's world. Collecting represents acquisitiveness and possessiveness, freed from lingering guilt and imbued instead with a noble sense of purpose and destiny. The rhetoric that collectors use to describe the development of their collections is not dissimilar to that used by religious converts to describe their calls to serve God. In the case of collecting, however, the god being served is often materialism -- a pure unadulterated fascination with getting and keeping things -- even when these things are intangible objects such as experiential memories. The process of collecting is legitimized and institutionalized through the fellowship of other collectors, collector organizations, public institutions, and dealers. This same community helps sacralize certain consumer objects through ritual, mystery, myth, and reverence.

The fusion and cathexis of work, play, and love that collecting represents often occurs in the service of self-enrichment through an idiom that consumer researchers have only recently begun to investigate. Collecting is a culturally sanctioned, anxiety-reducing way to present one's self with a gift (Mick and DeMoss 1990, Sherry and McGrath 1989). Freud was aware of his own penchant for giving gifts to himself, as an excerpt from at letter to a colleague suggests (Dudar 1990, p. 103):

> I got myself an expensive present today, a lovely little dipylon vase -- a real gem -- to fight my ill humor. (Spending money is indicated not only for states of fear.)

The nature of collecting as a gift to the self merits investigation in its own right. It may be one of the only forms of self-indulgence that resolves the demands of conflicting ideologies in a culture of consumption, because it seems to many to serve a higher purpose than other forms of consumption. It may be one of the few sacralization rituals that hallows the individual and enobles society in the same enterprise. Consequently, collecting manifests itself as an elegant way to serve beauty and utility, self and others. Through such giving, a relationship with the self is developed over time, and cultural values are affirmed in the bargain. In this sense, goods are truly good to think (Douglas and Isherwood 1979). While Freud, as many of us, may have had little to say in public about the personal significance of his collection, his harnessing of the discordant forces of his episteme and sublimation of them in both philosophy and practice were greatly facilitated through his collecting.

The history of collecting, its contemporary institutional aspects, and the societal functions served by collecting activity in large scale capitalist economies help explain the singular importance of collecting in contemporary consumer culture. For these reasons, to study collecting is not only to study the distilled essence of consumption, it is also to study the course of the modern consumption experience. Together with the intense focus of energies that collecting brings forth in the collector, these are important reasons to make collecting a key element in the consumer research agenda.

REFERENCES

Abbas, Ackbar (1988), "Walter Benjamin's Collector: The Fate of Modern Experience," *New Literary History*, 20 (Autumn), 217-237.

Ackerman, Paul H. (1990), "On Collecting--A Psychoanlyatic View," *Maine Antique Digest*, (May), 22A-24A.

Adler, Jerry (1988), "Cookie Jars of Oppression: Shades of Jim Crow Make it Big as Collectibles," *Newsweek*, (May 16), 75-76.

Alexander, Edward P. (1979), *Museums in Motion: An Introduction to the History and Function of Museums*, Nashville, TN: American Association for State and Local History.

Allison, Neil K., Linda L. Golden, Gary M. Mullet, and Donna Coogan (1980), "Sex-Typed Product Images: The Effects of Sex, Sex Role Self-Concept and Measurement Implications," *Advances in Consumer Research*, Vol. 7, Jerry C. Olson, ed., Ann Arbor, MI: Association for Consumer Research, 604-609.

Alsop, Joseph (1982), *The Rare Art Traditions: A History of Collecting and Its Linked Phenomena*, New York: Harper and Row.

Appleyard, Donald, (1979). "Home," *Architectural Association*, 11 (3), 4-20.

Aries, Philippe (1989), "Introduction," in *A History of Private Life: Passions of the Renaissance*, ed. Roger Chartier, Cambridge, MA: The Belknap Press of Harvard University Press, 1-11.

Aristides, Nicholai (1988), "Calm and Uncollected," *American Scholar*, 57 (3), 327-336.

Avery, Albert E. and Carl M. Colonna (1987), "The Market for Collectible Antique and Reproduction Firearms: An Economic and Financial Analysis," *Journal of Cultural Economics*, 11 (December), 49-64.

Baekeland, Frederick (1981), "Psychological Aspects of Art Collecting," *Psychiatry*, 44 (February), 45-59.

Balzac, Honoré (1848/1968), *Cousin Pons*, Harmondsworth, Middlesex, England: Penguin.

Barnes, Deborah M. (1988), "Breaking the Cycle of Addiction," *Science* 241 (August 26), 1029-1030.

Beaglehole, Ernest (1932), *Property: A Study in Social Psychology*, New York: Macmillan.

Beards, Dick (1987), "Antique Shop Narratives--Lost Treasure Found--and Lost," paper presented at Popular Culture Association Annual Meeting, Montreal, March.

Beckham, Sue Bridwell and Bradley Brooks (1989), "Mary Moody Northen and Mail Order Immortality," paper presented at American Studies Association International Convention, Toronto, November.

Behrman, S. N. (1952), *Durveen*, New York: Random House.

Belk, Russell W. (1982), "Acquiring, Possessing, and Collecting: Fundamental Processes in Consumer Behavior," *Marketing Theory: Philosophy of Science Perspectives*, Ronald F. Bush and Shelby J. Hunt, eds., Chicago: American Marketing Association, 185-190.

Belk, Russell W. (1986), "Art Versus Science as Ways of Generating Knowledge About Materialism," *Perspectives on Methodology in Consumer Research*, David Brinberg and Richard Lutz, eds., New York: Springer-Verlag, 3-36.

Belk, Russell W. (1988), "Possessions and Extended Self," *Journal of Consumer Research*, 15 (September), 139-168.

Belk, Russell W. (1990), "Possessions and the Sense of Past," this volume.

Belk, Russell W. and Melanie Wallendorf (1990a), "Of Mice and Men: Gender Identity in Collecting," *The Material Culture of Gender/The Gender of Material Culture*, Kenneth Ames and Katharine Martinez, eds., Ann Arbor: University of MIchigan Press.

Belk, Russell W. and Melanie Wallendorf (1990b), "The Sacred Meanings of Money," *Journal of Economic Psychology*, March.

Belk, Russell W., Melanie Wallendorf, and John F. Sherry, Jr. (1989), "The Sacred and the Profane in Consumer Behavior: Theodicy on the Odyssey," *Journal of Consumer Research*, 16 (June), 1-38.

Belk, Russell W., Melanie Wallendorf, John Sherry, Morris Holbrook, and Scott Roberts (1988), "Collectors and Collecting," *Advances in Consumer Research*, Vol. 15,, Michael Houston, ed., Provo, UT: Association for Consumer Research, 548-553.

Bellony-Rewald, Alice, and Michael Peppiatt (1982). *Imagination's Chamber: Artists and Their Studios*. Boston, MA: Little, Brown and Co..

Benjamin, Walter (1955), "Unpacking My Library: A Talk About Book Collecting," *Illuminations*, ed. Hannah Arendt, trans. Harry Zohn, New York: Brace & World, 59-67.

Berger, John (1972), *Ways of Seeing*. London: British Broadcasting Corporation and Penguin Books.

Berman, Morris (1981), *The Reenchantment of the World*, Ithica, NY: Cornell University Press.

Bernfeld, Suzanne C. (1951), "Freud and Archeology," *American Imago*, 8 (June), 107-128.

Bettelheim, Bruno (1975), *The Uses of Enchantment*, New York: Vintage Books.

Bloch, Peter H. and Grady D. Bruce (1984), "Product Involvement As Leisure Behavior," in *Advances in Consumer Research*, Vol. 11, ed. Thomas C. Kinnear, Provo, UT: Association for Consumer Research, 197-202

Bloom, John D. (1989), "Cardboard Images of the Past: Baseball Card Collecting and Fragmented Historical Memory," paper presented at American Studies Association Conference, Toronto, November 4.

Botto, Louis (1989), "A Night at the Opera:...Terrence McNally's Ode to Maria Callas and the Fanatical Fans Who Idolized Her," *Playbill*, 89 (November), 66-73.

Bossard, James H. and Eleanor S. Boll (1950), *Ritual in Family Living: A Contemporary Study*, Philadelphia, PA: University of Pennsylvania Press.

Brown, Julie (1988), "The Commodification of Information, Bureaucratic Structures, and Problems of Identity," paper presented at Popular Culture Association Annual Conference, New Orleans, March.

Bruch, H. (1968), *The Golden Cage: The Enigma of Anorexia Nervosa*, Cambridge, MA: Harvard University Press.

Bryant, John (1982), "Stamps and Coins," *Concise Histories of American Popular Culture*, M. Thomas Inge, ed., Westport, CT: Greenwood Press, 389-398.

Burk, Caroline F. (1900), "The Collecting Instinct," *Pedagogical Seminary*, 7, 179-207.

Butsch, Richard (1984), "The Commodification of Leisure: The Case of the Model Airplane Hobby and Industry," *Qualitative Sociology*, 7 (Fall), 217-235.

Cabanne, Pierre (1961), *The Great Collectors*, London: Cassell.

Campbell, Colin (1987), *The Romantic Ethic and the Spirit of Modern Consumerism*, London: Basil Blackwell.

Caplow, Theodore (1982), "Christmas Gifts and Kin Networks," *American Sociological Review*, 47 (3), 383-392.

Caplow, Theodore (1984), "Rule Enforcement Without Visible Means: Christmas Gift Giving in Middletown," *American Journal of Sociology*, 89 (6), 1306-1320.

Carmichael, Bill (1971), *Incredible Collectors, Weird Antiques, and Odd Hobbies*, Englewood Cliffs, N.J.: Prentice-Hall.

Caxton Publishing (1974), *The Pleasures of Collecting*, Lindsay Hamilton, trans., London: Derbibooks.

Chamberlin, Russell (1983), *Loot! The Heritage of Plunder*, London: Thames and Hudson.

Chase, Arlen F., Diane Z. Chase, and Harriot W. Topscy (1988), "Archacology and the Ethics of Collecting," *Archaeology*, 41 (January/February), 56-60, 87.

Chatwin, Bruce (1989), *Utz*, New York: Viking Penguin.

Cheal, David (1987), "'Showing Them You Love Them': Gift Giving and the Dialectic of Intimacy," *Sociological Review*, 35 (1), 150-169.

Cheal, David (1988), *The Gift Economy*, London: Routledge.

Christ, Edwin A. (1965);, "The 'Retired' Stamp Collector: Economic and Other Functions of a Systematized Leisure Activity," *Older People and their Social World: The Sub-culture of Aging*, Arnold M. Rose and Warren A. Peterson, eds., Philadelphia: F. A Davis Company, 93-112.

Clark, Kenneth (1963), "Introduction," *Great Private Collections*, Douglas Cooper, ed., New York: Macmillan, 13-19.

Clifford, James (1988), *The Predicament of Culture: Twentieth-Century Ethnography, Literature, and Art*, Cambridge, MA: Harvard University Press.

Cole, Douglas (1985), *Captured Heritage: The Scramble for Northwest Coast Artifacts*, Seattle, WA: University of Washington Press.

Connell, Evan S., Jr. (1974), *The Connoisseur*, New York: Knopf.

Cooper, Douglas (ed.) (1963), *Great Private Collections*, New York: Macmillan.

Cox, Meg (1985), "Emotional Investments," *Wall Street Journal*, (December 2), 20D.

Cox, Meg (1987), "An Unusual Collector Indulges His Craving for Rodin Sculptures," *Wall Street Journal*, July 14, 1,15.

_____ (1988), "At Sotheby's, It Only Cost $247,830 to Raid Warhol Cookie-Jar Collection," *Wall Street Journal*, April 25, 3,7.

Crispell, Diane (1988), "Collecting Memories," *American Demographics*, (November), 38-41, 60.

Crossen, Cynthia (1989), "You Call It Junk, But Denison Hatch Sees Gold in It," *Wall Street Journal*, September 25, A1,A5.

Csikszentmihalyi, Mihaly (1975), "Play and Intrinsic Rewards," *Journal of Humanistic Psychology* 15 (3), 41-63.

Csikszentmihalyi, Mihaly and Isabella Csikszentmihalyi, eds. (1988), *Optimal Experience*, New York: Cambridge University Press.

Danet, Brenda and Tamara Katriel (1986), "Books, Butterflies, Botticellis: A Life-Span Perspective on Collecting," paper presented at Sixth International Conference on Culture and Communication, Philadelphia, PA, October.

Danet, Brenda and Tamara Katriel (1988), "Stamps, Erasers, Table Napkins, `Rebbe Cards:' Childhood Collecting in Israel," paper presented at Popular Culture Association Annual Meeting, New Orleans, March.

Danet, Brenda and Tamara Katriel (1989), "No Two Alike: The Aesthetics of Collecting," *Play and Culture*, 2 (3), 253-277.

Danet, Brenda and Tamara Katriel (1990), "Glorious Obsessions, Passionate Lovers, and Hidden Treasures: Collecting, Metaphor, and the Romantic Ethic," paper presented at the International Conference on the Socio-Semiotics of Objects: The Role of Artifacts in Social Symbolic Processes, Toronto, June.

Dannefer, Dale (1980), "Rationality and Passion in Private Experience: Modern Consciousness and the Social World of Old-Car Collectors," *Social Problems*, 27 (April), 392-412.

Dannefer, Dale (1981), "Neither Socialization Nor Recruitment: The Avocational Careers of Old-Car Enthusiasts," *Social Forces*, 60 (December), 395-413.

Davis, Fred (1979). *Yearning for Yesterday: A Sociology of Nostalgia.* New York: Free Press.

de Dampierre, Pauline (1987), "The Center of Our Need," *Parabola* 12 (2), 24-31.

Defert Daniel (1982), "The Collection of the World: Accounts of Voyages from the Sixteenth to the Eighteenth Centuries," *Dialectical Anthropology*, 7 (September), 11-20.

Denzin, Norman K. (1989), *Interpretive Interactionism*, Newbury Park, CA: Sage.

Dewey, John (1922), *Human Nature and Conduct*, New York: Henry Holt.

DiMaggio, Paul (1987), "Classification in Art," *American Sociological Review*, 52 (4), 440-455.

Douglas, Mary and Baron Isherwood (1979), *The World of Goods*, NY: Norton.

Dragadze, Peter (1988), "Having it All," *Connoisseur*, 912 (January), 82-91.

Dreiser, Theodore (1925), *The Titan*, Cleveland, OH: World.

Dudar, Helen (1990), "The Unexpected Private Passion of Sigmund Freud," *Smithsonian*, 21 (5), 100-109.

Duggleby, C. V. A. (1978), "The Lure of Collecting," *National Westminster Bank Quarterly Review* (May), 57-64.

Dunn, Don (1988), "A Boffo Market for Movie Memorabilia," *Business Week*, July 11, p. 107.

Durham, Michael (1985), "Note from the Editor," *Americana*, 13 (July/August), 2.

Durost, Walter N. (1932), *Children's Collecting Activity Related to Social Factors*, New York: Bureau of Publications, Teachers College, Columbia University.

Eisenberg, Evan (1987), *The Recording Angel: Explorations in Phonography*, New York: McGraw-Hill.

Ellen, Roy (1988), "Fetishism," *Man*, 23 (June), 213-235.

Engelman, Edmund (1976), "A Memoir," *Berggasse 19: Sigmund Freud's Home and Offices, Vienna 1938: The Photographs of Edmund Engelman*, Edmund Engelman, ed., New York: Basic Books, 131-143.

Erikson, Erik (1959), *Identity and the Life Cycle*, New York: W. W. Norton.

Fenichel, Otto (1954), "Trophy and Triumph," *The Collected Papers of Otto Fenichel*, 2nd Series, New York: W. W. Norton, 141-162.

Fine, Gary Alan (1987), "Community and Boundary: Personal Experience Stories of Mushroom Collectors," *Journal of Folklore Research*, 24 (3), 223-240.

Flaubert, Gustave (1880/1954), *Bouvard & Pécuchet*, T. W. Earp and GA. W. Stonier, translators, New York: New Directions.

Forty, Adrian (1986), *Objects of Desire: Design & Society from Wedgwood to IBM*, New York: Pantheon.

Fowles, John (1963), *The Collector*, New York: Dell.

Freud, Ernest, Lucie Freud, and Ilse Grubrich-Simitis, eds. (1978), *Sigmund Freud: His Life in Pictures and Words*, New York: Norton.

Freud, Sigmund (1914), *The Psychopathology of Everyday Life*, New York: Macmillan.

Friday, Nancy (1975), *Forbidden Flowers*, New York: Pocket Books.

Fromkin, Howard and C. R. Snyder (1980), "The Search for Uniqueness and Valuation of Scarcity: Neglected Dimensions of Value in Social Exchange," *Social Exchange: Advances in Theory and Research*, Kenneth J. Gergen, Martin S. Greenberg, and Richard H. Willis, eds., New York: Plenum Press, 57-75.

Galsworthy, John (1906/1967). *The Man of Property*. New York: Signet.

Gamwell, Lynn (1988), personal correspondence quoting Freud's comments as recorded by Otto Rank in *Minutes of the Vienna Psychoanalytic Society*, February 19, 1908.

Gamwell, Lynn (1989), "The Origins of Freud's Antiquities Collection," *Sigmund Freud and Art: His Personal Collection of Antiquities*, Lynn Gamwell and Richard Wells, eds., Binghamton, NY: State University of New York, Binghamton, 21-32.

Gay, Peter (1976), "Introduction, Freud: For the Marble Tablet," *Berggasse 19: Sigmund Freud's Home and Offices, Vienna 1938: The Photographs of Edmund Engelman*, Edmund Engelman, ed., New York: Basic Books, 13-54.

Gay, Peter (1989), "Introduction," *Sigmund Freud and Art: His Personal Collection of Antiquities*, Lynn Gamwell and Richard Wells, eds., Binghamton, NY: State University of New York, Binghamton, 14-19.

Geary, Patrick (1986), "Sacred Commodities: The Circulation of Medieval Relics," *The Social Life of Things: Commodities in Cultural Perspective*, Arjun Appadurai, ed., Cambridge: Cambridge University Press, 169-191.

Geertz, Clifford (1973), *The Interpretation of Cultures*, New York: Basic Books.

Glaser, Barney G. and Anselm L. Strauss (1967), *The Discovery of Grounded Theory: Strategies for Qualitative Research*, Chicago, IL: Aldine.

Glasser, William (1976), *Positive Addiction*, New York: Harper and Row.

Golden, Linda L., Neil Allison, and Mona Clee (1979), "The Role of Sex Role and Self-Concept in Masculine and Feminine Product Perceptions," *Advances in Consumer Research*, Vol. 6, William L. Wilkie, ed., Ann Arbor, MI: Association for Consumer Research, 599-605.

Goldstein, Judith (1987), "Lifestyles of the Rich and Tyrannical," *American Scholar*, 56 (2), 235-247.

Gottschalk, Earl (1988), "Prices for Collectible Automobiles Surge Amid Wave of Speculation and Nostalgia," *Wall Street Journal*, June 29, 25.

Gotelli, Dolph (1988), "Santa Claus as a Collectible," paper presented at Popular Culture Association meetings, New Orleans, March.

Gould, Leroy C., Andrew L. Walker, Lansing E. Crane, and Charles W. Lidz (1974), *Connections: Notes from the Heroin World*, New Haven, CT: Yale University Press.

Gould, Stephen J. (1979), "Mickey Mouse Meets Konrad Lorenz," *Natural History*, 88 (May), 20-24.

Greenspan, Stuart (1988), "Visual Obsessions: Am I Good Enough to Own This Painting?," *Avenue*, 12 (February), 88-94.

Hebdige, Dick (1988), *Hiding in the Light*, London: Routledge.

Herman, Tom (1990), "Drexel Now Toots Mugs, Baseball Caps With No Refunds," *Wall Street Journal*, March 26, B5D.

Herrmann, Frank (1972), *The English as Collectors: A Documentary Chrestomanthy*, London: Chatto & Windus.

Hillier, Bevis (1981), "Why Do We Collect Antiques", *Our Pasts Before Us: Why Do We Save It?*, David Lowenthal and Marcus Binney, eds., London: Temple Smith, 70-82.

Hirsch, Julia (1981). *Family Photographs: Content, Meaning, and Effect*. New York: Oxford University Press.

Hodgen, Margaret T. (1964), *Early Anthropology in the Sixteenth and Seventeenth Centuries*, Philadelphia: University of Pennsylvania Press.

Holbrook, Morris B. (1988a), "The Psychoanalytic Interpretation of Consumer Behavior: *I Am an Animal*," *Research in Consumer Behavior*, 3, 149-178.

Holbrook, Morris B. (1988b), "Steps Toward a Psychoanalytic Interpretation of Consumption: A Meta-Meta-Meta-Analysis of Some Issues Raised by the Consumer Behavior Odyssey," in *Advances in Consumer Research*, Vol. 15, ed. Michael J. Houston, Provo: Association for Consumer Research, 537-542.

Humphrey, Nicholas K. (1979), "The Biological Basis of Collecting," *Human Nature* (February), 44-47.

Humphrey, Nicholas K. (1983), *Consciousness Regained: Chapters in the Development of Mind*, Oxford: Oxford University Press.

Impey, Oliver and Arthur MacGregor (eds.) (1985), *The Origins of Museums: The Cabinet of Curiosities in Sixteenth- and Seventeenth-Century Europe*, Oxford: Clarendon Press.

Jenike, Michael A. (1986), "Illnesses Related to Obsessive-Compulsive Disorder," in *Obsessive-Compulsive Disorders: Theory and Management*, eds. Michael A. Jenike, Lee Baer, and William E. Minichielle, Littleton, MA: PSG Publishing, 133-145.

Jensen, Jens (1963), "Collector's Mania," *Acta Psychiatrica Scandinavia*, 39 (4), 606-618.

Jobst, Helga (1978), "Freud and Archaeology," *Sigmund Freud House Bulletin*, 2 (1), 46-49.

Johnson, Ragnar (1986), "Accumulation and Collecting: An Anthropological Perspective," *Art History*, 9 (March), 73-83.

Johnson, Robert A. (1983), *We: Understanding the Psychology of Romantic Love*, San Francisco, CA: Harper and Row.

Johnson, Robert (1990), "Classic 'Muscle Cars' Replace Model T's as Hot Collectibles," *Wall Street Journal*, March 20, A1, A9.

Johnston, Susanna and Tim Bedlow (1986), *Collecting: The Passionate Pastime*, New York: Harper & Row.

Joline, Adrian H. (1902), *Meditations of an Autograph Collector*, New York: Harper.

Jones, Barclay G. (1986), "Experiencing Loss," in Barclay G. Jones, ed., *Protecting Historic Architecture and Museum Collections from Natural Disasters*, Boston, MA: Letter to Butterworths.

Jones, Ernest (1955), *The Life and Work of Sigmund Freud*, Vol. 2, New York: Basic Books, 393.

Jung, Carl Gustav (1921/1971), *Psychological Types*, trans. R. F. C. Hull, Bollingen Series 20, Princeton, NJ: Princeton University Press.

Jurnovoy, Joyce and David Jenness (1987), *American on Display*, New York: Facts on File Publication.

Kaplan, Wendy (1982), "R. T. H. Halsey: An Ideology of Collecting American Decorative Arts," *Winterthur Portfolio*, 17 (Spring), 43-53.

Kaylan, Melik (1988), "The Warhol Collection: Why Selling it is a Shame," *Connoisseur*, 915 (April), 118-128.

Kelly, Robert F. (1986), "Museums as Status Symbols II: Attaining a State of *Having Been*," in *Advances in Nonprofit Marketing*, ed. Russell W. Belk, Greenwich, CT: JAI Press.

Kilburn, David (1988), "Coca Cola Joins Japan's Prepaid Card Craze," *Advertising Age*, January 4, 22.

King, Arthur (1981), "Beyond Propensities: Towards a Theory of Addictive Consumption," in *The Changing Marketing Environment: New Theories and Applications*, eds. Kenneth Bernhardt, Ira Dolich, Michael Etzel, William Kehoe, Thomas Kinnear, William Perreault, Jr., Kenneth Roering, Chicago, IL: American Marketing Association, 438-440.

Kisly, Lorraine (1987), "Focus," *Parabola*, 12 (2), 2-3.

Klein, Frederick (1990), "Baseball Cards Worth a Mint," *Wall Street Journal*, February 2, A9.

Kline, Paule (1988), "Who, What, and Whys of Collecting," paper presented at Popular Culture Association meetings, New Orleans, March.

Kopytoff, Igor (1986), "The Cultural Biography of Things: Commoditization as Process," in *The Social Life of Things: Commodities in Cultural Perspective*, ed. Arjun Appadurai, Cambridge, MA: Cambridge University Press, 64-91.

Kozden, Sharon (1989), "Antiques and Collectibles: Childhood Revisited," *Antiques & Collecting*, 94 (December), 27, 55.

Krippendorff, Klaus (1989), "On the Essential Contexts of Artifacts or on the Proposition that 'Design is Making Sense (of Things)'," *Design Issues*, 5(2), 9-39.

Kron, Joan (1983), *Home-Psych: The Social Psychology of Home and Decoration*, New York: Clarkson N. Potter.

Kuspit, Donald (1989), "A Mighty Metaphor: The Analogy of Archaeology and Psychoanalysis," *Sigmund Freud and Art: His Personal Collection of Antiquities*, Lynn Gamwell and Richard Wells, eds., Binghamton, NY: State University of New York, Binghamton, 133-151.

Landis, Dylan (1990a) "Collecting in the '90s," *Chicago Tribune*, March 25, Sec. 15, 6.

Landis, Dylan (1990b) "Uneasy Pieces," Chicago Tribune, February 25, Sec. 15, 1, 4-5.

Lang, Alan R. (1983), "Addictive Personality: A Viable Construct?" in *Commonalities in Substance Abuse and Habitual Behavior*, eds. Peter K. Levison, Dean R. Gerstei, Deborah R. Maloff, Lexington, MA: Lexington, 157-235.

Laughlin, Henry P. (1956), "The Soteria: The Converse of the Phobia," *The Neuroses in Clinical Practice*, Henry P. Laughlin, Philadelphia: W. B. Saunders, 198-207.

Lehman, Harvey C. and Paul Witty (1927), *The Psychology of Play Activities*, New York: Barnes.

Lehrer, Jim (1990), "And Now, A Word of Praise for the Pack Rats Among Us," *Smithsonian*, 20 (March), 58-67).

Leptich, John (1989), "Counterfeit Baseball Cards Aren't Flooding the Market, But They Do Exist," *Chicago Tribune*, June 18, Section 3, 15.

Lynswander, Linda (1980), "Collecting: It's A Good Return on Your Investment," *Drug Topics*, October 1, 75-80.

Marlatt, G. Alan, John S. Baer, Dennis M. Donovan, and Daniel R. Kivlahan (1988), "Addictive Behaviors: Etiology and Treatment," *Annual Review of Psychology*, 39, 223-252.

Mascia-Lees, Frances E., Patricia Sharpe, and Colleen Ballerino Cohen (1989), "The Postmodernist Turn in Anthropology: Cautions from a Feminist Perspective," *Signs*, 15 (1), 7-33.

Maslow, Abraham (1968), *Toward a Psychology of Being*, second edition, New York: Van Nostrand.

McClelland, David (1971), *The Achieving Society*, Princeton, NJ: Van Nostrand.

McCracken, Grant (1988a), "Lois Roget: Curatoircal Consumer on a Modern World," in *Culture and Consumption*, Bloomington, IN: Indiana University Press, 44-53.

McCracken, Grant (1988b), "The Evocative Power of Things: Consumer Goods and the Preservation of Hopes and Ideals" in *Culture and Consumption*, Bloomington, IN: Indiana University Press, 104-117.

McKinnon, Gary F., Milton E. Smith, and H. Keith Hunt (1985), "Hoarding Behavior Among Consumers: Conceptualization and Marketing Implications," *Journal of the Academy of Marketing Science*, 13 (2), 340-351.

McNally, Terrence (1989), *The Lisbon Traviata*, directed by John Tillinger, Manhattan Theatre Club, New York, NY: Promenade Theatre.

Mechling, Jay (1989), "The Collecting Self and American Youth Movements," *Consuming Visions: Accumulation and Display of Goods in America, 1889-1920*, Simon J. Bronner, ed., New York: W. W. Norton, 255-285.

Menninger, William C. (1942), "Psychological Aspects of Hobbies," *American Journal of Psychiatry*, 99 (July), 122-129.

Meyer, Karl E. (1973), *The Plundered Past*, New York: Atheneum.

Michaels, Walter B. (1985), "The Gold Standard and the Logic of Naturalism," *Representations*, 9 (Winter), 105-132.

Mick, David and Michelle DeMoss (1990), "To Me From Me: A Descriptive Phenomenology of Self Gifts" *Advances in Consumer Research*, Vol. 17, Marvin E. Goldberg, Gerald Gorn, and Richard W. Pollay, eds., Provo, UT: Association for Consumer Research, 677-682.

Miller, Daniel (1988), "Appropriating the State on the Council Estate," *Man*, 23, 353-372.

Miller, Pamela (1982), "Hair Jewelry as Fetish," *Objects of Special Devotion: Fetishism in Popular Culture*, Ray B. Browne, ed., Bowling Green, OH: Bowling Green University Popular Press, 89-106.

Millership, Peter (1989), "Teddy Bears With Pedigrees Command Royal Prices," *Chicago Tribune*, December 24, Section 5, 6.

Mollenhoff, Fritz (1939), "Remarks on the Popularity of Mickey Mouse," *American Imago*, 1 (3), 19-32.

Money, John (1980), *Love and Sickness: The Science of Sex, Gender Difference, and Pair-Bonding*, Baltimore, MD: The Johns Hopkins University Press.

Moulin, Raymonde (1967/1987), *The French Art Market: A Sociological View*, Arthur Goldhammer, trans., New Brunswick, Rutgers University Press.

Mullaney, Steven, "Strange Things, Gross Terms, Curious Customs: The Rehearsal of Cultures in the Late Renaissance," *Representations*, 1, 40-67.

n.a. (1988), "Surf Detergent Plans Giveaway at Ballparks," *Marketing News*, 22 (9), 2.

n.a. (1990), "Socially Responsible Collecting," *Mother Jones*, January, 48.

Nason, James (1987), "The Determination of Significance: Curatorial Research and Private Collections," in *Material Anthropology: Contemporary Approaches to Material Culture*, eds. Barrie Reynolds and Margaret Stott, New York: University Press of America, 31-67.

Nathan, Peter E. (1980), "Etiology and Process in the Addictive Behaviors," in *The Addictive Behaviors*, ed. William R. Miller, New York: Pergammon Press, 241-263.

Neal, Arminta (1980), "Collecting for History Museums: Reassembling Our Splintered Existence, *Museum News*, 58 (May/June), 24-29.

Nichols, Deborah L., Anthony L. Klesert, and Roger Anyon (1989), "Ancestral Sites, Shrines, and Graves: Native American Perspectives on the Ethics of Collecting Cultural Properties," *The Ethics of Collecting Cultural Property: Whose Culture? Whose Property?*, Phyllis Mauch Messenger, ed., Albuquerque, NM: University of New Mexico Press, 26-39.

Novey, Theodore B. and Pat R. Novey (1987), "Clutter: Some Considerations on the Effects of Increasing Entropy in Human Relationships and Environments," *Transactional Analysis Journal*, 17 (October), 146-151.

O'Brien, George (1981), "Living with Collections," *New York Times Magazine*, April 26, Part 2, 25-42.

O'Guinn, Thomas C. and Ronald J. Faber (1989), "Compulsive Buying: A Phenomenological Exploration," *Journal of Consumer Research*, 16 (2), 147-157.

Olmsted, Al D. (1987a), "Gun Collectors and Gun Collecting: A Morally Controversial Social World," paper presented at the Popular Culture Association Annual Meeting, Montreal, March.

Olmsted, Al D. (1987b), "Stamp Collectors and Stamp Collecting," paper presented at Popular Culture Association Annual Meeting, Montreal, March.

Olmsted, Al D. (1988a), "Collectors and Collecting," paper presented at the Popular Culture Association Annual Meeting, New Orleans.

Olmsted, Al D. (1988b), "Morally Controversial Leisure: The Social World of Gun Collectors," *Symbolic Interaction*, 11 (2), Norman K. Denzin, ed., Greenwich, CT: JAI Press, 277-287.

Olmsted, Al D. (1989), "Pin Traders at the 1988 Calgary Winter Olympics," paper presented at Popular Culture Association Meeting, St. Louis.

Olmsted, Al D. (forthcoming), "Gun Collecting in Western Canada: The Influence of Popular Culture and History," *The Gun Culture and Its Enemies*, William R. Tonso, ed., Indianapolis, IN: Merrill.

Owen, David (1988), "The Museum of Failed Products," *USAir*, July, 61-65.

Parsons, Talcott (1951), *The Social System*, New York: The Free Press.

Paton, W. D. M. (1988), "Bibliomania: A Clinical Case Study," *Book Collector*, 37 (2), 207-224.

Payne, Judy (1988), "Hairweaving: An Example of Material Culture," paper presented at: Popular Culture Association Annual Conference, New Orleans, March.

Pearson, Anthony (1987), "The Grateful Dead Phenomenon," *Youth & Society*, 18 (4), 418-422.

Peele, Stanton and Archie Brodsky (1975), *Love and Addiction*, New York: New American Library.

Peele, Stanton (1985), *The Meaning of Addiction*, Lexington, MA: Lexington Books.

Peers, Alexandra (1988), "Forget Stocks; Invest in George Patton, Old Lunch Boxes and 'Good Luck Charm,'" *Wall Street Journal*, March 2, p. 25.

Pereira, Joseph (1989), "After 25 years, Toy Maker Enjoys Fortune of Soldier," *Wall Street Journal*, February 6, A1;.A5.

Phillips, Richard H. (1962), "The Accumulator," *Archives of General Psychiatry*, 6 (June), 96-99.

Praz, Mario (1964), *An Illustrated History of Furnishing from the Renaissance to the Twentieth Century*, New York: Brazeller.

Ransohoff, Rita (1975), "Sigmund Freud: Collector of Antiquities: Student of Archaeology," *Archaeology* 28 (2), 102-111.

Read, Eileen (1990), "One-Stop Shopping for Rock-and-Roll Memorabilia," *Wall Street Journal*, April 26, p. A14.

Reid, Dixie (1988), "And the truly bizarre winner is ..." *Sacramento Bee*, E1.

Rheims, Maurice (1961), *Art on the Market: Thirty-Five Centuries of Collecting and Collectors from Midas to Paul Getty*, David Pryce-Jones, trans., London: Weidenfeld and Nicolson, also published as *The Strange Life of Objects: 35 Centuries of Art Collecting and Collectors*, New York: Atheneum, 1961.

Rigby, Douglas and Elizabeth Rigby (1944), *Lock, Stock and Barrel: The Story of Collecting*, Philadelphia: J. B. Lippincott.

Rochberg-Halton, Eugene (1979), "The Meaning of Personal Art Objects," *Social Research and Cultural Policy*, Jiri Zuzanek, ed., Waterloo, ON: Otium, 155-181.

Rowed, Charles (1920), *Collecting as a Pastime*, London: Caswell.

Saarinen, Aline B. (1958), *The Proud Possessors: The Lives, Times and Tastes of Some Adventurous American Art Collectors*, New York: Random House.

Sachs, Hanns (1945), *Freud: Master and Friend*, London: Imago.

Saisselin, Rémy G. (1984), *Bricobracomania: The Bourgeois and the Bibelot*, New Brunswick: Rutgers University Press.

Salzman, Leon (1980), "The Neurotic Compromise of Addiction," in *Addiction--Theory and Treatment: New Approaches to an Old Problem*, eds. George D. Goldman and Donald S. Milman, Dubuque, IA: Kendall/Hunt Publishing, 3-20.

Sandor, Richard S. (1987) "A Physician's Journey," *Parabola*, 12 (2), 16-23.

Schaef, Anne Wilson (1987), *When Society Becomes an Addict*, San Francisco, CA: Harper and Row.

Schiffer, Michael B., Theodore E. Downing, and Michael McCarthy (1981), "Waste Not, Want Not: An Ethnoarchaeological Study of Reuse in Tucson, Arizona," in *Modern Material Culture: The Archaeology of Us*, eds. Michael Gould and Michael B. Schiffer, New York: Academic Press.

Schwartz Emanuel K. and Alexander Wolf (1958), "The Quest for Certainty," *A.M.A. Archives of Neurology & Psychiatry*, 81 (January), 69-84.

Seigel, Ronald (1989), *Intoxication: Life in Pursuit of Artificial Paradise*, New York: E.P. Dutton.

Sherry, John F., Jr. (1990a), "A Sociocultural Analysis of a Midwestern American Flea Market," *Journal of Consumer Research*, 17 June, 13-30.

Sherry, John F., Jr. (1990b), "Dealers and Dealing in a Periodic Market: 'Informal' Retailing in Ethnographic Perspective," *Journal of Retailing*, 66 (Summer), 174-200.

Sherry, John F., Jr. and Mary Ann McGrath (1989), "Unpacking the Holiday Presence: A Comparative Ethnography of Two Gift Stores," *Interpretive Consumer Research*, Elizabeth Hirschman, ed., Provo, UT: Association for Consumer Research, 148-167.

Silver, Stu (1987), *Throw Momma From the Train*, produced by Larry Brezner, directed by Danny DeVito, New York: Orion Pictures.

Simmel, Georg (1907/1971), "The Miser and the Spendthrift," *Georg Simmel: On Individuality and Social Forms*, Donald N. Levine, ed., Chicago: University of Chicago Press.

Singh, Martand (1988), "The Obsession of Collecting: A Comment," *India Magazine*, 9 (December), 86-87.

Smith, Janet Adam (1988), "Books in My Life," *Book Collector*, 37 (Winter), 479-502.

Smith, J. C. P. and M. J. Apter (1977), "Collecting Antiques: A Psychological Interpretation," *Antique Collector*, 48 (7), 64-66.

Smith, Robin (1986), "Television Addiction," in *Perspectives on Media Effects*, eds. Jennings Bryant and Dolf Zillmann, Hillsdale, NJ: Lawrence Erlbaum Associates, 109-128.

Snyder, C. R. and Howard L. Fromkin (1980), *Uniqueness: The Human Pursuit of Difference*, New York: Plenum Press.

Soroka, Michael P. (1988), "In Heaven There is No Beer, That's Why We Collect it Here," paper presented at Popular Culture Association meetings, New Orleans, March.

Spector, Jack (1975), "Dr. Sigmund Freud, Art Collector," *Art News*, (April), 20-26.

Spignesi, Angelyn (1983), *Starving Women: A Psychology of Anorexia Nervosa*, Dallas, TX: Spring Publications.

Spitz, Ellen II. (1989), "Psychoanalysis and the Legacies of Antiquity," *Sigmund Freud and Art: His Personal Collection of Antiquities*, Lynn Gamwell and Richard Wells, eds., Binghamton, NY: State University of New York, Binghamton, 152-171.

Stebbins, Robert A. (1979), *Amateurs: On the Margin Between Work and Leisure*, Beverly Hills, CA: Sage.

Stebbins, Robert A. (1982), "Serious Leisure: A Conceptual Statement," *Pacific Sociological Review*, 25 (April), 251-272.

Stenross, Barbara (1987), "The Meaning of Guns: Shooters, Hunters, and Collectors," paper presented at Association for Popular Culture Annual Meeting, Montreal, March.

Stewart, Susan (1984), *On Longing: Narratives of the Miniature, the Gigantic, the Souvenir, the Collection*, Baltimore, MD: Johns Hopkins University Press.

Stillinger, Elizabeth (1980), *The Antiquers: The Lives and Careers, the Deals, the Finds, the Collections of the Men and Women who were Responsible for the Changing Taste in American Antiques, 1850-1930*, New York: Alfred A. Knopf.

Storr, Anthony (1983), "The Psychology of Collecting," *Connoisseur*, 213 (June), 35-38.

Stout, Hilary (1990), "Selling American," *Wall Street Journal*, July 10, A1,A10.

Sumption, Jonathan (1975), *Pilgrimage: An Image of Mediaeval Religion*, London: Faber & Faber.

Sutker, Patricia B. and Albert N. Allain, Jr. (1988), "Issues in Personality Conceptualizations of Addictive Behaviors," *Journal of Consulting and Clinical Psychology*, 56 (2), 172-182.

Taylor, Francis H. (1948), *The Taste of Angels: A History of Art Collecting From Rameses to Napoleon*, Boston: Little, Brown.

Time (1989), "Bubble Gun Not Included," *Time*, 134 (July 17), 77.

Torgovnick, Marianna (1990), "Entering Freud's Study," *Gone Primitive: Savage Intelects, Modern Lives*, Chicago: University of Chicago Press, 194-209.

Trachtenber, Jeffre (1990), "Antique Fishing Bait is Making Investors of Nostalgic Anglers," *Wall Street Journal*, April 16, A1,A7.

Travis, Russell (1988), "Why People Collect: Motivational Tendencies and the Addiction Factor," paper presented at Popular Culture Association meetings, New Orleans, March.

Treas, Charles E. and Dalton E. Brannen (1976), "The Growing Collector Market," *Proceedings*, Atlanta, GA: Southern Marketing Association, 234-236.

Tuan, Yi-Fu (1978). *Space and Place: The Perspective of Experience*. Minneapolis, MN: University of Minnesota Press.

Tuan, Yi-Fu (1986). *The Good Life*. Madison, WI: University of Wisconsin Press.

Unruh, David R. (1983), *Invisible Lives: Social Worlds of the Aged*, Beverly Hills, CA: Sage.

Urry, John (1990), "The Consumption of Tourism," *Sociology* 24 (1), 23-35.

von Holst, Niels (1967), *Creators, Collectors, and Connoisseurs: An Anatomy of Artistic Taste from Antiquity to the Present Day*, New York: G. P. Putnam's Sons.

Walter, Eugene (1988), *Placeways: A Theory of the Human Environment*, Chapel Hill: University of North Carolina Press.

Walker, Andrew L. and Charles W. Lidz (1983), "Common Features of Troublesome Habitual Behaviors: A Cultural Approach," *Commonalities in Substance Abuse and Habitual Behavior*, Peter K. Levinson, Dean R. Gerstein, and Deborah R. Maloff, eds., Lexington, MA: Lexington Press, 29-44.

Warren, Lynda W. and Jonnae C. Ostrom (1988), "Pack Rats: World-Class Savers," *Psychology Today*, 22 (February), 58-62.

Wartzman, Rick (1990), "I Will Swap You a '52 Mickey Mantle for your '85 Buick," *Wall Street Journal*, May 11, A1, A4.

White, Robert W. (1959), "Motivation Reconsidered: The Concept of Competence," *Psychological Review*, 66 (5), 297-333.

Whitley, M. T. (1929), "Children's Interest in Collecting," *Journal of Educational Psychology*, 20, 249-261.

Wicklund, Robert A. and Peter M. Gollwitzer (1986), *Symbolic Self Completion*, Hillsdale, NJ: Lawrence Erlbaum.

Williams, Tennessee (1945/1984), *The Glass Menagerie*, Harmondsworth, Middlesex, England: Penguin.

Winston, Gordon (1980), "Addiction and Backsliding: A Theory of Compulsive Consumption," *Journal of Economic Behavior and Organization*, December, 297-324.

Wittlin, Alma S. (1970), *Museums: In Search of a Usable Future*, Cambridge, MA: MIT Press.

Witty, Paul A. and Harvey C. Lehman (1930), "Further Studies of Children's Interest in Collecting," *Journal of Educational Psychology*, 21, 112-127.

Witty, Paul A. and Harvey C. Lehman (1931), "Sex Differences: Collecting Interests," *Journal of Educational Psychology*, 22, 221-228.

Woodman, Marion (1982), *Addiction to Perfection: The Still Unravished Bride*, Toronto, ON: Inner City Books.

Wright, Richard (1989), "Front and Center," *Chicago Tribune*, July 9, Section 17, 1.

Yates, Alayne, Kevin Leebey, and Catherine M. Shisslak (1983), "Running--An Analogue of Anorexia?" *The New England Journal of Medicine*, 308 (5), 251-255.

Yin, Robert K. (1990), *Case Study Research: Design and Methods*, 2nd ed., Applied Social Research Methods Series, Vol. 5, Newbury Park, CA: Sage.

Yoshihashi, Pauline (1990), "Rare Document Field Sees Prices Spiral As a New Breed of Collector Signs On," *Wall Street Journal*, July 6, B1, B3.

Beyond the Odyssey: Interpretations of Ethnographic Writing in Consumer Behavior

Annamma Joy[1]

ABSTRACT

The literature on the use of naturalistic inquiry in consumer behavior focuses primarily on the researcher and the research process, although the ethnographic account and the reader are often implied. The focus of this paper is on the crafting of such interpretive accounts - realist, confessional, impressionist and jointly constructed. It is argued that ethnographic accounts are not only interpretations of a culture but texts that raise theoretical, philosophical, and epistemological issues. Ethnographies question some of the underlying principles of what is known in the field of consumer behavior and our ways of knowing. By using alternate frameworks and methodologies, they create the "other" in order to understand the "self." In consumer behavior, this has led to the critical evaluation of core concepts such as consumer loyalty and consumer involvement. Selected works in consumer behavior are examined insofar as they deal with issues of interpretation.

The last few years have witnessed both ideological and intellectual ferment in consumer behavior over what constitutes knowledge and how it is generated, interpreted, and generalized across situations (Anderson 1983; Belk, Sherry & Wallendorf 1988; Belk, Wallendorf & Sherry 1989; Hirschman 1986; Holbrook, 1987a, Holbrook, Bell & Grayson 1989; Hudson & Ozanne 1988; McCracken 1988; Mick 1986; Sherry 1987a, 1988; Stern 1990). To date, there are very few publications in the *Journal of Consumer Research* that use naturalistic inquiry[2] (although Sherry & Camargo 1987 predates the Odyssey project), and doubts remain in some scholars' minds as to the usefulness of such alternate paradigms and research techniques in the field of consumer behavior. There is some unease about such deconstruction processes[3] where knowledge creation and dissemination become the focus of analysis (Anderson 1986; Holbrook 1989).

Since the consumer behavior Odyssey Project (Kassarjian 1987), there has been a concerted effort to use alternate methodologies to understand consumption patterns, processes, and meanings (Arnould 1989; Belk, Sherry & Wallendorf 1988; Belk, Wallendorf & Sherry 1989; Hirschman 1989; Sherry & McGrath 1989). Without exception, all these accounts have questioned some of the underlying premises of what is known in the field of consumer behavior and our ways of knowing. They have used the ethnographic mode to rethink some key concepts and revise many of our long-held assumptions. This process of questioning our established ways of thinking is referred to in anthropology as "defamiliarization"[4] (Marcus & Fischer 1986:138). In consumer behavior, for instance, Belk, Wallendorf & Sherry (1989) do this in their study of the sacred aspects of consumption. They state that revelatory incidents directly experienced by the researchers caused them to reevaluate some of the field's fundamental constructs for understanding marketplace and consumer behavior. They provide three examples of such revelatory vignettes and explain that (1989:2),

---

[1]The author wishes to thank John Sherry, Melanie Wallendorf, Gary Johns, V. Baba, and Russ Belk for answering questions, and providing valuable insights to improve the manuscript.

[2]Belk, Sherry and Wallendorf (1988) define *naturalistic inquiry* as a set of methods that are used in a natural occurring context, which are typically qualitative and represent a systematic set of procedures for assessing the credibility of the findings.

[3]*Deconstruction* is an approach to literary interpretation which suggests that texts can generate a variety of meanings over and above what is intended. Further, the meaning of a text is generated by what it says as well as what it does (Stern 1990).

[4]Defamiliarization is a term used by anthropologists to critique our own culture, by examining the form and content of ethnographies written about cultures other than our own (Marcus & Fischer 1986:138). The authors describe two ways of doing so - through cross-cultural juxtaposition and through epistemological critique. The former makes use of data from other cultural contexts to probe and describe cultural reality at home. Defamiliarization by epistmological critique is more abstract and refers to the process by which knowledge generated on the periphery of a Eurocentric world can be brought back to examine the assumptions at the centre. This helps us to realize the culturally constructed and arbitrary nature of other societies as well as our own.

Highways and Buyways © *1991*
Association for Consumer Research

Each of these vignettes reflects a dimension of a buyer and seller world previously undescribed in consumer research. Each is an example of the ritual substratum of consumer behavior. These observations make it apparent that consumption involves more than the means by which people meet their everyday needs. Consumption can become a vehicle for transcendant experience; that is, consumer behavior exhibits certain aspects of the sacred.

The focus of this paper is on the crafting of such interpretive accounts whether they are narratives of one's own culture or of cultures other than one's own. Further, this paper incorporates some of the insights provided by feminist discourse that poses new challenges to the writing of ethnographies at home and abroad. Since the consumer behavior odyssey project was confined geographically to the U.S. the ethnographic narratives linked to this project primarily consider issues relating to the "self" and "other" in the context of one's own culture. Consequently gender concerns or cross-cultural issues are only peripherally raised. To fill this gap, I examine at some length Arnould's (1989) study of consumption in Zinder, Niger Republic, (cross-cultural) as well as Sherry & McGrath's (1989) comparative ethnography of two gift stores (Feminist discourse). In addition, I also make references to a few other ethnographies that help in elucidating key issues raised in this account.

While ethnographic writing is still in its infancy in consumer research, researchers, some of whom have training in fields with long histories of ethnography and case studies, have veered rapidly toward such rich documentation processes (Wallendorf & Belk 1989). It is my contention that the creation and production of the text is the logical outcome of the hermeneutic process[5] and should be given importance not only because it plays a major role in the dissemination of knowledge but because it raises ethical, political, and epistemological issues. One of the central concerns of this paper is to argue that by not reflecting on the text-writing process or on the reading of the text, we objectify the text. This self-reflexivity is central to the claims made by the naturalistic mode of inquiry (Belk et.al. 1988, 1989). Thus

the four components - the researcher, the research process, the reader, and the text - are inextricably entwined, and no one factor can be considered without the other. However, this form of demystification need not be confined to accounts using a naturalistic mode of inquiry but must be applied to texts written in a positivist mode as well.

There is a danger, however, in focusing on the textualization process.[6] Post-modernist[7] accounts suggest that writing is autonomous and that we can talk about the "other" without situating the discourse in a political context (Polier & Roseberry 1989). This approach contains an interesting blindspot - it refuses to be self-reflexive, even though it elevates the process of self-reflexivity[8] (Rabinow 1986:250). The very same argument is applicable to this paper as well. While I have had the opportunity to receive feedback from some of the consumer researchers whose works I have selected I, as the author, have the final say. The attempt at

_____

[5]*Hermeneutics* refers to the theory of interpretation that is based on a subjective understanding and significance of human actions, utterances, products, and institutions. It is associated with philosophical attempts to investigate the human condition and the nature of human existence.

_____

[6]*Textualization* is a term used by Ricouer (1973) to refer to the process by which unwritten behavior, beliefs, and practices become coded and classified as data, which then forms the basis for interpretation. It is embodied in field notes kept by researchers. It is thus at least once removed from the immediate situation in which the ethnographer participates.

[7]*Post Modernism* is a feature associated with advanced captalist societies and is a controversial term referring to experimental tendencies in the arts, social sciences, and architecture since the 40's. It is confusing as a term, since it suggests that modernism is over; yet what are characterized as sucessor movements are dependent on what has gone before (Mascia-Lees et al 1989). The post-modern condition is devoid of authority, unity, continuity, purpose, and commitment. In its place, there is rupture, fragmentation, and crisis (Marcus & Fischer 1986).

[8]*Self-Reflexivity* is a term commonly used by anthropologists to refer to the consideration of the "self" in the interpretive process. It arises out of the concerns with ways of knowing as presented in positivist philosophy and language. The "self" in such discourse, although recognized, is minimal and unintrusive. Hermeneutics challenges this notion of the neutral or objective self and consciously draws it into the research process such that knowing is contingent on the knower. The self thus becomes a vehicle of meaning transfer.

using a dialogic mode[9] remains partial because of the authorial voice I use.

To write a piece such as this at a critical time in the history of consumer behavior is also to highlight the political processes - at both a macro and a micro level. The macro level has already been alluded to in terms of discussing paradigm diversity arising out of dissatisfaction with existing theories and explanations (Anderson 1986; Firat, Dholakia and Bagozzi 1987; Holbrook 1989). At the micro level, power relations involve the university community and the publication process that includes informant readings prior to publication, editorial control, and the review process (Sherry 1988). Any discussion of interpretive textualization cannot be understood out of the social contexts of knowledge production (Crick 1982; Flacks & Turkel 1978).

In what is to follow, I explore, through a close reading of the ways in which each author has constructed the text, the ways that selected authors using the ethnographic mode arrive at their conclusions. It is subjective in that it is one reader's interpretation of the texts. Yet any interpretation is also a socially located activity and involves selecting the elements to be included, translating these elements into standard parts, and then arranging them into a text (Becker 1986). Such a process does not occur in a vacuum but follows from the conventions of a collective tradition - in this case, an anthropological/feminist approach. While the ethnographic mode is alive and well in sociology, and eminently applicable to consumer behavior, this paper focuses primarily on anthropological texts.

WHAT IS AN ETHNOGRAPHY?

An ethnography is a written account that arises out of fieldwork rather than from the description of the fieldwork[10] experience

itself (Marcus & Fischer 1986). It is the systematic description of a culture, based on first-hand observation. There are two facets to this - the actual observation and collection of data; and the transformation of such knowledge into the text. The written account of fieldwork in some form in the text is what distinguishes an ethnographic account from all others.

The writing of the ethnographic text has moral and ethical implications, since writing about other cultures involves participation in the culture, and first-hand knowledge of a culture belies any form of neutrality. Ethnographic accounts point to the numerous ways of defining what it is to be human. More recently, ethnography has been a way of talking about theory, philosophy, and epistemology while maintaining the traditional task of interpreting different ways of life (Marcus & Fischer 1986). One of the ways in which this is accomplished is by the conscious examination of "self" vis-a-vis the "other."[11] This "other" could be either one's own culture or a different one. In trying to explain differences however great or small, ethnographers have to deal with complex relations between their cultural constructions of reality and those of others.

How can these concepts of "self" and "other" be applied to consumer behavior? At a very general level, the "other" can be applied to the study of consumption in our own society as well as to those that are different from our own. In the first instance, we make the familiar strange; and in the second, we make the strange familiar. At another level, the "self" refers to constructs and methods that are dominant in the field (for instance, the construct of consumer involvement understood through a positivist mode of inquiry). This familiar construct can be made strange by subjecting it to scrutiny and re-

---

[9]The *dialogical mode* is used in ethnographic accounts that are jointly constructed. It provides cultural materials that are elicited in the interaction between informant and researcher and depends on the representation of the actual discourse of fieldwork (Marcus & Cushman 1982:43).

[10]*Fieldwork* refers to the systematic, first-hand participant observation and in-depth interviews that are conducted by researchers in the field. Prolonged contact and linguistic competence are generally considered necessary to the creation of an ethnographic account. Field notes and a field journal are systematically kept as tools for self-reflection, observation, and interpretation. They are the preliminary steps to the interpretive process.

[11]The terms *"other"* and *"otherness"* have been used extensively in the sociological and anthropological literature (Marcus & Fischer 1986). "Self" and "other" are seen as inhabiting the same world, although the "Other" lives a separate life, with its own centre distinct from the "self." The attempt in phenomenological understanding is to focus on the similarities of the self and other that make mutual understanding possible. Putting oneself in the shoes of another allows one to see the similarites between one's own behavior and that of the other. A particular twist to this process of understanding involves making the other strange. In other words, knowledge of the other is possible only through further defamiliarization of the strange or unfamiliar as part of the other.

analysis using a naturalistic mode of inquiry. Such an exposure to deconstruction and reconstruction of the meaning of this construct through an alternate framework brings forth new recognition and newer understanding.

Belk, Wallendorf & Sherry (1989:3) provide some insights into this process. They state, with reference to the use of naturalistic inquiry,

> This approach differs from surveys or experiments which assume that the researcher understands the phenomenon prior to doing the research, so that hypothesis and fully specified data collection and analysis plans are possible. In naturalistic inquiry, no such assumption is made. Instead, researchers build an understanding of the phenomenon as it occurs in situ, later testing the veracity of that understanding also in situ.

Later (p.31), regarding the construct of involvement, they observe,

> Involvement has been glossed as focused activation (Cohen 1983), whether its duration is situational or enduring (Bloch & Richins 1983). Even when it has been considered as more than merely repeat purchase, loyalty is reduced to a function of decision-making, utilitarian, evaluative processes (Jacoby & Kyner 1973)...We have described the sacred and the profane as conceptual categories that animate consumer behaviors. We have incorporated the spirit of these constructs into a more inclusive and culturally grounded process in which consumers routinely harness the forces of material and mental culture to achieve transcendent experience.

In reading a text, a person understands it not only in terms of his/her own individual concerns but also as a collective effort. Reading is a learned and socially organized activity (Becker 1986; Peterson 1976). As an anthropologist I am familiar with the set of conventions that has been used in interpreting a text. These conventions were developed over time and have changed over the years through debate over the problems of representation and interpretation (Becker 1986). When changes are made in conventions, it suggests that the authoritative voices of the past have been replaced by those of a new interpretive community. The political dimension in the interpretive process is thus crucial.

That being said, I must identify the conventions that I used to read and interpret the ethnographic texts presented below. For these purposes I rely heavily on articles by Marcus & Cushman (1982), by Flax (1987) and Strathern (1987), although I have developed my own style of reading and interpretation. On my first reading, I form a general impression of the text. In my subsequent readings, I flesh out the salient features identified in my first reading.

Salient Characteristics of Ethnographic Accounts

1. Its particular genre - realist, confessional, impressionist or jointly constructed.
2. The location of fieldwork, duration, number of researchers, reasons and choice of locale(s), references to establishing rapport, conditions of fieldwork, linguistic competence (if applicable), choice of key informants, methods used to gather data, as well as references to field notes and journals on which the account is based.
3. Organization of the text. How does the author establish a narrative presence? How does s/he present the problem (event, ritual, concept) and how is it analyzed? What stance does the author take on the subject?
4. Documentation on any prolonged contact with informants through revisits.
6. Field experience. While the writer may choose to exclude what happens in the field, the reader must be convinced that the writer presents a world that is known to him or her through first-hand experience. This includes not only written statements but maps, drawings, films, videos, and photographs as well.
7. Generalizations from particular sets of data. For instance are the cases presented for instance treated as "typical" or are they acknowledged for their individuality when the author tries to interpret them?
8. Linguistic competence in studying cultures other than one's own. I examine the ways the author uses contextual explications of native concepts in organizing the text.
9. The ways by which the author establishes his/her authority. In any interpretation, this means examining the individual's biases and prejudgments and the ways they are presented. How does the author

locate his/her study with interpretations that have gone before? What is the problem and how does it unfold? The concern here is with the story line and the fleshing out of the details. What point of view does the author take in narrating the story? Does the data presented stay close to the contexts from which the cultural materials are drawn or is it abstracted from the contexts in which it is elicited?

10. The form of cultural critique the text offers. Is it through cross-cultural comparison or through a critique of theory?

11. Gender implications - that is, the author's gender, the gender of the informants, and the types of questions that are asked that reflect gender concerns. This is very closely linked to the stance taken by the author(s). While this may not be critical to all texts, the sensitivity to such issues I consider crucial.

12. Closure, consistency, and formality of presentation.

13. Authenticity or plausibility of the explanation. I consider the sensitivity the author displays in presenting the informant's perspective. Does s/he use an "us-them" difference or a "me-they" form of contrast, and how is it presented in the text?

14. Audience. Is the author writing for a readership, some of whom are unfamiliar with this framework?

Having outlined the criteria I use for evaluating and interpreting an ethnographic account, I will now discuss the different genres available. They are expertly discussed by Van Maanen (1988), upon whose text I rely heavily for what is to follow.

Types of Ethnographic Texts

A historical description of ethnographic genres sets the stage for the examination of ethnographies in consumer behavior. Through these accounts, we have the benefit of knowledge that has gone before, thus providing a potentially greater variety of textual modes. Consumer ethnographies however combine elements of each of these genres while emphasizing one or the other.

Realist tales are documentary, are written in the third person, and make reference to typical individuals in the society under study. Ultimately what distinguishes this genre of ethnographic writing from others is the authoritativeness with which the fieldworker presents the culture. The formal rendition of the "I was there" narration

appears only in the introduction or the footnotes or the appendix. The informants and accounts are presented as abstract or ideal types, and the narrator fades into insignificance after the initial introduction (Marcus & Cushman 1982; Van Maanen 1988).

A modified attempt at realism is provided by Arnould (1989:241) in his study of consumption practises in Zinder, a province in the Niger Republic. He notes,

Data for this study comes from the author's fieldwork in Zinder province of the Niger Republic....Ethnographic data collection began in 1977 in several villages (Lepdo, Don Doukou, and Riga) and one urban neighborhood.....Multiple data sources (both quantitative and qualitative), constant working back and forth between hypotheses and reality tests of them, and intimate knowledge of a group's daily life earned through long-term participant observation provide internal validity checks on the data (Kirk and Miller 1986,pp.24-25). As in any discipline, peer review provides external validity checks for published material....For this study, formal interviews provided data about consumer behavior (Wallendorf & Arnould 1988).

Realist portrayals gave way to more conscious accounts of the encounter with other cultures and gave rise to *confessional* tales, written in the first person. They exist today, in a modified form. Confessional tales question the assumptions of objectivity in studying other cultures and, more importantly, attempt to deal with this issue in the writing of ethnography.

An example of a confessional is provided by Van Maanen (1988:83) in his study of the police. He writes,

Three rather personal and perhaps pivotal factors seem best to explain my particular choice to study the police. First, when I began thinking seriously of the police as a topic for research in the late Sixties, the police were prominently fixed in the imagery of the day....Second, however, not much seemed to be known about the police. Third, the available literature did not seem to square with my own random observations and run-ins with the police.

The Seventies witnessed a radical change in the role of ethnography and the importance of writing ethnographic accounts. In particular, *impressionist* tales made their appearance, exemplified by Geertz (1973). These writings were more reflexive, although episodic and complex, and reflected the tenuous nature of the link between researcher and informants (Van Maanen 1988).

The reader is aware of the nuances and subtleties of the culture as expressed in the vignettes of the ethnographer, establishing a rapport with the informants (Geertz 1973). The reader peeks over the narrator's shoulder much the way the narrator reads over the shoulders of informants in deciphering cultural principles. However, in this view, the independence of the text and its stable and structural properties are challenged. Detail and intimacy provide proximity between the ethnographer, the informant, and the cultures they each come from.

An excellent example of impressionist writing is evident in "the Balinese Cockfight." Geertz (1973:4) writes,

> In Bali, to be teased is to be accepted. It was the turning point so far as our relationship to the community was concerned and we were quite literally 'in.' ..Getting caught, or almost caught in a vice raid is perhaps not a very generalizable recipe for achieving that mysterious necessity of anthropological fieldwork, rapport, but for me it worked very well.

The process of editing informant voices out of the text has the effect of distancing the reader. Distancing lends authenticity to the text. Changes in the account are made in relation to prior knowledge and less from encounters in the field even in the skilled hands of Geertz (1973).

> What the cockfight says it says in a vocabulary of sentiment - the thrill of risk, the despair of loss, the pleasure of truimph...Attending cockfights and participating in them is, for the Balinese, a kind of sentimental education...If, to quote Northrop Frye again, we go to see Macbeth to learn what a man feels like after he has gained a kingdom and lost his soul, the Balinese go to find out what a man, usually composed and aloof, almost obsessively self-absorbed, a kind of moral autocosm, feels like when, attacked, tormented, challenged, insulted, and driven in result to the extremes of fury, he has totally truimphed or been brought totally low. The whole passage takes us back to Aristotle.

There are no exemplary impressionist narratives in consumer behavior although the article by Sherry & Camargo (1987:183) on

English language labelling in Japan provides some insights.

Marcus & Fischer (1986a) refer to the newer modes of impressionist tales as experimental ethnographies, or *jointly constructed tales*, which reflect on writing itself and the contrived nature of cultural accounts. These accounts use the dialogical mode, wherein the focus is on the actual discourse of fieldwork. They seriously question the substantiality and independence of the text and highlight the tenuous and collaborative nature of the ethnographic account (Crapanzano 1980; Clifford 1983, 1986a). They recognize the role of rhetoric in the persuasion process (Sangren 1988). Dwyer (1982:221) provides an interesting attempt to jointly produce a tale based on his fieldwork in Morocco. He writes,

> D: Now, I'd like you to think about this question. When I came here for the first time, when Bukhensha brought me here, what did you think then?
> A: I wasn't thinking anything. Just.. 'welcome,' that's all. What would be on my mind?
> D: You must have thought something.
> A: No

(Dwyer observes that this question leads to an immediate dead end. But since it is an important issue, he pursues it further.)

> D: Let's see - what did Bukhensha say to you then?
> A: Well, he said it in front of you: all things considered, this Rumi wants to come here and wants to rent your little room in the vilage. I have gotten to know him and I am making his concerns mine....

In consumer behavior, there are no exemplary accounts that use the dialogic mode, although Sherry (1990:33) provides some insights. The author introduces parts of the dialogue (not between himself and an informant as Dwyer does) that a consumer had with a vendor. He quotes,

> P: Will you take $10 for it?
> V: I'd feel like I was giving it away. I'd hate myself.
> P: I wouldn't hate you.
> V: I'd hate myself.
> P: I'll split the difference with you- $12.50
> V: What's it marked?
> P: $18
> V: Can't do it. I'll go [$] 14[00].
> P: Sorry, thanks.
> V: No, thank you.

The focus in such accounts is on using rhetorical devices rather than on rendering quoted speech. Inspired by the new literary criticism, these accounts show how rhetoric can be used to communicate the meaning of a text (Burke 1969). They also enhance the reader's understanding of the ethnographer's aim of communicating a point of view. Just as self-reflexivity regarding the role of the informant and researcher sharpened earlier renderings into meaningful accounts, the new rhetorical devices lend credence to the subversive possibility that the account is unstable, and indeterminate. But this must always be seen within a particular context.

Documenting culture is embedded in a specific way of creating knowledge. No text stands by itself; it is constructed within fields of power and privilege and must be seen as such (Mascia-Lees, Sharpe & Cohen 1989; Polier & Roseberry 1989:251). One way is to introduce elements of critical inquiry into the narrative, which becomes particularly important in cross-cultural contexts. A political economy framework, especially a feminist framework, provides insight into this process. *Critical tales* try to highlight the structural and historical connections among specific customs, institutions, or nations without adopting a normative commitment to social solidarity or stressing functional integration (Polier & Roseberry 1989:257).

To write about writing ethnographic accounts is itself a political process. In consumer behavior, the politicization of pluralism has been referred to as an unfolding drama - a clash of interests between paradigm bearers, the positivist, and post-positivist researchers (Thompson, Loccander & Pollio 1989; Sherry 1988; Belk 1990). The people have been identified, and critical incidents vary from the ACR presidential address to the Odyssey Project of 1986. While tensions mount, an impasse is avoided by reparation done to the situation, evidenced in major changes made to the *Journal of Consumer Research.* Sherry (1988) views this politicization process as a re-vitalization movement in the history of the discipline. The choice of the performative metaphor opens up the process of dialogue about social complexity rather than reducing it to the single argument of the writer (Marcus & Fischer 1986).

Standard Conventions in the Crafting of an Ethnographic Text

In the construction of a tale, there are some common conventions regarding data collection and interpretation observed by ethnographers, regardless of the genre. Field data in any form (audio and visual) and the keeping of a field journal are central to the interpretive process (Wallendorf & Belk 1989).

The preliminary process of recording data is the earliest act of interpretation. Field data are constructed from talk and observation. These field notes provide the opportunity for self-reflection, since the researcher has to make conscious choices as to what is to be recorded, how, when, and why it is to be recorded. Values and attitudes determine what are to be recorded as events. A good example of this process is provided by Belk, Wallendorf & Sherry (1988) in their discussion of revelatory incidents that helped them focus on the sacred aspects of consumption. These events or observations, in turn, do not speak for themselves. An interpretation is necessary because what we see or choose to see imposes constraints on us (Polier & Roseberry 1989). In combination with the journal kept by the researcher, it forms a powerful basis for the textualization process. This is why any interpretation is unstable and precarious.

Secondly, transforming oral and visual into written text can take many forms. Particularly in realist writings, the authors are conscious of the effort to represent the "other's" point of view. The authenticity of the text (realist tales) was expected by the interpretive community to be enhanced by the actual words, translated and edited by the author. Yet this form of polyphony was used not so much as a consideration of the uses of rhetoric as a desire to lend objectivity to the text.

Thirdly, textualization also raises the epistemological issue of visualism (Clifford 1986a,b; Fabian 1983). Hence the emphasis on quantification, diagrammatic representation, maps, and charts. By examining cross-cultural contexts which emphasize the importance of other human senses (Howes 1989), the arbitrariness associated with vision and cognition in our culture is revealed (eg. "I see" ...suggests "I understand"). In consumer behavior, Sherry & McGrath (1989), as well as Sherry (1990), pay attention to extra-sensory modalities in different retail contexts. Sherry and McGrath (1989:162) note,

> The reduction of atmospherics to just four sensory features--visual, aural, olfactory, and tactile notions are noted by Kotler (1974)--blunts the exploration of simultaneous perception and synaesthesia which more accurately characterize ambience.

A particular twist to visualization involves the recording of fieldwork in the form of photographs and videos. While this fits well with the visual metaphor and is used precisely for these reasons, it opens the possibility of evoking polyphony and the multidimensionality of the account. As Wallendorf & Belk (1989:72) note,

> In our experience, there is generally much more to gain in obtrusively, openly and honestly videorecording and talking to consumers than completely foregoing this opportunity and relying only on unobtrusive observation.

Audio and visual data challenge the givenness of the tale and speak with a different voice (McDougall 1978).

Jointly constructed ethnographies deal with the idea of polyphony in a different manner. They identify the philosophical issues of mediation and problems of meaning involved in presenting the informant's point of view. These authors know that the story can be told in a way in which the author wants to tell it. Expertise is not so much at issue as is the knowledge that he or she is both voice and vehicle of meaning transfer. The emphasis is on fragmentation and discourse, not on the text. Narrative form is not a prior issue but one that evolves from the dialogical process. In consumer behavior, there are no exemplary accounts, although Sherry (1990) provides some insights. He notes (37),

> The flea market is essentially a multilogue, as Emerson construes such discourse (Fernandez 1986:239), with many voices communicating. Or, rather, in keeping with the "alternative" status of the periodic market..As a polylogue, the flea market is a booming, buzzing confusion negotiated at the emic level by transactors, and at the etic levels by the analyst...The flea market is a polylogue whose semiotic intensity is apparent to all participants but whose multiple meanings may be apparent to only a few. The subject of this polylogue (and ultimately its object) is the nature or essence of the marketplace in contemporary U.S. society.

Recognizing multiple voices in the text further necessitates the use of an inter-subjective temporal structure which reduces the distance between the informant and the ethnographer. The assumption in such a situation is that both the researcher and the informants are equal and share the same concept of time (Fabian 1983). The difficulties of doing so have been identified earlier. At the present time it seems that the experience of the consumer researcher is given temporal anchoring in the past in order to lend logical credence to the description. Realism is preferred, as in the article by Arnould (1989:242). He notes,

The first case describes the historical context for contemporary consumer behavior in Zinder...In the nineteenth-century state of Zinder (or Damagaram), mass access to luxury goods was limited by macromarketing factors: the narrow span of the market system, long channels, cumbersome media of exchange (cowrie shells, foreign coins, and slaves), and the absence of written accounting systems (Baier 1974,1977)....

Later, in the discussion of contemporary contexts of consumption, the author states (p. 247),

> A critical periodic consumption event that provides scope for expression and innovation of preferences is the marriage ceremony.... A typical marriage today often involves expenses well in excess of annual per capita income.

Likewise, in the presentation of the account, the format used (expository substructures) varies, depending on the nature of the account. Thus Belk, Wallendorf, and Sherry (1989:2) observe,

> Explicit recognition of the sacred status accorded to many consumption objects illuminates aspects of contemporary North American consumer behavior that, while basic and pervasive, have not been explained by prior theory and research. The substantial body of social science theory on the role of the sacred in religion is used here in developing an understanding of sacred apects of consumption. . . However, the processes of meaning investment and divestment-the sacralization rituals we treat at length in this article-are resistant to such distanced exposition.

ETHNOGRAPHIC NARRATIVES

THE CONSTRUCTION OF "SELF" IN ONE'S OWN CULTURE

Ethnographies, among other objectives described above, construct the "self" in the process of constructing "otherness" (Marcus & Fischer 1986). This "other" can refer to a society very different from that of the ethnographer or can be the same one from which he/she comes. Instead of a cross-culturally based probing, "otherness" is constructed from within the researcher's own culture. This form of cultural criticism is not new and is predominant in such fields as anthropology, sociology, literature, and fine arts (Barthes 1973; Csikszentmihalyi & Rochberg-Halton 1981). There are two general directions in which this style of cultural criticism has evolved. The first involves the deconstruction of pure reason and the idea of social progress that results (Rabinow & Sullivan 1979). The second form of criticism arises from the study of social institutions and cultural forms. More recent studies, especially in sociology, deal with the production of cultural forms such as music, the text, and art (Becker 1986; Griswold 1987; Petersen 1976). The latest form of cultural criticism, a combination of the two styles, is self-reflexive, conscious about the positioning of the critique vis-a-vis one's own society, and provides alternatives to what is being critiqued (Marcus & Fischer 1986).

Thus a study of the researcher's own culture allows for the construction of "otherness" from a new vantage point. Being an insider and yet providing a cultural critique privileges one; on the other hand, it makes the researcher more vulnerable to cultural criticism. But the benefit of such a process is that it minimizes cultural chauvinism that has often accompanied the interpretation of an exotic "other." "Otherness" is comprehended as being both participant and interpreter. Secondly, by virtue of this dual position, the ethnographer is able to identify the various possibilities and alternatives as they exist in reality. However, such a perspective is not without problems there are a number of blindspots for the ethnographer studying her/his culture (Wallendorf & Belk 1989). Two examples are examined below.

A Naturalistic Inquiry into Buyer and Seller Behavior at a Swap Meet (Belk, Sherry & Wallendorf 1988)

The importance of this article can be appreciated when one considers the background information and critical political underpinnings of the consumer behavior odyssey project. Dissatisfaction with the existing logical positivist philosophy expressed by a number of consumer researchers since the early 80's eventually led to the coalescing of efforts by "a substantial and sociometrically-central minority" to question the appropriateness of this position (Belk 1990). This group then decided to embark on the Odyssey Project, which was to employ a variety of naturalistic methods to explore American consumption. In order to receive funding from the Marketing Science Institute (MSI), it was decided that a subset of the larger group would do a pilot project. The article on the Red Mesa Swap Meet was the outcome.

The purpose of the article on the Red Mesa Swap Meet is to document both the process and the outcome of interpretive research. It is essentially a tutorial and takes the reader through the various research stages encountered by the authors at a swap meet.

Consequently, the first half of the paper is an explanation of data collection methods, data recording techniques, the creation of field notes, and the keeping of the field journal. Together they form the basis for the written account. Since the purpose is not to focus on the crafting of the text itself, the latter half of the paper deals briefly with their findings.

It is the first account of its kind in the consumer behavior literature to deal explicitly and systematically with alternate methodologies and paradigms for doing research, although Hirschman's article (1986) attempts to do the same. The framework used is described as "naturalistic," although the authors are sensitive to current issues in the field of anthropology and sociology (Wallendorf & Belk 1989).

This account of the swap meet is a prelude to the Odyssey Project. It is based on traditional fieldwork at a single venue and explores a variety of significant actors, events, and processes. As in other ethnographic accounts, etic and emic differences are well documented.

The reader is introduced to the site and is provided with a map of the meet. This is followed by some general information about the organization of the vendor area. Next, a brief description of the line-up and ambience is provided. The authors provide a brief description of the sellers and buyers, followed by a discussion of the emergent themes and possible hypotheses that could be tested further.

The authors' concern with the scientific nature of the study is particularly important, given the newness of the framework in consumer research and the considerable hostility of some researchers in the field toward such a paradigm (Sherry 1988). The pilot was critical to the launching of the Odyssey Project. Too much was at stake and, as Belk (1990:13) notes,

> I doubt that MSI ever got more effort, energy, or material out of $1000 than they did out of the seed grant that got us started. It was partly a labor of love, partly that this effort promised larger rewards in potential funding for the summer project, and partly that it was now time to 'put up or shut up' about the project.

"Otherness" is represented by the alternate methodology and the paradigms that are used by the researchers. By juxtaposing the richer findings garnered from such alternative methods in specific consumption contexts to established concepts in the field, they raise havoc with our thinking and conventional modes of studying consumer behavior. In their words (p. 467),

The field has attained some elegance and precision but lacks soul, feeling and sensitivity to natural consumption contexts. ...But because naturalistic inquiry studies consumers in situ and provides thick qualitative insights, it can potentially inject the richness that Tucker saw as missing in our research.

The dialogic mode that is used is not so much the process of joint construction by informant and researcher as the dynamic chorus of styles identified by Bakhtin (1981), which includes both the team's voice and individual voices (e.g., p.462 they state "yet for each of these rules we saw several violations"); narrative action; the reported speech of informants (e.g., p. 461 : " if we come out here and spend $10, $15 or $20, it is money well spent"); the teller's commentaries (e.g., p. 461: "Bill is one of a group of people who sell miscellaneous furniture and used household items. When we first talked to them, they were sitting in upholstered reclining chairs drinking beer and appeared to have been all day"); evaluative remarks (p.461: "Bill had never heard of Wroe Alderson, but he nonetheless explained Alderson's sorting concept perfectly"); and interpretive remarks (p. 462: "Freedom is an important motivation for both buyers and sellers at the swap meet and often transcends economic motivations").

The use of field notes and journal excerpts in the text, especially by researcher's name, suggests self-reflexivity in the research and writing process. One introspective field note excerpt on p. 465 (some researchers separated field notes from the journal) is particularly poignant. It reflects a sensitivity to the informant as well as gender concerns that explicitly drew me into the text.

I talked to one young woman who was selling household items in the regular area. She moved to New York about a year ago and had flown back into town for the weekend to sort through the things that she had left here. She was trying to sell some of them at the swap meet.... A woman friend was helping her sell her things. She said the things that were sentimental she was shipping to New York. These things that she was selling were just things that could be used. I asked about an old waffle maker. She said that if she didn't sell that, she would take it with her because her grandmother gave it to her. But she said that she felt okay about selling it. It appeared to be a U.S.- made waffle maker rather than one that had come from Norway. It was, however, fairly old (1950's) and was probably given to her used [MW].

The instability and precariousness of the interpretation, the simultaneity and intimacy of the moment are all evoked in the reader. Wallendorf's interaction with the woman informant centres around the topic of personal and family ties and how sacred commodities are converted into profane commercial wares in impersonal market (public) contexts. The author is also sensitive to the ambiguity the woman informant felt about selling the waffle maker because it straddled both categories. It was sacred, Wallendorf argues, in that it was a gift from the woman's grandmother, yet it was not as sacred as those objects given to her that were made in Norway.

From such a poignant moment, we are drawn back into the team's effort to provide substantiality to the text and legitimize the process of naturalistic inquiry. We are told of the value of triangulation methods, of researchers, as well as of the usefulness of auditors. The ethnographic account as a record of facts also becomes apparent in the author's discussions of choice of site, the ambience at site, the profiles of buyers and sellers, and the themes that emerged over the course of doing fieldwork.

The map, the profiles, the categories, and themes are all intended to convince the reader of the factuality of the text. The blow-by-blow description of events and the process of temporal anchoring in the past lend validity to the description. The politics of writing culture is revealed only by examination of field entries by the researchers. The use of photographs and the video is an ingenious mechanism to suggest the presence of researchers and help in the interpretive process. However, while there is a commitment to the hermeneutic process, there is a preoccupation with establishing the credibility and legitimacy of naturalistic inquiry in consumer behavior. The field journals kept by some of these researchers suggest this dilemma. Sherry (1986:15) makes the following obervations regarding the use of video equipment:

I find that I am relying too much on video as aid to memory, and trying too hard to sustain the interview rather than absorbing all that is being said... The naturalistic context we are after is distorted by this intercept procedure and is being sacrificed to some extent in favor of producing a particular kind of product to the proposal package..Once again, I found myself quite conscious of the camera, in the sense that I attended more to directing the interview than I did to absorbing the sense of his discussion. This time-constrained research -- blitzkrieg ethnography is how I am coming to think of it -- with a video product objective is disrupting my own natural rhythm, and I'll have to monitor that closely.

In the final analysis, the pilot project accomplished what it set out to do, despite its explicitly exploratory goals. What's more, it helped to establish procedures that were to be used in the main project and became a tangible marker for what was to come for the larger number of researchers who were keenly awaiting the results.

The Sacred and the Profane in Consumer Behavior: Theodicy on the Odyssey (Belk, Wallendorf & Sherry 1989)

The editorial (although an extra-authorial intrusion over which the authors have little control) that accompanies the publication of this article signals the importance of the piece (Lutz 1989).

The use of vignettes as a rhetorical device at the very outset prepares the reader for what the authors try to do - that is, to question our taken-for-granted assumptions of the process of consumption as well as our day-to-day understanding of what is sacred and profane. The authors argue that consumption is more than the means by which individuals satisfy their material needs. It is a vehicle, they say, for a transcendent experience. Further, despite the recognition of sacrality associated with objects in North America, such concepts have not been explained by prior research and theory in consumer behavior.

The authors demonstrate that the use of naturalistic modes of inquiry is more suitable for revealing such fundamental aspects of consumer behavior. The iterative and discursive fashion in which they read the literaure and interpret their field experiences is an effort to explain, deconstruct, and reconstruct theories for us. In so doing, it is multi-discipinary and is intended as a conceptual contribution to parallel disciplines and as an empirical contribution to consumer research.

That being said, this is how they do it. While the pilot project used a conventional mode of data collection - participant observation at one site - the Odyssey Project involved several researchers and multiple sites. The intent was to pursue a phenomenon that transcended specific sites.

Having established personal authority through the identification of sampled sites, they launch into a discussion of the properties of the sacred as drawn from theories of religion. This section is tutorial in intent, since this material is presumed to be unfamiliar to researchers in consumer behavior.

Following this is a discussion of the shifting boundaries of the sacred and the profane. What constitutes the sacred is outlined at some length to tutor the reader and make him/her aware of the paucity of such data in the field. This knowledge, they claim, is new and powerful-not amenable to quantitative analysis but best understood through qualitative research. The closest analog in consumer research are the concept of consumer involvement and extended self, which barely touches upon the nature and experience of sacrality.

"How do certain possessions attain sacred status?" they ask. Through several processes, they answer, such as ritual, pilgrimage, quintessence, gift-giving, collecting, and inheritance. They flesh out these ideas through field notes and observations informed by cultural theory and provide a thick text of the processes of sacralization. Each of these topics requires much in-depth plumbing through field data and recursive reading of theories and material and is done, for instance, by Belk, Wallendorf, Sherry and Holbrook (1990) in their paper on collecting.

This section is followed by a discussion of how sacrality is perpetuated. This includes spatial and temporal separation, sustaining rituals, specialized uses of objects, gift-giving, bequests, and tangibilized contamination. Again, field notes are used to substantiate each of these methods of maintaining sacredness.

The Odyssey data included 800 pages of field notes, journals, 4000 still photographs and slides, 137 videotapes, a dozen audio tapes, and few dozen artifacts - a very impressive amount of information that supports both the significance and the generalizability of their observations. The insights drawn from religious theories, seem to provide ample insights into the phenomena they observed, allowing the authors to make "thick descriptions."

The use of field notes rather than reported speech is an important means by which they establish scientific authority and objectivity. For instance, on page 16, the authors state,

> He exhibited typical Japanese unwillingness to offend by claiming to have difficulty picking a favorite place he has been in America....He doesn't like the crowded areas and said that the West is like the real America for him.

The distancing of the account from the simultaneity of the moment is what gives it scientific authority. There is no question in the reader's mind that the authors were there. Of the 24 instances of fieldwork material woven into the tale, more than half were taken from the field notes themselves. These detailed observations sometimes include short statements by informants. On occasion, the name of the informant is provided (eg. p. 18: "John's favorite toy is..."). The rest were extracted largely from the interviews and presented within quotation marks.

A very interesting attempt to jointly construct the interpretation is done on pages 19 and 22 where the authors provide extracts from the interviews that use both voices - the questions they asked and the responses they received. A touching moment is presented in the text when they describe a woman selling handcrafted dolls (p. 22). They state, "She kissed the baby as she sold the doll (one object with two communicative voices)." Self-reflexivity is also evident on another occasion when they describe a situation in which they were corrected by their informants (p. 26). One other rhetorical device they use effectively is to bring the same informant into the text from time to time. By spreading the field notes and quotations from a single informant over the entire text, the reader begins to develop a sense of the person and not just the faceless "informant."

The discussion of triangulation of researchers and methods raises an element of reflexivity, although this is not pursued; the reader is told that they had a bi-gender team with multi-disciplinary specialists. In part, this can be explained by the fact that not all researchers were involved in the complete duration of the Odyssey Project (Belk 1990). Self-reflexivity is at its lowest when methodology and the theoretical discourse on the sacred and the profane are provided. The blow-by-blow description of the various stages of research and the interpretation process not only provides clinical description but helps to substantiate the text.

THE CONSTRUCTION OF "SELF" IN CULTURES OTHER THAN ONE'S OWN

Focusing on a culture different from the ethnographer's is critical for three reasons. First there are restraints placed by countries on the nature of the research to be conducted and questions as to the accountability of the researcher. Second the informant can read and contest the interpretation provided by the ethnographer. Finally, the political confrontation between white and non-white feminists have led to a reconsideration of theories of the woman and replaced them with theories of multiplicity (Mascia-Lees et al.1989:23). In particular, describing an alien society requires a complex and moral relationship between the researcher, his/her culture, as well as the informant and his/her culture (Marcus & Fischer 1986).

There are several ways of analyzing the "self" in the narrative. In the paper by Arnould (1989) that deals specifically with cultures other than one's own, the "self" can be identified through many means. In a general sense, "the self" refers to Arnould's cultural background. It also refers to the discipline that he is embedded in - consumer behavior. He is an ethnographer with anthropological training, creating ethnographic texts that challenge existing methods in the field of consumer behavior. It (the self) also refers to the central constructs and concepts in consumer behavior that are challenged by information gathered through such alternate ways of knowing. Most importantly, the interdependence between "self" and "other" as an outcome of a particular historical and cultural context is also brought to the fore (Dwyer 1982).

Toward a Broadened Theory of Preference Formation and the Diffusion of Innovations: Cases from Zinder Province, Niger Republic (Arnould 1989)

Arnould deals with the concepts of diffusion of innovation, economic development, and its impact on consumer behavior in Zinder, Niger. Here is a realist tale par excellence that does not detract from the centrality of the contribution this article makes. It builds, brick by brick, an argument that uses the "other" in the examination of the "self." The "other" refers to the people of Zinder and their consumption practices. Specifically, the article deals with the diffusion of innovation in Zinder consumption contexts. The "self," in addition to what I stated before, is also identified as the existing theory of diffusion outlined by Gatignon and Robertson in consumer behavior. The express purpose of studying consumption in Zinder is not only to highlight cultural peculiarities but also to allow the author to refine the existing model of diffusion of innovation developed primarily within a North American context to reflect these multicultural realities.

The discussion of field methods establishes incontrovertibly that the author was there. The authority of the narrator is established in the long-term field involvement in Zinder. He gathered information on household budgets, interviewed people at 70 weekly markets and various members of marketing channels, collected oral histories, carried on informal discussions, and had informants fill out a questionnaire. In addition, published data on earlier fieldwork provides the background, specific issues to which Arnould refers in this account.

However, other than this revelatory note on fieldwork, very little attempt is made to bring either his field notes or his journal into the narration. The style is documentary, and the people described are "typical people." There is little in the narrative that allows glimpses of Arnould, the participant observer in Zinder-ostensibly one of the poorest parts of the world. There is no descripton of actual encounters with informants in the field, although they figure prominently in the background. They are nameless and faceless, much like the author, who establishes that he was there and then disappears from the narrative. Another factor is the absence of reference to any material kept in a journal. While journal material does not always have to appear in the text, as a reader I am interested in knowing the context within which Arnould elicits and interprets information from the people he studies. Further the absence of the author from the narrative gives the false impression that the interpretation is objective.

It is from an elaborate set of data collected over several years that the author constructs a series of cases. The amount of time spent in the field (although duration does not necessarily guarantee good ethnography), the technical skill of the ethnographer, and the sensitivity in presenting the native's perspective render this narrative authentic. While concern with issues of validity and reliability are embedded in such thick description, the construction of cases from empirical data signals the scientific narrative presence of the author.

The author begins with a brief consideration of innovation and diffusion theory outlined by Gatignon and Robertson before critiquing some of the axioms underlying it. He takes a key concept in consumer behavior, such as diffusion of innovation, and systematically defamiliarizes it for us with materials from Zinder (discussed below). By tying in diffusion of innovation in consumption with larger forces outside of Zinder, he weaves together a more critical approach to the narrative structure. The juxtaposition of critical theory in a realist account makes the reader question the earlier assumptions of the substantive nature of the text. Such narration seems to raise a critique of the text by the author himself.

The first case he describes sets the stage for what is to follow-it provides a historical account of the economic and political changes and the accompanying alterations in consumption. Case 2 provides an example of a "typical" rural marriage today. It provides a detailed example of how cultural values are enacted in consumption processes. Social structure, stage in life cycle, bridewealth contexts, as well as the indigenous concept of "brilliance," provide a framework for acceptance of new products. Case 3 provides ample justification for the statement that rural adoption of cosmopolitan styles may be part of a broader pattern of

implantation of common, international, elite standards of operation and consumption within a global economy. Case 4 patiently takes the reader through a discussion of the importance of Hajj in preference formation.

Each subcategory of the diffusion concept is then examined in the light of field data, to either revise it or question its cross-cultural applicability. The revised propositions are smaller in number (16 rather than 29) but greater in scope and depth. This then leads into a discussion of a broader theory of preference formation and diffusion of innovations.

Here is a tale that is both realist and critical. This rendering provides concrete and complex images of Zinder. Yet in raising the embeddedness of the concept of diffusion of innovation in the light of a revised world systems approach, it alerts the reader to the subversive possibilities in the text. It is unpretentious and not experimental. The author does what he sets out to do - to provide an improved multicultural model for diffusion, and in that process transform the descriptive mission of anthropology into a paradigm-building one. He also contributes to the disciplinary goal of a comparative science of consumption rather than one of buyer behavior. This narrative is exemplary in the depth, breadth, and realism it conveys. Yet while what is "known" is substantial, the "knower" is unknown. In the final analysis, as a reader, I consider what is known to be contingent on the knower.

THE "OTHER" AS IRRECONCILABLE WITH "SELF"

If in realist, impressionist, and jointly told tales the self and other are seen as important elements to be dealt with one way or another, feminist discourse offers yet another dimension to ethnographic writing in its irreconcilable stance between "self" and "other."

Why should feminist discourse be a consideration in writing ethnographic texts in consumer behavior? The answer to that is as follows: if self-reflection is a cornerstone of ethnographic accounts, the uncritical examination of gender issues that invariably arise in fieldwork is not tenable (Rosaldo 1980; Strathern 1987). More eloquently stated,

Feminist theory is an intellectual system that knows its politics, a politics directed toward securing recognition that the feminine is as crucial an element of the human as the masculine and thus a politics skeptical and critical of traditional 'universal truths' concerning human behavior (Mascia-Lees, Sharpe & Cohen 1989:8).

The above authors state that constructing the "other" entails relations of domination. While post-modern anthropologists speak for the "other" (women in our culture, and both men and women in other cultures), the feminist speaks from the position of the "other" (p. 11). This insight is brought home to us with greater force when we consider the paucity of such analyses in consumer behavior (Schmitt, Leclerc, & Dube-Rioux 1988; Stern 1990).

Gender discourse refers not only to the ethnographer and the construction of gender in her/his own culture but also to the informants and their constructions of gender. In cross-cultural contexts, this becomes particularly significant, since universal theories of asymmetry are questionable. In consumer behavior, the construction of gender is not so much an issue as is its manifestation (eg.Jackson, McDaniel & Rao 1985). The key construct in feminist discourse is domination embodied in the general principle of patriarchy and, more concretely, in men. Men are the "other" in this discourse (Strathern 1987), and the feminist task is to expose and destroy the authority of the "other" in order to determine the female experience. Yet within feminist discourse itself, the dialogic process is pursued. The "self" and "other" are reconcilable, despite the varying interpretations and divergent cultural experiences of women. With men, however, there is no collaboration, no parity, only asymmetry. Dominance and patriarchy must constantly be recognized in order to maintain self and identity (Strathern 1987). The danger in such a perspective is the reification of the differences that are the sources of oppression that feminism is keen on destroying. One positive outcome of this binary thinking, however, is the emphasis on the worth of some of these "feminine" qualities (Holbrook 1989). It has countered the negative valuation of women, as well as provided a critique of general cultural values that foster aggression and narrow individualism (Hare-Mustin & Marecek 1989) and allowed women to speak for themselves.

In the consumer behavior literature, there are a few accounts that deal tangentially with some of the issues raised above (Fischer 1989; Sherry & McGrath 1989). It is to a discussion of this theme in the Sherry & McGrath article that we now turn.

Unpacking the Holiday Presence: A Comparative Ethnography of Two Gift Stores (Sherry & McGrath 1989)

While this article is not informed by feminist discourse that sees asymmetry and conflict, there is an attempt to recognize the role of the female voice and the female experience in the construction of the text.

Thus of all the texts discussed hitherto, this is the most self-reflexive regarding gender considerations.

The authors begin the narrative with the stated objective of studying the institutional focus of discovery and the production of meaning. The two researchers chose sites that are comparable, especially in relation to the backgrounds of the owners and clientele who shopped at the stores. Each week, for a period of two months, 12-24 hours were spent doing field work. The researchers' concern with short-term ethnography made them reluctant to give anything other than tentative generalizations and suggest explanatory frameworks. This sense of incompleteness and missing data set the mood for the reader, who could now join in the interpretive process. Multiple voices were also presented. For instance, the authors note (informant's voice),

- I'd love to receive a gift from here but would never buy anything here for myself. Buying here is a time investment. It shows that people really care if they take the time to shop here.

and

- This (expensive piece of jewelry) is a present from me to me.

The introduction to the two gift stores (Baubles and The Mouse House) is richly descriptive. There is detail and there is attention to preparing the reader for what is to follow. Expectations of the reader are met in the discussion of appropriate subtopics such as ambience, merchandise, history, choice heuristic, personnel, seasonal cycle, range of shopping activity, backstage activity, and giving to oneself. The differences in text, albeit very few, are apparent in the slight deviations in topics by the ethnographer of Baubles, who introduces subtle nuances in her discussion of the importance of place and the marketing mix involved.

The propositions they offer are illuminating. They also challenge some taken-for-granted assumptions in marketing. The importance of sense of place in understanding buyer behavior is evident in the authors' discussion of synaesthesia, which accompanies perception. Kotler's concept of "atmospherics," which refers to the use of the senses of touch, smell, vision, and taste, they argue, barely touches this issue.

Object - person relationships through gift-giving processes is a mechanism by which individuals make and re-make themselves vis-a-vis others, they note (Sherry 1983). The ludic and hedonistic qualities embedded in gift-giving activity is more important than its utilitarian function, they argue. Through rich descriptions, metaphor, and point of view, the authors allow the reader to share in the construction and narration of the text. Most importantly, the authors state that gift-giving is the work of women (Fischer 1989). Since gift-giving behavior is part of kin work that women do, they amplify our existing knowledge of kin work and, by extension, its importance to consumer behavior. Further, by raising this issue, they signal the importance of kin work and thus defamiliarize the concept of work itself and what constitutes men's work and women's work. They even suggest that a gendered mediation between gift exchange and market might provide a model for a more personalized political economy and more humane work place cultures.

CONCLUSIONS

The purpose of this paper is to provide a sequel to the discussions on naturalistic inquiry that have appeared in the consumer behavior literature. It suggests that the openness associated with such an endeavor, the process, once begun, must go on. The paper raises the issue of the links between the researcher, the research process, the reader, and the narrative.

In the above discussion, I explored some of the many ways in which ethnographic accounts are being crafted-be they realist, critical, impressionist, or jointly constructed tales. This paper is my interpretation of the selected accounts. Yet any interpretation is also socially constructed and is guided by conventions used by an interpretive community (anthropologists/feminists in this instance).

Ethnographic accounts reflect and construct cultural variation in an otherwise homogenizing world. They point to the multiplicity of being human. In the process, they question and challenge existing knowledge and the aims of such knowledge in consumer behavior. More recently, these have been mechanisms by which theoretical and ethical issues are discussed.

Writing an ethnographic tale does not occur in a vacuum. It is embedded in a specific way of creating knowledge. In particular, ethnographies in consumer behavior reflect the political turmoils within the field. While they provide alternate frameworks for an epistemological critique of the discipline, there are differences of opinion among the researchers themselves that reflect these larger concerns. The politicization of pluralism and the mission of legitimizing naturalistic inquiry have led some authors to restrict the textualization process. This gate-keeping function can limit the creativity of these accounts.

Based on the studies that have been discussed earlier, the following observations can provide some guidelines for interpreting a text:

1. The crafting of the text is central to the hermeneutic process because it raises theoretical, philosophical, and ethical issues.
2. Field notes are the first type of interpretation that occurs. It is close to what the informants say and do and reinforces the constructed nature of interpretation.
3. Field journals allow for self-reflection that informs not only of the keeping of field notes but also of the interpretive process. In conjunction with field notes, they are necessary manifestations of in-depth observation and interviews and form the basis from which the ethnography is written.
4. The visual metaphor that guides the creation of an ethnographic account contributes to the emphasis on diagrams, charts, and maps. However, they have the potential for using multiple voices and presenting the "other's " point of view and must be explored by researchers.
5. While photos and videos add to the substantiality of the text, they also evoke multiple readings of the text and must be plumbed for its uses. In addition, these videos/photographs may themselves be presentational media (as exemplified by the video "Deep Meanings in Possessions: Naturalistic Research from the Consumer Behavior Odyssey," (Wallendorf & Belk 1987).
6. The temporal structure that is essential to the structure of the text raises issues of inter-subjectivity in the crafting process. While informant and ethnographer share the same time during fieldwork, distancing occurs through the use of narrative structure.
7. Likewise, writing an account cannot be divorced from its political and social context. Concerns over legitimizing naturalistic inquiry, editorial control, and the review process may lead to the use of expository substructures that provide for more realist accounts.
8. The use of multiple voices depends on the stance taken by the researcher(s) and varies with the account. Realist accounts, such as Arnould's (1989), provide data on typical individuals in the field, yet offer a critical perspective. Polyphony is maximally evoked by

Sherry (1989) and presented differently in the dynamic chorus of styles in Belk, Sherry & Wallendorf (1988).

9. Finally, the mutuality of the "self" and the "other" is challenged in instances that are written in a feminist mode. The constructed nature of gender rather than the acceptance of gender manifestations is dealt with, at least tangentially, in Sherry & McGrath (1989) and offers us insights into how gender can inform writing in consumer behavior.

The writing of ethnographic accounts is recent in consumer behavior, hence there is not a large selection of documents. Importantly, research monographs that do justice to the multiple dimensions of the text are only beginning to be considered. Journal articles, however comprehensive, are constrained by the requirements made by reviewers in their ability to flesh out the multiple voices of informants, professional standards in doing fieldwork, the self-reflection of the authors, and the nature of field experience itslf.

This paper, it is hoped, will encourage researchers working within this tradition to reflexively consider the interpretive process. While Belk, Sherry, and Wallendorf (1988) provide guidelines for doing research, this paper poses questions about how such accounts are written and read.

REFERENCES

Anderson, Paul F. (1983), "Marketing, Scientific Progress and Scientific Method," *Journal of Marketing*, 47 (Fall), pp. 18-31.

_____ (1986), "On Method in Consumer Research: A Critical Relativist Perspective," *Journal of Consumer Research*, 15(1), pp.133-173.

Arnould, Eric J. (1989), "Toward a Broadened Theory of Preference Formation and the Diffusion of Innovations: Cases from Zinder, Province, Niger Republic," *Journal of Consumer Research*, vol. 16: no. 2, p. 239-267.

Bakhtin, Mikhail (1981), *The Dialogic Imagination: Four Essays*, M. Holquist, ed. Austin, University of Texas Press.

Barthes Roland (1973), *Mythologies*, London: Paladin Press.

Becker, Howard (1986),"Telling about Society," in *Doing Things Together*, Evanston: Northwestern University Press.

Belk, Russell (1986), Journal, Odyssey project. Unpublished text.

Belk, Russell (1987), "A Modest Proposal for Creating Verisimilitude in Consumer-Information-Processing Models, and Some Suggestions for Establishing a Discipline to Study Consumer Behavior," in *Philosophical and Radical Thought in Marketing*, eds. A. Fuat Firat, Nikhilesh Dholakia, and Richard Bagozzi, Lexington, MA: Lexington Books, pp. 361-372.

_____ , John Sherry and Melanie Wallendorf (1988), "A Naturalistic Inquiry into Buyer and Seller Behavior at a Swap Meet," *Journal of Consumer Research*, 14(4), pp. 449-470.

_____ , Melanie Wallendorf and John Sherry (1989), "The Sacred and Profane in Consumer Behavior: Theodicy on the Odyssey," *Journal of Consumer Research*, Vol. 16, No. 1 (June), pp. 1-38.

_____ , Wallendorf, Melanie, Sherry John, & Holbrook Morris (1990) "Collecting in a consumer culture," in *Highways and Buyways: Naturalistic Research from the Consumer Behavior Odyssey*, Russ Belk ed., Provo, UT: Association of Consumer Research. (in this volume)

_____ , (1990) "The History and Development of the Consumer Behavior Odyssey," in *Highways and Buyways: Naturalistic Research from the Consumer Behavior Odyssey*, ed., Provo, Utah: Association for Consumer research. (in this volume)

Burke, Kenneth (1969), *A Rhetoric of Motives*, Berkeley & Los Angeles: University of California Press.

Clifford, James (1983), "On Ethnographic Authority," *Representations*, Vol. 1 (Spring), pp. 118-146.

_____ (1986a), "Introduction: Partial Truths," in *Writing Culture: The Poetics and Politics of Ethnography*, eds. James Clifford & George E. Marcus, pp. 1-26, Berkeley, California: University of California Press.

_____ (1986b), "On Ethnographic Allegory," in *Writing Culture: The Poetics and Politics of Ethnography*, eds. James Clifford & George E. Marcus, pp. 98-121, Berkeley, California: University of California Press.

Crapanzano, Vincent (1980), *Tuhami: Portrait of a Moroccan*, Chicago: University of Chicago Press.

Crick, Malcolm (1982), "Anthropology of Knowledge," *Annual Review of Anthropology*, 11, pp. 287-313, Palo Alto, California: Annual Reviews Inc.,

Csikszentmihalyi, Mihaly & Eugene Rochberg-Halton (1981), *The Meaning of Things :Domestic symbols and the Self*, New York: Cambridge University Press.

Dwyer, Kevin (1982), *Moroccan Dialogues: Anthropology in Question*, Baltimore: Johns Hopkins University Press.

Fabian, Johannes (1983), *Time and the Other: How Anthropology Makes Its Object*, New York: Columbia University Press.

Flacks, Richard and Gerald Turkel (1978), "Radical Sociology". *Annual Review of Sociology* 4, pp. 193-238.

Flax, Jane (1987), "Post-modernism and Gender Relations in Feminist Theory," *Signs*, Vol. 12, No. 4, pp. 621-643.

Firat A. Fuat, Nikhilesh Dholakia & Richard Bagozzi (1987), *Philosophical and Radical Thought in Marketing*, eds. Mass: Lexington Books.

Fischer, Eileen (1989), "'This the Season to be Jolly? Tensions and Trends in Christmas Shopping," paper presented at *ACR*, October 1989.

Geertz, Clifford (1973), *The Interpretation of Cultures*, New York: Basic Books.

Griswold, Wendy (1987), "The fabrication of Meaning:Literary interpretation in the United Staates, Great Britain and the West Indies," *American Journal of Sociology*, Vol 92: 1077-1117.

Hare-Mustin Rachel & Jeanne Maracek (1989), "The Meaning of Difference", *American Psychologist*, vol.43: no. 6.455-464.

Hirschman, Elizabeth (1986), "Humanistic Inquiry in Marketing Research: Philosophy, Method and Criteria," *Journal of Marketing Research*, (August), vol: 23.,pp. 237-249.

_____ (1989), *Interpretive Consumer Research*, Provo, UT: Association for Consumer Research, forthcoming.

Holbrook, Morris (1987a), "What is Consumer Research?," *Journal of Consumer Research*, 14(1), pp. 128-132.

_____ (1987b), "From the Log of a Consumer Researcher:Reflections on the Odyssey," unpublished journal and fieldnotes from the Odyssey project.

_____ , Stephen Bell & Mark W. Grayson (1989), "The Role of the Humanities in Consumer Research: Close Encounters and Coastal Disturbances" in *Interpretive Consumer Research*, (ed) E.C. Hirschman. Provo, Utah: Association for Consumer Research.

Holbrook, Morris (1989), "President's column," *ACR Newsletter*, p.1-9.

Howes, David (1989), "Sensorial Anthropology," unpublished manuscript, Department of Anthropology, Concordia University.

Hudson, Laurel and Julie Ozanne (1988), "Alternative Ways of Seeking Knowledge in Consumer Research," *Journal of Consumer Research*, 14(4), pp. 508-521.

Jackson, Ralph W., Stephen W. McDaniel, and C.P. Rao (1985), "Food Shopping and Preparation: Psychographic Differences of Working Wives and Housewives," *Journal of Consumer Research* vol:12 (June), 110-113.

Kassarjian, Harold H. (1987), "How We Spent our Summer Vacation: A Preliminary Report on the 1986 Consumer Behavior Odyssey" in *Advances in Consumer Research*, vol. 14 (ed.) Melanie Wallendorf & Paul Anderson, Provo, UT: Association for Consumer Research: 376-377.

Lutz, Richard (1989), "Editorial" *Journal of Consumer Research*, vol. 16, no. 1.

McDougall, David (1978), "Ethnographic Film: Failure and Promise", *Annual Review of Anthropology*, vol. 7, pp. 305-426.

Marcus, George E. (1986a). "Contemporary Problems of Ethnography in the Modern World System," in *Writing Culture*, edited by James Clifford and George E. Marcus, pp. 165-93, Berkeley, California: University of California Press.

_____ and Dick Cushman, 1982, "Ethnographies as Texts." *Annual Review of Anthropology* 11, pp. 25-69.

_____ and Michael Fischer (1986), *Anthropology as Cultural Critique: An Experimental Moment in the Human Sciences*, Chicago: University of Chicago Press.

Mascia-Lees, Frances, Patricia Sharpe & Colleen B.Cohen (1989), "The Postmodernist Turn in Anthropology: Cautions from a Feminist Perspective,"in *Signs*, Vol 15:no.1, p.7-33.

McCracken, Grant (1988), *Culture and Consumption: New Approaches to the Symbolic Character of Consumer Goods and Activities*, Bloomington, Indiana: Indiana University Press.

Mick, David (1986), "Consumer Research and Semiotics: Exploring the Morphology of Signs, Symbols and Significance," *Journal of Consumer Research*, 13(2), pp. 196-213.

Peterson, R.A. (1976), *The Production of Culture*, Beverley Hills: Sage Publication.

Polier, Nicole & William Roseberry (1989), "Tristes-tropes: Post-Modern Anthropologists Encounter the Other and Discover Themselves", *Economy & Society*, vol. 18: no. 2. (May) p. 245-264.

Rabinow, Paul (1986), "Representations are Social Facts: Modernity and Postmodernity in Anthropology," in *Writing Culture*, eds. James Clifford and George E. Marcus, pp. 234-61. Berkeley, California: University of California Press.

_____ and William Sullivan (1987), "The Interpretive Turn: A Second Look," in *Interpretive Social Science: A Second Look*, eds. Paul Rabinow and William Sullivan, Berkeley, CA: University of California Press, pp. 1-30.

Ricouer, Paul (1973), "The Model of the Text," *New Literary History*, Vol.5, pp.91-120.

Sangren, Steven (1988), "Rhetoric and the Authority of Ethnography," *Current Anthropology*, Vol. 29, No. 3 (June), pp. 405-435.

Schmitt, Bernd H., France Leclerc, and Laurette Dubé-Rioux (1988), "Sex Typing and Consumer Behavior: A Test of Gender Schema Theory," *Journal of Consumer Research*, vol :15 (June), p.122-128.

Sherry, John F., Jr. (1983), "Gift-Giving in Anthropological Perspective," *Journal of Consumer Research*, vol. 10 (Sept.), 157-168.

_____ (1986),"Odyssey Pilot: Fieldnotes and Journal" unpublished text.

_____ (1987a), Journal and fieldnotes on the odyssey project, unpublished text.

_____ (1987b), "Keeping the Monkeys Away from the Typewriters: An Anthropologist's View of the Consumer Behavior Odyssey," *Advances in Consumer Research*, Vol. 14, eds. Melanie Wallendorf and Paul Anderson, Provo, UT: Association for Consumer Research, pp. 370-373.

_____ & Camargo (1987c), "May your Life be Marvellous: English language Labelling and the semiotics of Japanese Promotion." *Journal of Consumer research*, vol. 14. p. 174-188.

_____ (1988), Post-Modern Alternatives: The Interpretive Turn In Consumer Research," *Handbook of Consumer theory and Research*, eds. Harold Kassarjian and Thomas Robertson, Englewood Cliffs, NJ: Prentice Hall, in press.

_____ and Mary Ann McGrath (1989), "Unpacking the Holiday Presence: A Comparative Ethnography of Two Gift Stores," in *Interpretive Consumer Research*, ed. Elizabeth Hirschman, Provo, UT: Association for Consumer Research.

_____ (1990), "A Socio-cultural Analysis of a Midwestern American Flea Market," Vol. 17 (1) pp. 13-30, *Journal of Consumer Research*, vol. 16 (4).

Stern, Barbara (1990), "Literary Criticism and Consumer research : Overview and Illustrative Analysis," *Journal of Consumer Research*, Vol 16: 3, p. 322-335.

Strathern, Marilyn (1987), "An Awkward Relationship: The Case of Feminism and Anthropology", *Signs*, Vol. 12, No. 2, pp. 276-296.

Thompson, Craig J; William B. Loccander & Howard R. Pollio (1989), "Putting Consumer Experience Back into Consumer Research: The Philosophy and Method of Existential-Phenomenology," *Journal of Consumer Research*, vol. 16: 2, p. 133-146.

Van Maanen, John (1988), *Tales of the Field*, Chicago: University of Chicago Press.

Wallendorf, Melanie (1986), Journal observations on the Odyssey project, unpublished text.

Wallendorf, Melanie and Russell Belk (1989), "Assessing Trustworthiness in Naturalistic Consumer Research," in *Interpretive Consumer Research*, ed. Elizabeth Hirschman, Provo, UT: Association for Consumer Research.

Epilogue: Lessons Learned
Russell W. Belk

I have no regrets about having "done" the Consumer Behavior Odyssey, nor about recruiting others to come along. It was without doubt a more challenging and rewarding research experience than any I had undertaken previously. The experience was all-consuming and totally engrossing. I learned a great deal that would have been much more difficult to learn in other ways, and my teaching and research career has substantially and indelibly changed as a result. The Odyssey also forged or reshaped a number of friendships that I am confident will last a lifetime.

That said, if I knew then what I know now, it would not have been necessary to do the Odyssey. The Odyssey served its purposes well in shaking some colleagues and me out of our complacency, stimulating new substantive and theoretical insights, learning research methods that were new to most of us, and bringing the attention of the field to an alternative paradigm and research agenda. But, knowing what I know now, I would do things differently. This brief postscript outlines what I feel I have learned and how I would conduct the Odyssey in retrospect.

THE RESEARCH AGENDA

The initial intent was for the Odyssey to be an unfreezing experience. Whereas the standard anthropological task is to make the strange familiar, the task of the Odyssey was to make the familiar strange (Burgess 1984); to force us to see it with "new eyes." By taking the participants out of the environments with which we were most familiar and forcing us to encounter "alien" environments, it was hoped that we could learn to see things differently without the implicit taken-for-granted knowledge and blind spots that we all too soon adapt when we are comfortable with the situations in which we participate. We *did* learn to see with new eyes, to question what we previously accepted, and to open ourselves to more intense perception of the consumer behavior occurring around us. But, in retrospect, it was not necessary to encounter such a diverse array of otherness or to cover so much geographic territory in order to accomplish this unfreezing.

Some phenomena such as collecting and sacred and profane aspects of consumption, were undoubtedly explored much more thoroughly and completely by covering as much ground as we did. But other phenomena of a more concrete and site-specific nature were less thoroughly explored and less completely understood than they might have been. To really know the Amish,

art shows, horse ownership, house decoration, automobile ownership, or any of a number of other specific consumption behaviors examined, requires more intense study than the Odyssey was able to devote to any one of these phenomena. Thus, were I restructuring a summer-long project to awaken complacent researchers to new methods and new ways of seeing, I would choose a single consumption phenomenon and, if appropriate to this focus, a single research site. Ideally, the site(s) would be far enough away to constitute a field station, since much of the unfreezing experience would quite likely be lost by 9:00 to 5:00 research in which we all return to the familiarity and comfort of our home environments each evening (or each daytime or weekday in other instances). Locale, however, depends on the research focus, as does concentration on a single intact group and research site.

In concentrating the study more, longer term informant relationships become feasible and the researchers also have a greater opportunity to track dynamic behaviors over time. It is also more feasible to understand longitudinal processes and to detect misimpressions with a more extended period of time. It is not necessary to adopt the standard anthropological model of a year in the field in a foreign culture (although a Utah marketing Ph.D. student is now contemplating such a study and Arnould's 1989 study of Niger is based on repeated extended visits), but time should be allowed to reach closure at a site or with a phenomenon before moving on to the next engagement. In fairness to the Odyssey research, numerous projects stimulated by the Odyssey were continued after the initial project and some of these are still underway with further data collection and analysis planned. But for training new researchers, a more focused research project now seems preferable to the movable feast of the Odyssey. Only if the nature of the phenomenon studied requires it (e.g., changing residence, driving, vacation touring) would a moving research platform be preferred.

In fact, this lesson learned is reflected in my own subsequent research and that of a number of other Odyssey participants as well (some of which is presented in this volume). John Sherry has continued with research at a single swap meet. He and Mary Ann McGrath have continued a multiple-year project at two gift stores. Mary Ann and Deborah Heisley continued farmer's market work started prior to the Odyssey. Jeff Durgee, Melanie Wallendorf, and Morris Holbrook revisited the homes of several women interviewed on the

Odyssey, and Tom O'Guinn, Melanie Wallendorf, and I have revisited several men interviewed on the Odyssey about their cars. I have made a number of repeat visits to a man who accumulated three garages full of treasures, and was joined by Melanie Wallendorf during a term she spent in Utah on sabbatical. Melanie and I have also revisited informants cultivated at swap meets on the Odyssey and during the pilot study. Tom O'Guinn continued his work on "touching greatness" after the Odyssey, and together we have revisited Mann's Chinese Theatre and continued to interview visitors to various mansions. Tom and I also extended this work to a project at Heritage Village, U.S.A. following the Odyssey. Several of us have continued work on pets and collections. And four of the Odyssey participants (Deborah Heisley, Mary Ann McGrath, Scott Roberts, and John Schouten) have now completed qualitative doctoral dissertations with more prescribed foci. In addition, the majority of the Odyssey participants have taken up new qualitative research projects since the Odyssey, all of which are focused on narrower topics than the total Odyssey agenda. My own on-going or completed qualitative projects since the Odyssey also include studies of dating and gift-giving, Halloween consumption, automobile restoration, museum presentation and consumption, the meanings of possessions in India and among Indian immigrants to the U.S., possessions of early Mormon pioneers moving to Utah, sports fans, nouveaux riches consumption, in-home music listenership, and modern mountain men reenacting fur trade rendezvous. Many of these projects have been conducted jointly with others, including Joyce Arntz, Greg Coon, Janeen Costa, Raj Mehta, Tom O'Guinn, John Schouten, Sherri Stevens, Melanie Wallendorf, and Melissa Young.

Taken together, these research topics may not indicate less promiscuous research agendas by Odyssey participants, but they do reflect much more thorough and continuous data collection efforts than were possible during the Odyssey per se. One thing that has not changed since the Odyssey in selecting these topics is the continued focus on areas of consumption that are important to informants. It is not impossible to do good qualitative work on low involvement consumption (e.g., Tom O'Guinn has done a project on mayonnaise and I have done a project on footwear), but emotionally involving consumption is a far more neglected part of the consumer research agenda because non-naturalistic research such as survey and laboratory studies are inherently unsuitable for such work.

Despite these lessons learned, if someone reading this should want to do a variant of the Odyssey across multiple venues and multiple topics, please do! For besides choosing topics that are important and of interest to informants, it is imperative for good research that the topics be of all-consuming interest to the researcher as well. I have seen some videotapes of an excellent European Odyssey organized by Peter Gerlitz near Düsseldorf, in cooperation with Grey Advertising. Subsequently Peter did interviews with East Berliners coming to buy things in West Berlin just after the wall came down. This sort of adventurous and opportunistic spirit in research is precisely the spirit likely to lead researchers to quality research projects and to sustain them in the inevitably long hours of intensive work required by qualitative data collection and analysis. If piling into a recreational vehicle and heading cross-country is what gets you excited enough to muster this concentrated effort, by all means do so.

RESEARCH METHODS

Other Odyssey participants will confirm that we learned a great deal about how to conduct qualitative research during the Odyssey. These lessons range from types of equipment to use and fine points on interviewing techniques to broad philosophical positions on how to design and evaluate such research. The following enumeration begins with some of the finer points and builds toward broader considerations.

1. Bring two or more of each essential piece of equipment.

This means two video cameras and numerous tapes, multiple batteries, multiple audio recorders and tapes, multiple computers and lots of disks, duplicate still cameras, film, and lenses, spare clothes, and alternate transportation, as well as multiple human instruments. The human instruments are interviewers, camera persons, bulk film loaders, film editors, "donkeys" (who schlepp equipment), gofers (who go for things), cooks, drivers, map-readers, leaders, and gender representatives (for bi-gender research teams are a distinct advantage, as discussed in 2). Murphy's law applies here, and waiting for repairs or, worse, loosing key records of events, is a distinctly frustrating experience. One way to build-in extra human instruments is to have everyone cross-trained in as many research roles as possible (I admit that learning another gender may prove difficult). Equipment back-up is more expensive, but well worth the investment. There are few more anguishing experiences than watching an absolutely brilliant videotaped interview that has inexplicably lost all sound. All of this extra equipping should be done with an eye to minimizing weight and bulk without compromising quality.

2. Use a research team.

While it is not absolutely necessary for qualitative research to involve multiple researchers working together, there are substantial advantages to be gained through such a team. Because the researcher is the instrument in qualitative research, no two researchers are likely to elicit the same responses from informants or observe and interpret in precisely the same way. By building diversity into a research team, maximal triangulation of perspectives is possible. Specialization potential and adaptivity to research situations are also increased. If there is an informant who appears to respond better to a male or female or old or young researcher, the diverse team is able to call upon the best suited member. If technical expertise is needed for an interview or for operating a piece of equipment, a well-staffed and well-trained team is better able to provide it. If multiple informants (e.g., a family) are encountered, various research team members can work with the individual family members. And where multiple team members are present for an interview, not only is triangulation possible, but one researcher can concentrate in taking notes or running a video camera or tape recorder while another concentrates more on conducting the interview.

There is a further advantage in terms of the moral support offered by working in a group context. It remains a test of courage to initially approach a stranger to gain entry to a research situation or secure an interview, and having a coworker along does much to evoke and sustain the courage that is needed. Given the overwhelmingly cooperative nature of people I have interviewed, it is easy to dismiss this need for moral support in retrospect. But on the Odyssey and a number of research projects since, I have been grateful to have someone at my side during many research experiences.

At the same time, there is generally a subtle competition between research team members to get the best "stuff" -- insightful interviews with probing questions and revealing answers, rapport with informants, detail in fieldnotes, and sensitivity and insight in journals and analysis. It is here that much of the pride in research skills that may not directly show in a research report, nevertheless is expressed in the daily procedures visible to team colleagues. This brings up the interesting question of whether doctoral dissertations can utilize team research. The concept is not entirely unprecedented and has been employed in sociology. A less radical alternative is

cooperative exchange of researchers helping on one another's projects. Tom O'Guinn and I have successfully worked with each other in this way.

There are two changes I am beginning to make from the ways in which research teams were used in the Odyssey. One is that the research team should remain as intact as possible. In working with the same people you get to know one another's strengths and skills and also develop a comfortable, and usually humor-laden, style of working together. This knowledge and working relationship is disrupted by changes in the research team as was common on the Odyssey. It also disrupts the developing synergy of the research team and the ability to be able take advantage of the right person for a given research task. The other change in the use of teams I would recommend is, as much as possible, to assure beforehand that the research team members have compatible work styles and either similar objectives or agreement that the different researchers have differing objectives which should be jointly pursued by all. Different work styles relate not so much to relatively minor things like waking hours and neatness as to such broad considerations as need for closure and adaptability to different conditions. I tend to have a high tolerance for ambiguity and do not feel I benefit from attempts to analyze data too early in the research process. When I am asked to do so prematurely (to my mind), I feel the research quality is compromised and the mode of reasoning has inappropriately shifted from intuition to the assembly of facts. However, such differences are less likely to be a problem in a long-standing research team in which members have gotten to know one another's research strategies and patterns more fully and to work out ways respect these differences and work together most effectively.

3. Plan to take longer.

Qualitative research requires more time and effort than quantitative research. Data collection takes longer, data management is more complex, and data analysis is lengthier and far more challenging than with quantitative research. Time in the field may well be 24 hours a day when research is underway. For every hour of data collection, two or three may be spent in doing fieldnotes and journals. Transcriptions take longer. There are often photos, videotapes, audiotapes, and artifacts to index and organize. Producing a 40-minute videotape report of the Odyssey took months, including some all-night efforts with Deborah Heisley, Tom O'Guinn, and Melanie Wallendorf, with later assistance from Scott Roberts. Data analysis is aided by specialized text retrieval programs such as ZyIndex and WordCruncher and by coding programs such the Ethnograph, TAP, and HyperQual, but these programs do not analyze in the sense that quantitative statistics packages do (Tesch 1990). The result is that such research involves longer and more challenging time periods than survey and experimental work. There is also less certainty as to when the project will be complete since emerging design means that the focus may evolve and saturation of conceptual categories cannot be scheduled in advance. Ideally time should be allowed for co-researchers to be together during data analysis as well as during data collection. The payoff that justifies such time and effort is not entirely dependent upon project completion however. Work with informants and colleagues can be rewarding and gratifying in itself in ways that seldom occur in quantitative research.

4. Use more participant observation.

While participant observation was employed on the Odyssey (e.g., by selling and assisting sellers at swap meets), there was not adequate time spent at any one site to do sufficient participant observation. Subsequent research has taught me that additional perspective and emotional involvement is gained through extended participation in a research site or phenomenon. Having spent the past summer making and wearing buckskins needed to participate in rendezvous and other modern mountain man activities, I can attest that in this case interviewing is not an adequate substitute for doing. The Odyssey did employ in-situ observation of phenomena of interest, but seldom as full participants. We stopped short of the "blitzkrieg ethnography" Ray Rist warned against (1980) and we came to understand well a number of phenomena that cut across research sites and groups of informants. But the summer-long cross-country Odyssey did not allow the luxury of intimate knowledge of any single site visited.

5. Make fewer compromises with positivism.

Naturalistic inquiry, as presented by Lincoln and Guba (1985) and as largely adopted by the Odyssey, contains a number of compromises with positivism, including the counterparts of reliability and validity for qualitative research. A paper by Wallendorf and Belk (1989) explains how these methods were adapted by the Odyssey and offers a mild critique of such procedures as audits and member checks. I now feel that even these adapted procedures make the mistake of attempting to present research in a way that will be more acceptable to positivists who assume that there is a singular underlying objective reality which can be confirmed by

triangulation, audits, member checks, peer debriefings, and other such methods. The mistake is not in these methods per se, which may do relatively little harm to the research enterprise, but in the homage these methods may pay to a set of philosophical assumptions that are antithetical to the ethnographic enterprise. As Smith and Heshusius (1986) argue, to attempt to bring the qualitative and quantitative research traditions together in this way does great violence to the premises of relativism that underlie virtually all qualitative research traditions. It is more imperative to recognize that reality is socially constructed, that the qualitative researcher is related to the research and to informants in an impassioned and emotional way (Denzin 1989), and that truth is neither a matter of validity or of simply applying the proper research methods. Although reflexivity is a significant post-modernist issue in ethnography at the present time (e.g., Clifford 1988, Clifford and Marcus 1986, Jackson 1989), implicitly or explicitly adopting the philosophy of positivism is certain to lead to the same sterility that quantitative positivism has produced in consumer research.

THE IMPLICATIONS OF QUALITATIVE RESEARCH FOR THE FIELD OF CONSUMER RESEARCH

It is too easy to leave this assessment of Odyssey implications at the workbench level of tips for conducting qualitative and naturalistic research. But the Odyssey methods also have broader implications for the potential course of consumer research. For more than just adding to the methodological tool kit of consumer researchers, qualitative methods enable research into issues and problems that have proven difficult or impossible to assess with survey and experimental research. The topics made accessible by such methods include macro issues in consumption (e.g., the development of consumer culture around the world, the phenomenology of holiday consumption), interpersonal aspects of consumption (e.g., gift-giving in dating, social networks involved in modern mountain man rendezvous), and considerations of what happens after advertising and purchase (e.g., the meanings of possessions, the emotions involved in disposition). In part, the new array of topics opened to investigation by qualitative research presents itself because these methods are more sensitive and can probe for deeper and "squishier" feelings than are likely to be tapped by quantitative measures. In addition, a new set of topics emerges with qualitative methods because these methods are more emergent and informant-focused and are less apt to impose an inappropriate a priori agenda of concepts, perspectives, and topics. Very often this results in informant discussions of products rather than brands, product use rather than purchase, and personally and socially constructed consumption meanings rather than marketer-constructed message processing.

Visual artists often speak of finding ways to solve problems in representing their visions. It is in this sense that qualitative methods have been especially useful to me. I struggled for more than ten years trying to find meaningful ways to investigate collecting and pet ownership before my eyes were opened to qualitative methods. Qualitative methods proved the solution to many problems I was having in trying to understand gift-giving phenomena (cf. Belk 1976, 1979 versus Belk and Coon 1991). Qualitative research is not appropriate for all consumer research problems, but I find that it is the key to many of those problems I find interesting.

It is also potentially significant that qualitative methods have gained popularity in consumer research at just the time that consumption topics are becoming legitimate in a variety of other disciplines that more fully embrace qualitative methods: sociology, anthropology, communications, history, popular culture studies, American culture studies, semiotics, literary studies, phenomenological psychology, and others. It is becoming increasingly apparent that consumer research does not occur solely within the membership of the Association for Consumer Research or the pages of the *Journal of Consumer Research*. Both in order to be conversant with the new genres of consumer research and consumer researchers and in order to avoid having ACR and *JCR* come to be narrowly perceived as interested only in micro consumer behavior issues and quantitative research methods, it seems opportune that qualitative studies have begun to permeate the ACR/*JCR* nexus of consumption research.

Thus, the more subtle impact of the Odyssey may be more substantive than methodological. There is a broad unexplored world of consumption waiting to be investigated and I hope that the Odyssey has in a small way helped us to be better prepared for this greater journey.

REFERENCES

Arnould, Eric J. (1989), "Toward a Broadened Theory of Preference Formation and the Diffusion of Innovations: Cases from Zinder Province, Niger Republic," *Journal of Consumer Research*, 16 (September), 239-267.

Belk, Russell (1976), "It's The Thought That Counts: A Signed Digraph Analysis of Gift-Giving," *Journal of Consumer Research*, 3 (December), 155-162.

Belk, Russell W. (1979), "Gift-Giving Behavior," *Research in Marketing*, Vol. 2, ed. Jagdish N. Sheth, Greenwich, Connecticut: JAI Press, 95-126.

Belk, Russell W. and Gregory S. Coon (1991), "Can't Buy Me Love: Dating, Money, and Gifts," *Advances in Consumer Research*, Vol. 18, Rebbecca H. Holman and Michael R. Solomon, eds., Provo: Association for Consumer Research, 521-527.

Burgess, Robert G. (1984), *In the Field: An Introduction to Field Research*, London: Allen & Unwin.

Clifford, James (1988), *The Predicament of Culture: Twentieth-Century Ethnography, Literature, and Art*, Cambridge, MA: Harvard University Press.

Clifford, James and George E. Marcus, eds. (1986), *Writing Culture*, Berkeley, CA: University of California Press.

Denzin, Norman K. (1989), *Interpretive Interactionism*, Newbury Park, CA: Sage.

Jackson, Michael (1989), *Paths Toward a Clearing: Radical Empiricism and Ethnographic Inquiry*, Bloomington, IN: Indiana University Press.

Lincoln, Yvonna S. and Egon G. Guba (1985), *Naturalistic Inquiry*, Beverly Hills, CA: Sage.

Rist, Ray C. (1980), "Blitzkrieg Ethnography: On the Transformation of a Method into a Movement," *Educational Researcher*, 9 (2), 8-10.

Smith, John K. and Lous Heshusius (1986), "Closing Down the Conversation: The End of the Quantitative-Qualitative Debate Among Educational Inquirers," *Educational Researcher*, 15 (January), 4-12.

Tesch, Renata (1990), *Qualitative Research: Analysis Types and Software Tools*, New York: Falmer Press.

Wallendorf, Melanie and Russell W. Belk (1989), "Assessing Trustworthiness in Naturalistic Consumer Research," *Interpretive Consumer Research*, Elizabeth Hirschman, ed., Provo, UT: Association for Consumer Research, 64-84.